CHANGE MANAGEMENT IN ACTION

The *InfoManage* Interviews
(December, 1993–November, 1998)

*Industry Leaders Describe How They
Manage Change in Information Services*

BY
GUY ST. CLAIR

Special Libraries
Association
www.sla.org

SLAPUBLISHING

Special Libraries
Association
www.sla.org

Published by Special Libraries Association
1700 Eighteenth Street, NW
Washington, DC 20009, USA
1-202-234-4700

DEDICATION

To Andrew Berner, Beth Duston Fitzsimmons,
Evelin Morgenstern, and Meg Paul

. . . four colleagues and friends
whose commitment to positive change
in information services
much influences our profession

CONTENTS

Foreword xiii
by Eugenie Prime, Hewlett-Packard Company

Introduction xv

**Chapter 1: Change Management in Information Services:
            "Results-Focused and Opportunity-Focused"** 1

Chapter 2: Conceptualizing Change 33

    William D. Walker at NYPL's SIBL: It's state-of-the-art
information, and "the pieces are coming together" 36

    Relaxed at the revolution: **Ken Megill** takes us into
information resources management 41

    Pat Molholt's bold CHIPS project 47

    Ann Lawes: Thinking about the information manager
as change agent 53

    Knowledge management: The third "era" of the
information age? **Lois Remeikis** at Booz-Allen
& Hamilton thinks it is 59

Making the case for a national engineering information
system: **David Penniman** has found his challenge   67

That much-anticipated change in American
librarianship is now going to happen and **Bob Klassen**
is supervising the job   74

Jerry King at NIH sees a new information profession
being born—and it's happening right now   81

Deanna Marcum at CLIR: Moving us ever closer to that
seamless web of information resources   89

Anne Woodsworth at Long Island University's
Palmer School: Change management and leadership
are now the profession's basic competencies   96

Judith J. Field: Information educator, president
of the Special Libraries Association, and mentoring advocate 104

**Chapter Three: Management Practices in Information
                        Services—Organizing** 103

"It's the staff." **Catherine A. Jones** talks about LC's
Congressional Reference Division 116

Ruth K. Seidman at MIT's Engineering and
Science Libraries: Managing international information
issues at the Institute 121

Mimi Drake at Georgia Tech: Ten years online and
the future is NOW! 127

Marching into the new millennium:
Lois Weinstein is leading the charge at the
Medical Library Center of New York 134

Teacher / Librarian / Copyright & Intellectual Property Expert:
Lolly Gasaway continues to tackle new challenges 140

At America's new state-of-the-art specialist library,
an optimistic **John Ganly** says it's the content
that provides a role for librarians 148

Allan Foster: At Keele University, information convergence
is the key concept for managing information 155

Tom Pellizzi at InfoSpace Consultants in New York:
Showing information managers how to optimize space 163

Team-based organizational management in
the research libraries environment: **Carla Stoffle,**
Shelley Phipps, Michael Ray, and **Carrie Russell**
describe the process at the University of Arizona 170

**Chapter Four: Entrepreneurial Management
in the Information Environment** 187

Inmagic's **Betty Eddison**: adding value to information services . . . 189

Mark Merrifield's entrepenuerial approach to
public librarianship 194

Judy Macfarlane at the Price Waterhouse Business
Information Center: An intrapreneurial approach to
providing information for the Montréal business community 199

Victor Rosenberg teaches information people
how to be entrepreneurial. He also runs his own
company—it's a combination that works 205

The "entrepreneur" in "entrepreneurial librarianship":
Perhaps **Mike Gruenberg** at Disclosure can provide some tips 211

Claudia Lux at the Senatsbibliothek Berlin:
Looking at information services with a political eye 217

**Chapter Five: Management Practices in Information Services—
Planning** 225

Mary Park thinks "partnering" is a good idea
—if the partner is senior management 227

"Determined"? "Driven"? Perhaps even "relentless"?
At Arthur Andersen in New York, success in the company's
Business Information Center connects to **Lucy Lettis**'s
own career path 233

A high-visibility focus at the Los Angeles Times:
In the editorial library, **Tom Lutgen** and his staff
have put it all together 239

Mary Dickerson: At the Ontario Legislative Library,
change management calls for directional planning 247

Planning: it's the critical "essential" in the library
transformation process and **Ethel Himmel** and
Bill Wilson are the planning and transformation experts 254

**Chapter Six: Management Practices in Information Services—
Implementing Change** 261

John Wilson at JMW Mosaic talks about internal consultants 263

Peter Emmerson at Barclay's Bank: Training records
managers for value-added service 269

Does "moving up" mean "moving out" for
information professionals? Not necessarily.
Ellen Miller at J.P. Morgan is no longer a "practicing"
librarian. But information management is still very
much part of her work. 273

At London's V&A, **Jan van der Wateren** is enthusiastic about
moving Britain's National Art Library into its new space
—and about the managerial challenges the move provides 279

Andrew Berner at the University Club of New York:
Library management includes customer service, a team focus
—and library promotion, done subtly 287

Lany McDonald at Time Warner (I)
Changing the culture in the editorial/corporate environment:
You start with the information staff, and, "you share the vision" . . 295

Lany McDonald at Time Warner (II)
Changing the culture in the editorial/corporate environment:
Now you target the information customers—
"research informs the story" 305

Chapter 7: Customer Care in the Information Environment 311

The information independent organization:
Carol Ginsburg's bold approach 313

Meg Paul talks about information in Australia,
and about the satisfied customer as advocate 317

Matching corporate information services to
corporate information needs: At Coopers & Lybrand
Trish Foy is reinventing information services 322

The service / management / leadership continuum:
Is SLA's **Jane Dysart** the model for specialized librarianship? 328

Quality reference delivery is critical—and as society
moves into the digital age, **Anne Lipow** has some
provocative ideas on the subject 335

Chapter 8: Quality Management in Information Services 343

Ted Slate at *Newsweek*: He likes the look of
what he's leaving . . . and where he's going 346

Andrew Ettinger at Ashridge Management College;
Total quality learning for managers 352

Defining the corporate library: **Richard A. Willner** at
Lehman Brothers 358

Ann Wolpert at the Harvard Business School:
Introducing new managers to information values 363

Wayne Wilson at the Amateur Athletic Foundation:
Olympic-class management for an Olympic-class
sports information facility 370

Barbara Spiegelman at Westinghouse Energy Systems:
TQM and competency-based management—it's a
synergistic relationship 378

Chapter 9: Preparing for the Future 385

Looking to the 21st century: **Joe Fitzsimmons**
and UMI take on the big issues 388

Taking on those "big" information issues
Joe Fitzsimmons at UMI—Part II 392

Sylvia Piggott at the Bank of Montréal: Reengineering
information services for the 2nd era of the information age 397

Gabriele Greve at Berlin's Bibliothek des Kammergerichts:
Taking the initiative and confidently confronting the challenges . . 402

Looking at information services from a communications
perspective: It's the possibilities that intrigue **Bob Frye** 407

David Bender at the Special Libraries Association:
Visionary leadership for the information industry 415

Monica Ertel at Apple's Advanced Technology Group:
Building the infrastructure for an information-intense world
. . . and enjoying it 423

Robert Nawrocki is ARMA International's President
and he's sounding a wake-up call for records managers 432

Martina Reich at Roland Berger & Partner:
Here comes the new generation of European
information managers—they're confident, they're experts,
and they like what they are doing 440

Seamless information delivery is coming to
Colonial Williamsburg—and Library Director
Susan Berg is doing her part 448

Beth Duston Fitzsimmons: Policy development for
the information future 456

Sources and Selected Bibliography 467

FOREWORD

Change sucks. This is a normal response to unwanted, unexpected, unplanned, unorchestrated change or change processes. Yet we live and work in a turbulent environment where unanticipated change has become the norm, where the rate of change has accelerated to a pace that is dizzying in its impact, where we are no longer assured of the comfort that comes with a sense of continuity or predictability, where the future is no longer what it used to be. Our profession has not and cannot expect to be immune to these changes. That is one reason why I readily embraced the opportunity to write the foreword to this book. The issue of change is a vital and compelling one that demands the attention of any manager who wishes to be successful or any leader who chooses to be effective. The other reason I welcomed this task is the fact that the career path of the editor, Guy St. Clair, is evidence that he creatively embraces change.

"No company is safely and permanently successful in today's business environment. For many organizations, perhaps most, doing business now has become a new game with new rules." Karl Albrecht wrote that statement in the preface to his book *The Northbound Train*[1] in 1994. Today, five years later in 1999, no one would dare to contest that statement. We as librarians and information professionals are working in an environment that demands that we do some different things and that we do some things differently. And that other things we do not do at all.

Change is sometimes painful. But failure to change will result in far greater and more excruciating pain. Change is most times risky. But the alternative means taking a far greater risk, the risk of professional suicide. Change is absolutely essential. It is our only option. Indeed, it is the only option that assures us that our profession will prosper and survive. In actuality, the only guarantee of our survival is to do more than simply accept or embrace change. Our guarantee lies in our willingness to be creators or co-creators of the new game and the new rules.

Change Management in Action is not a theoretical treatise. This book deals with real people in real situations. This book shows us not theorists, but doers in the act of doing. We see people dealing with change, attempting to manage change, creating change and facing both the intended and unintended outcomes of their decisions and actions. We get a taste of the 'real thing' through the experiences of academic, special and public librarians and other information professionals, in large, small and medium sized organizations.

In Trina Paulus' *Hope for the Flowers*[2], Yellow asks "How does one become a butterfly?" and is told: "You must want to fly so much that you are willing to give up being a caterpillar. You mean to die? Yes and no. What looks like you will die but what's really you will still live. Life is changed, not taken away. Isn't that different from those who die without ever becoming butterflies?"

These people show us that "We can fly! We can become butterflies!"

EUGENIE PRIME
Manager, Corporate Libraries
Hewlett Packard

---

1. Albrecht, Karl. *The Northbound Train: Finding the Purpose; Setting the Direction; Shaping the Destiny of Your Organization* Amacom, 1994.
2. Paulus, Trina. *Hope for the Flowers.* Paulist Press, 1972.

INTRODUCTION

*W*hen it became clear in the early 1990s that a new publication, dealing with information services management in all its various manifestions, and not limited to one or another "branch" of information services, was needed in the profession, it never occurred to any of us associated with this venture that the newsletter would be a "one-subject" newsletter. And in truth it has not been, for much of the material published in *InfoManage: The International Management Newsletter for the Information Services Professional,* is not limited to any one subject or area of interest. Strangely enough, though, there was one subject that soon became a theme in every issue, and it wasn't long before *InfoManage* (originally subtitled *The International Management Newsletter for the Information Services Executive*) was being read for—among other subjects—its attention to change and change management in information services.

And why not? Is there any subject that commands as much attention in the professions and work groups affiliated with information delivery? No, and as these five years of publication have demonstrated, the more librarians and other information practitioners can read about change management, the more they want (and perhaps need) to read about it. In fact, it soon became apparent that change management was the subject that *InfoManage* is about, and one of our editorial advisors still says to me, on an almost monthly basis, something along the lines of "Oh, Guy, you and your change management. That's what these newsletters are really about." And she's right, of course.

It gives me much pleasure to offer these interviews to the information management community, for there is much in them that will be directly applicable to almost any management situation in the information services arena. These people—chosen to be interviewed because they *are* the leaders in the information industry—have much to say to us as we attempt to bring change to the organizations in which we have information delivery responsibility. And, as I hope has been made clear in all of the issues of *InfoManage* (in the interviews as well as in the "back-of-the-book" material published in each issue), the concepts and ideas put forward in the newsletter are applicable to every type of information delivery operation. Yes, there are those who will say that "This interview doesn't mean anything to me, because I work in an academic library and this person manages a records management department," or "That interview is interesting, but all that talk about entrepreneurial information management isn't of any value to me in my public library."

Nonsense. It takes very little skill or ability to read what one information manager is doing and to adapt or "translate" those concepts and ideas to any information delivery environment. All it takes is the will, and an interest in providing the highest levels of information services that can be provided. For those information managers who have that will, and that interest, the content of these interviews will be of much value, regardless of the branch of information services in which they are employed.

A few comments about the technical production of this material is in order. All of the interviews, with one exception, were written by me. Although other people work on *InfoManage* and contribute much important material for the newsletter, I am (as anyone who knows me can attest) first and foremost "a people person." I delight in spotting people who are making a particularly important contribution to the information management field and getting to know them through the interview process. And of course one of the great benefits of this particular methodology is that I get to know these people and learn from them. It is a rewarding intellectual and professional experience from which I gain much.

The one exception to the "Guy-St.Clair-as-interviewer" model is the David Penniman interview. David and I have known each other a long time, and as we attempted to set up a time and a place for our interview, and as I attempted to learn more about the subject he wanted to discuss (the development of a national engineering library), we realized that I had much to learn about his field of work. So he took the initiative and presented *InfoManage* with a very well-written "interview" that was, for all intents and purposes, almost ready for publication. As an editor and publisher, I was not about to turn away that kind of initiative, and I'm not so sure that my interview with David Penniman would have been as good as the one he provided, so we used it.

Speaking of interviews and interviewees, it should be noted that there have been many changes in the careers of some of the interviewees, and when known, we have attempted to refer to these new positions in the biographical notes. Similarly, it should be pointed out that early interviews did not include biographical notes, and since the current book is not presenting the interviews in chronological order, there seem to be inconsistencies. In fact, what is printed here is what we have, representing what was included in the original presentation of these interviews.

A comment should also be made about our publishing routine at SMR International. We have always felt that it is not our place to engage in investigative journalism, and for that reason, we do not look for weaknesses in our interviewees to expose, or for failures that we can call to the attention of professional colleagues. In fact, we have sometimes been accused of being too "kind" to our interview subjects, for there are in the profession those who want to have their colleagues' professional shortcomings made public.

That's not what we do. In fact, even in our discussions of books and other products that are being made available to the profession, we do not engage in "reviews" as such (when we write about books, we refer to the articles as "bibliographic essays"). Here at SMR International, we have long felt that it is our job to tell people what is good about the profession, what works, and to leave the investigative reporting and the descriptions of failed enterprises to others. Our company is also in the consulting business, and perhaps our publishing philosophy is somehow related to that work, for we have long known that our readers want to learn from those who are successful, who are managing well, so that they can refer to these people and benefit from knowing about them. They are not interested in reading about failure. So the tone in the interviews is often one of admiration and, hopefully, constructive, because we feel that it is to our readers' advantage to know about these people. Exposing failings does no one—or the information management field—any good.

With respect to the content of the interviews, it is possible that some of the material in this book has appeared in other contexts. As one who works as a consultant, trainer, educator, author, and frequent public speaker, I am obviously going to leverage some of the material I gather and move it into the different types of work I do. Generally speaking, however, most of this material is appearing in this form for the first time, and if the content of some of these interviews had made its way into other books, speeches, presentations, and consultation reports that I wrote or that my company produced, I apologize. As I say, however, I don't believe any of this material has appeared exactly as it appears here, as reprinted interviews from *InfoManage*.

Also related to the content of the interviews, I have attempted to arrange these sixty contributions in broad chapters that reflect, to some degree, the general focus that each of these leaders has to offer. While there is much to be said for a strictly chronological order (these interviews cover the period from December 1993 to November 1998), it seems to me that the best way to read these interviews is to think about them—the interviewees and what they are saying—in a particular context relating to the overall subject of change management. I think the arrangement offered here is the best one for providing instruction, guidance, and inspiration for librarians and other information practitioners who are attempting to come to grips with change and change management in their organizations. I hope it is a useful arrangement for the reader.

The list of acknowledgements that I wish to make is long, and I fear greatly that I am going to leave someone out. If that happens, I will be very sorry, for I am very proud of *InfoManage* and the fine newsletter that our company produced would not have been possible without the continuing help of many people.

First of all, editorial consultants Andrew Berner and Beth Duston Fitzsimmons worked with me for about two years before the newsletter was born in December 1993. We thought long and hard about what we were doing, for we wanted to create and produce a newsletter that would meet the information and professional development needs of information managers. So it was a big undertaking for the three of us, and I thank them for their help. And I should note here that it was Beth who came up with the name for the publication, and I am delighted to acknowledge that contribution. Both she and Andrew have been stalwart colleagues as this newsletter has developed, and I am much indebted to them.

The original group of editorial advisors to *InfoManage* included some of the most prominent people in the information industry, and I am happy to acknowledge their contribution to the newsletter's success. They were: Michel Bauwens, Antwerp, Belgium; Mary E. Dickerson, Toronto, ON, Canada; Miriam A. Drake, Atlanta, GA, USA; Joseph Fitzsimmons, Ann Arbor, MI, USA; Carol L. Ginsburg, New York, NY, USA; L. Susan Hayes, Ft. Lauderdale, FL, USA; Ann Lawes, London, England; Judy Macfarlane, Montréal, PQ, Canada; Emily R. Mobley, West Lafayette, IN, USA; Nigel Oxbrow, London, England; Mary Park, Baltimore, MD, USA; Meg Paul, Melbourne, VIC, Australia; Martha P.B. Schweitzer, New York, NY, USA; Ann J. Wolpert, Cambridge, MA, USA; Mark Vonderhaar, Bethesda, MD, USA.

In September 1994, Bruce Hubbard of Taastrup, Denmark, joined the group, as did Lou Parris of Houston, TX, USA, in October, 1997. In November, 1997, Keitha Booth of Wellington, New Zealand, Marion Dupper of Cape Town, South Africa, and Evelin Morgenstern of Berlin, Germany became Editorial Advisors to *InfoManage*. I am grateful to them all for their advice and for their contributions. These Editorial Advisors have had a great deal to do with the newsletter being as good as it is, and I appreciate what they have provided. As the publisher and the person with overall editorial responsibility for *InfoManage*, I am extremely grateful to these people for their ideas, support, and commentary during these five years of the newsletter's publication.

Also, a word of thanks should go to the many people who have contributed articles and other leads to stories for the newsletter, even though much of that material is not represented in this collection of interviews. While I have written the interviews, the newsletter itself is the result of the combined efforts of many people. Marisa Urgo, as a regular contributor to the newsletter and as *InfoManage*/SMR International's Information

Resources Coordinator, has been responsible for website creation and maintenance, including adding the *InfoManage* table of contents and content summary each month, and she has done a terrific job with this. I am grateful to her for her participation in the newsletter's production.

And a word of thanks goes to Jeffrey and Annette Miller, good friends who always seem to enjoy being the "last eyes" before the issue goes to press. They not only enjoy reading the newsletter, but their sharp attention to detail has, on several occasions, prevented a possibly embarrassing situation. I'm grateful to them for their continued interest and support for our work.

Finally, a special word of thanks should go the four individuals to whom this book is dedicated. Andrew Berner and Beth Duston Fitzsimmons (already mentioned) have been faithful supporters of *InfoManage* and the dissemination of its message. Additionally, Meg Paul in Melbourne, VIC, Australia, and Evelin Morgenstern in Berlin, Germany—both editorial advisors to the newsletter—have been exceptionally helpful in advising me about the content that readers want (and need) to see, and I am indebted to them for their good advice and support. Additionally, Andrew, Beth, Evelin, and Meg are good personal friends and I rejoice in our good friendship. These are the best kinds of professional colleagues one can have. I thank them for their inspiration and I look forward to many more years of sharing ideas, concepts, and concerns with them.

GUY ST. CLAIR
New York, NY USA
October 1998

CHANGE MANAGEMENT IN INFORMATION SERVICES
"Results-Focused and Opportunity-Focused"

Introduction

In 1994, writing about the "age of social transformation," Peter S. Drucker describes what the editors of *Atlantic Monthly* called "an economic order in which knowledge, not labor or raw material or capital, is the key resource." In the essay, as he writes about the rise of the knowledge worker, Drucker makes it clear that the move toward a "knowledge economy" is more than simply a rearranging of the workforce:

> The rise of the class succeeding industrial workers is not an opportunity for industrial workers. It is a challenge. The newly emerging dominant group is 'knowledge workers.' . . . the great majority of the new jobs require qualifications the industrial worker does not possess and is poorly equipped to acquire. They require a good deal of formal education and the ability to acquire and to apply theoretical and analytical knowledge. They require a different approach to work and a different mind-set. Above all, they require a habit of continuous learning. (Drucker, 1994)

Of course the definition of what those workers do has changed in the intervening years since 1959 when Drucker first defined these people and their work. But the basic elements of the knowledge workers' tasks and their contributions to the organizations and companies that employ them are fundamentally where they were then. The primary difference is that today's knowledge worker is empowered, indeed, even expected to take responsibility for the work that he or she performs [see sidebar on page 3], and is expected to recognize that he or she adds value to the achievement of organizational goals by knowing how to handle the exceptional cases.

For today's knowledge worker, it is difficult to imagine a more interesting or more exciting career than the one librarians and other information services professionals get to enjoy. Every day brings new responsibilities, new challenges, new products and services, new opportunities, and new expectations and perceptions from their information customers and patrons. Even new compensation and reward structures are now experienced as a matter of course. Yesterday's information professional would hardly have expected to participate in the successful financial management firm's end-of-the-year bonus offerings; today's librarian or other information manager won't consider employment at the firm unless a respectable bonus package is included.

It is not hard to see why the information professional's career picture has changed. In any organization (or community, for those employed in public library work), information is the critical component in organizational and community success, and that fact is now commonly recognized. Managers know it, the information customers know it, the vendors and suppliers know it, and all other information stakeholders know it. Most important of all, the information managers and librarians know it (the special librarians have known it all along), and they are now quite comfortable in stating unequivocally (and backing up their statements with solid documentation) that their function in the organization or the community is to provide the information that leads to success in the achievement of the organizational or community mission.

Obviously, such a happy state of affairs has not come about without attention to change: changes in the information marketplace, changes in information delivery mechanisms (and philosophy), changes in the organization's attention to the role of information in the organization's functional structure. Related to this, of course, are changes in society at large,

Knowledge Workers: The New Definition

"*The* value, and values, of American workers have changed dramatically over the past few decades. The shorthand phrase to describe the change is the 'knowledge economy.' While technically accurate, the description is misleading. Hearing it, people tend to assume that the economy rewards only the highly educated elite, and that there's no longer a place for Everyman. . . . But many economically valuable forms of knowledge aren't taught in school. They're valuable, in fact, because they're difficult to articulate and therefore to teach. Formal education may indicate the ability to acquire such tacit knowledge, but it doesn't convey the knowledge itself.

"Consider the three groups of jobs identified by the Bureau of Labor Statistics as likely to be the fastest growing over the next decade. The first is 'professional specialty occupations,' projected to increase by nearly five million workers between 1996 and 2006. These jobs include such obvious areas as computers, engineering, and health care, but also special-education teachers, social workers, physical-training instructors, musicians, and designers. Next come technicians and related support positions, a smaller group that complements the first. Finally, there are service occupations, which include such fast-growing jobs as home health care aides, child care workers, and manicurists. . . . These three categories are projected to make up about 36% of the total work force by 2006, or about 54 million jobs, a jump from about 30% in 1996.

"What all these jobs have in common, regardless of their education requirements, are specific skills and a great deal of employee discretion. Many also reward the ability to interpret and respond to the unpredictable moods and actions of other people. In short, they all employ knowledge workers.

"That knowledge may be gained in school or passed down through apprenticeship and custom. Whether caring for the sick elderly person, writing music for a TV commercial, or repairing a photocopier, none of these employees can be constantly supervised or told in advance exactly how to do their jobs. All belong to 'communities of practice,' in which they share knowledge by recounting war stories and soliciting advice from people in similar jobs, though not necessarily with the same employer. . . . These employees add value by their ability to handle the exceptional cases." (Postrel, 1998)

far too many to be enumerated here but, for our purposes, a few of which can be identified. Such things as the attention to cross-border information flow, the growing significance of the overall global information marketplace, the expectations of information customers, and the industry's own move toward excellence in customer service and its self-determining emphasis on quality information management have all combined—with numerous other change forces—to position librarianship as a critical element (and its practitioners as key players) in the modern information environment.

How information services and information delivery have changed, and how the general library community has advanced itself from what is commonly referred to as "traditional librarianship" to its present place in the information industry is not hard to discern. The emphasis on information delivery (and—connected to that—information services management) in those organizations in which information specialists provides the information is two-fold: the delivery of information is limited to mission-critical information, and information professionals, especially special librarians, provide customized information for their customers, a form and a standard of information delivery that David R. Bender has referred to as "just-for-you" information delivery. (Bender, 1997)

To meet this standard of service has required, and will continue to require, that information services management change. The entire information industry must now think differently about itself—and, indeed, must totally restructure itself. As this happens, the tenets and characteristics of change management, as practiced in any society or any industry, must be brought to the information services environment. Those industry leaders who are the subjects of the interviews captured in this book have done so; those who have not yet been able to do so can look to these people for guidance.

Defining information services

Who these people are and the organizations for which they provide information delivery represent what is becoming increasingly identified as an information-services "umbrella." This is not a particularly new concept, and it has, in fact, been much written about in the pages of *InfoManage* and other information management literature. Such new information services management "issues" as convergence and integrated information, innovation and risk taking in information delivery, excellence in customer service, and advocacy and the achievement of power and influence in information management have all been frequently written about. Their underlying premise, their basic foundation, goes back to service excellence, that focus on customer service that Michael Barrier identified several years ago as the first "essential" of total quality management and which this author adopted as the first essential in what has become known as QIM—quality information management. (Barrier, 1992; St. Clair, 1996)

But QIM is more than customer service (although the primacy of that particular "essential" must not be diminished in any way), and as a subset of organizational management and as a specific management methodology for providing the highest standard of information delivery to an identified user base, the other attributes of this information delivery technique must be given attention. These attributes have been described in a number of published books and articles and the six components can, quite usefully, be summarized here. Generally speaking QIM—quality information management—builds on the four "essentials" of quality management with two additional characteristics:

- Intense focus on customer service
- Accurate measurement
- Continuous improvement
- New work relationships based on trust and teamwork (Barrier)

To these must be added:

- A desire for quality on the part of all information stakeholders
- The commitment and enthusiasm of senior management in the organization or community (St. Clair)

These characteristics of quality information management all come together in a standard of information delivery that today's (and tomorrow's) information customers are expecting and are, in many environments, demanding. Called "one-stop shopping" in some industries (and which, in some information delivery operations, practitioners speak of as providing customers with "a single point of entry" to information), this level of service recognizes from the outset that the driving force in the information transaction is the information customer. Information customers don't want to be told by an information worker that the information they seek is not here but somewhere else. They want to ask their question once and have the information delivered from one source, and it's not difficult to understand why: from the information customer's point of view, as Elizabeth Orna has so brilliantly put it, information can be defined in very basic terms. For her, the "touchstone" for identifying information is simply: "Is this something that people need to know and apply in their work, to achieve their and the enterprise's objectives?" In her definition—and it is one that is particularly appropriate to the delivery of information in the contemporary information services environment—Orna does not limit herself to traditional concepts about the subject. Instead, she points out that within the organization, information will be found everywhere, "not just in formal repositories like libraries or information systems, and not just in those functions where people spend a lot of time reading, writing, or interacting with computers." The list of items that meet Orna's criteria is long. It includes such things as customer records, financial records, internal information, external information, technical information, and information about the environment in which the enterprise operates, and significantly, the "form" in which the information is held is irrelevant. Certainly Orna's definition makes much sense as information managers attempt to incorporate the basic tenets and philosophies of change and change management into their work, and as organizations seek to move toward knowledge management and achieve the organizational successes built into that valuable concept, her encompassing definition becomes even more valuable to information specialists. (Orna, 1990)

Just how valuable this broad-based definition can be is demonstrated as we think about how these universal information applications are put to work in the corporate information environment. Len Ponzi, in an unpublished paper on the role of information policies in corporate knowledge management, describes corporate information policy as having three distinct components for management, components which associate smoothly with Orna's definition. Ponzi's three components, and his explanations for use are described in the sidebar on page 7.

Connected to Orna's definition and to Ponzi's identification of the necessary components of corporate information policy, is a further refinement for all information workers. It is that they understand (that is, those who are successful in their work understand) that for each of them, regardless of the branch of the information industry in which they are employed, their role is but one component of an overall information services umbrella. This concept, too, has been described (St. Clair, 1996) and

Corporate Information Policy for Knowledge Management: Three Components

1. *Determine what knowledge work will be useful for improving future knowledge products as well as for critical business decisions and preserving corporate memory.* These knowledge works will include structured information (for example, presentations, case studies of best practices, etc.). It will also include unstructured information such as client contact notes and interview notes.

2. *Create a description of how to code finished knowledge works.* This description includes an explicit direction on indexing vocabulary. A knowledge work is of no use if each department classifies competitive marketing strategies differently.

   After successfully entering the work, the knowledge worker who created the piece enters his or her name as the owner of the record, thus allowing future users to access the owner in order to leverage valuable tacit information located in the mind of the knowledge creator. In addition, this link lets the owners see where their work is being used and how it is rolled up into other deliverables.

3. *Define measurements in order to monitor use and value-add of the created knowledge.* Establishing measurements to track usage patterns and data requests will not only result in the purging of the system but will allow management to create financial incentives for those knowledge workers to get their works entered accurately and completely.

   Defining measurements for any process is difficult. Traditional measures can be categorized into: cost, time, product quality, service quality, and customer satisfaction. Each of these has its own set of individual measures.

   However, measures for corporate knowledge and knowledge bases are just being developed. Most thought leadership is being developed in some of the most well-known knowledge companies or service firms. In fact, several professional services firms, including Andersen Consulting, Booz Allen & Hamilton, and McKinsey, have all begun major efforts to capture and share knowledge around the organization. Their information quality measure is a simple concept: Each consulting firm's management reviews the information that is entered by each consultant. Information quality is measured by the number of times their knowledge work is accessed and used as value-add on other consulting engagements. (Ponzi, 1998) the advantages of positioning each information delivery specialty within the broader information management industry, within this "splendid information services continuum," has particular implications in terms of change and change management in information delivery.

This concept of information services includes various and multitudinous subsections of information provision and management as it is practiced. There is now a new understanding of what constitutes "information services," and of what is meant by "information services management," a concept of information, and of the provision of information, that now influences much of what is understood about the delivery of information services and products. Workers in this industry can be employed as information managers, as information providers, or as information specialists, and their work environment might be in information technology, in telecommunications, in traditional librarianship or specialized librarianship, in records management, in corporate or organizational archives, in information brokerage, in publishing, in consulting, or in any of the many other branches of the information industry that participate in or provide service to the information community.

Connected to this new definition of information services is a new understanding of the work that its practitioners do. In 1994, Woody Horton admonished those who have been educated as librarians to "extend their domain." In a short monograph that explores how librarians, especially special librarians, might look at their role in the information workplace and come away with workable and achievable objectives for the profession (it was published by the Special Libraries Association), Horton poses six assumptions that can be expected to greatly impact the delivery of information in the near future. These assumptions relate directly to the services that all librarians and other information workers strive to provide. Recognizing them enables these information workers to plan future services with more precision and, of course, with more flexibility. Horton's six assumptions are these, and with a little clever rewording, they can be made to fit any kind of information work, not just special librarianship:

- Knowledge is needed by all segments of information societies, at all levels.

- Organizations are undergoing fundamental and radical structural transformation to cope with external changes in the environment.

- Within organizations, operating functions are becoming far more information intensive than they've ever been before—and they demand a far higher degree of information literacy.

- Special librarians, while positioned to be the premier information experts in their organizations, are thwarted by stereotypes about what librarians do, by the attitudes of employers who do not understand librarianship, and by the attitudes and behaviors of the librarians themselves.

- Librarians and other information services professionals must shift their primary focus from describing, organizing, and cataloging objects to planning and managing the information requirements of the decision-makers in their organizations.

- Librarians and other information services professionals must move out of the traditional library domain into the organizational domain. (Horton, 1994)

To be successful in the modern information environment, all information workers must understand the ideas that Horton has identified and incorporate them into their thinking and planning as they develop information policy. If they do so, their work will quite naturally take on a new meaning —and match the new information demands—for the organizations in which they are employed, which in itself might be a new definition of change management for information services.

Enabling technology and the new information environment

Much of the change that is being experienced in information services management is connected to the new and different media through which information is delivered. No longer does information management simply refer to the delivery of information that has been located in appropriate books, journals, or reports. Indeed, in many libraries, the media of traditional librarianship is no longer appropriate, and has been replaced with the convenience and timeliness of electronic-based information delivery.

And this is a good thing, having this new media at hand, as Sylvia Piggott has so eloquently described. Piggott, eternally optimistic (and well she should be, in this case), points out that this is a very exciting time for information services, simply because information managers are working in what she calls the *second* era of the information age. They've passed through the childhood and adolescence of electronic delivery, and as a consequence of *enabling* technology, businesses and professions are reengineering. Special libraries and other information operations can benefit from applying the same concepts leading to the realization of what Piggott—and many others in the industry—have for their organizations: a library or information center that exists as a seamless, borderless service, "a place where information can be sought from wherever it exists and can be used immediately by local or remote customers." (Piggott, 1995)

Nevertheless, there's still the dichotomy of service that requires information specialists to recognize and to understand that the medium is only that, a medium and a conduit. For many generations to come, information seekers will continue to look to traditional media (e.g., the printed word) for finding the information they require or (in the case of that "piece" of information gathering we call "reading for pleasure") desire, and information management—as a management construct—continues and will continue to incorporate the management of traditional library services, that is, those information delivery activities that are print-based as well as those in which information delivery is provided through the new media.

It's not a problem. If information workers (and those who employ them) will look at the competencies required for success in the 21st century it becomes clear that those employees who have these competencies are well-prepared for providing excellence in information delivery, regardless of the medium through which the information is disseminated. They are being educated, trained, and employed as special librarians and, as the required competencies demonstrate, they are expected to be managers and to undertake managerial responsibility in the delivery of information.

Such a perspective becomes clear when looking at the competencies document published by the Special Libraries Association in 1997. In her description of how competencies can be used as a performance appraisal and compensation tool, Barbara Spiegelman makes the case for identifying and utilizing staff competencies in the workplace, particularly in the information workplace:

> Core competencies grow out of the aggregated skills of people. Just as a corporation must identify, develop, and leverage its competencies, each individual within the corporation must identify and develop their own key competencies to help make the business successful. (Spiegelman, 1997)

It doesn't matter whether we're talking about information-delivery competencies in the "business" community, to use the term Spiegelman used in the book, or in any other environment in which information services are provided and information is delivered. Whatever the environment, the competencies identified by SLA are critical in the successful achievement of the information mission. And while it is not necessary here to quote all 24 of the SLA competencies (11 professional competencies and 13 professional competencies), it can be a useful exercise to think about how they might be summarized. To this end, we can condense the SLA Competencies statement to five broad component issues, with these five keywords: *resources, content, media, manager* (or management), and *advocate* (or advocacy). The information management specialist has:

- expert knowledge of information *resources* within a specific subject field or fields
- has specialized knowledge of the *content* of these resources
- understands and implements information delivery *media*
- performs as a manager within the organizational entity, whatever it is; and
- serves as an information *advocate* within the organization or community at large (St. Clair, "Exceptional . . . " 1997)

When working with change and change management, it is the fourth of these that demands our attention, for information specialists are expected to be "an effective member of the senior management team and a consultant to the organization on information issues." (Spiegelman, 1997). As the information industry changes, these managers with information delivery responsibility (that is, managers of information departments in their parent organizations, managers of resources, of people, of quality information delivery) must meet a variety of challenges having to do with change and change management. No longer can the individual who "likes to read" consider librarianship, much less special librarianship or any of the more specific information-delivery functions, as a career. These new information professionals are managers, and as managers they have responsibilities that absolutely *forbid* their sitting quietly on the sidelines, enjoying their bookish peacefulness, working diligently at the profession's stereotypical pursuits while the "real" responsibilities for information delivery take place elsewhere. Even those information workers with responsibility for traditional library collections must take the managerial center stage, as Peter Likins at the University of Arizona has noted:

> In the current information age, life on the sidelines is no longer an option. But life center stage doesn't mean we're alone. We just have to give up the idea that organizations can be managed according to Newtonian mechanics, where everything is clean, pure, beautiful, orderly, deterministic, and comforting. Instead, we have to look to the model of the chaos theory and find comfort in the drama of stars, supporting cast members, and the audience being all in it together. (Likins, 1998)

And "being all in it together"—for information professionals as managers—provides unique challenges and splendid opportunities. The crunch comes, however, when these managers are required to take those challenges and opportunities and incorporate them into their daily managerial work.

It is not, however, a crunch that we can avoid, for we are living and working in a "post-traditional" society, a society in which our institutions and organizations and communities are crying out for change and for the successful implementation of change management methodologies in their libraries. In the next few years, and as we move into the twenty-first century, players in the the information industry will be dependent—literally—on the success we achieve in bringing change into their libraries and other information services organizations. Why? Because we live in and are moving further into a society in which the old choices are no longer working, and the scenario in which choices were made for us no longer exists. Or if it does, will not exist long into the twenty-first century. Just as the knowledge economy and its knowledge workers have been redefined, so have our responsibilities as information services managers, and we now recognize that old assumptions and old systems for information management no longer work. We no longer follow precise paths to organizational success, and choices are no longer made for us. It's *our* responsibility now, and the sooner we learn—and are willing—to make choices, the sooner we'll be prepared for managing those information organizations, including libraries, that will be (at least for a while yet) our responsibility.

It is Anthony Gibbons, author of *Beyond Left and Right* and the director of the London School of Economics, who offers insight for those of us who work in libraries and information services. In an issue of the *New Yorker*, Robert S. Boynton captures Giddens eminently accessible philosophy in a paragraph that almost obliges us to attach it to what is happening in libraries and other information management operations as we move into the twenty-first century:

> The modern world, according to Giddens, is not only fully global but 'post-traditional,' a term he uses to mean that, although tradition endures in a society, it has lost the privileged status that once enabled it to trump all other contenders. Traditions must now justify themselves in the same manner as any other points of view. Everything is 'constructed' in a post-traditional society, and nothing is 'given': one must choose every facet of one's life, from the nature of one's personal or sexual identity to one's profession or religion. The tradition-minded days when a woman's marriage prospects were calculated with an eye toward her family's finances, or a man was expected to take up his father's profession, are over. In a post-traditional world, men and women simply don't have predefined natures. Even the decision to forgo the dizzying collection of options afforded by the modern world, and conform to the *status quo ante*, is itself a decision. 'Individuals have no choice but to make choices'. (Boynton, 1997)

As citizens in a post-traditional society (and as information services managers), we are required to make choices, choices in everything we do, including choices in the workplace. And as post-traditional managers in the information industry—regardless of the branch of the industry in which we are employed—the choices include an acceptance of change, an understanding and an acceptance of the *value* of change and change management. It was David S. Ferriero and Thomas L. Wilding who in 1991 recognized that—in information management—change is both inevitable *and* desirable, a recognition that continues and will continue to have much influence in how information managers succeed in their work. Change is good, and can—for any information delivery entity—lead to enhanced information delivery which is, after all, why we went into the information industry in the first place:

> Change is not something we can choose or not choose. As information services managers become part of the power structure, their leadership in the change process is recognized and they become heroes within the organization. They become known as 'information leaders.'

As such, they put to rest the misperceptions of those who would relegate information services provision as just another 'service,' and the subservience one associated with the organization, management, and delivery of information services and products is, thankfully, lost forever. (St. Clair, 1994)

Change, change management, leadership, and innovation

For the successful information manager in the twenty-first century, these concepts are all linked, a point made succinctly and appropriately in one of Peter F. Drucker's essays. Writing in another context with immediate application to many "specialized" management entities, Drucker pointed out that "The goal of most organizations . . . is not just to deliver services but to foster change and to improve lives. . . . We have to learn in our organizations what is needed to perform and to innovate." In information services organizations, performance and innovation are uniquely connected, for the information specialist—the organization's or the community's information manager—is continuously seeking to find better ways to provide information delivery to the identified information customers. And the "discipline of innovation," as Drucker calls it, is the critical link to providing better information delivery. Such excellence of service—in Drucker's terms—is accomplished by doing three things, three actions that managers must take (and require their direct reports to take):

- Focus on the mission
- Define the results we are after
- Assess what we're doing and how we do it

And in a sentence that could have been penned specifically for those information workers employed in the library profession (particularly librarianship as it has been perceived—and continues to be perceived—by many laypeople, people not versed in the basic attributes of information delivery), Drucker deflates the historical "innately good" characteristic customarily applied to libraries:

One of the tasks of leaders is constantly to make sure that we put scarce resources of people and money where they do the most good. We have to be results-focused and opportunity-focused. Good intentions are no longer enough. (Drucker, 1998)

Change management requires leadership, and it is the managers in any organization who determine whether change will succeed or fail. They do that by providing—or not providing, when change fails—leadership, and the leadership responsibilities of management must be built into and recognized as a critical element of the managerial function.

There are many resources for identifying what it is that managers do, but in attempting to characterize the information specialist as a manager, and to connect his or her work with leadership in the change management process, a useful essay from 1994 provides appropriate guidelines. In that essay, Christopher Bartlett and Sumantra Ghoshal looked at "three challenges senior managers face as they strive to develop an energizing corporate purpose":

- embedding corporate/organizational ambition
  (defined as capturing the employees' attention and interest, getting the organization involved, and creating momentum)
- instilling organizational values
  (described as building on core values, "sowing the message," and measuring progress)
- giving meaning to employees' work
  (described as recognizing individual accomplishments, committing to develop employees, and fostering individual initiative)

In thinking about change and change management for information practitioners, it is relatively easy to substitute certain words and phrases in order to move Bartlett and Ghoshal's management configuration into the information arena. "Embedding corporate ambition," for example, becomes an admonition to look at the information services unit's mission, to identify and codify what the unit is expected to bring to the parent organization of which it is a part, and determine how those expectations are related to the "ambitions" and goals of the unit's manager and those to whom he or she reports. "Instilling organizational values" relates the work of the information services unit to the mission (and understood values) of the parent organization and the values of the employees in the organization who make up the identified customer base for the information unit. And finally, "giving meaning to employees' work" is almost a formula for competency-based management for the information services unit, insisting as it does on attention to the competencies of the staff, to the further growth and development of these competencies and skills, and to their innovative skills. Bartlett and Ghoshal themselves relate these three challenges to the modern work environment, and information practitioners, with their profession's characteristic desire for service in the workplace, readily agree with their conclusions:

> In the end, every individual extracts the most basic sense of purpose from the personal fulfillment he or she derives from being part of an organization. Creating that sense of fulfillment is the third challenge senior managers face as they strive to develop an energizing corporate purpose. Institutions like churches, communities, even families, which once provided individuals with identity, affiliation, meaning, and support, are eroding. The workplace is becoming a primary means for personal fulfillment. Managers need to recognize and respond to the reality that their employees didn't just want to work for a company; they want to belong to an organization. More than just providing work, companies can help give meaning to people's lives. (Bartlett and Ghoshal, 1994)

Giving meaning to people's lives, especially in the workplace and especially in a working environment as tradition-oriented as librarianship and information services is, brings special challenges to those who are responsible—the managers—for the successful delivery of information products, services, and consultations. Yet managers in all professions and disciplines are struggling with this very issue, for change management is resisted at every turn. Peter Senge, reacting to the Drucker essay referred to above, made it clear that these challenges require special planning and special thinking from information managers. "Peter Drucker," he wrote, "has elegantly presented the three ingredients of the discipline of innovation: focus on mission, define significant results, and do rigorous assessment. But if it sounds so simple, why is it so difficult for institutions to innovate? . . . " For Senge, the search begins with the mission. "It is very hard to focus on what you cannot define and my experience is that there can be some very fuzzy thinking about mission, vision, and values. Most organizations today have mission statements, purpose statements, official visions, and little cards with the organization's values. But precious few of us can say our organization's mission statement has transformed the enterprise. And there has grown an understandable cynicism about lofty ideals that don't match the realities of organizational life." To move beyond the cynicism, Senge suggests, requires that managers recognize that the essence of leadership ("what we do with 98 percent of our time," he says), is communication: "To master any management practice, we must start by bringing discipline to the domain in which we spend most of our time, the domain of words."

And Senge has further advice for information services managers who have responsibility for bringing change to their information delivery operations: ". . . there is a big difference between having a mission statement and being truly mission-based. To be truly mission-based means that key decisions can be referred back to the mission—our reason for being. It means that people can and should object to management edicts that they do not see as connected to the mission. It means that thinking about and continually clarifying the mission is everybody's job because . . . it expresses the aspirations and fundamental identity of a human community. By contrast, most mission statements are nice ideas that might have some meaning for a few but communicate little to the community as a whole. In most organizations, no one would dream of challenging a management decision on the grounds that it does not serve the mission. In other words, most organizations serve those in power rather than a mission." (Senge, 1998)

Senge is equally pragmatic in advising managers (and in this context, managers with information services responsibility) on how to deal with Drucker's second and third ingredients of "the discipline of innovation," defining significant results and employing rigorous assessment. Managers must naturally concentrate on results, but they must do so carefully and conscientiously: "The danger is that short-term goals can obscure larger purposes. Here again, language matters. After all, vision—an image of the future we seek to create—is synonymous with intended results. As such, vision is a practical tool, not an abstract concept."

And as for assessment, Senge simply reminds information managers that assessment has two components: measurement and interpretation. "The problem is that the second and more difficult component of assessment—interpretation—requires understanding, participation, and physical presence. Statistical measures of an activity may be disappointing, but if you're actually involved, you may see that people are engaged and learning. They may be on the brink of a breakthrough. Incomplete or premature assessment destroys learning. . . . assessment is fundamentally about awareness and understanding, without which any set of measures can mislead. Someone sitting on the outside judging, rather than fully understanding, can make effective assessment impossible." Which explains why the most successful information services executives find their way to the service points in their organizations for occasional visits and observation. They probably don't interact with the customers (after all, for many information executives, information delivery skills were lost long ago),but their very presence in these occasional observations gives them information about what goes on "on the floor" that they need to have.

Dealing with change and change management

Many influences affect the work that information services managers do and the delivery of information products, services, and consultations that they and their staffs are expected to provide. And they are required to recognize that in the change management process these influences become part of the environment within which managers are expected to function. By now most authorities agree that change is a response, a planned or— sometimes—unplanned response of an organization to pressures. These may be internal or external pressures, and they may be positive or negative, but they are circumstances that require the organization—the library or other information services unit—to do something differently.

So a first step in the change management process requires looking at these influences, and examining the overall organization and its *readiness* for change. Rick Maurer has noted that most change efforts fail because of employee resistance, and his recommendations for attacking employee resistance to change (see sidebar on page 19) are built on an understanding that change is an "ongoing capability, not a series of recurrent events." His advice seems to be very applicable to the library and information services environment, for as an industry known for its interest in (but not necessarily success with) participative and/or team-based management, the information services field does seem to be one in which Maurer's recommendations can be put to good purpose. For example, Maurer recommends that as the change management process develops, those with responsibility for ensuring that the change is successful should think about a two-pronged approach. First, they should assemble a group of

Change-Ready Assessment

For librarians and other information services managers, the success of any change management process depends on, first, determining the information organization's readiness for change. Rick Maurer offers specific guidelines that apply very well in an information services environment. To determine if the library or other information is ready for change, information managers should seek to achieve the following:

1. Build a foundation.

Ask: To what extent did we:

• Cultivate strong working relationship with those most affected by the change before we asked anything of them? (Too often, we go to people only when we need something from them. If trust has been low, this transaction-based approach seldom builds the healthy relationships necessary to carrying out major changes.)

• Use this change as an opportunity to build relationships with other stakeholders?

2. Communicate with constituents.

Ask: To what extent did we:

• Provide a context and compelling business case for the change process? (In other words, did people see why this change was important?)

• Engage in face-to-face conversation regarding the change and its implications?

• Find ways to communicate informally with people at all levels in the organization throughout the change?

3. Encourage participation.

Ask: To what extent did we:

• Identify all the individuals and groups that had a stake in the outcome?

• Find ways to involve them in the planning of the change?

• Involve them in making decisions regarding implementation?

4. Expect resistance. No matter how well a change is planned, resistance will occur.

Ask: To what extent did we:

• Monitor people's acceptance or resistance to the proposed changes?

• Engage people in dialogue to understand their concerns when resistance did occur?

5. Create rewards and benefits for stakeholders.

Ask: To what extent did we:

• Search for ways to make this a mutually beneficial change?

• Demonstrate to people how the change benefited them?

6. Lead the change skillfully.

Ask: To what extent did we:

• Create alignment among diverse interests?

• Invite critical feedback?

• Articulate a compelling vision (or work with others to create a shared vision)?

• Anticipate and respond appropriately to resistance?

• Keep people informed? (Maurer, 1998)

people "who have their fingers on the pulse of the organization—people who know what is going on and are willing to speak candidly." But Maurer doesn't ask information managers to rely on these people exclusively: "Alternatively," he writes, "feedback can be gathered through anonymous sources. . . . Pick at least two past change efforts—one you consider wildly successful and one that failed." (Maurer, 1998)

Change management expert Rosabeth Moss Kanter also has good advice for information managers who must lead change in their information delivery units, and she, too, understands the value of organizational readiness when change is required. Asked how a manager can recognize whether or not his or her unit is a change-adept organization, Kanter had this to say:

> A change-adept organization is one that is constantly investing in three things. One is innovation. You can look at how many experiments an organization has underway at any one time. How many projects are people doing that are pushing them in new directions and teaching them something new?
>
> Two, the organization is attuned to learning and professionalism. It's constantly getting better at what it's already doing, especially serving its customers. My slogan for a change-adept organization: Do it better the second time, a play on the quality slogan, Do it right the first time. That is, change-adept organizations are constantly improving on what they're doing and spreading that knowledge through an organization. You know an organization is going to be good at handling change whenever it spends more time educating people, exchanging best practices, looking for the best model or role model, and making sure that the models are spread to other places. It's attuned to learning.
>
> Three, a change-adept organization is better at collaboration. It works closely with customers, suppliers, and other partners—not only to do today's work well, but also as a source of ideas for innovation. They're much more open to external influences." (Kanter, 1998)

To make change management work, information services managers are wise to refer to Ferriero and Wilding—of "inevitable-and-desirable-change" authority —and to think about the Ferraro and Wilding strategic planning model for libraries and information services organizations. It is important to recognize that there are several specific steps in the change management process that have been identified for us. In the first, of course, managers plan to plan. In information services, this simply means that they recognize—from whatever source—that a change is required, and they know that they must devise some sort of methodology for incorporating that change into their managerial structure, they must "plan to plan" how they are going to manage this particular change. Following the plan to plan comes the environmental scan, which leads to what Ferriero and Wilding call the "envisioning" process, that stage of the exercise that is the most creative, wherein the information services manager develops a comprehensive vision of what the library or information services operation is to be. This step is followed by the development of an action plan, an implementation plan, and, finally, a procedure for evaluating the change as it is implemented. (Ferriero and Wilding, 1992).

Throughout the entire process, these managers are seeking to identify specific steps that they can take, as managers, to ensure that the changes that must be made *are* made. To go from the very theoretical to the very practical, Susan C. Curzon in her excellent book on change management for libraries offers this list of steps for the manager to take the change process from its initiation to its successful conclusion:

1. Conceptualizing

2. Preparing the organization

3. Organizing the planning group

4. Planning

5. Deciding

6. Managing the individual

7. Controlling resistance

8. Implementing

9. Evaluating (Curzon, 1989)

When dealing with change and change management, managers of libraries and other information services units must recognize the enormous role that organizational culture plays in the process, a point made repeatedly in the work of John Cotter as he studies organizational change. "Culture," Kotter has written, "refers to norms of behavior and shared values among a group of people. Norms of behavior are common or pervasive ways of acting that are found in a group and persist because group members tend to behave in ways that teach these practices to new members, rewarding those who fit in and sanctioning those who do not. Shared values are important concerns and goals shared by most people in a group that tend to shape group behavior and that often persist over time even when group membership changes." (Kotter, 1995). There are few institutions in which norms of behavior and shared values play a stronger role in shaping organizational success than information operations, and the manager seeking to instill a change management process who ignores this role does so at his or her risk, for the change simply won't proceed until the influences of norms of behavior and shared values are recognized.

Organizational change, in Kotter's terms, must be "anchored" in the culture, which means that those responsible for bringing change into the organization must make every effort to understand the culture before they attempt to make the change. Supporting his contention, Kotter has published an eight-stage formula for "creating major change" that is eminently applicable for library and other information services organizations (see sidebar on page 23). Those with change management responsibility need only to transfer Kotter's eight-stages into the information environment to benefit from his work in this area.

Kotter also suggests that successful change management has four identifiable characteristics, and they are characteristics that are particularly appropriate in the information environment:

1. Successful change depends on results, since new approaches usually sink into a culture only after it's very clear that they work and are superior to old methods.

2. Successful change requires a lot of talk, for without verbal instruction and support, people are often reluctant to admit the validity of new practices.

3. Successful change may involve turnover, since sometimes the only way to change a culture is to change key people.

4. Successful change makes decisions on succession crucial, since if promotion processes are not changed to be compatible with the new practices, the old culture will reassert itself. (Kotter, 1996)

When confronting cultural change, however, there can be fearsome barriers, and in the library and information services field, the struggle

The Eight-Stage Process of Creating Major Change

John P. Kotter

1. Establishing a sense of urgency
- Examining the market and competitive realities
- Identifying and discussing crises, potential crises, or major opportunities

2. Creating the guiding coalition
- Putting together a group with enough power to lead the change
- Getting the group to work together like a team

3. Developing a vision and a strategy
- Creating a vision to help direct the change effort
- Developing strategies for achieving that vision

4. Communicating the change vision
- Using every vehicle possible to constantly communicate the new vision and strategies
- Having the guiding coalition role model the behavior expected of employees

5. Empowering broad-based action
- Getting rid of obstacles
- Changing systems or structures that undermine the change vision
- Encouraging risk taking and nontraditional ideas, activity, and actions

6. Generating short-term wins
- Planning for visible improvements, or wins
- Creating those wins
- Visibly recognizing and rewarding people who make the wins possible

7. Consolidating gains and producing more change
- Using increased credibility to change all systems, structures, and policies that don't fit together and that don't fit the transformation vision
- Hiring, promoting, and developing people who can implement the change vision
- Reinvigorating the process with new projects, themes, and change agents

8. Anchoring new approaches in the culture
- Creating better performance through customer- and productivity-oriented behavior, more and better leadership, and more effective management
- Articulating the connections between new behaviors and organizational success
- Developing means to ensure leadership development and succession

(Kotter, 1995)

often comes down to a battle of wills. Management wants to bring about change, in fact is insisting on it. And staff, together with many of the organization's information customers, comfortable with the way things are, have great difficulty moving beyond the first stages, the first conversations about a changed process or a changed culture.

Good advice is at hand. Rosabeth Moss Kanter, for example, when asked how organizational leaders get past "the rhetoric of change," replied with characteristic directness, and offered three key steps for information managers:

- They put actions behind their words; talk is cheap. Leaders that do the best job of leading change—first of all, they have a vision of where they want to go that's well-articulated, communicated wisely, and communicated repeatedly. That way, everyone has a sense of the destination. There's no point in talking about change if you don't know where you want to go.

- Second, they look for exemplary practices—innovations—that are already occurring in the company that reflect the new way that they want to operate. Leaders put those in front of people as tangible models of what can be done.

- Third, they organize to manage a change process in which projects help move the company to a new state of being. And they put real resources into it. Leaders give people responsibility. They set in place new measures that tell people what the standards are and measure progress toward the goals. They give feedback to an organization. They look to see whether policies, practices, systems, and structures support the change goals. (Kanter, 1998)

But the information unit's leader/managers can't do it alone. They must have the support and, if at all possible, the enthusiasm of others who participate in the information delivery process. It isn't easy, and in fact there are many who will suggest—with considerable authority—that change cannot take place because certain staff members can prevent change before it even gets beyond the planning stage. If that is the case (and it might be in some organizations), how does management persuade staff to support change. After all, as one advertising slogan phrased it, "Change imposed is change opposed." Is change—and the change management process—already defeated if there are staff members who are uncomfortable with change?" Not necessarily.

The wise information manager starts with the people in the first place. Of course the mission of the organization (and of each individual subunit of the organization) is important and must be given attention. And of course the information customers must be considered. But doing that is only what is supposed to be done anyway, and the proposed change, if it is being offered for the right reasons, only reflects that attention to the organizational mission and the information customers. The missing essential at this point, however, is the staff, the people who will not only continue to enable the organization to achieve its mission and provide the customers with their information, but will, of course, be the organizational stakeholders who will implement the change and participate in the transition. This is an enormous responsibility, and for these people, participating in the process from the very beginning is essential. It is also only right from a moral perspective as the staff are the people who will ultimately be responsible for the success that the change will bring.

To acknowledge the role of these people is to acknowledge that change produces anxiety. Such acknowledgement does not have to be a debilitating exercise, however, as Katherine Kott has observed in a paper that looks at anxious response to change. First of all, Kott helps us all—management and staff alike—by taking some of the mystery out of anxiety and offering suggestions, based on the work of Dr. Murray Bowen during the 1950s and '60s and now being further developed at the Georgetown Family Center in Washington, DC [see sidebar on page 26]. For Kott, the establishment of values—what she calls "the defining of self"—is the foundation for leadership in the change management process, and it requires, above all else, that "the individual rise to the challenges of defining principles, taking stands, and thinking before acting" in order to make the change process work. (Kott, 1998)

Maureen Mackenzie, too, has recognized that resistance to change is an almost universal reaction, and her approach is to understanding that resistance through the study of cognitive factors. "The information professional who studies the technology which stores, processes, and retrieves information," Mackenzie writes in a 1998 paper, "may find substantial value in studying the storage, processing, and retrieval mechanisms of the human mind. Why? Because within our study of the human

Anxious Response to Change

*A*nxiety is a basic human condition. There are two categories of anxiety, chronic and acute. Acute anxiety is "real" anxiety, generated by stressful occurrences. Chronic anxiety is the "fretting" people do over imagined worries. How well an individual manages anxiety has a strong impact on ability to function. An individual's definition of self is closely related to the ability to manage anxiety. A well-defined self is an understanding of one's own principles, and an ability to think about one's own feeling and decide how to behave before acting. Individuals interact in relation to others in terms of "relationship systems." Like individuals in families, individuals in organizations spend enough time together to form relationship systems. The primary unit of the relationship system is the triangle. Triangles are the most stable emotional unit for people, as intensity in one-on-one relationships often causes one or the other person to bring in a third to bring the anxiety down to a manageable level.

The unpredictability of change generates anxiety. When people perceive that they do not have control over what happens to them, they experience stress, which causes psychological and behavioral changes such as loss of mental flexibility and heightened sensitivity to stimuli. In times of rapid change, anxiety generated by uncertainty can show up in altered cognitive processes, such as inability to make decisions and in exaggerated responsiveness to the environment, such as 'personality clashes' or sick building syndrome. As individuals attempt to rid themselves of anxiety, they find ways to involve others in the issues that are perceived to be causing it. In this way, anxiety travels through the relationship system.

Bowen theory posits that any individual in a relationship system can calm an anxious system by 'defining a self.' In organizational relationship systems, an individual has the most influence on the relationship systems at the same hierarchical level, below and just above. The more highly placed an individual is in the organization, the greater the influence he or she can have on agitating or calming the system.

An individual defines a self in the organizational context by explaining his or her position and setting the expectation that each individual has responsibility for his or her own behavior. To do this, the leader must be certain of his or her own principles and stand and take the time to state them clearly and calmly. When difficult relationships must be managed, the calming leader stays connected to all parties but expects the individuals involved to solve the problem. (Kott, 1998) mind, we will identify the judgmental biases that contribute to the resistance of change." Building on the work of M.L. Johnson Abercrombie on "the anatomy of judgment" (the title of Abercrombie's 1960 study), Mackenzie provides a useful analysis of the relationship between schemata formation and success in change management. She writes:

> People remark that an individual may have good or bad judgment, yet may be unaware of the intricate processes at work to form such judgment. Most people are blind to the assumptions that are programmed into their minds. These assumptions are constantly at work filtering new information and unconsciously making decisions of classification that influence future judgements.

> Abercrombie established his hypothesis stating that "we may learn to make better judgements if we can become aware of some of the factors that influence their formation. We may then be in a position to consider alternative judgments and to choose from among many instead of blindly and automatically accepting the first that comes; in other words, we may become more receptive, or mentally more flexible." Abercrombie introduces us to the schemata, which is the scheme in a person's mind that allows information to be organized.

> Within the deep-seated activity of the human mind new information is being sorted and neatly classified so it fits into what is already known and accepted. As information is presented to an individual, the human mind scans all current schematas to find a match. The mind may distort new information to make it fit into a current assumption or schemata. Information that does not fit may be omitted. Our minds may not necessarily remember information as presented, but rather misremember it, allowing it to flow into a melting pot, forming our individual perspective on what we think we saw, read, heard, or learned.

> Schematas are formed slowly as the result of our experiences beginning at birth, and these experiences ultimately influence our perspective. . . . [and] context severely influence the filtering and perception of new information. The state of mind or general attitude of the individual will also influence the actual information received and how it is interpreted. . . . During an organizational change, the context of the work environment as well as the human relationships experienced therein may severely change for the employee. Unconscious or conscious resistance may be the outcome.

An important component of change management strategies is communication. Open, ongoing communication is advised. But [it should be recognized], an employee's schemata may distort the communication message, resulting in an interpretation that is flawed. An employee may not be aware that certain schematas exist and that they are filtering or distorting information. Because the employee, as Abercrombie put it, "is not aware of them, he or she does not question the validity of using them . . . ."

Management faces the challenge of constantly making changes to processes and procedures. Employees must respond to these changes but may struggle because their work schematas have been well formed. The employee may have received recognition for his or her ability in performing work and achieving outstanding results. This successful, ingrained schemata will not easily change.

When management must install change, the strategy should be to help the employee unlearn the old schemata or even destroy it, before establishing new schemata. Allowing employees to gain a fuller, deeper understanding behind why change is needed, and why the old schemata is wrong, may help to erase the established schemata. Simply retraining may not be sufficient. Experienced employees may revert back to the old procedures (schemata) as they move away from the training. Perhaps this is the reason a newly appointed CEO may replace the current senior staff rather than try to change their schemata! (Mackenzie, 1998)

The obvious next step then, for information managers who want success in the change management process, is to go to the information staff (or whoever the information stakeholders are) and invite their participation. As Maurer puts it in his essay:

Use people's insights into both the successful and unsuccessful change efforts to develop guidelines for future initiatives. For example, one action plan might be, 'As part of the planning process we will identify all stakeholders and determine ways to involve them in the process early on." Formulating several such goals will produce an effective agenda for implementing your next change effort.

The most common finding from such exercises is that most leaders pay attention only to the technical aspects of a new initiative. They treat the change as a purely rational, linear process and seldom address the human impact of the changes they seek. On the other hand, the leaders of successful change efforts take a more systemic approach. They recognize that technical and financial planning, while essential, are not enough; cultivating relationships, communication, participation, and shared benefits is equally important.

> For effective organizations, change is an ongoing capability, not a series of recurrent events. That requires us to take a clear look at ourselves, and build on practices that have already worked. No organizational change is easy, and as leaders we need all the help we can get. Often that help is close at hand—if we ask. (Maurer, 1998)

For Kanter, the road to success in change management comes back to the manager/leaders, who " . . . do many tangible things and keep repeating them. Those who are good at mastering change keep putting the goals and the progress in front of people."

And to get straight to the point, an interviewer asked Kanter how leaders get the needed buy-in. Kanter had an answer:

> One of the best ways is to begin with the needs, interests, and points of view of the people in an organization and use that to guide changes. You don't announce a new vision or new changes until people have been asked, "What do you think? What are the challenges facing you in your job? What are the new opportunities or threats that come from the external environment?" The best way to get buy-in is to involve people in the process of defining the future. (Kanter, 1998)

Or, very specifically in terms of change in an information environment, we develop an organizational culture that will support change, according to Meg Wheatley, by getting people involved:

> Human beings are the only species to consider change, creativity, and learning to be problems . . . . Independence is not a biological construct, but a political one. The lone visionary leader who pulls the reluctant organization into the future by sheer force is a flawed concept. People only support what they create. (Wheatley, 1998)

For the information leaders interviewed in *InfoManage*, the concepts, directions, guidelines, and visions put forward by such management experts as Drucker, Maurer, Kotter, Wheatley, and the like relate directly to excellence of service in information delivery. Their talents connect in these pages, and librarians and other information workers can now benefit from their combined expertise. It is, indeed, a very good time to be in the information management business.

References

Barrier, Michael. "Small Firms Put Quality First." *Nation's Business*, 80 (5), May, 1992.

Bartlett, Christopher A. and Sumantra Ghoshal. "Changing the Role of Top Management: Beyond Strategy to Purpose." *Harvard Business Review*, November-December, 1994.

[Bender, David R.] David Bender at the Special Libraries Association: Visionary Leadership for the Information Industry.*InfoManage: The International Management Newsletter for the Information Services Professional.* 4 (7), June, 1997.

Boynton, Robert S. "The Two Tonys,"*The New Yorker* October 6, 1997.

Curzon, Susan C. *Managing Change*. New York: Neal-Schuman, 1989.

Drucker, Peter F. "The Age of Social Transformation." *Atlantic Monthly*, November, 1994.

Drucker, Peter F. "Discipline of Innovation." *Leader to Leader*, No. 9, Summer, 1998.

Drucker, Peter F. *Landmarks of Tomorrow* New York: Harper, 1959.

Ferriero, David S., and Thomas L. Wilding. "Scanning the Environment in Strategic Planning." *Masterminding Tomorrow's Information— Creative Strategies for the '90s*. Washington DC: Special Libraries Association, 1991.

Horton, Forrest Woody. *Extending The Librarian's Domain: A Survey of Emerging Occupation Opportunities for Librarians and Information Professionals*. Washington, DC: Special Libraries Association, 1994.

Kanter, Rosabeth Moss, quoted in "A Conversation with Rosabeth Moss Kanter About Leadership," by Donna J. Abernathy.*Training & Development* 52 (7), July, 1998.

Kott, Katherine. "Anxious Response to Change." Unpublished paper delivered at the conference, "Living the Future II: Organizational Changes for Success," University of Arizona Library, Tucson, AZ, April 22-24, 1998.

Kotter, John P. *Leading Change*. Cambridge, MA: Harvard Business School Press, 1996.

Kotter, John P. "Why Transformation Efforts Fail." *Harvard Business Review*, March-April, 1995.

Likins, Peter, quoted in "Living the Future II: Organizational Changes for Success," by BethAnn Zambella. *C&RL News*, 59 (7), July/August, 1998.

Mackenzie, Maureen L. "A Cognitive Look at Change Management." Unpublished paper, August, 1998.

Maurer, Rick, "Building the Capacity for Change" *Leader to Leader*, No. 8, Spring, 1998.

Orna, Elizabeth. *Managing Information Flow Within the Organization*. Westport, CT: Ashcroft, 1990.

Piggott, Sylvia E.A. 1995. Why Corporate Librarians Must Reengineer the Library for the New Information Age. *Special Libraries* 86 (1), Spring, 1995.

Ponzi, Len. "The Role of Information Policies in Corporate Knowledge Management." Unpublished paper, August, 1998.

Postrel, Virginia. "The Work Ethic, Redefined."*The Wall Street Journal*, September 4, 1998.

Senge, Peter. "The Practice of Innovation." by *Leader to Leader*, No. 9, Summer, 1998.

Spiegelman, Barbara, ed. *Competencies for Special Librarians in the 21st Century*. Washington, DC: Special Libraries Association, 1997.

St. Clair, Guy. "Exceptional Information Delivery: The TQM/QIM/SLA Competencies Connection," *Information Outlook*, 1 (9), August, 1997.

St. Clair, Guy. *Entrepreneurial Librarianship: The Key to Effective Information Services.* (London and New Providence, NJ: BowkerÐSaur, 1996).

St. Clair, Guy. *Power and Influence: Enhancing Information Services Within the Organization,* (London and New Providence, NJ: Bowker-Saur, 1994).

Wheatley, Meg, quoted in "Living the Future II: Organizational Changes for Success," by BethAnn Zambella. *C&RL News,* 59 (7), July/August, 1998.

CONCEPTUALIZING CHANGE

For change management to begin, someone in the organization must be thinking about what the organization is, what it is to become, and where it is on the journey to that goal. In information services management, that means that someone—certainly someone in authority—must be willing to think about not just how quality information delivery is implemented in the present circumstances, but how that quality delivery can be improved upon. In other words, visionary thinking is called for.

Visioning is fun, and because it's fun, conceptualizing change is the easy part of the process. In today's information management arena (and indeed, in society at large), change and the management of change have now been established as critical elements in any success in any endeavor whatsoever. And the general acceptance by those with management responsibility for successful information delivery that change is both inevitable and desirable has become the driving force for improved library and information services management. This is true regardless of the environment in which the information operation functions. The viability of inevitable and desirable change and the implementation of successful change management in the information workplace are now fundamental management concepts in information management.

What we see in the interviews in this chapter (and, indeed, in any information workplace that succeeds in fulfilling its mission) are individuals who understand clearly that their impact in the successful delivery of information in their organizations connects to Drucker's three "actions": they focus on the organizational mission, they know what results they are seeking, and they are able (and willing) to assess what they and their organizations are doing to achieve success. Conceptualizing change cannot begin without a commitment to these three activities. Not surprisingly, for many leaders in the information industry, the pursuit of these activities is so ingrained in the way they work that they are not even consciously aware of that commitment. It's just there.

For some, as with William Walker, when he was putting together SIBL, the Science, Industry, and Business Library of The New York Public Library Research Libraries, the change process started with a totally new concept, a level and a focus of information management that had not been attempted before. Pat Molholt, too, was able to envision a new framework for information delivery and curriculum development at Columbia University Health Sciences. These industry leaders were willing to go where no other information professionals had gone before.

Ken Megill and Ann Lawes, on the other hand, are not looking at information delivery as it relates to a particular institution or customer base, but at the entire realm of information management, and how it will be performed in the very near future. Both of them strongly advocate new roles and new responsibilities for information practitioners, roles and responsibilities that, in many cases, will require a drastic "letting go." That new information future will bring, according to Jerry King at the National Institutes of Health, not just new roles and responsibilities but something a lot of people aren't comfortable with, a totally new information management profession, an altogether new management entity. It will, of course, incorporate the best of the past but, when necessary, it will move beyond what is no longer working. In the new information management profession, what is "traditional" (as noted earlier in another context) will survive only as long as it contributes.

The information leaders who are leading the industry into this new discipline are very aware of what is going to be required. Deanna Marcum, for example, at the Council on Library and Information Resources and Robert Klassen at the U.S. Institute of Museum and Library Services are rewarded with the knowledge that their vision for improved and enhanced information delivery in the new global arena is one that—despite much struggle to get the vision accepted by the authorities—is one that, now in place, bears valuable fruit. And while the National Engineering Information System that David Penniman wants to see organized is yet to be, his cause is strong and will attract much attention.

What form information takes has, in the past, been a major stumbling block for quality information delivery. Libraries dealt with books and journals, records management staff dealt with current records, archives with noncurrent records. Museums took care of artifacts, and video, reel-to-reel tape, vinyl recordings, film, and similar "audio-visual" materials were given "special" treatment. No more. As Lois Remeikis makes clear as she describes knowledge management, the distinctions between the conduits that contain the information are no longer valid distinctions. Remeikis has led the way in bringing specialist librarians and other information professionals into the knowledge management environment, and since the interview with her was published, knowledge management and its companion discipline content management have evolved into motifs of major emphasis in the information industry. Remeikis recognized early on that this now-popular information management concept would be important, and it was her vision that contributed much to its acceptance in the modern information environment.

But in this new information management profession, who will be the practitioners? Two of those who are interviewed in this chapter are quite skilled at challenging the current education/training situation, and both Anne Woodsworth and Judith J. Field have their own ideas about how information workers will be taught to ensure that they provide their best work. Woodsworth's vision of education for information services is remarkable, and what she has put in place at Long Island University's Palmer School of Library and Information Studies sets a standard that other organizations with educational responsibility in the information industry will look to and, eventually, emulate. When that education vision meets Judy Field's attention to mentoring and coaching, the future of training for excellence in information delivery looks very promising indeed.

None of this happens accidentally, and those who conceptualize change in the information industry open themselves to challenges that even they can't predict. But the very act of conceptualization is the first step, and when that action is taken with the vigor and assurance that these people have brought to the process, the successful—changed—operation that they bring about simply confirms their leadership.

WILLIAM D. WALKER at NYPL's SIBL:
It's state-of-the-art information and "the pieces are coming together"

Two and a half years ago, when plans for the New York Public Library's Science, Industry and Business Library were announced, the excitement in the information community was almost palpable. Few people could think of any library or information services project that had been proposed on such an enormous scale, and the fact that the library was planned, from the very beginning, to be "the most comprehensive and sophisticated information center of its kind in the world," was enough to make every information services professional sit up and take notice.

Administratively, SIBL is one of the constituent elements that make up The Research Libraries of The New York Public Library, and William D. Walker, Associate Director, is the manager who has direct responsibility for bringing SIBL into operation. In a conversation with *InfoManage*, Bill Walker talked about some of the issues connected with the organization of this major new facility.

Originally published in *InfoManage : The International Management Newsletter for the Information Services Professional* 1 (7), June, 1994.

The concept of a large-scale, state-of-the-art specialized library and information center for the business and scientific community had been kicking around for a long time and, in fact, by 1989 (when Walker came to The Research Libraries), the then-President of NYPL, the late Timothy Healy, was already looking for a site for the projected library. By then envisioned to be the largest public information center in the world devoted solely to science and business, and now with the goal of serving an international as well as a local constituency, the new information mega-center was on its way.

It has been Bill Walker's job to coordinate it all, and the magnitude of the effort is nothing short of spectacular. SIBL will come in at $100 million, of which $84 million is for planning and construction and $16 million is for the SIBL endowment and operating expenses. Now, half-way through the project (the opening is planned for late 1995), the purchase of the space has been concluded, the design of the first phase of a two-phase restructuring is complete, and $59 million of the $100 million is in place, with the remaining guaranteed by various private/public partnerships.

"It is a unique funding arrangement," Walker notes, "and it enables SIBL to have its financial planning in place through the year 2000." But funding isn't Walker's only interest. His enthusiasm for the totality of the project comes through in any conversation about how NYPL is bringing this new information center to life.

"SIBL is a new model of library service," he says, "for the rest of The New York Public Library and hopefully for others as well. What we're doing here is a complete re-thinking of what business we're in. We want to seize the opportunity to incorporate information technology—both existing technology and that of the future—into one program." Paper-based materials will continue to be used, of course, and that's not a prospect that bothers Walker, for he has no doubt that there will be a "bridge" period when both hard-copy materials and electronic-based resources will be needed. And certainly any initiative to move to that new age of information services must be built on what already exists.

Any library, information center, or research operation being created today begins with paper-based materials, and SIBL is no exception. All along the idea has been to combine the huge NYPL science and business collections in order to make up the core hard-copy materials for the library. Just about a year ago, however, another important decision was made, to include at SIBL the materials and services of the Science and Business Collections at the Mid-Manhattan Library, the NYPL branch located at Fifth Avenue and 40th Street, just across from the Research Libraries building. Among the various findings that have come from its user studies, NYPL's managers have discovered that as far as science and business are concerned, New Yorkers aren't interested in making distinctions between "research-level" services, and "branch-level" services (with their circulating materials). So now the total SIBL materials collection will encompass some two million research-level volumes and a circulating collection of 80,000 books, a mighty impressive beginning for a "new" research facility.

As a major research center, SIBL is designed to serve a diverse, international audience of users. In addition, a series of targeted information services has been identified in order to ensure optimum service to special constituencies. Among these special programs will be a Small Business Information Service, an International Trade Information Resource Center, a program of Partnerships with Science Education, and a Premium Services research program.

So of course, by this point in the conversation, the visitor has begun to see that this is an extremely ambitious undertaking. In organizational and logistical terms, putting together an information center of this scale must be roughly akin to the kind of organization and logistics that go into building something like the new tunnel under the English Channel, or a major new skyscraper. Certainly it is an almost superhuman effort, in terms of working with staff, creating support, and dealing with change.

"Change is always threatening," Walker says, but he quickly points out that the way to get staff involved, with productive results, is to give them the opportunity to "buy in" to the project. During all the planning, the staff has not been left out, and in fact there has been a major emphasis on teamwork, on putting together planning teams, focus groups and the like to study the pros and cons of individual pieces of the project.

"One of the first things we did," Walker says, "was to get everyone hooked into an E-mail system to enable them to communicate with one another." In a place as large as The New York Public Library, face-to-face communication is often not possible and almost always difficult, and E-mail has turned out to be "the great democratizer" for the organization.

Along those same lines has been an investment of some $350,000 in individual work stations for all staff, simply because, as Walker tells it, you can't change attitudes if people don't have the right equipment for doing the work they need to do.

Among the management techniques NYPL has employed as SIBL comes closer to reality is the empowerment of some of the newer staff with high-level responsibilities, breaking down of some of the vertical, hierarchical management structure in the organization. One of the major challenges of the project, naturally, is to support the staff through a period of massive change, to prepare them for the time when "change is the constant," Walker says, describing what's coming in the information scene of the future.

In the preparation for SIBL, there is much emphasis on what Walker calls "long-range gratification strategies" for the staff, and with the creation of processing and planning teams, there has been a positive and very gratifying change in staff attitudes about the project, just in the short time they've been working together. People are now more enthusiastic about SIBL, about the changes that are coming, and in fact one of the problems is that the changes aren't coming fast enough for some.

There is a major emphasis on staff development for SIBL, and approximately $500,000 has been committed to the effort, because, as Bill Walker puts it, the library is required "to develop the information professional of the next century, to develop competencies for creating and distributing information in a digital format." Four initiatives stand out.

First, all SIBL employees will be required to adhere to basic competency standards. Second, there will be some 70-80 databases up and freely accessible to the public; staff must be expert at working with the public in using these databases. Third, there will be much networked information, and navigational and resource development skills will be required.

Employees will need to know the content of the 'Net, as well as how to evaluate the information that they access through it. Finally, there will be a required core of staff with advanced competencies in digital information management. These staff members will provide an expert knowledge base and they will not only be able to distribute information but create and package it for the specific constituent customers who will require it.

Clearly, customer service figures into the picture as well, and the work has already begun, with every staff member having had two full days of customer service training. The goal for SIBL—indeed for NYPL as a whole—is a modified TQM module, and the state-of-the-art information services at SIBL will be designed to meet the needs of the customers.

"The customer is at the focus of it all," Walker says. "The library is committed to a very formal customer service training program for all staff, and it is not an option."

Is it going to work? A few minutes' exposure to Bill Walker's infectious enthusiasm about SIBL puts to rest any doubts. He's seen it start, he's seen it come to this point, and he is optimistic about the future.

"All the pieces are coming together now," Walker says, and its obvious that the pride he and his staff have in the undertaking is genuine, and deserved.

On the other hand, that same enthusiasm might lead a visitor to conclude that SIBL is "his" project, but that would be a serious misreading of the situation, for a conversation with Bill Walker begins and ends with clear references to the teamwork, interest, and support of the staff of The Research Libraries.

"SIBL is possible," Walker says, "because all of the staff are pulling together. I can't single out any one person or any one group for special commendation. Not now. It's working because everyone is involved and determined to succeed."

The project is working because innovative, enthusiastic, and, yes, risk-taking people at NYPL have been able to envision what the institution can do. They knew that they could build an information structure that would meet the information needs of the scientific, industry, and business community in New York, and in the world.

The people at The New York Public Library have set out to succeed, and they won't stop until they do. With Bill Walker at the helm, there's no doubt that SIBL will be what it plans to be, a major international reference center and the preeminent information resource of its kind in the world.

Meet Bill Walker

Formerly Associate Director for the Science, Industry, and Business Library, New York Public Library Research Libraries and now Vice-President and Andrew W. Mellon Director of The Research Libraries, New York Public Library . . . Director of the Medical Library Center of New York from April, 1979-August, 1989 . . . Prior to that, Head of the Information Services Department and Assistant Professor at the University of Illinois at the Medical Center, Chicago, Library of Health Sciences, and Visiting Associate Professor at the University of Illinois, Graduate School of Library and Information Sciences, IL . . . Undergraduate degree from Lock Haven University, Lock Haven, PA . . . Graduate work at Pennsylvania State University . . . A.M.L.S., 1974, from the University of Michigan School of Library Science . . . To enhance his research regarding the development of SIBL, Bill Walker was awarded The Astor Fellowship of The New York Public Library in 1991, in order to study three areas: the redefinition of the role of librarians, the integration of information technologies into the reference and document delivery processes, and service and technology models that facilitate access for off-site users. In his private life, Bill Walker is an avid bridge player, but his main avocation is travel, especially to the Far East.

Relaxed at the revolution:
KEN MEGILL
takes us into information resources management

Someone once said of Ken Megill, "He's so relaxed he could come from Los Angeles." Well, that might be an arguable point, because, first of all, just how "relaxed" is Los Angeles these days, and, more important, Ken Megill would be this relaxed no matter where he came from. He's just not the kind of guy who gets too excited about things.

He is excited about information resources management, though. Megill has been pondering this subject for several years now, and the more

Originally published in *InfoManage: The International Management Newsletter for the Information Services Professional* 1 (10), September, 1994.

he thinks about it, the more excited he gets. With its emphasis on the client/user/patron, its empowering and decentralizing management structure, its integration of all information as its primary task, and its commitment to automation and electronic data transfer for providing better information products and services for those clients, well, it's a pretty exciting prospect, and a good field to be working in these days. "Aha!" you exclaim. "Automation. That's what information resources management is. It's just another tag for what we all think about all the time. It's just another name for technology."

No. Ken Megill won't let you off that easy.

"Technology-driven, but not about technology." That's how Megill describes information resources management, the new way of looking at information that recognizes information as an "identifiable, measurable, manageable" resource.

And while the concept is certainly—for today's information managers—a "new" way of thinking about information, it's not necessarily a new idea. It fact, "IRM" (as it has been affectionately acronymed) has been around for many years, since just before the turn of the century if you count the Cockerell Committee's report of the high cost of copying documents back in 1889.

But it was only in the 1970s that IRM became a subject for serious consideration in the information services management field. That was when the Conference Board published an important report entitled *Information Management: Some Critical Implications for Decision Makers*. In the report, Edward Glaser wrote that "Information may be considered a resource. Unlike other resources, it is not consumed in the process of use." This was new territory, and for many information services managers in industry and in government, the report crystallized their thinking. Now they could understand—and work with—the concept that information is a specific resource, to be dealt with as such. It was a major breakthrough in the study of information management, an event of such magnitude, in fact, that it has been described by some participants as just about the most important information activity in this century.

Megill describes information resources management as "a movement in the government to manage information and make it available to the people of the United States." But isn't that too limiting? Is IRM just about government information, and is it only American? After all, Megill is being interviewed for a newsletter with a strong international readership, and information services managers outside North America won't take too well to an idea that doesn't transfer across borders. Not to worry. Megill just smiles that easy-going, relaxed smile that seems to be characteristic of all his conversations.

"Information resources management is about information," he said, "lots of information, big blocks of information, the kind of information that is needed by governments, yes, and by huge multinational corporations as well. Any organization, anywhere, that is dealing with large quantities of information and big information structures can benefit from knowing about IRM."

Megill makes this very point in his new book, *Making the Information Revolution: A Handbook on Federal Information Resources Management* (published in 1995 by AIIM, the Association for Information and Image Management). IRM, he makes clear, is a concept that looks at information as a resource. How that concept is applied, in whatever environment, is up to the people dealing with the information. And as a direction for managers, IRM has many components that relate to the very ideas information services managers concern themselves with every day: accessibility and openness, cost, distribution and delivery, and, not least of all, the value of information within the organization or community it supports.

In a way, talking with Ken Megill about IRM and the "role" of information is a little like talking with a calmed-down Tom Peters or a revved-up Elizabeth Orna, for like Peters, Megill is quick to point out that information must be available and accessible to as many people as possible, and like Orna, he demands that the organization be structured around how information moves through the organization. It all makes sense, and when you look at what Megill refers to as the "principles" of IRM, it makes you wonder how any business or organization has functioned without recognizing these tenets:

- Information is a resource. Like other resources it has value and can be managed.

- Information gains value with use.

- Since information gains value with use, it should be available to the broadest possible audience.

- Information should be organized to meet the needs of the user; organizations should be organized around the flow of information.

- Work will be fundamentally transformed if: information is managed as a resource; information is organized for dissemination; work is organized around information flow.

Megill first got interested in IRM as the Records Manager at the U.S. Comptroller of the Currency, the Administrator of National Banks, where he observed first-hand the ramifications of working with large quantities of information. While in that position, Megill began to realize that there was, within the federal government, a group of people, a cadre, if you will, or a community, of "IRM people," government employees who took very seriously their responsibilities as information services practitioners.

Centered at the General Services Administration, the group was formalized into an IRM Task Force at the Department of Commerce and included colleagues from several government agencies. In its "Final Report" (August, 1989), the Task Force found that while program managers were beginning to "aggressively manage their information to realize benefits and cost savings," responsibility for managing information was fragmented. Most units had not delegated responsibility for the development and administration of an IRM program to a single central authority or organization, coordination among the various organizations to which IRM authorities and responsibilities had been delegated was limited, and, importantly, no formal communication channels existed for the exchange of knowledge, experiences, technologies and information across operating unit lines.

It was to address this last, of course, that the IRM training programs came into being, and Megill was there to be part of it, for he had come to Washington's Catholic University of America to put together an IRM program. He did it with great success, not only adding a course and a series of monthly seminars on the subject for the regular students at the school, but by directing an annual "institute" on federal librarianship/information management that has attracted growing attention and support from a broad range of participants.

Thanks to its location in the nation's capital, Catholic's IRM training program has had the benefit of not only Megill's leadership, but the local cooperation of a variety of government and former government information people, including Sarah Kadec, whom Megill refers to as the "god-mother" of the IRM movement. Long known for her innovative and creative approach to information services management, Kadec has teamed up with Megill to bring the program to information services professionals in the Washington area, including of course many government people, but also including members of the business world as well. And he put some of them to even more work, for several became collaborators in his book, including Kadec (who had served in the Carter White House when the Paperwork Reduction Act was conceived and implemented), Marilyn S. McLennan from the National Archives and Records Administration, Rose Cummins from the U.S. Department of the Interior, Michael McReynolds from the National Archives, Bob Woods, who manages the federal government's long-distance telecommunications program, and Tom Horan, an official of the General Services Administration. Together they are an impressive group, and Megill has brought them together to produce an IRM handbook that is, in no uncertain terms, a revolution in information management.

Megill's involvement in IRM continues. The training effort is now a major component in the graduate library program at Catholic University. And as a member of the National Committee on Non-Serial Publications of the Association for Information and Image Management, Megill takes seriously his role as a "go-between" for IRM, as a unique discipline in the field of information studies, and AIIM's goal to be more proactive in bringing to its members (and to the public at large) the kind of up-to-date, hands-on information they need to do their work more effectively. This connection explains why, in an unusual arrangement, the royalties from the sale of the book will go to a special fund at CUA to assist students in its IRM program.

Certainly it all makes sense, this connecting up of technology and customer needs, and certainly any information services manager seeking to develop a business or management plan for the information unit he or she supervises needs to include in it a strategic technology plan. Can it all work? Ken Megill thinks so, and he's staked a big chunk of his career and his reputation (and his employer's reputation) on information resources management. If, in fact, the IRM "philosophy," for lack of a better term, can be sold to senior managers in corporations, government organizations, academic institutions, or any other facility or institution that deals with information on a serious basis, Megill and his crowd will have achieved their basic goals.

And what are those goals? They're summed up in Megill's "working guides" for information resources managers: Business needs must drive technology, not the other way around, and our goal, as information professionals, is to do work better, not just, as Megill puts it, to do dumb things faster.

They're mighty fine goals. And they're what we all want, or we wouldn't be information services managers to begin with. Will we get there?

Ken Megill says we will.

Meet Ken Megill

The first Director of IRM at the School of Information and Resources Management at The Catholic University of America (since 1992) . . . Ph.D. in philosophy from Yale University in 1966 . . . Attended German universities for two years . . . After joining the faculty at the University of Florida, he spent eight months at the Institute of Philosophy in Budapest in 1968, where he wrote his first book, *The New Democratic Theory* (Macmillan, 1970) . . . Also wrote more than a dozen professional articles in philosophy that were published in several languages . . . From 1972-1982, chief organizer and, later, president of the United Faculty of Florida, representing more than 8,000 faculty and professional employees in the State of Florida . . . Came to Washington in 1982 and worked with a number of different organizations, including the National Education Association (where he founded *Thought and Action*, the largest-circulation academic journal in the United States) and the Virginia Association of Towing and Recovery Operators (where he was named the Outstanding Towing Executive in the Country by *Tow Times* magazine) . . . Received his Master of Science in Library Science from Catholic University of America in 1987 . . . Became a Certified Records Manager in 1993, one of 450 CRMs in the United States . . . Co-owner, with his companion, of the Straits of Malaya, an award-winning restaurant in the Dupont Circle neighborhood of Washington, DC.

PAT MOLHOLT's
bold CHIPS project

Think about an organizational structure that's not the usual square, or triangle, or even lots of little boxes all flattened out. Pat Molholt doesn't use those, for her way of doing things is smoother. When you walk into her office at Columbia University you observe that her work table is an oval where everyone sits together. They pass things back and forth without worrying about egos or the hierarchy getting in the way. They relate to one another without being concerned about rank. In other words, Molholt's managerial structure is an oval.

"Some people liken it to an egg," Molholt says with a grin. "But whatever you call it, it works. The various functions are distributed within the space, and the management framework is built on interdependence, collaboration, and shared responsibility."

Pat Molholt has used her oval managerial structure to create—in just over two years—an information entity that is generating major excitement in the profession. It's not finished yet, and perhaps it will always be a "work in progress." But what she is doing at Columbia University Health Sciences is going to have a mighty impact on information delivery in the future. By coming to Columbia to pull together the two connected but diverse fields of curriculum development and information services, Molholt has found herself in the enviable position of creating an information entity that is needed, supported, and anticipated with much enthusiasm by her co-workers in the academic community (and perhaps in the private sector as well, but that's a story for another time).

Molholt's new venture is well under way, which is not surprising when you consider that she had begun developing the concept from day one, when she arrived in 1992 to assume this new position with the cumbersome but aptly descriptive title of "Assistant Vice President and Associate

Originally published in *InfoManage : The International Management Newsletter for the Information Services Professional* 1 (12), November, 1994)

Dean for Scholarly Resources." She came to create an information services operation that not only met the needs of faculty and students, but would lead them, without distress, into the effective and efficient utilization of new information resources and media as they are developed in the future.

So how do you do it, when you come in with an idea that is going to affect broad segments of your community, segments that are not necessarily in tune with what you want to do?

Pat Molholt doesn't hesitate for a moment. "Two things are required," she says, "vision and a public forum."

Molholt had the vision by the time she got there, for as far as curriculum and information were concerned, she had already been discussing what needed to be done with various members of the faculty and administration. As for the public forum, Molholt was eager to test whether her concept was valid, so she eagerly accepted speaking engagements whenever they came up. By the spring of 1993, she was speaking to both library and medical groups. The approach paid off, for wherever she spoke the concept of connecting curriculum development with information services (as well as the specific design of the program she was putting into place) was received with considerable enthusiasm. When she describes the project, you can see why.

"At Columbia, we are creating an 'electronic curriculum,' a program designed to accompany students through their professional training and into their practice. It's student-centered, it's a network-based curriculum environment, and it functions from an underlying knowledge model linking information resources unique to Columbia and those elsewhere in the world."

"The user can view the curriculum from many perspectives, say that of a student of nursing, for example, or medicine, public health, or dentistry. Or it can be connected to a student's learning style. The program can thread an idea across various 'courses,' across years and disciplines, or it can be approached from the perspective of a faculty member wanting to augment a lecture or an administrator compiling a report for an accrediting agency."

As Molholt sees it, this educational environment reverses the usual learning model that assumes the writers of texts or the individual giving the lecture knows what the student needs and in what order. She and her colleagues take the view that students are capable of directing much of their own learning and that they can learn more effectively and efficiently when self-directed. What she's doing, in effect, is bringing customer services to medical education.

"And," she says, "in an environment that combines aspects of the library, aspects of tutoring and testing, and the added benefit of 24-hour, anywhere access."

The program is now organized sufficiently to have a structure, and it is administered as an extension of the Health Sciences Library. Of course it has an acronym: CHIPS, which stands for the Columbia Health Information PerspectiveS project, and it soon becomes obvious that much thought and planning has, indeed, gone into the work. In effect, what Molholt has done is to recognize that there is now an opportunity to connect curriculum planning with information services planning.

"The tie is technology," she says. "With an automated, integrated information program, the library can become a true 'service' operation, combining the faculty perspective with the librarians' perspective. It's an opportunity we've not had before."

Molholt notes that while libraries have been called the heart of a university, it's not always so, especially in the area of curriculum support. "That's where we see most clearly how libraries play a supportive, secondary role," Molholt says, and that's where she sees an opportunity for major change.

"While we librarians are worrying about the costs of publications, the lack of standards in CD-ROM products, teaching Internet skills and the like, our parent institutions are facing major problems in the delivery of education. I contend that librarians have skills and resources that can be an important part of the solution to the cost-effective delivery of instruction."

So the CHIPS project is an attempt to find a way to provide faculty with "meaningful support" as they go about creating new courses, revising old ones, and making choices about what to include and what to put aside.

Using librarians to provide workable alternatives for delivering information to supplement the lecture environment, Molholt offers a promising picture of how librarians and faculty can work together.

"There is a constant need to incorporate new information and to rethink existing information in the curriculum, particularly in professional education. Among medical schools, for example, there is currently a major effort across the country to get students out of the large lecture hall and into problem-solving groups. Our information delivery should match that. Do you realize how rare it is for students in higher education to be involved in collaborative work? Especially in college, where it tends to be labeled 'cheating'? Yet teamwork is vital, critical, in the world of professional practice. So as we move into revising the curriculum, we need to consider how we can make the revisions rational, interwoven, connected, and continuous."

And the "continuous" part has to do with the attention that continuing education must now be given in one's professional life. Here, too, the goals of the CHIPS project match up with the needs of its user community.

"The half life of a bachelor's degree in engineering is five years," Molholt points out. "In my estimation, that of a librarian's master's degree is even less, considering the changes in media and technology and the explosion of knowledge to be acquired, organized, and made accessible.

"The medical profession, and interestingly enough medical librarianship as well, have recognized the need for continuing education in their certification and credentialing processes. If, as will be the case for Columbia, we train health science professionals in a different way, by using more technology and reassessing the role of memorization, can we not also provide graduates with continuous updates to their knowledge? The learning process doesn't stop at graduation, but our information-based relationship with the student does. With the Internet and increasing connectivity, might we not have options for a longer-term relationship and a more extended/protracted role for the alma mater in life-long learning?"

So how is the CHIPS project coming together? Here we come back to Molholt's oval, that management structure that works so well. As she described how she works with her staff, making that reference to "interdependence, collaboration, and shared responsibility," it becomes obvious that this project is going to succeed because the team is geared up to work together, to achieve a common goal that all team members agree is the way to go.

Molholt has four people on her management team, and each of them has different responsibilities and a different "piece" of the project (the total effort involves some 60 FTE employees). All of the four are at the director level. One, for example, directs the Health Sciences Library and coordinates library-related issues into the CHIPS scenario. Another directs the Center for Academic Computing. A third directs the Center for Curriculum Evaluation and Faculty Support and the fourth, as might be expected, is the Business Manager. Together, with Molholt, they ensure that those different perspectives she talks about all have appropriate representation within the enterprise.

One benefit of this arrangement is that library and information services have acquired a much closer affiliation with the rest of the campus, have become more "mainstream," and have thus created within the university community a heightened awareness about the role and value of information. This awareness, in turn, has helped to develop the identity of the Office of Scholarly Resources as an agency for change within the university, a development that has been good both for the CHIPS project and for Columbia University.

So that oval management structure makes a great deal of sense, and it says much about Molholt and her approach to this monumental project she's involved with. It also makes sense in the environment in which she and her people are attempting to create this new information entity.

"It's all part of a broader information context within the university at large," she says, and she hastens to give credit where it is due. Dr. Herbert Chase, for example, coordinates the first-year curriculum for medical students and has worked closely with Molholt's staff not only in directly connecting curriculum development with information services, but also in finding grant support for their work. Similarly, Elaine Sloan, University Librarian, is engaged in what Molholt characterizes as a "full frontal attack on digital library issues," and brings to the table an attitude and an approach that enables Molholt and her people to do their work in a context in which creativity and innovation represent something akin to a "requirement" for success in this particular arena.

And from the very beginning, there was internal support to move ahead, emanating from Dr. Herbert Pardes, Vice-President for Health Sciences, on down throughout the administrative side of the university. As far as the immediate community was concerned, there was no need to deal with that usual barrier to innovation, the need to persuade authoritative information stakeholders within the community to "buy in" to the idea. In this case, the stakeholders were ready to buy in—they just needed someone to bring them the concept. Pat Molholt was that someone, and CHIPS was the concept.

So what will it look like—this CHIPS project—when it's up and running? Molholt expects three stages of implementation, the first of which is simply an electronic counterpart to the library's collection of books and journals. Then there is the curriculum model, and it is here that Molholt and her team can rightfully be very proud of what they are doing, for in order to work the curriculum model requires nothing less than changing the culture. There's no room here for the usual "turf wars" that characterize so much activity in the academy, for everybody has to cooperate. So while medicine is the first thrust in this new curriculum model, Molholt is quick to point out that it will go much further, "eventually encompassing the schools of dentistry, nursing, and some aspects of public health."

Linking defines the third stage, for CHIPS exists, if for no other reason, "to bind the information resources, the images, the animation, the video, and whatever other resources become available, to the skeleton that is the curriculum model. And we'll create only those information resources that we cannot acquire from others, whether commercially or on an exchange basis. The whole purpose of the linking is to build pathways to enable the students to move about among the resources, perusing new knowledge, taking tests on material, being tutored, and so forth."

So the time has come, it seems, to recognize that libraries and other information services activities are, yes, as vital as they have always been. But in our new information environment in which every medical student, every practicing physician, every dentist, nurse, and, eventually, every public health practitioner will have access to the systems he or she needs for acquiring information, the passive, reactive delivery of information won't work anymore. Information customers will be seeking information as they themselves want to find it, on their own terms. By building an information services operation that is based on customers' needs—and on their own perceptions of their needs—Pat Molholt and the CHIPS project at Columbia are moving in a thrilling new direction for information workers.

Will it be the best of both worlds? That depends on many different factors, and not all of them relevant to this description. But no matter how much—or how little—CHIPS succeeds, it does things with information and education that have not been done before. And in the doing, the students, the teachers, and the information services professionals are all better off for it. That, in itself, is a remarkable achievement for Pat Molholt and Columbia University Health Sciences' Office of Scholarly Resources.

Meet Pat Molholt

Since 1992, Assistant Vice President and Associate Dean for Scholarly Resources, Columbia University Health Sciences . . . Previously Associate Director of Libraries (1978-1992) and Affirmative Action Advisor to the President (1988-1992), Rensselaer Polytechnic Institute, Troy, NY . . . 1987-1988 Sabbatical Term spent as a Senior Research Analyst in the Office of Library Programs at the U.S. Department of Education . . . Other career service as the Director of the Science and Technology Library at the University of Wyoming, Director of the Physics Library and Director of the Woodman Astronomical Library at the University of Wisconsin at Madison . . . Has held a variety of offices in the International Federation of Library Associations and Institutions (IFLA) . . . Was President of the Special Libraries Association, received SLA's John Cotton Dana Award in 1989 and is an SLA Fellow . . . Currently serves on the New York Regent's Visiting Committee on the State Archives and as a member of the Editorial Board of Electronic Networking. Research, Application, and Policies . . . Ph.D. Dissertation: "Standardizing Inter-Concept Relationships in Knowledge Structuring" . . . Frequent author of articles in professional journals . . . Often speaks to professional organizations about technology and the implications of new technology in information services . . . Makes her home in Scarsdale, NY.

ANN LAWES:
Thinking about the information manager as change agent

In London's information community, Ann Lawes has built up something of a reputation as a pragmatist / philosopher / mentor. With particular responsibility for TFPL's professional development services, Lawes is frequently called upon to express her opinions about the information services field and where it is going. She's a modest person, though, and when asked, she hastens to tell you that she is not delivering any great "truths" about information services management.

Originally published in *InfoManage : The International Management Newsletter for the Information Services Professional* 3 (1), December , 1995

"Don't expect me to be some sort of theorist," she says. "My outlook about all this is pure 'man in-the-street,' strictly practical. I've been involved in information services management for a long time, most of it in the business and industrial community, and my outlook is based purely on practical needs."

Well said. And true. But in fact that attitude, as sincere as it is, is just a little disingenuous, for Lawes has been flirting with some pretty serious subjects over the last few years. As she's seen the professional development programs at TFPL, Ltd. grow into the enormous success that they are now (the firm's training suite is seldom vacant, and the list of information management / information services-related courses on offer is fairly staggering), Lawes has come in contact with a great number of practicing librarians and information services workers. That exposure has given her a unique vantage point for observing how the library and information services profession is being practiced, and—at the same time—has provided her with a unique perspective for thinking about what the profession needs.

"I'm not a pessimist by nature," Lawes says, "and I am really uncomfortable beginning this conversation by commenting about some of our failures in the library and information services field, but I really think we don't seem to recognize what enormous change agents we are. There is so much change going on in society at large—and in the information field—that the words 'change' and 'change agent' have almost become devalued. We say them so much that we don't really think about what we're saying. But in fact we information managers have a tremendously important role. We are the very people who influence others in how they use information, who change the way they access information. And it is incumbent on us to recognize and manage how the changes we introduce affect our users.

"That's a formidable responsibility," Lawes continues. "We've got people coming into our organizations, coming out of university and other training programs, and they're going to have key roles in these organizations in the future. And look at how comfortable they are with information. They come to work with us, and they're so comfortable with information it's almost as if they've got computers hanging off the ends of their fingertips. They are a far different breed than the people for whom we have previously provided information."

Lawes has thought about this, and she knows what she is talking about.

"It's not so neat yet," she says, "and I'm not sure I've got it all worked out. But there are some trends, some factors that affect the way we are going to be managing information. We have to step back and think about them, about how they affect the way we do our work, and about how they affect users of information.

"The first bit, for example, has to do with what I just said, the people who are going to be looking for information, the people who will be managing organizations in the future. Right now they're the end-users, and they want fast information. And we must give it to them, that is, we must give them the means for finding it, show them how to get it themselves. And that means we must persuade them to change their working practices, to change how they use information, to think about things that they weren't thinking about before. If they're going to be end-users—and if we are going to be working with them to help them find information—they must change how they think about information. And that's our job, to show them how to change and to convince them that the change is worthwhile.

"We have to do it, because if we are going to be working in knowledge-based organizations—which we know we are—then the whole organization becomes information focused. And the information is not limited to external information or internal information or what the librarian finds or what the records manager finds. Those categories will become irrelevant, as information customers begin to demand one-stop shopping in an integrated information environment. There's just no way information staff will be able to deliver all that information by using traditional methods, so we've got to transform the information customers into information end-users and give them the help that they need to get the information they want. Look at what's happening: now we're talking about a massive consultation and training job, and it's the information professionals who will be called upon to do this work. And as they do this work, they do it while bearing in mind the huge changes they're asking people—the information customers—to undergo."

This is getting serious, and Lawes stops to focus her thoughts.

"At the same time," she continues, "there's another thread to this, and that's the hodgepodge of delivery mechanisms that we're all frantically trying to keep up with all the time. They're changing so fast that even information services staff can't keep up, so how must the end-users feel? That's what we've got to know, and then we have to work with them so they can learn to use and exploit these changed delivery mechanisms."

Even then, it doesn't get easy, for there are other factors Lawes has identified that influence the way we work with these "new" information customers. For example, we all talk a great deal about the amount of information that is becoming available, about how information as a commodity is increasing—globally—("by leaps and bounds" is the way Lawes puts it) and how it is not just the amount of information that is increasing but the access points, the amount of accessibility that is also increasing incrementally. So there are more challenges for librarians and information managers: how to keep up, just so they can advise the end-users who will come to them for advice, for if it's hard for the information professionals to keep up, the end-users aren't going to have a clue, except in those specific areas of expertise in which they work. The information professionals are going to have to lead the way.

"Well, not just the librarians," Lawes points out. "It's very much a cooperative arrangement, for in fact it's the librarians and the information technology people working together who become the change agent. The information workers who understand the content of the information—the librarians, the records managers, the archivists, and people like that—will need to join forces with the IT people, and together they take on that enormous responsibility I'm talking about, showing people how to manage and use information."

Obviously what Ann Lawes is looking at is a new—and very different—role for librarians and information services managers. It's a role that, at the risk of trivializing the concept, moves them almost into a "pop psychology" realm, a realm where they are to take responsibility for the satisfaction of their information customers in their—the customers'—quest for information. That's a very different thing from what most librarians and information services professionals are trained to do. In fact, one can't help but wonder if librarians and information professionals, educated as they are currently being educated, are up to these tasks, to taking on this "ownership," this almost psychological direction they're being asked to embrace.

It's not a question, as far as Ann Lawes is concerned.

"We don't have a choice," she says. "This is a different situation than we had two years ago, when I first spoke to *InfoManage*. Then, we were just thinking about these change agents, and wondering what was going to happen. Now we know. They're all coming together, and it's nothing less than a revolution for the information services profession. And how we got there isn't important. Recognizing that we're there is what's important, and that means letting go of a lot of baggage. We've simply got to do it."

As an example, Lawes describes the excitement in the UK now that the Labour Party's leader, Tony Blair, has obtained a commitment from British Telecom for getting libraries and schools wired into the Internet. The uproar is political, of course, about whether Labour can really do it and why the Conservatives didn't do it, and the brickbats are flying back and forth like crazy, as they usually are in British politics. But the point is not whether it's going to happen or not. It's going to happen, and what will be needed will be changed mind sets about information, especially within the library and information services community. The implications, Lawes is quick to point out, are tremendous, because when the change comes, it will give focus to the 'Net. And when there is focus, there is a market. This is a pretty powerful paradigm for information workers, and again Lawes raises the question: can the library and information services profession—as now structured—provide the people to do this work?

So you end up, according to Lawes, with a picture of the current state of information services management that is almost visual: on the one side, you've got these change factors, the things that are influencing how information is delivered, the "new" end-users, the disorganized and uncoordinated delivery mechanisms, the huge amount of information and the multiplicity of access points, the cooperation (required—not optional—according to Lawes' way of thinking) between the IT people and the content people, and the integration of information. At the other end of the spectrum, you've got the information customers, the people who need the information, and they're people who, in a knowledge-based organization, are going to be required to find that information for themselves. And smack in the middle of the line, linking it all together and making it happen, are the change agents, the librarians, the archivists, the records managers, the information managers, the information specialists, the IT people, the information scientists.

And the big issue for the folks in the middle, the people who are, as Lawes is very quick to point out, the people who make it work, is taking on board how the information customers—the end users—feel about change, how they react to change. No, it is not easy, and it is not going to be easy. It requires the leading players in the information services field to take on a vision of information delivery that makes the end-users the focal point, recognizes them as the key, and requires information managers to act pro-actively across the entire organization. It's a vision that requires an information services operation that isn't static, isn't a stand-alone operation, and is—along with other departments—organic to the organization as a whole.

At the end of the day, it's a vision of information services that asks a very important question. And while it's an easy questions to ask, it's a tough one to answer. Nevertheless, Ann Lawes insists it be asked:

Where do we find the people, the information workers? If we are going to meet the challenges that Lawes has identified, where do we find the people who will be the information managers of the 21st century?

Obviously some information services workers will be educated and trained in graduate business schools, other professional educational programs, in continuing education and professional development courses and seminars, and even in vendor-sponsored programs. On the other hand, information services managers—those "leading players" Lawes talks about—will continue to be educated in graduate programs of library and information science. Certainly the ones headed for careers in public, academic, and school libraries will be educated in these institutions, and as long as some of these graduate schools continue to give attention to specialized librarianship (as most are now doing, at least to some extent), many of the leading players in the business and organizational information community will be educated at the library schools as well.

So now the question becomes one of direction, of accountability and of responsibility, and it's a question Ann Lawes is very comfortable in asking: Are the library schools willing to provide the information workers the fiercely competitive information community is going to need? She admits she doesn't have all the answers, but she demands that the question be asked for, as she puts it, "If they don't, someone else will."

Meet Ann Lawes

Director, Professional Development, at TFPL, Ltd., London . . . Began career at the Science Museum Library in London, but quickly moved into the chemical industry, working in competitive intelligence and marketing information systems . . . Then moved to the advertising industry and later worked as an information consultant, with expertise in the management of small special libraries . . . Joined TFPL when the company was organized in 1987, coming on board as a Director, with special responsibility for courses, conferences, and seminars . . . Writes and lectures on a variety of subjects related to records management and the management of information services . . . Edited *Management Skills for the Information Manager* (Ashgate, 1993) . . . Active member of the Records Management Society (edits *The Records Management Bulletin*) . . . Member of the *InfoManage* Editorial Advisory Board . . . Like many professionals working in the City, Lawes keeps a flat in London, but retreats to Gloustershire on weekends to enjoy her garden.

Knowledge Management: The third "era" of the information age?
LOIS REMEIKIS
at Booz-Allen & Hamilton thinks that it is

As the information services discipline has developed, one of the most striking attributes of this new line of work has to do with how its practitioners handle the massive changes taking place in the workplace. Dealing with change causes untold worry for many information services workers, and they aren't very happy with the disruption and uncertainty that change brings to their jobs.

On the other hand, there's a group of information professionals who seem to relish the challenges and demands of the "new" information workplace. For them, the negative, old-fashioned, "things-aren't-what-

Originally published in *InfoManage : The International Management Newsletter for the Information Services Professional* 3 (10), September, 1996

they-used-to-be" point of view is just boring. They want to move forward, and they are excited and stimulated by the changes that are taking place in society and, of course, in their work. For these people, the changing information workplace simply provides an opportunity to shine, a chance to put forward their own positive perspective about how good information delivery can be.

For these people, there are no lingering doubts about whether working in information services is a positive or a negative experience, about whether the glass is half-empty or half-full. They know where the future of information services lies, and they plan to participate fully in getting the profession there.

One of these people is Lois Remeikis, who just might turn out to be one of the ringleaders in the movement to position information services management as the critical function in the organizational framework. Remeikis has spent the last couple of years working with her staff and the other employees of Booz-Allen & Hamilton around the world in thinking about information management from a very broad-based point of view, in getting comfortable with the idea that information and information delivery are important in the grand scheme of things, and that information and knowledge are a critical part of the big picture that leads to organizational success. Change and change management are key elements in the work that Lois—and Booz-Allen as a whole—are doing.

"It's not something we can even be concerned about any more," she says, referring to the role of change in today's workplace. "And certainly I understand that as well as anyone. For a long time I was pretty uncomfortable with dealing with change. Not to make too big a deal of it, I was referred to by friends as 'stubborn,' as someone who wouldn't yield. But you can't take that kind of attitude into the business world, into the workplace. You come to a point where you realize that there's so much change in the business world, you simply have to accept it and move on. You simply have to learn to be comfortable living with a lot of ambiguity."

Remeikis warms to her subject, and it becomes clear that sometimes all the talking about change and change management just gets in the way. It's not the change management that has to be concentrated on, it's the work that has to be done. So it's best to move beyond change and change management as quickly as possible.

"Look," she says, and you can tell by her tone of voice that this is a subject that has been talked about a great deal in her presence. "Change is good. It's not something to worry about."

But then Remeikis's face lights up, and she laughs as she remembers the approach taken by another of the senior information managers she knows in the corporate world.

"One of my colleagues has the right idea," she says. "She just tackles it head-on. She just tells her people to quit bitching and to look at this positively: change is going to happen, and if you give it the right twist, it can be a whole new adventure. So you might as well just accept it and get on with what you have to do."

This "new adventure" is exactly what Remeikis has taken on in her work. For one thing, she and the 79 people she supervises in her global group have to look beyond the immediate work that they do, because Booz-Allen & Hamilton is a global firm, a big firm with a strong international presence, and the information professionals can't expect to limit their work to just the day-to-day sorts of assignments. They have to think in "big picture" terms, and it's that moving toward the big picture, toward understanding the implications of the global marketplace and global information issues that has led Remeikis and her people into exploring knowledge and knowledge management.

"What we're attempting to do," she says, "is to define, create, capture, use, share, and communicate the company's best thinking about the many different subjects that impact the company's work. Obviously this activity, this quest, is a little different in each organization, in each of the sub-units of the company, but that doesn't mean it doesn't have to be looked at, or that we don't try to pull it all together."

And "pulling it all together" is pretty good way to define the concept of "knowledge management" that Remeikis is bringing to her company, and, not to be dismissed too lightly, to the information services field at large. Of course other people are doing work in knowledge management as well, and there are now employees in many organizations and corporations identified as "knowledge managers." What Remeikis is doing, though, is going beyond the basic—and now somewhat established—knowledge management concepts within this or that specific organization and bringing the knowledge management discipline to the information services community at large. She is specifically interested in seeing that the information practitioners—the special librarians, archivists, records managers, even MIS staff—get involved in knowledge management, simply because they are, to her way of thinking, best qualified to do this work.

Which explains why she has thrown herself into leading the effort to establish a networking group within the Special Libraries Association, the international organization that just happens to be her own primary professional association. For Remeikis and her colleagues at Booz-Allen & Hamilton, knowledge management is an idea whose time has come, and it just makes sense, they think, for SLA to have some mechanism, some organizational sub-group, available for people who are interested in learning more about (and applying in their own organizations) the principles of knowledge management.

"There are many, many people working as special librarians who are qualified to be knowledge managers in their organizations," she says. "Bringing knowledge management into the SLA organizational sphere seems to make a lot of sense."

Apparently some of SLA's leaders think so, too, for thanks to Remeikis's efforts, her work came to happy fruition in the spring of 1996, when SLA's Library Management Division authorized a Knowledge Management Section as a sub-unit of the division. With more than 50 charter members, the Section is on its way to becoming a strong networking focus for people interested in knowledge management.

Certainly there were plenty of special librarians who were thinking along those lines at SLA's 87th Annual Conference. At that conference, held in June in Boston, MA, there was a program—billed in the conference program as a "roundtable discussion"—on knowledge management, and several hundred people showed up. All of them wanted to learn more about knowledge management and, particularly, they wanted to learn how they could take the idea of knowledge management forward in the companies and organizations where they have management responsibility for some phase of information services. It was an amazing show of interest, and it sent a very clear message to Remeikis and her colleagues that knowledge management, as a management discipline, is a subject that has great potential in the information services workplace. The session, which Remeikis chaired, looked at the three key issues that relate to knowledge management (information technology, processes, and change management), and the meeting ended with all participants wanting to know more about the specifics and management applications of knowledge management as a new focus in information services.

Of course there were those in the audience who had come out of curiosity, who just wanted to know what knowledge management is, and how it is applied in today's information services environment. The answer had actually been supplied some months earlier, in a paper Remeikis wrote for *The Business and Finance Bulletin*. In the Fall, 1995, issue, in an article entitled "Knowledge Management—Roles for Information Professionals," Remeikis had very clearly defined the concept:

"Simply put, knowledge management is the creation, capture, exchange, use, and communication of a company's 'intellectual capital'— an organization's best thinking about its products, services, processes, market, and competitors. Closely related to a company's other information activities, *Knowledge Management* involves gathering internal information, such as financial and marketing data, and combining it with related external data, such as competitive intelligence. It goes beyond simple records management in that the information captured may include ongoing discussions, corporate stories, and other facts not typically documented."

What Remeikis is working with is, of course, closely related to the integrated information management that some of the leaders in information services have been attempting to bring to the attention of organizational and corporate management for a number of years. Certainly knowledge management relates to the work that Elizabeth Orna did back in the late '80s when she identified information as "anything" that people need in order to do their work, regardless of where and how that information is captured, and then related that entity, that commodity, to the organization's achievement of its stated mission. But knowledge management goes further than that, for it also ties in to the concepts that Ken Megill and others put forward when they ushered in the Information Resources Management effort that not only linked all the various information "elements," as it were, but added to them a philosophy of information delivery that demands that organizations should be organized around the flow of information, and that work is essentially transformed—for the better, in organizational terms—when this happens.

As Remeikis sees it, what the knowledge management "piece" adds to the equation is that "best practices" framework, and that, she says, is where each organization (and the information professionals in the organization) can begin their move into knowledge management.

"It's a beginning point," Remeikis says, "sharing best practices, lessons learned, benchmarking, and that kind of thinking. In fact, I think what is different about knowledge management is that it requires people to change their behavior, specifically to change how they work within the organization or the company and how they share what they know. It means that they have to be willing to break down what I call the "knowledge fiefdoms,' those little individual power bases that get built up in every organization, every department of every organization, even in individual offices. Knowledge management takes a look at the concept of teamwork—which we've all agreed is highly valued in today's workplace if the company is going to be successful—and moves that thinking about teamwork into the way we handle information."

It's a very powerful paradigm, and it just very well might be moving information services management into what some would call the third "era" of our information age. Certainly it evolves directly from the so-called second "era" that Sylvia Piggott (as described in the February, 1995, issue of *InfoManage*) and others have suggested we're in now, an era in which we've outgrown our earlier fascination with technology as technology. In this second era, according to Piggott and the "second era" thinkers, we recognize that the technology is important, but we recognize that technology is an enabler that permits us to reengineer our processes, to concentrate on the needs—and the authority—of the information customer, and to move our best efforts into meeting those needs.

What happens with knowledge management—if Remeikis and her colleagues are right—is that it moves information services into a third realm, in which the organizational or corporate goal is not just the delivery of information, but the literal, seamless integration of internal and external information that links directly to the achievement of organizational success. A powerful paradigm, indeed.

But can it work?

"The whole effort requires core knowledge teams," Remeikis says, "and that's exactly where the concept either works or it doesn't. People must be willing to take a leap of faith that they are doing the right thing, that moving organizational information services efforts toward the integration of information, and seeking out and sharing best practices, is good for the company.

"So of course part of it is finding 'like souls,'" she continues, this time with a grin that tells you she likes this part of the job. "You have to recognize that all organizations are going to be different, and the people are going to be different, but that's o.k., too. Knowledge management can be very much a 'grass roots' sort of effort. It doesn't necessarily have to involve senior management or even have senior management support. But ideally, of course, it would have top-level support.

"In any case, knowledge management is not something that needs to be off-putting, or something to be afraid of. What it is, in effect, is a marvelous opportunity for information services practitioners to take responsibility, to be interested in moving the organization's information management ahead. Certainly that's what we do at our company: we enthusiastically encourage staff to take responsibility for information involvement, and if they do, we'll help their develop their careers. It's that kind of organization and that kind of culture."

Core knowledge teams. Leap of faith. Sharing best practices. "Grass-roots" effort. Responsibility for information involvement. For information services professionals who want to make a mark in their organizations, who want to position themselves as the information leaders that they know they are, knowledge management makes a lot of sense.

Keep your eye on knowledge management. And on Lois Remeikis. This is a combination that is going to pay off for the information services community.

Meet Lois Remeikis

Lois A. Remeikis is Director of Knowledge & Information Manager for Booz-Allen & Hamilton, and is based in Chicago. She is responsible for global management and leadership of the company's Information Professional Community and its knowledge and information infrastructure, including oversight of Knowledge Online operations and processes, practice information/knowledge management and research services activities, and library automation and external information systems. She is a member of Booz-Allen's Core Knowledge Team.

Prior to coming to Booz-Allen, Remeikis was Assistant Executive Director and Head, Nutrition InfoCenter for the National Center for Nutrition and Dietetics (NCND) of The American Dietetic Association. Information management responsibilities and administrative responsibilities encompassed the design, implementation, and direction of an ongoing consumer nutrition hotline, automation of office functions and library services, and the development, implementation, and management of a fee-based research library. Earlier work experience included service as a Product Manager and the

Information Service Department Director for the Bank Marketing Association, where she developed and marketed the FINIS (Financial Industry Information Service) database for the Association. Previously, she worked in reference positions in other business libraries.

Remeikis holds the Bachelor of Arts (Anthropology) and Master of Library Science degrees from the University of Wisconsin. Her memberships include the Special Libraries Association, for which she is Chair of the new Knowledge Management Section of the Library Management Division, the National Federation of Indexing and Abstracting Services, and the Chicago Council on Foreign Relations. She is a Past-Chair of SLA's Food, Agriculture, and Nutrition Division and the Trade and Professional Roundtable of SLA's Business and Finance Division. She is the author of "Knowledge Management—Roles for Information Professionals" (*Business and Finance Bulletin*, Number 100, Fall, 1995), and she has taught in graduate library and information studies programs.

Lois Remeikis lives in Chicago, and her personal interests include cooking, gardening, and opera.

Making the case for a national engineering information system:
DAVID PENNIMAN
has found his challenge

You should, at the very least, give Dave Penniman an "A" for tenacity. He's been promoting the idea of a national system to serve engineers' information needs since his early days as a young engineer at Battelle Memorial Institute. It was there that he had his first experience with government-supported "information analysis centers" and saw the real power of effective information delivery systems on design and development work. It was also there that he worked on a project sponsored by the National Science Foundation to look at the feasibility of a "United Engineering Information System"—a project conducted in the late 1960s that provided a framework for the type of system needed by engineers, but never implemented.

As the saying goes: That was then, this is now. Penniman moved on from Battelle to a job overseas, and then to OCLC, and then to AT&T Bell Laboratories where he was in charge of the company's internal information systems. But he never forgot the idea of a national system that could serve the needs of engineers. In fact, along the way he became even more convinced of its need. Then, in 1991, he became President of the Council on Library Resources (CLR), and he had the chance to propose and promote the idea of the national system again. Penniman has now moved on from CLR, to the Center for Information Studies at the University of Tennessee, but he is still committed to the idea that engineers' information needs can be met more effectively than they are met now, and whenever he can, he presents his ideas at national meetings and other forums. *InfoManage* caught up with Penniman after he had delivered a presentation at the recent Special Libraries Association's Annual Conference in Boston. It was a good opportunity to learn more about his thinking.

Originally published in *InfoManage : The International Management Newsletter for the Information Services Professional* 3 (12), November, 1996.

Penniman quickly admits that his ideas about information systems for engineers were shaped by Harry Goodwin, a fellow Battelle employee and an early advocate of user-centered design (based on experience with information analysis centers). Goodwin published an article (in the November, 1959, issue of *Special Libraries*) that described what a good information system should do. He said users should:

- get the information they desire
- get it at the time it is desired (not before and not after)
- get it in the order of importance
- get it with auxiliary information attached
- get it with indications of reliability included
- get it with the authority of the information source indicated
- get it while exerting minimum effort to obtain the desired information
- be screened from undesired / untimely information
- know that negative results mean the information doesn't exist

Penniman likes to point out that it has been almost forty years since that article was published, and American engineers still don't have a system that meets their information needs in the way Goodwin described. The "information analysis centers" of the 60s and early 70s began to do this, but it was at tremendous expense (paid for at the time by the U.S. Government). The problem was, the expense was explicit but the benefit—in dollars saved—was not, much like in libraries today. And also as with today's libraries, the promise of automation ultimately did in the labor-intensive operations of the analysis centers.

In his talks, Penniman uses Goodwin's ideal characteristics as a framework for a comparison between today's libraries, the emerging World Wide Web, and the old information center concept.

The problem, Penniman points out, is that many managers and senior executives believe that the new Internet-based World Wide Web will solve the information problems of engineers (and scientists) and save money when it comes to locating needed information.

"Not so," Penniman says. "In fact, the dollars spent in time and effort searching the Web are not known. Unfortunately, the dollars spent on a library in an organization are known all too well, while the benefits are seldom measured in dollars. So you end up with a model in which a library is identified as having explicit costs and hidden benefits, while the Web is shown with hidden costs but with explicit benefits (the fact that it reaches everyone, for example, or that it appears to provide comprehensive information, or, worse yet, that it appears to eliminate the need for a library). Within this scenario, it is not surprising that many who should know better say that the engineering information problem is solved, or that the need for a national effort is not a real need."

At this point in the discussion, Penniman's commitment to his quest becomes dramatically evident, for he is prepared to take on what he calls "the big vested interests." He explains that the reason the idea of a United Engineering Information System didn't succeed back in the 60s, and why it still has not been supported, is that the larger professional societies don't want to collaborate to make it happen.

Now that's a pretty strong accusation. Why don't these organizations want to collaborate?

"It's pretty basic," Penniman says. "Each society wants to be the "one-stop shop' for its own members, and for any market it can reach beyond its own members. Each of the large societies relies on its own sale of publications for as much as fifty percent of its revenue. And, each of the large societies doesn't want to trust a unified distribution system that could serve all engineers. If they did, they would have done so before now. Unlike medicine, agriculture, and education, there is no National Engineering Library. And if there were, it would have to focus on engineers and their needs—not scientists and general science information—to really be useful."

In fact, how engineers and scientists seek information is a subject of some controversy and confusion, and not recognizing that engineers and scientists seek information differently is the cause of some of the problem. Many people involved in establishing information policy in their organizations seem to think that engineers and scientists have the same information-gathering behavior.

Penniman suggests that this is not generally the case, and to make his point, he likes to refer to a book written by Tom Allen, a scholar at MIT. Written in the late 1970s, the book (*Managing the Flow of Information*) is still in print, Penniman says, because it has useful information about engineers. He shares a quote:

> "Engineers are not scientists. . . . It is just that failure to recognize the distinction that has resulted in so much misdirected policy. In the field of information science, it has often resulted in heavy investments in solutions to the wrong problem. . . . The engineer's technique for acquiring formal literature is very informal. If the material is not available in his own work area, he either seeks it from a colleague or conducts a personal library search. Only on very rare occasions does he resort to such formal aids as a library assistant or a technical abstract."

So of course the question has to be asked: Are Allen's ideas still valid, a couple of decades on?

"Of course," Penniman replies, and his tone of voice lets you know this is a subject he feels strongly about. "Here's a recent report, one that I sponsored when I was at the Council on Library Resources. It's available from CLR as *Communication by Engineers*. It summarizes more current research on the distinction between engineers and scientists. Listen to this: "Engineers first consult their personal stores for information; then, they seek out co-workers inside their organization; next, they consult colleagues outside their organization. If these strategies do not yield the necessary information, the engineers use the literature resources found in a library. Only as a last resort do they consult a librarian.

"Now that's what worries me," Penniman says. "I want to change that. I want to give engineers faster, more cost effective access to information from any source, and I want to see a national system that serves them—and one that involves librarians in its design and operation."

Penniman also believes that much of the engineers' 'attitude' about information is formed early on.

"In my opinion, engineering schools need to design into their course work more projects requiring the use of information and data not distributed in the classroom," he says. "Engineers need to learn from the outset that external information sources can save them time and money."

But that won't happen, Penniman says, as long as there's no cooperation toward a United Engineering Information System.

"With each major professional society wanting to create its own one-stop shop, and with no coordination among these societies, the number of such sites on the Web is proliferating. There are at least a half dozen sites now offering "comprehensive access' to engineering information and dozens more are offering some smaller pieces of the information-resources puzzle. But with so many "one-stop shops,' there is really no "one-stop shop.' And without some coordinated national effort, the Web is creating more—not fewer—places to look for information, and making the search process more—not less—frustrating. It's yet another reason why a national system for engineering information is called for."

Penniman is also concerned that many of the functions previously provided by libraries and traditional publishers will be lost in the uncoordinated development of information sources. He wants to know, for example, who will perform such library-related activities as the identification of user needs, the organization of information, public services (free access, the sharing of resources, help/training, and single-access-point delivery of information), and collection development. Similarly, Penniman is worried about who will provide the traditional publishing functions, which he is quick to list:

- editorial work (the review and screening of texts)
- production (design, format, and layout)
- legal (contracts, copyright, etc.)
- financial (again, contracts, author payments, reprint payments, etc.)
- operations / clearinghouse
- marketing, promotion, distribution, distinctive imprint, etc.

Looking back at the performance scorecard he referred to earlier, Penniman also points out that the factors of reliability, authority, screening, and confidence are all quality-related characteristics—and that's where the discipline of a coordinated approach, a national library, can really contribute. And finally, Penniman talks about the rising costs of information. Resource costs are rising, not only in terms of price but more so in terms of the time spent by engineers in learning about and locating material, let alone reading it and analyzing it.

"Unfortunately," he notes, "this cost is seldom discussed, while the cost of operating a library (electronic or otherwise) is seen as an "overhead' expense."

Just before he left CLR, at the end of 1994, Penniman brought together a group of top-level individuals from a variety of government, non-profit, and professional organizations. They met at the National Academy of Engineering to see if they could support the idea of a United Engineering Information System.

"The results were disappointing," Penniman says, "though not surprising. Some of those attending thought the Internet would solve all the information access problems of scientists and engineers. Others thought their own products or services provided what was needed, and that no further effort was required. Others—as you have with all groups—opted for a 'wait-and-see' attitude."

Not Penniman. The meeting only spurred him on to find a different strategy for making his United Engineering Information System a reality. And while he looks, he continues to speak about the idea at meetings whenever he has an opportunity and an invitation.

"With the number of engineering jobs in the U.S. hovering at around two million," Penniman says, "the benefit to the nation of a "virtual national engineering library' is obvious. When it is built on a collaborative basis by those who could use it the most, the engineers and their supporting organizations, it will be smart for the profession. In fact, it would be smart for both professions, for engineering and for information services. And it surely would be smart for the nation."

So how does Penniman propose making the United Engineering Information System come about, particularly since he has identified those "strong vested interests" in the larger professional societies as working against the idea? His answer is surprising, but it makes sense.

"We turn to other engineering societies, not so big as the top ten or fifteen," he says. "There are over 500 engineering societies in the U.S., and most could use an improved and coordinated way of distributing information to their members."

By building a coalition among the second tier of engineering societies, those with specialized niches to serve, Penniman believes enough engineers could be engaged to make the idea a reality. And he believes that by focusing on the economic consequences to the nation of the currently fragmented system, top level support for the idea could be achieved.

If you agree, let him know. Dave Penniman is looking for all the grass-roots support he can get.

Meet W. David Penniman

W. David Penniman is Professor and Associate Director of the School of Information Sciences at the University of Tennessee and Director of the Center for Information Studies, an interdisciplinary research component of the University. He also serves as a consultant to senior management in information systems, resources, and services. His experience spans over thirty years serving government, industry, educational institutions, and not-for-profit organizations. He has served as President and CEO of the Council on Library Resources, was a director at AT&T Bell Laboratories, and was Vice President at OCLC. He has worked as a research scholar at the International Institute for Applied Systems Analysis in Austria and as an information scientist at Battelle Memorial Institute, where he also led the group responsible for the development of the BASIS online retrieval and data management system.

Penniman's professional activities include serving as Chairman of the Board of Engineering Information, Inc., and as President of the American Society for Information Science. He is a senior member of the IEEE and a fellow of the American Association for the Advancement of Science.

Penniman holds an undergraduate degree in engineering from the University of Illinois and a Ph.D. in behavioral science from Ohio State University. He is a registered professional engineer and has published over sixty articles and papers in the areas of information systems research, development, and operation, and has lectured throughout the world on information-related topics.

During his spare time from information science matters, which is not plentiful these days, Penniman enjoys hiking the trails around Oak Ridge, Tennessee, where he and his family now live. He also is restoring a 1927 Chevrolet depot hack (a wooden station wagon).

▎▎

That much-anticipated change in American
librarianship is now going to happen and
BOB KLASSEN
is supervising the job

Librarianship has long been thought of as a profession that resists change,
a profession made up of workers who want to keep things just as they are.
According to the common view, we're told, the librarians, the practitioners in the library science field, are people who are not interested in doing
anything differently, people who couldn't care less about moving their
beloved book-centered careers into a future that incorporates high-quality
and fast-paced information delivery, regardless of format.

Balderdash! Such ideas are just plain silly, and most information services workers and their satisfied information customers know it. Of
course there are some library workers—just as there are workers in any
profession—who are weak in interpersonal skills and who come across as
losers, but they would be losers in any business or profession. By and
large, most professional librarians would jump at the chance to be a part
of the "new" librarianship, but they aren't given the resources to do what
needs to be done. In fact, more often than not, it's not the practitioners
who resist but the people who interact with them: the library's users (who
in their ignorance continue to think of a library as a place where "just
books" are stored) and the library's governing authorities, those decision
makers who are willing to find a little money here and there for what is
commonly referred to as "traditional" library services and who want
"their" libraries to continue to provide those services.

All that's going to change now for American librarianship, for the primary Federal incentive funding program for libraries has now been
repackaged. Although the last session of the U.S. Congress was not
exactly noted for its social programs (and will in fact probably go down in

Originally published in *InfoManage : The International Management Newsletter for the Information
Services Professional* 4 (3), February, 1997.

history for its anti-social legislation), it did approve on the last day of the Congress what appears to be the only progressive social program passed in the session, the Library Services and Technology Act of 1996. Built into the legislation is language that transfers the Office of Library Programs—administered for forty years through the U.S. Department of Education—to a new, independent agency, the Institute of Museum and Library Services (IMLS).

To date the transfer has gone largely unnoticed, but that's about to change. As state library administrators prepare their five-year state plans (due April 1st), they are discovering, much to their surprise, that the requirements of the new legislation are much different than the previous requirements had been. Bob Klassen, current Director of the Office of Library Programs, is responsible for seeing that the transition to IMLS goes smoothly.

"I'm here trying to manage the process," Klassen says with a wry grin, and it's easy for a visitor to see that there's more than a little enthusiasm in his comment. This is a pretty exciting opportunity and Klassen is enjoying his role in moving American librarianship—at least the Federal government's contribution to that move—in a direction that will benefit all American citizens.

"What we're doing," Klassen says, "is setting up a program that creates equality of access to information, and this new legislation does just that. What we needed for a long time was a consolidated package of legislation, one that talks about linkages, and that's what we now have."

That's the key—"linkages." And if you spend any time with Bob Klassen, you're going to come away with the idea that what's good about this Library Services and Technology Act of 1996 is that it will foster linkages.

But it also requires changes, changes in the way libraries do business, in the way funding authorities use funds. It's not going to be easy, and there are certainly going to be barriers to its implementation, but its purpose is to create information access for the entire community, to connect schools, libraries, academic institutions, organizations, special libraries, and any other operational entity that handles or distributes information.

"It's a blurring of the institutional lines," Klassen says, and in implementing the requirements of LSTA, he and his staff are going to be confronted with fascinating and, perhaps for some, difficult challenges. But they are challenges worth addressing.

"Of course," Klassen says, and there's just the beginning of a frown on his face. "It's turning out to be a very strange year, for the management process is complicated with current funding under the old programs and planning for the new LSTA program. It will not be without some stress, but what we will accomplish is so far beyond what's being asked of us. There's no question about our commitment to the process."

Take the transfer, for example. With the administrative move to what was the Institute of Museum Services, an independent agency under the leadership of Director Diane Frankel, the United States Government is now taking a position that identifies American librarianship—with some additional emphasis on information delivery—in a cultural role. And the new role is one that may not necessarily connect the profession and its services to the educational establishment.

"Oh, the educational function is still there," Klassen notes, "for certainly museums today are seen as educational institutions. And the field of museum education is a field that has gained much strength in the last couple of decades, and provides a good match for what the library profession is attempting to do with information delivery. So in that respect the "marriage' between libraries and museums is a good one, and offers good prospects for the future of both institutions."

The question comes up, though (as it does in other countries where librarianship is being connected with museology, places like Australia, New Zealand, Canada, and South Africa), as to whether the museum/library connection is valid with respect to other types of information management and delivery. In some places, librarians who work in specialized libraries, information workers whose information focus is quite different from that of those who work in the museum or traditional library fields, are very concerned about librarianship being seen as part of the cultural community, just as they were concerned when librarianship was seen as part of the educational community. What about those people, and their concerns? Will the marriage between museums and libraries leave them out?

"Not at all," Klassen says. "In fact I was at a meeting just the other night when someone asked me if special libraries are included in the Library Services and Technology Act of 1996. Of course they are, for the whole focus of the legislation is to create a program of library services that looks at community-based information needs, and special libraries and the organizations that support them are part of the community. Obviously special libraries and their librarians and managers must determine themselves what information is proprietary and what can be shared, but that is not a responsibility that they would shirk. Again, remember what the legislation does. It has been passed to set up a mechanism for creating linkages. We want to link all information in the community that should be linked, to insure equal public access to information."

Klassen is probably too modest to admit it, but in fact his affection for special librarianship and his interest in ensuring that specialized librarianship and its practitioners be included in the new information picture being drawn by the U.S. Federal Government is well founded. He has long been involved in special librarianship, and for many years his work at the Office of Library Programs was focused on working with the special libraries community. He has been a frequent participant in the activities of the Special Libraries Association, and served two terms on its Board of Directors, so if there is anyone at the senior level in American government who understands the connections between the requirements of specialized librarianship and traditional librarianship, it's Bob Klassen. And it won't come as any surprise if—at some future date—the successful implementation of the Library Services and Technology Act of 1996 is used as a prototype for other countries as they attempt to unite librarianship-as-culture and librarianship-as-information-delivery. It makes sense for them to be one and the same, and practitioners will wake up to the fact that it is to their—and their information customers'—well-being to unite them. When that happens—and it will—Bob Klassen and the staff at the Office of Library Programs will be happy to be participants.

But will there be problems?

Klassen is optimistic, but he is also a realist. He's worked in government library support programs for his entire career, beginning with his early work at the California State Library. At that time, as a budding librarian, Klassen had the opportunity to see the U.S. Federal Government's very first, tentative steps in library support, when the Library Services Act of 1956 was first put into play. After seven years at the state level, Klassen went to the U.S. Department of Education, where he's been involved with the Office of Library Programs for nearly 29 years.

So he knows about government support of libraries, and he knows what some of the problem areas are, and indeed, what some of the mine fields are.

"First of all," he says, "let's make it clear what we're talking about here. Yes, the funding provided by this office sounds like a lot of money—over $135 million for FY1997—and if those funds were put into any single project it would be quite a windfall. But let's remember that it is divided up among many different programs, and in fifty different states, so no one state or program is going to be receiving a great deal of money from this. What we offer is pump-priming money for incentives. Think about how library services are supported in this country. The figures vary from speaker to speaker, but the general numbers for all public library support, for example, are something like 1.4% from the Federal government, 13% from state governments, and the rest from local support. So it's local support that makes things happen. What we do here is provide monies that encourage local funding authorities to do their part.

"And that's where we have to be careful, for what the new legislation creates is not funding that is specifically for public libraries. It's funding for equal access to community-based information, and that's where we have our work cut out for us. It's our job to educate—or re-educate, if you will—state and local library authorities to think less in terms of the public library from an institutional perspective, to think in broader terms, in terms of how information can be accessed on a community-wide basis. That is why we're talking so much about linkages, and why 'linkages' is the key concept here. If, for example, a doctor in a rural community in North Dakota can access information that he or she requires through some database that we've provided leverage dollars to support, we will have succeeded in achieving this mission. That is our mission: to encourage communities to build on the federal funds we provide, and the state funds that come from their own state, to strengthen what they can do locally."

So the problem, insofar as there is one, is to educate state and local funding authorities to the advantages of thinking in broader support terms, to get them to thinking about community-wide information resources.

"Exactly," Klassen says. "And we think we can do that, for in the long run, state and local authorities want to provide community support for information access from a wider base. It's just that they might have to have their awareness raised about what can be done."

And the librarians? The practitioners within the profession?

"In some situations, that might be another concern, for there are some who might not want to participate, who will resist the linkages that we're talking about. We're the same agency, but we have a new mission, and that mission is to provide the opportunity for the library community to be the gateway to the information age.

"Our society is poised for a new information age. That's a reality, and it's not going to change. What has to be accepted—by all the players—is that the linkages to create better access to information resources go beyond types of libraries."

Giving up—or giving new consideration to—the whole idea of "turf" in information services work is something that Klassen had obviously given much thought to, and he clearly understands that the new legislation is moving the profession toward change.

"This legislation," he says, "this Library Services and Technology Act of 1996, can be the vehicle for moving libraries into the information-providing business for the next forty years. I won't be around to see it, and in fact many of us won't be around to see it, but what we have here is the foundation for information delivery, based on equality of access to information, that goes beyond traditional types of library service. If there is a problem here, it's with the public perceptions of libraries and what they do, and with the librarians themselves when they don't choose to participate. It's going to happen. There is going to be information delivery built around community-based information needs, and if librarians don't jump in and participate in this, someone else will do it. It's a very crucial time for us as librarians, for our profession. We have the opportunity to promote the linkages that will make the new information age work. And that's what I'm in business to do."

So it is, indeed, a crucial time for librarians. And equally crucial for their customers, those members of the American public who are seeking information. For both groups of people, poised as we are at the virtual gateway to tomorrow's information delivery, it is comforting to have a man as skilled and as conscientious as Bob Klassen to help us through.

Meet Bob Klassen

When interviewed, Robert L. Klassen was Director of the Office of Library Programs at the U.S. Department of Education, where he was employed for nearly 30 years. Long a leader in the library community in the United States, Klassen's focus for many years was in the specialized library area, where he served as a liaison between the special libraries community and the more general library profession. He was a member and later Chair of the Public Affairs Committee of the American Society for Information Science (ASIS), and for the Special Libraries Association he served on the Board of Directors and was President of the District of Columbia Chapter. Bob Klassen has also had a long and prominent membership in the American Library Association, serving on the ALA's Research Committee, the Committee on Organization, the Awards Committee (which he chaired in 1987-1988), and a variety of other committees and study groups. An active member of the several programs connected with his work at the Office of Library Programs for the U.S. Department of Education, Klassen was an Observer at the White House Conference on Library and Information Services in 1979 and again at the second White House Conference in 1991. Klassen makes his home in Arlington, VA, where he lives with his wife, Beverly. An avid traveler, Klassen has traveled much for his personal enjoyment, and he has represented American librarianship on several trips abroad, including travel to the USSR in 1970 and 1972, to Poland and Rumania in 1976, and in two of the Citizen Ambassador Program People-to-People Delegations, to Russia and the Czech Republic in 1995 and to South Africa in 1996.

JERRY KING

at NIH sees a new information profession being born—
and it's happening right now

At the U.S. National Institutes of Health in Bethesda, Maryland, Jerry King is putting into practice the "umbrella theory" we write so much about in *InfoManage*. According to this theory, a single information services profession is emerging, and it's a profession based on the belief that good customer service is built on one-stop shopping.

Sometimes it's possible and sometimes it's not, and a great many variables have to be taken into consideration as an organization looks at this approach to information delivery and attempts to move to what is, by definition, a customer-focused perspective. And that's what Jerry King is doing, looking at the variables.

For the past few years, he's been playing with these ideas, and he's concluded that the time has come for the many and varied professions that relate to information delivery to come together, to create a new and all-encompassing profession that he calls "information management."

King is in charge of the Medical Record Department at the Warren G. Magnuson Clinical Center at NIH, and in the eighteen years that he's been at NIH, he's seen information management—as a distinct administrative operation—go from simple, primarily clerical (and cumbersome) file-keeping to a sophisticated and content-based management function that links to the organizational mission. In other words, successful information delivery is now as much a part of the NIH management operation as all the other management "pieces" that contribute to that massive organization's success.

It's a natural sort of evolution, according to King, and his career at NIH and his current management responsibilities reflect the progressive

Originally published in *InfoManage : The International Management Newsletter for the Information Services Professional* 4 (4), March, 1997.

movement toward what is, after all, a very reasonable way of thinking about information and information delivery.

"Don't look at what I do as medical records," he says. "It's information management, and it involves all organizational records, research records, medical staff records, medical records, vital records, protocol review, privacy act management, the whole spectrum, in fact, of information management as we do it at NIH."

In fact, he's too modest. For many generations, medical records was referred to patient records, and in King's operation, that little distinction went by the boards a long time ago. For King and the management at the Clinical Center, the term "medical records" has become "record management" and may now refer to any information-delivery practice that connects to the work of the organization.

In a way, King's own title reflects the scope of this work, for while he is indeed described as "Department Head, Medical Record Department," his business card also shows that he is the NIH "Privacy Act Coordinator," so anyone who sees it quickly learns that his brief from management is a broad one. And it's not hard to see how it came about, this wide-ranging management responsibility of King's, for as he talks about his work, it's clear that the man has a vision of what he (and the Clinical Center) can do with respect to information delivery.

"Of course." he says, and his tone of voice implies that it's a given.

"For first of all you have to have an understanding of what you do, you have to have a vision. For us—for me and my staff—our vision is pretty simple: we do information management well, and we do it anywhere in the organization we're asked to do it. Yes, we were formerly responsible for performing just a records management function, but that has changed over the years and now we do more. Because we can do more."

King pauses for effect, to let you know that he's about to tell you just why his department can do more. And then a grin comes on his face, for he's figured out how to say something that information managers everywhere need to know.

"Being of value to the organization is easy," he says. "All you have to do is look around for the jobs that are difficult, dirty, time-consuming, detail-oriented jobs that others are not anxious to take on. Then you take them on, and you do them well."

That's what happened at the Clinical Center, and it's what leads King to believe that a new, inclusive information services profession can come into being. In fact, he says, it's being created right now, and it's being created in those places where certain ideas and certain considerations are allowed to flourish.

"Basic to the whole idea," he says, and you can hear the admiration in his voice as he speaks, "is that there has to be a very supportive boss. I work with a man who is willing to let us innovate, to look for new ways that we can contribute to the information picture here."

King is referring to Dr. Thomas L. Lewis, Associate Director for Information Services at the Clinical Center, a physician who, early on, became interested in clinical computing and was responsible for the implementation of the first whole-house computerized medical information system at the Clinical Center and one of the first in the nation.

"Tom is nationally recognized as a leader in medical computing," King says. "And most important, for me, is that he has served as a tremendous mentor over the past 14 years. He has always given me total access and shared his time, his intellect, and his interest with me. No matter what the project or the problem, he has always been supportive and encouraging in developing innovative ideas and pursuing new responsibilities."

As King speaks, it soon becomes obvious that this is also a working relationship—this connection between King and Lewis—that plays out well for each of them. Or, as King puts it with a self-deprecating laugh, "He sees that I get excited about the work we're doing and he lets me play out my excitement."

But the laugh isn't just self-deprecating. There's pride there, too, for he likes describing the good people he works with, and he is very comfortable pointing out that the support of senior management is critical.

"I've been really lucky," he says, "and I think that's the first thing that has to be established, if information management is going to be a broader-based profession. The lines of communication between what we do in the Medical Record Department and senior management are direct and open, and I can't imagine innovation taking place if that's not the case."

The second component in King's move toward a more unified profession has to do with what we're all calling these days "enabling technology." It's a term that is fast becoming a cliché, but it's becoming a cliché because—like all clichés—it grows out of something that is real and that is happening, in this case the technology that enables Jerry King and his staff to do not just more work, but work that is implicitly more important.

"We've been able to move to a system that combines paper and electronic records management, and, yes, it's a dual system and a lot of people have problems with that. But we know what our customers need (and want), and we understand that for some users and some records a paper-based document is what is going to be used. Still, with the growth of information technology, we've been able to move forward into electronic records, and now approximately 90-95% of our records work is electronic.

"Paper is not maintained for inactive files," King continues. "Archives are in microform at the present time, and that's been a good move. And we may be moving to totally electronic archives one day. But whether we'll ever get to a total electronic environment any time soon is questionable. For example, one of our primary records, the physician's notes, what we like to refer to as the 'guts' of the patient record, has historically been written by hand. Similarly, the subsystems of record-keeping are often paper-based, for when you have a decentralized environment, the record-keeping process starts with a paper, a hand-written document or a filled-in form, and that's not going to change for a long time to come."

King goes on to point out that another reason why total electronic record keeping is not immediately forthcoming has to do with the health services field itself. Like the legal profession, the medical profession has been historically conservative, and often slow to recognize the value of computerized information. Certainly in health services the practitioners have always been ready to use automation in related fields, as in keeping lab records and notes, in managing their libraries for procuring external information, in billing systems ("No surprise there," King says, and there's that grin again), and with automated medical devices such as electrocardiographs and other measuring devices interfaced with computers. But in the practice of medicine itself, there was a certain reluctance to go to automation because the physicians themselves often didn't see themselves as delivering information to others, or as creating information that would be used by others.

But that is changing, and King talks about pioneers such as Homer Warner, Sr., Larry Weed, G. Octo Barnett, and others who focused attention on the value of integrated clinical information systems, including

Turf Wars or Cooperation?
Jerry King's Management Perspective

"With increased automation," Jerry King says, "there are changes in the way people work. What has happened with us is that we have been able to move to fewer purely clerical functions. And at the same time, the professional staff has increased dramatically, going from 6 records administrators to 28 in eighteen years. Obviously a lot of this coincides with computerization, and we are forced to recognize that it's computerization that permits us—enables us—to let the machines do the routine work and use the professionals and their minds and skills do the 'out-of-the-box' work."

Nevertheless, there's a caveat, and King, despite his enthusiasm, must speak to it.

"Obviously computerization is not always a good thing, for computerization reveals the structural and record integrity problems that are inherent in many of the non-automated record-keeping functions, and that has to be addressed. We've looked at many different approaches for getting at this, and some have worked and some have not. For example, over the years we've looked at some TQM approaches to what we do. And like everybody else who's spent any time working with TQM, there have been some real failures, some real let-downs. But the effort was good—and a valuable one for us here at NIH—for one very simple reason: even when TQM was not always successful, just doing it, just setting up the process and getting into it allowed us to shift the focus from our belly buttons to the customer. And that, in a nutshell, is what I mean when I say we can do what we do

well anywhere in the organization it's needed. If we can look beyond ourselves, if we can concentrate on the information customer, we can get past the limitations and get on with getting the information that the customer needs to the customer when it's needed."

It's that "getting past the limitations" that separates Jerry King and his staff from others who talk about integrated information services but can't seem to move themselves there. And King thinks he knows why some information services managers can't move to providing customers with seamless, one-stop information delivery:

"It's turf," he says. "As long as people see themselves as working in only one of the subunits of the information services profession, and not being linked to the others, those turfs, those little boxes are going to continue to be important and the turf wars will continue. I strongly believe that if the concepts that apply to general records management are sound—and I believe they are—they can be applied in other information services work. If the records management people can move out of records management, as such, and work in other information-related functions, their skills and their expertise will improve those other functions. On the other hand, there is no reason why a well-trained corporate records manager cannot become a good medical records manager, or vice-versa, but for this to happen, the practitioner—and the practitioner's boss—have to be willing to move beyond the usual way of doing things."

clinical documentation, expert systems, and ambulatory care. Evidence of their important work—and that of others—can be seen at Latter Day Saints Hospital, the University of Vermont Medical Center, the NYU Medical Center, Mass General, Maine Medical, the University of Illinois, and elsewhere.

So as he and his staff take on more information management responsibility, King is becoming increasingly comfortable with the changes that are taking place in the professions that make up information services.

"More and more," he says, "we're moving to a heavily automated information environment, with a much more diverse content. I don't see that as particularly threatening to an information manager."

Obviously not, if the new information manager is willing to recognize how the basics of information organization and management in one of these subfields of information delivery can match those at work in the others. And that's where King sees the birth of the new information management profession, in its connections between the different information delivery subgroups, so to speak, and their shared goal of successful information provision.

"Where we're different," King says, "is in our commitment to the integrity of the data, our concern about content, the consistency of capture, and the replicability of information. Not all information workers are part of this, and certainly information systems specialists do not see that as a priority or even as a responsibility. The major differences between a new information management profession based on customer service and other practitioners in the information field—the information systems people, for example—is that the new information management professionals are concerned with the consistency, integrity, and replicability of the information content. The information systems people aren't. In fact, they even have a language for this lack of interest in content. They say things like 'garbage in, garbage out,' meaning that what they're working with is the machinery to move the data around, regardless of what the information is. Information management professionals don't think like that. What we bring to the practice of information delivery is a concern with how data will really be used and whether it is reliable. We are interested in where the data came from, and how it will be used. That's how we define what I'm calling the new information management professional."

King likes the idea of this new profession, and he begins to deliberate about how it will be structured. Almost immediately he finds himself looking at certification, at how the practitioners will be able to demonstrate their qualifications.

"In fact," he says, "it would be a wonderful move forward if there could be a single information management profession, with subspecialties requiring certification for each of their practitioners. And it makes a certain amount of sense, the creation of this new career and this new career title: the Information Management Professional. Certainly it makes sense from the point of view of the customers and the organizational managers.

"Whether it can happen will depend on a lot of things, and particularly on the certification process. It will also have much to do with the professional organizations and how they are structured. At the present time, most of the professional organizations in the information services fields—or their members and their leaders—don't understand the distinctions. What we need is one organization of information management professionals, a single entity that will be made up of practitioners and professionals from all the different subfields that make up information management.

"Will it happen? I don't know. I don't know that information professionals today—separated as they are into so many different professional organizations—can come together to create a new profession. What they need is some kind of federation of organizations to bind them together, but I don't know if that's a viable scenario. There are an awful lot of turf wars going on out there, and I don't know if the information professionals are even willing to try to come together. But if they would, if they would form a federation of sub-professions to work together in a single Information Management Profession, it would make a serious difference in the way information is managed. And the information customers would be better for it."

Not a bad idea, this. In fact, King's proposal for an overarching information services profession—a federation of subspecialties—is very much like what happens in the medical profession itself, and that wouldn't be a bad model for what information services workers want to do. After all, while information delivery isn't quite on the same societal plane as quality health care services, it is nearly as ubiquitous, and perhaps there is indeed a model for information services in the medical profession. Should information workers aspire for such professional heights?

Jerry King thinks they should.

Meet Jerry King

Jeremiah P. King is Department Head and Privacy Act Coordinator for the Medical Record Department at the Warren G. Magnuson Clinical Center of the National Institutes of Health, a position he has held since 1983. Jerry King was educated at Towson State University, where he was awarded the Bachelor of Science degree in 1979. His list of certifications is impressive, and includes certification by the American Health Information Management Association as a Registered Records Administrator, certification by the U.S. Department of Health & Human Services as a Federal Project Officer, for Small Purchases, for Basic Acquisition, and for Managing Total Quality. He is a Certified Medical Staff Coordinator, from the National Association of Medical Staff Services, and his designation as a Certified Records Manager from the Institute of Certified Records Managers is pending. He has had clinical faculty appointments at the University of Pittsburgh, the State University of New York Institute of Technology at Utica/Rome, the College of St. Scholastica, the University of Kansas, and at Temple University. In 1996, King received two important awards, the National Institutes of Health Merit Award, and the NIH Clinical Center Director's Award for Administration. His personal interests include golf, skiing, and tennis. And, "I love to eat—good French food is my favorite." He is an avid reader (currently reading *Angela's Ashes*, by F. McCourt, an account of growing up poor in Ireland during the Depression). He attributes his career success to his wife: "I would never have entered the field of Records Administration if my wonderful wife, Nancy, had not encouraged me to take a real risk, and change careers, despite the responsibilities of a young family and a hefty mortgage payment, eighteen years ago."

DEANNA MARCUM
at CLIR: Moving us ever closer to that
seamless web of information resources

July is here, and the Council on Library and Information Resources (CLIR) is now officially in existence. This is good news indeed, especially for those in the information industry who have—for so long—toiled to bring together the many and various components of information services into one linked and connected community of interests.

For those industry leaders who have struggled to achieve the information convergence that Allan Foster talks about, the integration of information and the information customers' perspective that Elizabeth Orna pushes for, the information services "umbrella" that is written about so often in these pages, and the new information management profession that defines information as anything that anyone needs to know, the creation of CLIR is a much needed and much anticipated move to that successful information future we're all looking for. To all who have—willingly or not—fought the information turf wars, the time for change has come, and Deanna Marcum is our change master

July 1, 1997.

What a good day this is for information managers!

For the uninitiated, the Council on Library and Information Resources is an outgrowth of the merger of two important organizations, the Council on Library Resources, founded in 1956 and a child of the Ford Foundation, and the Commission on Preservation and Access, organized first as a program of CLR which then, in 1986, became a separate organization.

"Over the years," according to Marcum, who was hired in 1995 to serve as President of both CLR and CPA, "the two organizations in partnership with libraries, archives, and other information providers have advocated collaborative approaches to preserving America's intellectual

Originally published in *InfoManage : The International Management Newsletter for the Information Services Professional* 4 (8), July, 1997.

heritage and strengthening the many components of the nation's information system. CLIR was founded to continue this tradition of support for a national information system and a seamless web of information resources, of which all libraries and archives are a part."

And the emphasis is on the "all," for if you take a look at the handsome new brochure which has been put together to describe CLIR (again under Marcum's supervision, for she definitely has a feel for how information organizations should be presented to their constituent markets), you're immediately impressed with the organization's statement of its mission [see sidebar on next page]. Particularly impressive is that attention to information without boundaries, that "seamless web" that Marcum talks about so enthusiastically:

"CLIR," the brochure states boldly, "embraces the entire range of information resources and services, from traditional library and archival materials to emerging digital formats, and the entire network of organizations that gather, catalog, store, preserve, distribute, and provide access to information."

It is a serious mandate, not to be taken lightly. To achieve it, Marcum made it clear when she came to her bifurcated position that hers was to be the unifying role. Her job was to take the two organizations—both with noble aspirations and highly respected reputations—and move them toward a single entity that would bring benefit to all parties.

It was a challenge, and hearing Marcum describe some of the components of that challenge gives new meaning to the phrase, "change management."

"Of course," Marcum says with a smile, and her visitor can quickly deduce from the smile that some hard decisions had to be made, decisions that—perhaps—all the players didn't necessarily agree with.

"In the first place," Marcum says, "I had to look at the governance structure for the two organizations, and I saw that I had to do two things. I had to work with the board members of both CLR and CPA to establish criteria for board membership, and we had to establish term limits. We could not achieve what we had to achieve with a self-perpetuating board, and before we could even begin to think about what CLIR was going to do, we had to determine who the players, the people in authority and with responsibility, would be."

The Council on Library and Information Resources (CLIR)

"*Information is a public good and great social, intellectual, and cultural utility.*"

The Goals

- To identify the critical issues that affect the welfare and prospects of libraries and archives and the constituencies they serve.

- To convene individuals and organizations in the best position to engage these issues and respond to them.

- To encourage institutions to work collaboratively to achieve and manage change.

Initial Program Areas

- *Commission on Preservation and Access.* Continuing the effort to rescue as much of the 19th-century publishing record as possible and preserving information that exists in digital form, including an international program working with institutions beyond North America to disseminate knowledge of best preservation practices and to promote a coordinate approach to preservation activity.

- *Digital Libraries.* Supporting pilot projects and experiments whose fundamental purpose is to build confidence in the digital component of hybrid libraries. As part of this effort, CLIR serves as the "administrative home" to the National Digital Library Foundation, establishing the conditions necessary for the creation, maintenance, expansion, and preservation of a distributed collection of digital materials accessible to scholars and the wider public.

- *The Economics of Information.* Helping librarians and other information managers better understand the consequences of the choices they face, so that the investments they make in resources that support scholarship and teaching will be cost-effective and enduring. As part of this effort, CLIR maintains a Small-Grants Program in the Economics of Information to stimulate research, encourage the collection of data, and promote the economic analysis of library operations and services.

- *Leadership.* Providing support and education so that successful library leaders can integrate the mix of education, culture, information resources, and community center with ease, knowledge, and enthusiasm. As part of this effort, CLIR has undertaken a series of case studies—Technological Innovation on College Campuses—to determine how liberal arts colleges are employing new technologies and delivering information resources to faculty members and students more efficiently than in the past.

Financing was next, for the two organizations were currently operating with two sources of funding, foundation support for special projects, with the steady income for operations provided by contributions from 108 institutional sponsors. Since neither organization had an endowment, the first thing on the agenda—with respect to financial operations—was to bring the two organizations together financially, and once that was resolved, to move on to programs.

"CLIR is focusing on four program areas," Marcum says, and she goes on to list them: leadership, digital libraries, economics of information, and preservation and access. "We obviously can't solve all the problems associated with all of these program areas, but what we can do—what we are doing with CLIR—is to think about the well being of the library/archival type of organization and to bring all these issues to what I like to think of as a neutral place for discussion. It's not going to be easy, and, yes, there will be those who won't be satisfied with some of the decisions we'll be making, but our role is to make the 'library' as important as the 'digital'—when we use that phrase, for example—and to see that all of our constituent publics, all of the information stakeholders, understand that one component isn't necessarily more important than the other."

It appears to be a monumental job, and one with far-reaching implications.

"Of course it is," Marcum says, and you can tell that, even after two years, she is still inspired by her work and the challenges it embodies. And it's the size of those challenges and those implications that pleases her so much.

And why shouldn't she be pleased? It is, after all, a pretty important responsibility, as she is very comfortable in describing:

"We represent those institutions," she says, "that society has entrusted to protect its cultural heritage."

It doesn't get much more important than that, and any information manager, regardless of the institution, organization, or enterprise in which he or she operates, and regardless of the type of information which he or she manages, is going to be challenged in the position Deanna Marcum finds herself in. For Marcum, it is a job to love:

"We're finding ourselves, both as an organization and as information professionals, grappling with our role, trying to articulate what our role is, what we specialize in, or even if we are going to have a role. It's a serious position to be in, and if it doesn't make too much of it to say so, our profession, the whole information services industry, is at a very important crossroads. For librarians and others entrusted with the nation's cultural heritage, we have to look at these important issues. There are others out there ready to move into the field, if we don't do what we're supposed to do, so we mustn't quibble over the small, little details. At this time in our history, we have to look at the big picture."

For example, CLIR will be looking at the work that is being done in public libraries, a relatively new area of interest, started when David Penniman was President of the Council on Library Resources.

"We're going to go further with this," Marcum says, "for lots of reasons. First of all, it's a good thing to do. Public libraries are perceived as good, but we have some problems in that technology has been oversold, and we have to do a much better job of explaining to our communities why the librarians' organizational skills make a difference in how the libraries succeed. The technology is important, of course, but there's more to it that just the technology, and we'll be looking at how some of our programs can help public librarians as they work with the managers in their communities.

"What we have to be looking at," Marcum continues, "is the way people use information and information products. As I see it, we need to do two things. We need to recognize that people need specific knowledge and the specific information that will lead them to that knowledge, and we need to understand one another's culture and traditions. So if we're going to be thinking about managing the information resources of a campus, say, or a region or a state, the librarian needs to know about the information policies that affect that campus or region or state. More importantly, these librarians need to know how to work as an information team. And that's what we're trying to do with CLIR. Everything we work on, everything we do, we try to bring in all the categories of people to work together."

It's a unique organization, this new Council on Library and Information Resources. For one thing, there's no specific constituency, no membership that Marcum can identify as the single "core" group she and her staff are attempting to serve. In the truest sense of "broad-based," what CLIR does is attempt to provide thinking—and planning, let it be said— for information management in the future. And that thinking and planning is for anyone and any organization that is going to be involved in information management. It's a tall order.

A Forum for Change

The work of CLIR is greater than the sum of its component programs. In collaboration with many associations, networks, and scholarly societies, CLIR serves as a forum for change. This convening role is central to CLIR's mission. It brings together experts from around the country and around the world and asks them to turn their intelligence to the problems that libraries, archives, and other information organizations are facing as they integrate digital resources and services into their well-established print-based environments.

CLIR urges individuals to look beyond the immediate problems and imagine the most desirable outcomes for the users of libraries and archives—to be rigorously practical and to dream.

"Of course it is," Marcum says with a laugh. "And we recognize that we can't do everything, but with our new organizational entity, we at least now have a framework that recognizes the playing field we're on."

A good example took place at the end of May, when Marcum went to the U.S. Department of State to participate in a program which was being billed as "Bridging the Atlantic." While reports about the program did not show up in the popular press, its purpose was nevertheless important to people interested in information management and information transfer. With Marcum there to describe the work of the National Digital Library Federation, it was an opportunity to encourage groups to sponsor joint meetings to look at such subjects as best practices, standards, protocols, and so forth, each and every one of vital concern as information managers look to establish how international information transfer will take place in the future.

These are the kinds of programs that Marcum and her staff and the many industry leaders who work with her are trying to put together. It's an impressive array of activities, and there's no doubt but that the new CLIR will play an increasingly important role in the much-talked-about "information future," now that—as of July 1—it is a chartered and authorized entity.

Of course there are problems, the first of which is endemic to any organization or any person who "thinks big": With CLIR's small staff and limited operation, it's just not possible to do everything Marcum and her board members want to do.

"There are so many things we could be doing," she says, "and it is hard to say no. It's hard to choose the things we will be working on, so we have to give a lot of thought to what we can do, and of course we have to consider what else is being done, who else is working on this or that subject. Because for us, we can't do what someone else is doing. We have to make a difference."

Make a difference? Of course CLIR is making a difference, and that is one of the beauties of this particular operation that Deanna Marcum is leading. She wouldn't be doing it if it didn't make a difference.

And that, perhaps, leads to what some might think of as another "problem" with respect to this work, but which, for Deanna Marcum, is not a problem at all. In fact, if it is anything, it's a benefit of the job:

"For some," she says, "it might be a downside, what I refer to as the extraordinarily personal agenda that this job requires. Is it a problem? I don't think so. If you're going to do this job, you have to be personally committed, and that's fine with me. I'm working on those things I believe in."

Indeed she is, and as Deanna Marcum takes on the leadership of the Council on Library and Information Resources, and as the specific agendas of the Council on Library Resources and the Commission on Preservation and Access are embraced into CLIR's new mission, that seamless web of information resources doesn't see so remote, so far away. With Marcum at the helm, it's just quite possible that CLIR will show us how to achieve that happy consequence.

Meet Deanna Marcum

Deanna Bowling Marcum is President of The Council on Library and Information Resources, a new (July 1, 1997) organization created through the amalgamation of The Council on Library Resources and The Commission on Preservation and Access, both of which she has served as President since 1995. Prior to coming to the two organizations, Marcum was Director, Public Service and Collection Management at The Library of Congress, and prior to that she was Dean, School of Library and Information Science, The Catholic University of America, Washington, DC. Before going to CUA, Marcum had served as Vice-President at The Council on Library Resources, had worked in academic libraries, and had been employed as a consultant and as a trainer. An accomplished writer, Deanna Marcum is the author of *Good Books in a Country Home: The Public Library as Cultural Force in Hagerstown, Maryland, 1878-1920*, published by Greenwood Press in 1994. She is also the author of many important articles, including "The Preservation of Digital Information" in *The Journal of Academic Librarianship* (November, 1996) and "Redefining Community Through the Public Library," published in *Daedalus* (Fall, 1996). Marcum makes her home in Washington, DC.

ANNE WOODSWORTH
at Long Island University's Palmer School:
Change management and leadership are now
the profession's basic competencies

Can a traditional "library school" turn out information practitioners to meet the demands of today's (and tomorrow's) information industry? Can a curriculum in information studies be developed—within a framework of "traditional" library services—that can bridge the gap between the needs of public, school, academic, and special librarians and their information customers who have no use for or interest in "traditional" library offerings?

Absolutely yes, to both questions. If the library school is the Palmer School of Library and Information Science and the school's leader is Anne Woodsworth, there is no question but that it can happen. It is happening.

At the Palmer School, located on the beautiful C.W. Post Campus of the Long Island University in Brookville, NY, 25 miles east of Manhattan on Long Island's famous Gold Coast, Anne Woodsworth has taken up a massive challenge, one that affects not just how the program at the Palmer School is being developed, but one that impacts the overall training of all information workers. In the six years since Woodsworth was called in to save the master's program (literally, for the Palmer School had lost its accreditation), there has been a remarkable turnaround in the school's fortunes. Graduates now leave with the highest caliber education, the faculty is one of the best around (and more and more of the real "thinkers" in the profession are being attracted to LIU to be part of this effort), and, as impressive as anything else, the school recognizes market forces and offers education in information studies at all levels.

A well-received undergraduate program in information transfer was inaugurated in 1996 and has drawn large numbers of enthusiastic

Originally published in *InfoManage : The International Management Newsletter for the Information Services Professional* 4 (11), October, 1997.

students who want simply to know more about information work. The new doctoral program, just approved by the New York State Board of Regents, has already been well-subscribed, and the school's popular "institutes" in the summer, together with the Senior Fellows Institute (which Woodsworth inaugurated) extends the school's offerings into the lifelong learning end of the spectrum. And of course the school's master's program, which was—of necessity—totally revamped, now offers any number of excellent courses for graduate students preparing to work in the information industry. Link these successes together with the programs offered at the university's Manhattan and Westchester campuses, and you have an information studies program that is, indeed, impressive.

"It had to be done," Woodsworth says, with no hesitation. "When I came here, we had to look at the entire market for information studies. Of course I wanted to move toward a doctoral program from the very beginning, but our first job was to get the master's program accredited. Then we could think about a doctoral program."

That's what happened. With accreditation reinstated in January, 1993, Woodsworth and her colleagues were ready to begin talking about how they could move to a doctoral program. In February, 1993, she did just that.

"An interesting thing happened, though," she says. "As we began to explore the idea of the doctoral program, we began to realize that there was also a need to address the idea of an undergraduate program. Early on, in our discussions, we found ourselves dividing the intellectual content of our work into three groups: the undergraduate, the master's level, and the doctoral level.

"It wasn't something we set out to do. It was just part of the discussion. We spoke with many different people, in casual conversations, in focus groups, in other types of meetings. And as we would spend time—the faculty and I—in these conversations, as we looked at the general information environment, at the way the world is turning in business management, in offices, in manufacturing, we realized that we had a wide group of people out there looking for education—at several levels—in information studies."

This kind of thinking all comes together when you spend some time with Anne Woodsworth, for in any conversation with her it soon becomes clear that she's excited by the changes in the information services industry, and she wants the Palmer School to be the leading educational institution preparing people for careers in the field. For example, as good as they are, she is not content with the excellence of the several summer institutes and the very prestigious Senior Fellows Institute, which brings present and emerging leaders from academic and research libraries together for four weeks exploring the critical issues related to information delivery in higher education.

"Absolutely not," she says with a laugh. "We're very proud of these programs, and it's really fine work, but in terms of lifelong learning and post-graduate studies, we must do more. And we are. In fact, we're already putting together a pilot course for an online post-graduate program. The technology is not in place yet, but when it is, we'll have selected faculty and students using shareware to work together to achieve some sort of 'advanced' certificate. It's the wave of the future. We've just got to do it."

And it's that "wave of the future" that seems to characterize what is happening at Long Island University, for this is not the proverbial academic "things-are-fine-just-the-way-they-are" situation. With the enthusiasm and support of a visionary university administration, Woodsworth and her team at the Palmer School are literally encouraged to innovate, to move forward, to think "out of the box." In just one example, of the 16 full-time faculty, two are joint appointments in Educational Technology and one is a joint appointment in Computer Science, a level of cooperative thinking and collaboration that isn't readily apparent at many other institutions offering programs in information studies.

"That idea," Woodsworth says, "is best described in the way we approach our program. First of all, we do, yes, have a very supportive university administration, a group of academic leaders who are quite serious about bringing the university into the twenty-first century in a leadership position. And it's that supportive environment and that collaborative relationship I gave a lot of thought to when I was asked to be the Acting Dean of the School of Education last year. To do that I had to "stretch' myself—perhaps a little further than I should have!" she interrupts with a laugh. "But I did it because I knew that in the long term it would pay off for the Palmer School."

And will it?

Anne Woodsworth in Print . . .

"*T*here is more information made available through more technological sources than most people can fathom. The information resources and delivery mechanisms that are now available have gone through decades of exponential growth . . . . The kinds of formats and the kinds of ways in which information can be obtained are now so complex and rich that experienced scholars and researchers encounter difficulties in their quest for information. Even information workers, trained to develop these information systems, often do not realize their full potential . . . .

"Information services can most simply be described as a combination of information, technology, and people. . . . information services or information centers are defined as a set of activities that provide individuals with relatively easy access to data or information."

—*Managing the Economics of Owning, Leasing and Contracting Out Information Services* (Ashgate, 1993) [with James F. Williams II]

◆ ◆ ◆

"Information policy is an area in which librarians must lead opinion. Ethical uses of information and evaluation of the validity and accuracy of information are two domains in which librarians have a deep and vested interest . . . .:

—"New Library Competencies" in *Library Journal*, May 15, 1997

"As a change agent, information technology is almost without peer. Whether the change itself is evolutionary or revolutionary may be a semantic distinction best decided by history. What is indisputable today is that the opportunity exists for all information service and information systems units to form a partnership and use the technologies to manage the change creatively."

—"Re-investing in the Information Job Family: Context, Changes, New Jobs, and Models for Evaluation and Compensation," (*CAUSE Professional Papers Series # 11*, 1993) [with Theresa Maylone]

◆ ◆ ◆

"Future user services will be characterized by
• proactive identification or anticipation of user needs,
• provision of access to almost all information at the level of the user's workstation,
• collaboration with faculty in developing new and customized services, and
• delivery of faster, more convenient access to bibliographic information and physical forms of information, irrespective of location."

—"The Model Research Library: Planning for the Future," *The Journal of Academic Librarianship*, 15 (3), 1989 [with Nancy Allen, Irene Hoadley, June Lester, Pat Molholt, Danuta Nitecki, and Lou Wetherbee]

"Yes, because the "library school' is not seen as a stand-alone, aloof part of the campus. We're recognized as being innovative and forward-looking, because that's what all of the departments on the campus are trying to be."

Those innovations can be seen in the remarks Anne Woodsworth makes about the curriculum at the Palmer School.

"We work very hard," she says, "to ensure that the intellectual content of our programs meets the students' needs, but we don't specifically break out our courses into "traditional' and "non-traditional' librarianship. Yes, it's true that most of our students (because of our geographical location, probably) go to work in public libraries and as school media specialists, but that doesn't mean we ignore the content components that carry across from special librarianship. What we try to teach at the Palmer School is a curriculum that isn't 'type-of-library' specific, and it works."

Certainly it works in the summer institutes. At these, the guest instructors, the adjunct and visiting faculty who come to Brookville to offer programs in such subjects as "Advanced Library Management," "Entrepreneurial Librarianship," and "Transforming Tradition: Leading Library Change" are delightfully surprised to find that their institutes' attendees aren't necessarily training to be entrepreneurs, senior managers, or research directors. Indeed, as the instructors get to know them, they discover that these are people working in small public library branches, in law firms, as hospital librarians, as media specialists in elementary schools, and as children's librarians in community libraries. They work in "traditional" environment, but they want to do that work from a larger, broader perspective.

"It's leadership," Anne Woodsworth says. "We're teaching leadership at the Palmer School, and when these people go into the workplace, or back to the jobs from which they've taken a break to attend an institute, they become the people who are leaders in their organizations. They become the people who can analyze problems, teach technologies, work with their colleagues. It's all part of a movement, not only in our profession but in society at large, to provide the workplace with people who can lead others to what they need."

She's on a roll now, and it's obvious that Dean Woodsworth enjoys making these connections.

"We're not talking about just leadership, though," she says. "We talking about preparing people to be change managers, to be visionary about what information services will be for the community. What we're really trying to do, I think, is to teach people how to fuse themselves with their communities, regardless of what those communities are. If they're in academic libraries, they want to be able to work with the faculty to have leadership roles on their campuses. If they're in public libraries, the same goals apply. We want Palmer School graduates to be the leaders in their communities, whatever those communities are."

She pauses for a moment, and Anne Woodsworth's visitor can tell that she's wondering whether she should continue. She decides to go for it, and her face lights up with a mischievous smile.

"And one of the techniques we use, not without a little nervousness from time to time, is simply our irreverent attitude. We say to our students, 'Challenge us as much as we challenge you; you must learn for yourself and adapt what you learn to your needs.' For us and them, it's a reciprocal arrangement. And it has to be if we're going to succeed at what we—and our university's leaders—want to do."

Woodsworth is, in effect, talking about competencies, that subject that seems to come up more and more often in the various professions working with information delivery. Certainly the Special Libraries Association, with its published list of competencies for the 21st century, has been moving in this direction, and members of ARMA International, the organization representing some 10,000 records and information management professionals worldwide, will be discussing the subject at its 42nd Annual Conference in Chicago later this month. Other professional information organizations as far afield as Germany and Australia are looking at the competencies required for their members to be successful in their work. But Woodsworth sees the need for an emphasis on competencies as more encompassing than those efforts, and she is looking at a broader perspective: specific competencies are required for all information workers.

"Change is running rampant in libraries," she wrote in a recent issue of *Library Journal*, and technology, she asserts, is the "driving force" for change. Of course.

And all workers in information services—whether the education required for the job is undergraduate, graduate, doctoral, or post-graduate—must confront the competencies challenge if they are going to be successful.

In fact, it's leading change that Woodsworth characterizes as a basic competency: "True competency," she says, "entails being able to lead change within the organizations and communities that libraries serve, as well as internally within libraries. Leaders in information services, the very people we are educating at the Palmer School, must have the communication skills and the understanding of teaching methodologies sufficient to empower users, staff, and peers to have access to information. When we look at the competencies required for truly succeeding in information delivery, we are looking at change management and leadership."

These are not challenges to be dismissed lightly. In fact, in today's information marketplace, those who will succeed in the future of information delivery will be required to have mastered change management and leadership, but in doing so, they will—as the student body at the Palmer School attests today—be providing their information customers with the highest levels of quality service that can be provided. Challenges, yes, but not challenges that Anne Woodsworth and her team at the Palmer School will let "slip" into complacency and routine.

Is she sure? Isn't that the natural result of any change, any "move" toward a "different" way of doing things? No matter how innovative and exciting it all is today, will the innovation and excitement last? How long will it be before the "new" Palmer School settles in, to become a recognized and taken-for-granted constituent in the Long Island University community?

"Never!" Woodsworth says. "I hope it will never settle into place. For several years now, the constant word around here has been 'change' and that's the way it has to continue, if we're going to succeed. Change is ongoing, and there's no time, no reason, in fact, to settle in. That's not what the Palmer School is about."

Meet Anne Woodsworth

At the time she was interviewed, Anne Woodsworth was Dean, Palmer School of Library and Information Science, Long Island University, C.W. Post Campus, Brookville, New York. Prior to coming to the Palmer School, Woodsworth held a variety of positions in the information industry, including that of Associate Provost and Director of University Libraries at the University of Pittsburgh and Director of Libraries at York University in York, Ontario. Employed earlier in a variety of positions at the University of Toronto, Woodsworth had put her management skills into practice as President of Information Consultants, Inc. from 1974-1983, before moving back into the academic community when she went to Pittsburgh.

The author of many important articles, Anne Woodsworth is also known for coauthoring (with J.F. Williams II) one of the most important books in the industry, *Managing the Economics of Owning, Leasing, and Contracting Out Information Services*, published by Ashgate (and reviewed in this newsletter's first issue in December, 1993). Her other writings include scholarly articles about the role of academic libraries, about the future of libraries and information services as a profession, and, naturally enough, about education for the information industry. Especially noted was her contribution to a collaborative article, "The Model Research Library: Planning for the Future," published in *The Journal of Academic Librarianship* in 1989, and an article about competencies required for success in information work published as "Educational Imperatives of the Future Research Library: A Symposium," by Woodsworth and June Lester, published in *The Journal of Academic Librarianship* in 1991. A regular columnist for *Library Journal*, Wordsworth's often-pungent comments about the library community are eagerly awaited by *LJ*'s readers.

Woodsworth makes her home in the Victorian community of Sea Cliff, Long Island, where—time permitting—she tries to indulge her hobby of restoring fine old houses. Her current home is her fourth such restoration, and with it, she says, she'll take a break for a while and enjoy her other hobbies of reading and travel.

JUDITH J. FIELD
information educator, president of the Special Libraries
Association 1997–1998, and mentoring advocate

"It's a critical management tool for the information industry," she says.

Mentoring. It's a term that is frequently bandied about, both within the information industry and in the general management field at large. But mentoring is also a concept that isn't easily explained, at least to folks who haven't had any workplace experience with it, and many managers, seeing the preponderance of material on mentoring in the literature and hearing so many colleagues speak about the subject, would like a little guidance.

For those who know her, and who have known and worked with her throughout her long career in specialist librarianship, Judy Field is the person to provide that guidance. Having discovered early on that mentoring is an important ingredient in any successful management endeavor, Field takes special pleasure in putting forward her ideas about mentoring and its critical importance to organizational success. As an educator with a particular interest in the management of special libraries and information centers and, now, as President of the Special Libraries Association, Field is delighted that she has her own forum for endorsing the mentoring process as a critical management tool.

"Of course I'm delighted," she says, with her words conveying the special enthusiasm for her work for which she is well known. "And why shouldn't I be delighted? My interest in mentoring was a direct response to the way I was welcomed, guided, and invited to become involved in SLA when I was a new member of the Indiana Chapter."

That welcome in Indiana was Field's first experience with SLA, the 15,000-member professional association that now includes a strong contingent of the movers and shakers in the international information

Originally published in *InfoManage : The International Management Newsletter for the Information Services Professional* 5 (4), March, 1998.

management community. Within six months of joining the Indiana Chapter of SLA, Field found herself in a responsible volunteer position (assistant editor of the chapter's newsletter) and, as a result of that appointment, finding herself positioned for getting to know many people and, concurrently, obtaining from them much helpful advice as she developed her first library.

"I assumed this was standard operating procedure," Field says, "and I was pretty happy with what was going on. But then I moved to another chapter and discovered that this behavior wasn't the norm. In my new chapter, at my first chapter meeting, a few people waved "hello' across the room, and then went back to conducting their own business. At first I thought there was something wrong with me, or that it was my own insecurity, but as I saw others join the chapter, I saw the same thing happening. So I decided to do some of the things that had been done for me in Indiana. I set up tables for the 'foreigners' at the meetings, and we exchanged phone numbers and arranged car pools, that sort of thing. Pretty soon I found myself pre-emptively volunteering, on behalf of myself and the other 'newbies,' for projects that gave us plenty of opportunities to do some good work but, at the same time, to get to meet a great many different people. And incidentally, this is something I still try to do, with the library school students I teach, since I feel that these activities are required for professional health. And it was the same when I started attending conferences. I found I was again able to implement these same strategies for getting involved, and the ball was rolling. It soon became clear to me that folks involved in SLA are willing to share, to extend that helping hand, to be involved in the mentoring process. But they have to be asked. The problem, as I discovered in those early days, is that special librarians must have both the expertise and the time to share their expertise. At chapter meetings and conferences, it is natural to want to spend time with your friends, and so you don't see the new people. For mentoring to work, attention has to be given to the fact that one is talented and has special skills and expertise and that, given that, time can be found for the sharing."

The mentoring concept, as a management—or perhaps as a sociological—phenomenon, has been defined. Back in 1985, K.E. Kram and L. Isabella explained the mentoring process and the relationships in a mentoring situation by referring to the "career-enhancing functions" that mentors provide, such as sponsorship, coaching, facilitating exposure and visibility, and offering challenging work or protection. All of these, according to Kram and Isabella, help the person being mentored establish a role in the organization, learn the ropes, and prepare for advancement. And there are psychological payoffs in the Kram and Isabella model as well: the mentor offers role modelling, counseling, confirmation, and friendship, helping the person being mentored develop a sense of professional identity and competence.

Field doesn't disagree, and in fact much of her thinking about the subject of mentoring builds on these concepts and ideas. In particular, Field connects the sponsorship, and facilitated exposure and visibility, as important elements for success in information management in the commercial sector:

"Since the process of sharing knowledge or providing guidance—the very basis of the information worker's function—gives you the opportunity to rethink what you have done," she says, "I feel that mentoring is one way for professionals working in the information industry to leverage their expertise. And this is especially important in the smaller special libraries where there is little opportunity to interact with others in your specific line of work. So I feel strongly that mentoring is one way to continue your own professional growth. Having said that, however, I agree with the types of relationships that Kram and Isabella use to help define their concept of mentoring."

But there can be dangers, as Field is quick to note. Many of these same concepts were questioned, and quickly discarded, she points out, as "mentoring" became a proscribed activity in many corporations in the latter part of the 80's.

"Originally, there was a lot of literature out there describing elaborate programs that companies were using for mentoring, including writings about such topics as the assigning of mentors and so forth. A year later, unfortunately, we were reading about how many of these mentoring activities had not only failed but had created considerable disharmony within the organizations. The whole idea of mentoring left a bad taste in a lot of people's mouths.

"For example, one negative idea had it that by being a mentor you could be guilty of 'consorting with the enemy,' unwittingly sharing corporate intelligence. Would someone, for example, attempt to become a mentee just to position himself or herself to obtain competitive intelligence? Well, this is a pretty unpleasant thought, but let's face it: in the 'real' world, some people are always trying to find a short cut to fame and glory, and that kind of thinking, and some of the other things that went on, put the whole mentoring idea on pretty shaky ground. But that doesn't seem to have been the case in information services. As far as our profession is concerned, those negative situations don't ring true. Our profession practices what is purported to be—and what I believe is—a higher standard of ethics in the workplace. Librarians and other information professionals are more ethical than many other workers. For example, as we learn in our basic professional education about the ethics of information delivery, librarians and other information workers are going to be careful about sharing confidential information, including sharing one client's request with another. On the other hand, in the dog-eat-dog world where many corporations operate, mentoring is something to be feared, as if mentoring means you are training a person who wants your job. I'm happy to say that is not the situation we, as information professionals, find ourselves in, and for us, mentoring seems to be a very natural and appropriate technique for bring newer or younger professionals 'up to speed.' Mentoring works for information workers."

Just how well mentoring works in the information services profession is demonstrated when Field speaks about some of the characteristics associated with successful mentoring.

"First of all," Field says, "mentoring is not a top-down process where an 'expert' passes down the wisdom of the ages. When mentoring is interpreted in that manner, it soon withers on the vine. A true mentoring relationship is one in which there is a two-way exchange of ideas and feelings, with the confidence that this exchange is private, just between the involved parties. While it may initially start out as more advice going from A to B, as the relationship deepens there will be more brainstorming sessions, with both A and B profiting from the exchange. This idea can also be explored in a group environment, much like the 'group mentoring' that we're hearing about these days. When it's done in a group situation, you get what is happening in many of SLA's chapters, where there are subgroups, ad hoc groups that organize themselves to meet together and have lunch on a regular basis. The goal is to provide a mechanism so that everyone who participates can refine their professional and managerial skills, and the beauty of this particular activity is that no one is in immediate competition for the same position. It is also within this type of setting that those who are already participating will bring new information professionals in for a courtesy lunch, to acquaint them with their colleagues who are located in the immediate geographical area and, of course, to enable the members of the group to find out a little more about the person. Later one or two of the original lunch group may do some follow-up with this person, especially if the 'new' person is employed in a single-staff or solo-type operation. It's group mentoring at its best."

So there is a place for mentoring, even group mentoring, with the information services profession?

"Of course," Field answers, and her tone of voice indicates that the answer couldn't be more obvious. "And much of what I'm talking about here highlights some of the career-enhancing functions, a subject of much interest to all information workers. For example, we all know that many people attend local meetings of their professional associations, but they don't go to hear the speaker. That's the bonus. The real reason they're there is to build friendships and to connect again with others in the profession, to reaffirm their own professional identity. It's something we all do, and we don't even think about it when we're doing it. Entering into such a situation, what we can now characterize as a 'group' mentoring set-up, enables several people in the group to take from these opportunities whatever it is they currently need. New information professionals, for example, need to develop a feeling of professional regard from others, a feeling that will be used to reinforce their own sense of competency and professionalism. Others will gain other—and sometimes quite different, or quite unexpected—results."

And it's the unexpected results that lead, of course, to a word a caution about mentoring, whether it is one-on-one or group mentoring.

"Be careful," Field says, "about your expectations, whether you are a mentor or a mentee. Pre-programmed expectations are dangerous, simply because these are still personal relationships. To have fixed goals about where they can lead can be self-defeating. And disappointing."

Despite such caveats, however, Field likes to report that there can also be very fine rewards from participating in the mentoring process, and sometimes the process itself becomes very subtle. In a series of articles in *Library Management Quarterly*, co-authored with Sharon L. Mosenkis and published in 1992 and 1993, Field gave attention to a specific "subset" of mentoring that has attracted a considerable amount of attention. There are situations, it seems, in which those being mentored realize that identifying with winners is a useful and valuable learning technique, and they go that route.

In their series, Field and Mosenkis gave credit to authors Joan Jeruchim and Pat Shapiro for raising their awareness about this idea, for it was in Jeruchim and Shapiro's book, *Women, Mentors, and Success*, that the whole idea of "symbolic mentors" as a source of guidance for people who work alone (or in situations in which they have few professional peers) first came to light. It is often possible, Jeruchim and Shapiro wrote, to identify with and model one's own career on the careers of others who are admired and respected, particularly when a nearer role model is not available.

The whole object, of course, is for managers—the very people who find themselves in such mentoring situations—to be careful about underestimating what they can learn from observation. Such "symbolic" mentoring should not only be encouraged, it should be openly encouraged. Field agrees, as she makes clear when she describes her personal situation:

"I very much believe in identifying with winners," she says. "In my inaugural speech, when I became President of SLA, I described from the podium how following Rosabeth Moss Kanter's career, reading what she wrote, listening to her presentations, had helped me to keep intact my personal beliefs about the future of information services and where our information management profession needs to go. I simply couldn't consider compromising my ideas, even though some of the people around me thought my expectations were too high for the field in which we work. I don't think they were—or are—too high. I think they make a great deal of sense when we think about where librarianship and information services—as a profession—has come in the last decade or so. And where it's going to go in the immediate future. That's the kind of influence people like Kanter can have in our lives.

"And this kind of activity continues, in a sort of reverse mentoring situation. In my latest information professional role, my role now as a teacher, I hear former students describe how they are emulating me, and while it is nice to hear (it is, after all, ego-pleasing!), it is also scary. I have to ask myself: Am I leading them astray? Am I giving them wrong ideas?

Judy Field: Mentoring Tips for Information Managers

*B*eing comfortable in a mentoring situation requires more than just thinking about it. *InfoManage* asked Judy Field to offer a few suggestions for organizational managers with information services responsibility, about how they might implement a productive mentoring process in their units. Here are Field's ideas:

1. Mentoring is not top-down. As I said in the interview: mentoring is a two-way learning relationship. Both parties must benefit for there to be a true mentoring relationship.

2. A manager can't be everyone's mentor (well, unless you're working in a two- or three-person workplace environment). Scope out the staffing situation in your operational unit, and make some attempt to identify those employees who would most benefit from having a mentoring relationship with you (and from whom you would obtain some benefit—see above). If the staff is larger than two or three people, work with others to ensure that there is a mentoring system in place that covers all employees. Be careful about setting up a formal or codified 'buddy system,' however. There's advantage is a certain amount of looseness.

3. Mentoring relationships develop over time. Just as an information manager can't mentor everyone on the staff, neither can he or she start the process and drop it two weeks later. Mentoring is a subtle, on-going process, and a successful mentoring experience will go through several developmental stages before it's 'in place.' And even then the relationship will change, strengthen, and—it is to be fervently hoped—grow.

4. Related to this, recognize that coaching is one aspect of mentoring. It labels one as the 'expert' but for this relationship to flourish, at some point the role of expert needs to be discarded for a less-threatening role of advisor, or 'listening ear.' The mentor needs to also ask for input as the relationship develops—everyone has some knowledge or expertise they can share. This is an area where the manager can take a lead role in visibly being a coach.

5. Mentoring isn't limited to information services. Just because this is your area of expertise and management responsibility, don't forget that there are people in other units in the organization who might benefit from a mentoring relationship with you (just as some of your staff will benefit from a mentoring relationship with another manager or staff member who might work in a different department). A little common sense is called for here (you're hardly going to be of much help to the person who manages the company's parking garage, but on the other hand . . . who knows?). Recognize that mentoring beyond your formal boundaries helps increase your visibility—and thus your net worth—to the organization.

6. Long-term mentoring can be seen as an 'on call' situation. After one set of problems has been resolved or solutions are being implemented, things may drift for awhile. Then, when the need is felt again, the mentoring relationship will fall into place again.

I don't think so, for over the years I myself have identified with many 'winners,' either emulating them or holding them up as examples for others. They didn't give me wrong information or lead me astray. So I think the people I'm influencing are going to be OK.

"But if there is a downside here, it's this: there just isn't enough of this sort of thing. I wish there were more of it, this mentoring and reverse mentoring, this formal and informal mentoring, at all stages in all our careers. Let's face it: We work in a profession in which practitioners do not easily (and certainly not wholeheartedly) praise other people's success. And that—when you stop to think about it—is kind of strange, considering how eager we are to share our expertise and even, when called upon to do so, our resources. But we're not very generous with praise, and as we move into a mentoring situation with those who work with us, with those with whom we come in contact in our professional organizations, I think it's important that we praise those who succeed and put them forward for recognition. It's how others, those coming up in the profession, will identify their place in the future of the information management field."

So what we have here, clearly, is an information professional—now in an international leadership role—who isn't shy about attributing her success to the kindness and interest of people who "brought her along." Now she wants us to do the same for others, and to do it in whatever format, whatever framework works for us in our particular management situations. It doesn't seem to be such an unreasonable request, when you think about it. If we're going to bring—as we say we are—the best and the brightest people into information management, we have to be willing to nurture them along until they are ready to practice on their own, and then, in turn, to show others how to practice as well. It's all part of the profession's maturity, and with Judy Field encouraging us along, we'll do it, and we'll do it well.

Meet Judith Field

Judith J. Field is Senior Lecturer, Library and Information Science Program, Wayne State University, Detroit, MI, where she teaches courses in special libraries and business information resources. Her degrees, all from the University of Michigan, are an undergraduate degree in business administration and the A.M.L.S. and the M.B.A. In addition to her work as an educator, Field has over 25 years as a practitioner in corporate, academic, government, and public libraries, including Head, General Reference Department, Flint Public Library, Flint, MI, and Director, Legislative Reference Library, Minnesota State Legislature, St. Paul, MN. Currently, in addition to her teaching, Field works as a management consultant.

Judy Field was President of the Special Libraries Association 1997-1998. A member of SLA since 1963, Field has been an enthusiastic champion for the organization. Her volunteer activities for SLA have included numerous committee and planning assignments, as well as the Chairmanship of the SLA 1994 Annual Conference, held in Atlanta, GA. In addition to SLA, Field has memberships in ASIS (President of the Michigan Chapter, 1991-1993) and the American Library Association. For ALA, she served on the ALA Ad Hoc Committee on the 1991 White House Conference on Library and Information Services, and she was a member of the ALA Committee on Accreditation from 1993 to 1997.

Field's personal interests include travel with her husband Than, spending time at their vacation house on Lake Huron, a great deal of reading (mostly history and fiction), and participation—"when I can get away," she says—in archaeological digs in various places throughout the world. A tournament backgammon player with hopes to do the full international backgammon circuit someday, Field also travels extensively to participate in backgammon play.

3

MANAGEMENT PRACTICES IN INFORMATION SERVICES—ORGANIZING

O rganizing for change management requires taking a look at what is already in place, and then making a calculated judgment as to whether that existing operational organization "works" and, if it does not, determining how to change it so that it *will* work. Organization—and accepting responsibility for the organizational function—has always been an essential activity for management staff, and in today's information services environment, organizing for change management is but one part of that activity.

The acceptance of change management into the general management context has grown from an honest determination of information services staff to provide—and to continue to provide—the very highest levels of information delivery that can be offered. It is no coincidence that the high (indeed, almost elegant and idealistic) standards of information delivery of the library profession are now being routinely pursued in the other information services disciplines. Librarians, since the very inception of the profession, have always maintained the highest standards of information delivery, and while their high standards were sometimes compromised by circumstances which they could not control, librarians—as service providers—have never lost sight of their essential goal, to provide

113

the highest levels of service that could be provided. Thus it is no surprise that these same qualities were shifted into the business information field (and later, into any kind of "specialized" subject field) as practitioners in these disciplines discovered, starting early in this century, that "special" librarians could provide them with information that no one else—and certainly no one else with their level of expertise and their commitment to quality in information delivery—could provide. At the end of the century, we have many, many others in the information industry seeking to emulate the quality information management and dissemination that specialist librarians provide with unwavering consistency.

How people who succeed at quality information provision organize the units for which they have operational responsibility and incorporate the management of change into their work is the subject of the interviews in this chapter. The late Catherine A. Jones was quite specific about how it is the commitment of the staff which enables a high-profile and many faceted information "factory" to succeed. At the Congressional Reference Division, which Jones managed with great success, codifying what is expected of staff is the only appropriate way to ensure that staff members know that their individual integrity is respected. It's sincere, and it's how Jones and her direct reports got their employees to do their best work.

In this day and age, of course, much of the success that organizations achieve has much to do with the expanding technical universe, and that is exactly what has enabled people like Miriam A. Drake at the Georgia Institute of Technology and Lois Weinstein at the Medical Library Center of New York to bring success to their work. In such environments, change management cannot be an option. With information technology providing new products and services on an almost-daily basis, information staff simply must be coached in managing change, and the results—the effective delivery of information to the operation's defined user base—cannot be compromised.

But *using* information technology is not the only link in the change-management-to-successful-organizational-operations chain. Acknowledging and taking advantage of what information is doing in society at large also plays a role in the new information workplace. At the Massachusetts Institute of Technology's Engineering and Science Libraries, Ruth K. Seidman has long been an advocate for increased attention to the role of international information delivery in the information workplace (it was the theme of her presidency of the Special Libraries Association and the subject of an important book which she wrote). Having identified specific "hallmarks" that distinguish successful international information products, she has put them to work in the delivery of information at her operation.

Laura Gasaway, too, has been able to identify certain trends in information delivery that now affect service provision. As she thinks about how copyright and intellectual property issues are handled in different information environments (the variety, say, between compliance levels in the public library community as opposed to the small business community), Gasaway has good words of advice for information managers.

Some of this thinking links to what people like Allan Foster are doing. At Keele University, Foster has been able to organize a unique convergence of information delivery that reflects quite closely that "new" information management profession that Jerry King, quoted earlier, sees on the information horizon. Much of this comes together in Tom Pellizzi's work, as he seeks to show managers in the information industry how space can be arranged to create the best design for information flow. It all fits uniquely in the work that John Ganly and the management team at The New York Public Library Research Libraries Science, Industry, and Business Library are doing at America's foremost state-of-the-art "specialist" library. The conceptualization of that information entity, described in the William D. Walker interview in the previous chapter, comes full flower in the Ganly interview here. It is, indeed, an object lesson in planning for change and organizing for change management.

Obviously, all successful change management activities do not develop in a totally new entity. Indeed, for most information services managers, change and change management must be inculcated into a pre-existing structure, and the redesign of a managerial structure is the framework for most large-scale change management efforts. That was the situation at the University of Arizona Library, and the move to team-based management at that institution is a case study that many research libraries and other large information organizations will watch closely. Dean Carla Stoffle, Shelley Phipps, Michael Ray, and Carrie Russell describe how, at the University of Arizona, it was their challenge to work with the organization to develop the organization, and their success, reported here, provides many a lesson for budding change managers in the information industry. The specifics—the move to team-based management—might be controversial in some quarters, but the process for organizing change at the University of Arizona Library cannot be considered as anything but successful.

"It's the Staff"
CATHERINE A. JONES
talks about LC's Congressional Reference Division

An afternoon spent with Cathy Jones brings out the best in you. If energy, enthusiasm and effectiveness are management qualities that appeal to you, and if big-time, high-quality information delivery is your particular focus, she's the person you want to meet. And the first thing you'll observe, and carry with you throughout your visit, is that her delight in her work is directly linked to her relationship with her staff. The considerable success of the Congressional Reference Division is staff driven, and Jones never lets you forget it. She knows how good these people are.

As Chief of the Congressional Reference Division, one of nine divisions making up the Congressional Research Service at the US Library of Congress in Washington, DC, Jones manages the organization, staff and resources for handling upwards of 350,000 annual requests from legislators, legislative committees, and the many staff assistants and analysts who provide support for them. The large and diverse staff of CRS (currently over 700 people and including a wide assortment of information services professionals, technicians, and administrative staff) are all trained to use appropriate research techniques and tools in all subject areas. In the Congressional Reference Division, the emphasis is on specific information, and it is the staff's goal to provide answers in the shortest possible time, frequently on the same day. It's not an easy task, and in fact the constant time pressures and deadlines forced upon them make information delivery a highly charged affair.

"Sometimes," Jones says, "the atmosphere is more like a newsroom than a library. We just don't have the luxury of a generous turnaround time." Certainly the standard RUSH order means just that: the information is delivered today or tomorrow; nothing else is permitted. Other

Originally published in *InfoManage : The International Management Newsletter for the Information Services Professional* 1 (2), January, 1994.

deadlines, such as delivery by a specific date, are adhered to, and standard non-rush designation for "Member" requests (as in "Member of Congress") and committee requests means that the information will be delivered "as completely as possible in the shortest amount of time." One week's turnaround time is the outside limit.

So speed is a priority, but so is accuracy. The user group is specifically defined ("all Members and committees of the U.S. Congress in support of their legislative, oversight, and representational functions"), and information from the Congressional Reference Division is frequently provided for the working press, the public, and of course for floor debates. In fact, the quality of the response is so important that special quality review programs are in place. It has to be good information, if it's going to Congress.

Although there's a level of seriousness in the work the CRS staff does, there is also, within this huge operation and throughout its various reading rooms and reference centers located throughout the Capitol area, a positively pleasant ambiance with respect to the work and the contribution the staff is making to the legislative effort. After ten minutes with Jones, it's easy to see why. Her comfortable manner with people, the satisfaction she takes in seeing the organization function so well, and, yes, her remarkable energy have a definite influence on the way people behave. It's obvious that she sees the staff as the primary asset in the success that the division achieves. When asked why, she has a ready response.

"It may sound corny," Jones says, "but as far as our staff is concerned, we respect the integrity of the individual." She goes on to describe how she and her staff do what they can to help their employees do their best. "It's important," she says, "for jobs to be codified as much as they can be," so CRD managers and supervisors are careful to tell their people just what is expected of them. Someone once said that the best way to succeed in management is to hire the best people, tell them what to do, and then let them do it. That same concept could be the theme for human resources management at CRD. Employees are taken very seriously, shown a great deal of respect, and "no one looks over anybody's shoulder."

Nevertheless, expectations are high. It is not an easy job, working for the Congressional Reference Division, and a brief read through the booklet of carefully designed training plans for all technicians and reference librarians, the awesome list of titles of reference materials "each employee is expected to know," and the 60-plus page "Guidelines for Work in

CRD," makes it clear that employment in CRD is not for the faint-hearted. These people work hard, and they have to. This is one information services organization where "wrong" or "bad" information would spell disaster, and every staff member knows it.

On that subject (and although she would like you to think she's joking), Jones means it when she says "When we say the answer is no, the answer is no." At the Congressional Reference Division, the resources, the procedures, and the staff commitment are so organized and so carefully calibrated that there really isn't any need to look elsewhere if the answer can't be found. While the vast majority of requests for information are responded to quickly and accurately, when there is that occasional question for which there is no answer, as Jones points out, there is no answer. If there were, the CRD people would have found it.

How did it come about, this attitude about information? What motivates Jones and her senior staff to create and manage an organization that can be so responsive? And what influenced Jones in her career, to look to providing such a high level of service?

"First of all," she says, "I trained under people for whom the delivery of information wasn't a luxury. It was always a case of 'now or never.'" She tells how, in her early career, she worked with Ruth Fine and Elisabeth Knauff at the library of the old Bureau of the Budget. In those days, when the economists, speechwriters, policy makers and other analysts who came to the library needed a piece of information, they needed it, and Fine and Knauff knew how to provide it. So in terms of customer service, and learning about customer service, when Jones came along she couldn't have apprenticed with a better team. She learned to give the library's users what they wanted, and that idea, of course, is what drives the Congressional Reference Division under her leadership.

But one could still ask: isn't there more to it than that? What about Congress itself, the institutional culture? Don't the Members have some influence on the approach to information?

Jones smiles. "Information is power," she says, "and we're here to provide information to the people for whom power means a lot." It becomes quite clear that Jones regards the work she and her staff do for Congress as a pretty high calling. It's an idea, of course, that has motivated her and her people to organize and implement their very sophisticated system of information management for responding to the Members' information needs. For example, as part of what they call "workload management,"

CRD staff created their famous Info Packs, those prestocked packets of information on popular issues. By using them, the information staff is not always busily re-inventing the wheel for each of the 1500 legislative assistants who might want some basic information on, say, the European Community, as they did when that was a "hot topic" in 1992, or, during the late summer and early fall of last year, NAFTA. Such Info Packs—Jones refers to them as "prepared background information"—not only relieve the staff from re-answering the same question, they frequently provide the requester with just what he or she needs and the satisfactory information transaction is complete. On the other hand, if the Info Pack stimulates a request for more in-depth information, or a more detailed look at some aspect of the subject, that request, too, can be responded to.

And while the Info Packs are but one product of the highly responsive information structure at the Congressional Reference Division, they are an example of the serious level of information delivery that is achieved. In fact, the highest form of flattery is accorded to much of the effort at CRD: throughout the world, parliamentary and other legislative libraries have adopted CRD's methods and even some of its products, and CRD staff members have been successful in working with a variety of other legislative information delivery programs. It is now common, for example, to see article packets, bibliographies, Info Packs, and similar information products created at CRD turning up in Polish, Scandinavian, Russian, Spanish, and other non-English language versions, and service to the international legislative community is now recognized by Congress and the Congressional Research Services staff as part of the division's legitimate mission.

Much of the success of the Congressional Reference Division can be attributed to Jones and the management qualities she brings to the operation. Quietly estimating that probably as much as 75% of her time is spent in administrative work, it becomes clear, as she talks, that it is working with the staff that she sees as her primary mission at the Library of Congress. Planning—in the traditional managerial sense—is not typically part of the process, simply because appropriations for funding CRD programs are organized only on an annual basis, since that is the way Congress operates. So it is difficult to do much serious planning when the timeframe is so limited. There are no five-year plans, no long-term strategic plans.

On the other hand, as far as staff tasks, functions and responsibilities are concerned, planning is organized and honed to a fine art, resulting in such satisfactory products as the recent reclassification of several staff positions in the division. The changes were needed, Jones points out, because much of the work that is done by the "librarians" on the staff is, in fact, analytical and managerial in nature and not very related to the strictly "information provision" work of traditional librarianship. In addition, vastly increased access to information through electronic sources adds to the complexity of the work and expands the variety and types of questions that staff are expected to respond to. So for several years Jones and her managers campaigned to have some of the "librarian" positions reclassified to a new title, to better reflect their responsibilities and contributions to the division. They've been successful, so henceforth, for those who qualify, the professional staff will include several professional employees with titles like "information research specialist" and "information management specialist," as well as a formalized title of "team leader" for the people who do that work. Jones is particularly proud of the success of this effort, the result of several years of innovation and initiation on her own part, as it will ensure that the titles of the employees at the Congressional Reference Division, at least the ones so affected, more accurately describe the work that these information services professionals perform.

It's all part of the job for Jones, who from this perspective is unique in her work as a manager. In her work as an information services executive, she is particularly talented in being able to see the bigger picture, to envision for her specific users just what it is that she and her staff can provide for them. Yet at the same time, the ambiance at the Congressional Reference Division clearly reflects a leader/manager who understands the personal role in the provision of information and in the management of the information unit itself. The combination of the two, a vision of service and an interest in the people who provide it, results in a remarkable information organization for a very important clientele.

Catherine Jones, who died in January 1998, was Chief, Congressional Reference Division, Library of Congress, Washington, D.C.

RUTH K. SEIDMAN
at MIT's Engineering and Science Libraries:
Managing International Information Issues at the Institute

For many people working in the information services field, international information issues are still a little removed, still just a little "beyond" what they do every day. For these folks, all the talk about a "global information highway," "borderless information exchange," and the like simply conjures up images of hightech CIA operatives putting together esoteric data that only they and their compatriots can access or, for that matter, understand.

Then there are the folks who have jumped in feet first, recognizing that the world is changing drastically, and that as it changes, so does the delivery of information. These are the folks who, like Ruth Seidman at the Massachusetts Institute of Technology, are so in tune with the role of information in a global society that they don't even know how to think provincially any more. In the work they do (and Seidman is typical in this respect), it's this "big picture" that drives the decisions.

At MIT, that big picture is the reality that determines how information services are provided for students, faculty, and the many scientific and technical researchers who make up the vast network of users for the MIT Libraries. Seidman has responsibility for the Engineering and Science Libraries, a combined operation that pulls together the major components of the scientific and technical collections. And with three other special collections under her authority, the Aeronautics and Astronautics Library, the Schering-Plough Library (materials in neurosciences, medical research, biomedical imaging, and consumer health information), and the Lindgren Library (collections in earth, atmospheric, and planetary sciences), you might say that Seidman is pretty much required to have a "big picture" outlook on information services issues. After all, there's not much in the scientific and technical fields—the very subjects in which

Originally published in *InfoManage : The International Management Newsletter for the Information Services Professional* 2 (5), April 1995.

research information has such global implications—that she is not responsible for, at least at MIT.

The connection with international information is not necessarily a new interest for Seidman. After a healthy stint in the science field (her previous job, before coming to MIT, was as Director of the U.S. Air Force Geophysics Laboratory Research Library and, prior to that, as librarian for the New England Region of the U.S. Environmental Protection Agency), Seidman was brought to MIT to facilitate a major reorganization, the administrative merger of the Science Library, located in the Charles Hayden Memorial Library Building, and the Barker Engineering Library, located on the fifth floor of the famous domed building that faces Memorial Drive and the Charles River. While operating in two separate spaces became Seidman's first challenge, it wasn't really a major one and it was easily overcome when she set up shop with an office in each library. And with the buildings physically connected ("nice during the New England winter," Seidman says cheerfully), she is able to do her work without feeling too schizophrenic, as long as she doesn't mind the walk.

When she came to MIT in 1988, combining the libraries seemed like a natural progression, due to the increasing cross-disciplinarity between engineering and science. Since then, of course, a number of external and societal changes have taken place, changes which—while not necessarily connected to information services—have certainly had an influence on the way scientific and technical information is delivered. Now it makes a lot of sense to have combined the libraries.

"For one thing," Seidman points out, "there is less money to support graduate students and scientific research, so a certain amount of downsizing is required. The post-Cold War situation, the drop in the amount of Department of Defense work, and a change in the way the government computes indirect costs to support research have all had a serious impact on the way we do business. Here at MIT, we are entering the third year of a three-year, institution-wide cut of 2% a year, so the move to streamline the library function with respect to engineering and science subjects now appears—in hindsight—to have been a very wise move indeed."

It might have been wise, but it wasn't necessarily an easy task to bring the libraries together administratively. For one thing, with two separate facilities, the entire concept of "turf wars" takes on a very realistic structure. When asked how she dealt with these very basic managerial issues, Seidman seems a little surprised that the subject is important enough to discuss. Her attitude seems to be: Well, it was a problem and we fixed it and that was that. But when pressed, she is obviously pleased with the results.

"Certainly the first thing we did, as I've mentioned, was setting up an office in each space," she says. "It's very important that all staff know that where I am, that I am available, and that as a manager I can be located when I'm needed. But probably more important than the two offices was the establishment of joint meetings between the employees of the two libraries. One of the first things we looked at was staff competencies, where there was expertise in such things as subject specialty, reference skills, hightech competencies, and collection development, and we put the two staffs together so that staff with like functions could meet and learn from each other. Also, all librarians are scheduled at both the Engineering and the Science reference desks, regardless of their primary subject areas."

Has it worked?

"Absolutely," Seidman says, and the finality of her response tells you she is satisfied with the job she did.

But of course the effort continues, and at the Institute, which you don't refer to as "Tech" ("No one ever calls it 'Tech' nowadays," Seidman says with a laugh. "It's either 'MIT' or 'the Institute,' but never 'Tech.'"), Seidman and her senior staff are looking carefully at ways in which the delivery of information can reach beyond traditional borders to bring information services and products to the users from wherever it is found. It all comes around again to Seidman's interest in international information issues, an interest that she has maintained throughout her career but which took on a significantly different perspective just a few years ago, when she was president of the Special Libraries Association. Prior to her inauguration, Seidman had chosen a presidential "theme" of looking at international information issues, specifically with respect to information professionals, the people who provide the information.

The thematic focus paid off, for everywhere she went in her presidential travels, Seidman saw examples of how "exciting initiatives" (as she referred to them later in a book she wrote on the subject) were being undertaken by special librarians in their pursuit of international information. These people were getting involved in visits, job swaps, consultation, corporate networks, interlibrary exchange agreements, and other similar activities, and their work was not always necessarily involved in the delivery of information, per se. Quite often, in fact, information professionals were becoming interested in what their colleagues were doing, and they wanted to know how international projects were initiated and how they were implemented. It soon became obvious that Seidman had tapped a powerful—and mineable—vein in the information services profession's corporate lode.

One result of this work was that Seidman identified several specific characteristics (she calls them "hallmarks") that distinguish successful international information projects. Among these are, of course, such expected attributes as advance planning and flexibility, but equally important was another characterization she identified, the value attached to what might be called "equal" or "nearly equal" points of view. In all of these successful projects, Seidman makes clear, what works best is a combination of the consultant's knowledge and expertise with "information and insight possessed at the local level."

In fact, such an approach might also characterize Seidman's management style at MIT, for "combined" expertise seems to distinguish her work. A look at the several reporting relationships on the management chart for the various libraries under her authority quickly reveals that the people who work with her are engaged in an ongoing series of mutually supportive relationships. Much of this work, it soon becomes clear, involves the delivery of information products and services from wherever they can be obtained and this, of course, includes much international activity.

One such project—in which MIT is participating with eight other universities—is the so called TULIP project, looking at a prototypical electronic journal delivery system. The publisher of 38 materials science journals (Elsevier Publishing in the Netherlands) sends scanned images of journal pages and citation records to participating universities, which then have the responsibility of making this electronic information available to their materials science researchers. At MIT, Suzanne Weiner, assistant engineering and science librarian, works closely with the materials science faculty. She is watching the progress of the project carefully, for it has serious implications in the delivery of international information, especially in terms of intellectual property rights, costs, and similar important issues.

"What we're seeing here," Seidman points out, "is the amazing effect that the Internet has had on information exchange. In almost every area in which our reference librarians work, the librarians use online sources to access information for the users. And of course it is international. When you surf the World Wide Web, how is the menu arranged? By continent. And as Suzanne Weiner has pointed out in an article about the Web, it was always intended to be international. It was created in Switzerland and it exists to provide that borderless information exchange we all hear so much about."

A similar approach defines the Japanese Science and Technology Information Project, sponsored by the MIT Japan Program and the MIT Libraries. Although currently being brought up at the Dewey Library, MIT's social sciences and management collection, the project will be a cooperative project and ultimately will involve much coordination with the librarians at the Engineering and Science Libraries. Seidman is enthusiastic about the prospects for the project, which will lead to the creation of a national online resource for Japanese science and technology information when it is completed. Funded by the U.S. Air Force Office of Scientific Research and planned to include information on electronic resources, print collections, directories, bibliographies, document delivery and translations services, the project is expected to grow as research needs are assessed and responded to.

All of which is keeping Ruth Seidman busy, for not only is she managing the "doublesided" information delivery process at the Engineering and Science Libraries, she continues in her efforts to bring information services professionals together through the literature. Her book was just one step in this direction, and she has other such interests that keep her busy. For several years, Seidman has chaired the Editorial Committee of *MIT Libraries' News*, and in November, 1994, she became the new editor of *Science and Technology Libraries*, the quarterly journal that the Haworth Press has been successfully putting out for fourteen years.

"This is a challenge I am very excited about," Seidman says. "The journal plays an important role in contributing to a dialogue that clarifies issues, and it provides needed information for those working to develop creative solutions."

Among those solutions, as might be expected, is a serious focus on the globalization of information, specifically in terms of science and technology libraries worldwide.

"The goals are simple," she says. "We want to use the journal to broaden the awareness of information professionals and to facilitate resource sharing, and we also want to look at the changing nature of scientific communication, experiments in electronic publishing (such as the TULIP project), and national and international information policy."

Seidman noted that in the past much of the emphasis in *Science and Technology Libraries* has been on collection development, and that will continue, but now she intends to have the journal look at all sides of management in scientific and technical libraries, including such subjects as personnel management, a look at who runs scientific and technical libraries and how they do things, and, a subject of specific interest, how librarians and their users interact.

"We're specially interested in, say, how engineers and librarians work together," Seidman said. "And to find out, we expect to use librarians who have subject expertise or experience. In looking at engineers, for example, we are about to publish a study by a librarian with an engineering background, and that should give us many useful and interesting ideas about the way engineering libraries might be managed. And we hope to do that with a variety of subject disciplines that have traditionally been information intensive and have turned to libraries for information support for their work."

Certainly there can be no doubt that the big picture concept Ruth Seidman is bringing to her work is one that is going to impact information decisions for many generations to come. By acknowledging the changes that society is bringing to information delivery, and by embracing those changes as a positive force in the work that she and her staff are doing at the Engineering and Science Libraries at MIT, Seidman is, in fact, embarking on a whole new approach to the management of scientific and technical information. It's an approach that bodes well for the information users, and that's good for the Institute.

Meet Ruth Seidman

Head, Engineering and Science Libraries, Massachusetts Institute of Technology, Cambridge, MA . . . Has written and lectured on library management, integrating technology into library operations, and staff development . . . Began her career as a subject specialist, as Librarian of the Russian Research Center at Harvard University, where she had completed a Master's degree in Soviet Area Studies . . . Contributor to Massachusetts statewide and New England regional efforts in library cooperation over the past two decades . . . Served as New England Regional Librarian for the U.S. Environmental Protection Agency and participated in the onset in the development of the national EPA Library Network . . . At EPA, in addition to library responsibilities, was Federal Women's Program Coordinator and implemented innovative equal opportunity programs involving upward mobility, cooperative education, and opening up nontraditional careers for women . . . As Director of the Air Force Geophysics Laboratory Research Library, participated in the implementation of an Air Force-wide library management internship and two-year training program . . . President of the Special Libraries Association, 1990–1991 . . . Author of *Building Global Partnerships for Library Cooperation*, published by SLA in 1993 . . . Other interests: Seidman is a child care advocate and the founder of two child care centers. She enjoys the wonderful arts life in the Boston area-especially music and theatre.

MIMI DRAKE
at Georgia Tech: Ten years online and the future is NOW!

Miriam Drake is Dean and Director of Libraries at the Georgia Institute of Technology, where the future of information services for the Institute is debated and delighted in every day. In fact, Mimi (as she's known to most of her colleagues in the information services profession) is pretty much leading the charge in both the debate and the delight, and you don't have to talk with this lady very long before you realize you're speaking to an information services executive who is a futurist to the tips of her toes. She knows what information delivery has been, she knows where it is now, and she anticipates with much enthusiasm and pleasure where the information services field is going to be in the next few years. The future of information, in fact, is one of the subjects she truly enjoys talking about.

"Not too long ago," she says, "I was asked to spot some 'themes,' you might call them, for the next few years in information services." Drake speaks with an authority that tells her listener that this is a subject that she's given more than a little thought to. "I came up with four: The first is that our world will be increasingly multimedia and interactive. The second is that we need to bring structure and organization to knowledge and content. The third is that technology has enabled and will continue to enable huge increases in productivity. And finally, the information world, our world, will be customer-driven, with products and services tailored to individual needs, interests and mind sets."

Is it any surprise, then, that information services at Georgia Tech reflect these themes? In fact, they're pretty much organized along lines that incorporate these directions into the information products and services that are made available to students, faculty, staff, and researchers at the Institute. It's all part of Drake's commitment to an information services picture that is client centered, that looks at information delivery

Originally published in *InfoManage : The International Management Newsletter for the Information Services Professional* 2 (6), May, 1995.

(even in large research organizations like Georgia Tech) in terms of the individual information customer's needs.

"When customer concerns are paramount," Drake says, "each person is recognized as unique and information services are organized accordingly."

Rightly so, and the concept has been elaborated on in her speeches and published writings, most notably in her essay on academic libraries in the book she edited with James Matarazzo in 1994. Drake made it clear that an individualized approach to information services is precisely what is required: "Value-added information services," she wrote, "are not mass-market items. They are based on the desire to satisfy each customer. Customers don't want standardization."

Was she throwing down the gauntlet for managers of academic and other large information organizations? Not really, for the more time you spend with Drake, the more you realize that—despite the fact that there's an iron fist in the velvet glove—she has a great deal of respect for her colleagues and for what they've done. She's just very interested in doing better in the future.

Part of that future, of course, is thinking about what information the customers need. "One of the issues we have to address," she points out, "is how we are going to deal with the past. Much important basic work was done in the past (in civil engineering, for example), and we need to be able to access the records of that work, not just as a historical archive, but as basic, foundation material which is and will continue to be referred to by practitioners in that field for a long time to come. But that doesn't mean we don't look for progress, that we don't move forward when we have the opportunity. That's part of the whole customer-driven focus. We have to recognize that even though we must prepare for the day when things will be different, when the Nintendo kids have completed their PhDs and are running our classrooms, we will continue to have customers who want to come to a library building to smell and touch the volumes."

Drake has been directing information services at Georgia Tech since 1984, and she's proud of what they've done in those eleven years. You can hear the excitement in her voice when she talks about how information is delivered there.

"Georgia Tech students are among the nation's best and brightest. They deserve a great library and first-rate information services and they get them. One of my personal goals is to ensure that every Tech grad is information competent. I feel especially pleased when a colleague from industry tells me that our grads have a competitive edge in this area."

While her own polite modesty prevents her from demonstrating too much pride about her personal role in the Institute's success, as far as its information delivery programs are concerned, it soon becomes evident that Georgia Tech owes a great deal to Drake. This is an information executive who has an astute ability to cut through the layers, to look at the delivery of information products and services from the user's point of view, and who can, at the same time, enjoy a football game with the Institute's movers and shakers in the President's Box and come away with a promise for a major funding commitment. It's just another example of how she makes it work.

"Let's not make too much out of that President's Box story," she says with a laugh. "That's where I sit for all the games. It's just that sometimes some of the needs we have come up at that time, and who am I to stop the conversation if it turns to information?"

Obviously. And such positioning certainly pays off, whether it is casual happenstance or part of a serious and planned-out campaign, for the information services operation that Drake heads up is nothing if not successful. That success has a particular focus to it right now, as Drake and her staff—and the entire research community at Georgia Tech—prepare themselves for a little celebrating.

"May is a special month for us this year," Drake reports. "It was ten years ago that we went online with the Georgia Tech Electronic Library. Georgia Tech and Carnegie Mellon were the first universities in the nation to make a catalog and leased databases available to all faculty and students on the campus-wide network. Now our students, faculty, and researchers just take for granted an information-delivery system that was something of a big deal when it started ."

It was with the Georgia Tech Electronic Library ("GTEL®," as it's known) that the Institute, under Drake's direction, began the transformation of the library from a collection-based entity to a customer-based library. Directing such a move is completely in character for Drake, for as a great proponent of quality management in the information services field, a commitment to customer-focus fits right into the scheme of things.

The Georgia Tech Library has a long history of innovation," Drake reports. "We were a MARC 1 pilot site in the nineteen sixties. Twenty-five years ago the card catalog was replaced with a computer-produced micro-fiche catalog which was distributed to all campus departments.

"GTEL® was a logical step. The system includes the catalog, a variety of bibliographic, abstracting, and indexing and full text databases as well as directories and gateways to other sources. There is a gopher service for the Internet with suggestions for the best sources. The system also includes modules to request documents to be delivered, ask a reference question, recommend items for purchase, and suggest improvements in the system.

"Our goals for GTEL® have not changed in ten years. The most criti-cal goals are to make the maximum amount of information available to our students and faculty on the campus-wide network and to increase fac-ulty and student productivity. GTEL® is available to our customers in their offices, dormitories, and homes 24 hours a day, 365 days per year."

It soon becomes obvious, in any conversation with Mimi Drake, that it's the customer that she and her staff think about first.

"Absolutely," she says. "Our customer focus, GTEL®, and our contin-uous quality improvement program have made a difference for Georgia Tech. Our staff of 115 people have a strong commitment to internal and external customers and to quality service. They make magic happen every day."

The success of GTEL® on the Georgia Tech campus fits neatly into a pattern that seems to be in place there (after all, they've had document delivery for faculty for 25 years), and it is an appropriate venue for Drake to be looking at another of those future themes she identified, our pro-fession's (and society's) need to bring structure and organization to knowledge and content. A great admirer of Peter Drucker, Drake is quick to relate what we are doing in the information field to Drucker's concepts about the knowledge workers and their use of knowledge to create pro-ductivity, innovation, and competitiveness.

"It's an incredible challenge for us," she says, "because it means that we must rethink some of our ideas about our profession and what we do as information professionals. How many librarians, for example, understand the implications of knowledge work and productivity? How many librarians concern themselves now with the productivity of their customers, clients, and users? How many librarians and computing staff are prepared to make the changes necessary to manage information and actively contribute to a learning society and a knowledge-based economy?"

These are not easy questions to answer, but Drake makes it clear that she thinks about them. She is, in fact, comfortably optimistic about how the changes will come about.

"First of all," she says, "strategic planning becomes more and more critical in the work we do as information services professionals. All libraries and information systems and services units must now plan strategically in order to lead in knowledge, productivity, and information transfer and diffusion. And these strategic plans must be part of a vision that relates the information units' missions, goals, strategies, and action plans to those of the parent organization. The days of the library or the computing center existing by itself and for itself are gone."

Which means, of course, that staff training in information services is a much more serious matter these days than it was in the past.

"Of course," Drake replies. "I came to Georgia Tech in 1984, and I can see a change just in that short period of time. Jobs are different now, and will continue to be different as time goes on. Staff training must focus on how to handle the different types of work we expect of the employees. As with our customers and their needs, our training can't be standardized either. We have to prepare for the unique situation, but it has to be within a context of customer-focused service."

Drake is particularly sensitive, she says, to the whole idea of change these days, for she finds herself having to work with two major change-management challenges within the next few years. For one thing, planning has already begun on a new library facility, expected to be under construction no later than 1998 or so. But for the immediate future—as anyone who has heard the word "Atlanta" in the last couple of years is bound to know—the 1996 Summer Olympic Games are to be played in Atlanta, and specifically, for several sports, at Georgia Tech.

"If you want to talk about the challenges," Drake says with a laugh, "let's talk about 1996. For security purposes, there will be three layers of fences around the campus, and access to all university buildings, including the library, will be limited. While some faculty won't be teaching that summer, for those who will be teaching and for the Institute's usual researchers, work can't stop, and courses will be taught at suburban campuses. So although access to the library will be limited, research work will continue and the library will be accessible to our faculty and students remotely. We are preparing now to supply what will be needed for the six or eight weeks that the library will be closed in 1996. All information delivery will be electronic. It will have to be."

For this native of Boston, this library manager with her background in industry and her work in economics, the challenges of total electronic delivery for the summer of 1996 and a new building by the end of the century seem to be eminently do-able. Mimi Drake is not a person who looks for an easy way out, and she's certainly not an information executive who would want a job that didn't include challenges. In fact, she looks like she's the perfect person to be running information services for Georgia Tech these days, and if her enthusiasm and her interest in her operation's future success are any benchmark to measure by, these next few years are going to be remarkable. And fun.

Meet Mimi Drake

Miriam A. Drake is Dean and Director of the Libraries and Information Center at the Georgia Institute of Technology, Atlanta, GA. Drake is responsible for the operation of the Libraries, Institute Records Center and Archives, and a variety of information services programs. Drake began her career as a transportation economist and spent 14 years in industry as a consultant and market researcher. Prior to joining Georgia Tech in 1984, Drake served as Assistant Director of Support Services at Purdue University Libraries and Audio Visual Center. She received her BS in Economic Analysis and MLS from Simmons College and did graduate work in Economics at Harvard University. The author of more than 50 journal articles and book chapters, Drake has also presented more than 70 conference papers on management and the management of information technology and services. An Editorial Advisor to *InfoManage*, she also serves on the editorial boards of *Database*, *Online Libraries and Microcomputers*, *Science and Technology Libraries*, and *Research & Education Networking*. In her work with higher education, Drake serves on visiting boards for the Lehigh University Libraries, the MIT Libraries, and chairs the Visiting Board for Information Services at Case Western Reserve University. Drake was Chairman of the OCLC, Inc. Board of Trustees, 1980-1984. She is immediate past president of the Special Libraries Association, and she was the 1992 recipient of ALA's Hugh Atkinson Memorial Award for Management and Risk Taking, and the first recipient of the Kent/Meckler Lifetime Achievement Award. In 1994 she was awarded an Honorary Doctorate of Humane Letters by Indiana University, on which occasion Gerald Bepko, Chancellor, IUPUI said, "Miriam Drake was quick to recognize . . . that the natural leaders of efforts to navigate the Information Age were librarians. And among those navigators, she has been a captain. At a time when few other professions were called upon to adapt to new technologies so quickly and without costly mistakes, librarians like Ms. Drake were ahead of the automation game and saw the tremendous opportunities and challenges that lay ahead."

Marching into the New millennium:
LOIS WEINSTEIN
is leading the charge at The Medical Library Center of New York

"Passion" is a word that isn't generally associated with our profession, and truth to tell, there are probably information services workers who would be uncomfortable with the idea of being passionate about the work they do. *Enthusiasm* and *enthusiastic* cross the desk from time to time, and we nod our heads appreciatively. But *passion*? Isn't that a bit of a stretch for librarians, records managers, archivists, and the other information providers we've come to identify as the people who make up the information services field?

Well wait 'til you meet Lois Weinstein. This is a lady who is not only excited about her work. Her excitement goes beyond enthusiasm and, yes, "passion" seems to be a good word to describe what Lois Weinstein is about these days. After spending a few minutes listening to her describe the UCMP Project she's currently working on, you're begin to realize that it is, indeed, a kind of passion that has crept into her professional life, and she even—you guessed it—uses the term when she talks about what she and her associates at The Medical Library Center of New York (MLCNY) are doing to prepare themselves for in for ma tion delivery in the 21st century.

"We're a consortium here," she says, "and putting together this project has brought out the best in all of us, our staff, our board, the participants in the UCMP. All of us. The project has become a passion."

The project she is describing is the UCMP ONline Project, UCMP being—for those who don't seek medical information in their work—the Union Catalog of Medical Periodicals. The genesis of the project was simply an extension of The Medical Library Center's basic goal: to provide access to the continually increasing volume (frequently characterized as an "unprecedented explosion") of medical and health literature. While physicians, nurses, researchers, and other health professionals and stu-

Originally published in *InfoManage : The International Management Newsletter for the Information Services Professional* 2 (9), August, 1995.

dents have always recognized the value of information, they simply are not able to maintain private libraries and older materials get discarded. Then when they need these older materials, most health professionals must rely on hospital, research, and medical school libraries, but they too, can't maintain older collections indefinitely. So back in 1959, the deans of the medical schools and the heads of the New York Academy of Medicine and what are now known as the Memorial Sloan-Kettering Cancer Center and The Rockefeller University decided to establish one place where the older literature could be stored, retrieved, and rapidly dispersed. The Medical Library Center of New York, characterized by its founders as a consortium and a central repository library, was the result of the decision, and Weinstein stresses this characterization.

"MLCNY is a consortium," she says with emphasis. "Which means that when we're talking about strategic planning, management decisions, and the like, we're talking about a membership organization with seventy different institutional members. We're talking about a Board of Trustees made up of representatives of the deans or presidents of the founding institutions, people who at their institutions serve as Vice-President of Business and Finance, say, or Vice-President for Academic Administration, Associate Dean for Educational Affairs at a medical school, Assistant Dean for Information Resources, or Assistant Vice-President and Associate Dean of Scholarly Resources. Those are the kinds of people we have on our board. It's a strong group of leaders, and having a consortium structure means that each and every opinion has value. Everyone has his or her own viewpoint, and each viewpoint matters."

Currently, access to the holdings of the 750 medical libraries that participate in the Union Catalog of Medical Periodicals is through *UCMP Quarterly*, published on microfiche. While remarkably complete (and used all over the world), it was Weinstein's feeling—after she had been on board for a while and had begun to grasp some of the problems the information stakeholders in her user community were grappling with—that something could be done to make the process faster and more effective. Using *The UCMP Quarterly* requires searching over 40 pieces of microfiche to find the correct journals and then identifying the libraries that have the necessary volume and issue, and when the information is found, it must then be written down on a piece of paper before the librarian or other information worker can go to DOCLINE, the National Library of

Medicine's electronic journal ordering system. But that process is just too cumbersome in today's medical information gathering scene. Change was needed, and Weinstein found herself in the role of change agent.

"When I took this job," she says with the knowing smile of hindsight, "I sort of thought it was going to be another 'library' job. Oh, I knew it would be somewhat different, because I knew something about the kind of work that was done here, but I had no idea it was going to be such a challenge. Not only do we deal with the delivery of information products, I found myself responsible for real estate decisions, compensation matters, and, the big surprise for me, fund raising. At the time I was a little taken aback be cause, as a corporate librarian, I had never done any fundraising, but in fact it has to be done. So now I just look at fund-raising as another part of my job."

It's the fund-raising, of course, that has enabled MLCNY to move forward with the UCMP ONline Project, for although there is an annual operations budget of about $1 million, there was no way the costs of doing something as special and as innovative as the project could be financed from general operating funds. So to raise the money, Weinstein learned about fund-raising, and the most important thing she learned is that networking is the key to successful fund-raising.

"That I learned when I explained the Center's need to the founding Director, Erich Meyerhoff," she says. "His immediate reaction was, 'Count me in. I'll help.'"

And help he did, by introducing Weinstein to foundation presidents, one of whom, Dr. Thomas Meikle, of the Josiah Macy, Jr. Foundation, arranged for a $100,000 challenge grant from his Board of Directors.

Marketing, too, has turned out to be one of Weinstein's major occupations in the nearly six years she has been at MLCNY, and, in fact, it was through the marketing efforts that she and her board members realized how important it would be to improve the product—*The UCMP Quarterly*—that goes out. Some 30% of MLCNY's funding is realized through the sale of subscriptions to the publication, and that number was going to drop drastically if some changes weren't made.

How did she know?

"We asked," Weinstein says. "We did the usual information audits (which we're now doing annually), and we discovered that our customers wanted this information online. In 1992, we surveyed subscribers and participants and we had a better than 35% response. Of those responding, over 58% said they wanted an online UCMP. A follow-up survey the next year showed that the numbers were up. 51% of the surveys were returned, and of those who responded, more than 90% not only expressed a favorable interest in online distribution but wrote additional comments describing options they wanted."

As things began to fall into place, it became clear that Weinstein's vision was built around some pretty innovative thinking. Then there was that ability she discovered she had in spades: she could not only market The Center's products to the customers, she could motivate the trustees and the other information stakeholders to buy in to her vision. She was, in fact, defining herself as an entrepreneurial librarian, a role she hadn't exactly expected.

"Entrepreneurial?" she asks, surprised that she's been so characterized. "Yes, I suppose so, for the basis of entrepreneurial librarianship, in my opinion, is the quest for business results. We had to look at the whole system as a business: when you're making money, you stay in business—when you're losing money, you go out of business."

She continues with the story. "We were on the verge of losing money," she says, "and we needed to prepare MLCNY for serving its customers in the new millennium. We had no choice. If we didn't do something, there would be no Medical Library Center of New York in the future."

That sounds pretty drastic. Was it?

"Yes," Weinstein answers with a decisiveness that explains why she can be so enthusiastic and so passionate about this work. "Every entrepreneurial librarian/manager has a vision about what should be done. Or they should have. And if that person doesn't have a vision, he or she is in the wrong profession."

It's a theme that obviously interests her. "I've always been a 'vision' kind of person. It's something that I think about a lot, and it comes easily to me. I'm not always so good at the details of a situation, the nitty-gritty, but I can see the way I want something to be and I can figure out how to work toward it. And that's what happened at MLCNY. I could see what it should look like, this database, and I could see who would be using it in the next century. The people looking for this information will be document delivery providers for institutions, librarians, information managers, managers in health care organizations, health system executives, a wide range of end users. And we can provide them with what they need, but to do so we have to change our way of doing things."   Weinstein's vision is pretty impressive, for as she worked with her trustees, with MLCNY's staff (especially Robert Dempsey, Automation Services Head: "The vision would not be realized without him," Weinstein says), with various advisors from the member institutions of MLCNY, and with others, it became apparent that they were all in agreement that this was a direction that MLCNY had to go in. Yet part of entrepreneurial librarianship is handling the risk, and taking risks—even a calculated risk—is often the challenge that many information professionals balk at. It wasn't even a question for Weinstein.

"What risk?" she says with a laugh, but you know she's dead serious. "I didn't think I was taking a risk. To me the risk would have been to do nothing. We would have been out of business."

But weren't there times when it seemed she was taking a risk? Weren't there times when it got scary?

"Of course," she says. "When I realized that I would have to hand the vision over to someone else, and he or she would be required to bring it to fruition, that's when the risk came into the situation. I had to accept that I would have to work with someone else who would actually plug in the parts I was unable to do. I had to trust them to do something I couldn't do, and that became a little worrisome. For example, there was the time I was required to make a decision about which of several alternatives to choose. It was a half-million dollar decision, and I certainly didn't want to make the wrong decision. It's times like that when you're out on the high wire, and it's a long way down!"

The safety nets are there, though (if we can carry this analogy a little further), because in fact Weinstein had not only the strong support of the MLCNY's Board of Trustees, as well as advisory support from interested staff at several of the member institutions ("our 'sounding-board' of experts," she calls them), she also had a consultant who was reliable and committed to the project. The consultant's relationship with Weinstein and her staff was and continues to be totally and mutually supportive, and she gives him high marks for his skill and his overall ability to put together such a massive project. In effect, it was the consultant Weinstein was able to turn to for bringing this vision to fruition, and she and her team are very grateful. There have been no regrets.

Equally strong were the MLCNY staff, and it's a group of people Weinstein can't praise enough. There are eighteen of them, and Weinstein positively beams when she talks about the role they have played in the project.

"They're unquestionably the most phenomenal, hard-working group of people I've ever known," she says, and you know she is absolutely sincere, because these people are working with her to make her—and their—vision of what MLCNY can be happen. "I had no idea I would be so lucky. They have been wonderful to work with, and I'm grateful to them for their efforts."

So there are a lot of points coming together in this remarkable project they're working on at the Medical Library Center of New York. When you put it all together, connecting Weinstein's entrepreneurial librarianship with its innovation, its risk-taking, its vision, there's no surprise in finding enthusiasm and passion as key elements in the picture. In fact, for many of us in information services, if becoming passionate about our work can help us to achieve those things we are expected to achieve, perhaps it's time for a little re-thinking about how we look at our work. Of course we can get by just going into the office every day. But is that all we want? Don't we want to do more than that? If we want to be really successful, we need to get excited about going to work each day, and then we can leverage those parts of the job we're passionate about.

Meet Lois Weinstein

Lois Weinstein is the Director of the Medical Library Center of New York, with management responsibility for day-to-day operations, budgeting, strategic planning, MLCNY's research and development efforts, marketing, and fund-raising for the support of special projects. Prior to coming to MLCNY in 1990, Weinstein's previous professional experience had been in a variety of information settings, including the American Museum of Natural History in New York, the University of Miami Rosenstiel School of Marine Science in Miami, Florida, and the Maritime College of the State University of New York at Fort Schuyler, New York. Her primary experience, however, was in the corporate world where she worked with Lederle Laboratories in Pearl River, NY, and, from 1977 to 1988, with General Foods Corporation in White Plains, NY. At General Foods, she successively worked as Supervisor of Technical Services, Manager of Technical Information Services, and Technical Information Consultant, this last a special assignment to identify and capitalize on opportunities to use automation to reduce the time it takes for a product to go from development to production. An active member of the professional community, Weinstein has been a chapter president and frequent committee member in the Special Libraries Association, and she is well known for her work with the Medical Library Association. An author for professional publications, Lois Weinstein is also a popular instructor in continuing education and professional development programs for a variety of organizations. She lives in Larchmont, NY, and—aside from enjoying the cultural riches of living and working in the New York City region—Weinstein looks forward each year to the warm weather, in order to better indulge her week-end beach habit.

Teacher / Librarian / Copyright & Intellectual Property Expert:
LOLLY GASAWAY
continues to tackle new challenges

When you ask people about Laura Gasaway, the popular Director of the Law Library at the University of North Carolina, the responses all have a theme: "She's really excited about her work," you hear. Or, "This is a lady who really enjoys what she does." And the best one: "Lolly has so much fun—maybe we should all go into law librarianship!"

Perhaps. But unless we can all bring Gasaway's enthusiasm and excitement to the job, we might hold off on that mid-career change. Much of her success is, of course, connected to the fact that she is very good at what she does, and to the fact that law librarianship—at this particular point in time—is a very stimulating and attractive discipline to be working in, but all law librarians do not have Gasaway's enthusiasm, and it would be a mistake to assume that they do.

Lolly Gasaway is unique, and what makes her unique is that her personality (which is where the excitement and the enthusiasm come from, of course) enables her to look at her work from a point of view that makes law librarianship exciting. For most of its history, law librarianship would not have been characterized as "exciting," and certainly law librarians would not have been characterized as "enthusiastic." That's changing now, and Lolly Gasaway must take credit for much of the change.

First of all, there's that cheerful nickname. Nobody called "Lolly" is going to be a sourpuss, and Gasaway's cheerfulness matches the name. She is fun to be with.

But there's more. For example, this is a person for whom a career choice was not a major life crisis. "Indeed not," Gasaway laughs. "I think I'm the only person I know who is doing exactly what I set out to do. I

Originally published in *InfoManage : The International Management Newsletter for the Information Services Professional* 3 (4), March, 1996.

always wanted to be a librarian, and I decided in my freshman year of college that I wanted to be a law librarian."

So what people say about her is true. She really likes what she does.

"Absolutely," she says. "And right now, law librarianship and training in legal information studies and management—as a subject to be working in—is full of opportunities for innovation, for bringing new techniques and new methodologies into the picture. There are major changes taking place in the field, and it's a good time to be involved."

As a librarian and teacher, Gasaway is in the enviable position of being able to study legal information issues from the practitioner's point of view (she not only teaches future lawyers, she has a law degree herself) as well as from the perspective of the information provider. It makes her very aware of what the changes are.

"For one thing," she says, "legal bibliography was formerly taught as a sort of 'package,' a body of literature that was offered to the students 'as is,' so to speak. Now there's a refocusing to teach about the different kinds of legal information. The change has come about, I suppose, because teaching methods have changed, and not just what is taught. In the past, faculty thought in terms of concepts, theories, and the like. But even concepts change, so now efforts are being made to begin students on a knowledge quest."

As a member of the law faculty herself, and as a spirited observer of the societal changes that have been taking place in our culture, Gasaway can see where the new methodology is coming from.

"It's a whole new way of teaching," she says, "and much of it has to do with changes in the educational structure itself. Law schools have been—and many continue to be—very hierarchical, but the same new technology that enables lawyers (and law students) to acquire information differently than in the past is enabling these people to look at information much differently. For example, with the new technology, the law faculty are becoming more like 'coaches,' and less like esteemed jurists pontificating from the podium.

"Of course, there is some loss," Gasaway says, and then adds with a grin, "Well, from some points of view, it might be seen as a loss, for the formerly entrenched 'respect' factor so characteristic of law school—the whole 'Paper Chase' idea, and so forth—is pretty much slipping away. Now students question the teacher, and we don't have that iron-clad, 'total-acceptance-or-else' point of view. But I think it's a better situation, because the teacher now has the opportunity to ask if the student is questioning the law, the concept, or the answer to the teacher's question. It makes for a better educational process, in my opinion."

There are other changes as well, and these, too, appeal to Gasaway. It's an attitude that comes through as she describes some of them.

"In training for law librarianship, for example, legal research and legal writing were always taught, but the point of view is slightly different today. Now we are teaching information management, which means there can be changes in the way librarians in law libraries can be used. For example, we're all agreed—well, most of us anyway—that the need for technical services librarians is decreasing. Quite frankly, despite what some of the more hysterical library leaders would have us believe, the age of the technical services librarian is over. We simply don't need to train people to be technical librarians. Of course there is a role for the people who have been doing this work, the technical services librarians, in organizing information, but fewer people will be needed to do that. If they are not working as technical librarians, who then—in a law library, for example—is better qualified to teach law students information and how to manage information? These people have solid job security, if they are willing to take what they are good at and 'transfer' it to a new discipline."

So in the legal field, librarians are not about to be replaced?

The look of surprise tells you the answer is self-evident.

"Of course not," Gasaway says. "Librarians will always be needed, and as a profession librarianship will always have a place in the legal structure. Just look at it from a business point of view, from the perspective of managing a law practice as a business. All lawyers can't be experts in everything, and it is simply not cost effective to have lawyers do all of that research. Of course there's a certain fascination with end-user searching but as the lawyers become more experienced and their billable rates go up, it just is not practical to have them doing all of their searching. So in that one area alone—literature searching—lawyers will always need librarians.

"But there's more to it than just searching," Gasaway continues. "For one thing, the subjects will change. While the lawyers might be able to find the specific legal materials, there is so much related to the different cases that librarians will be needed to find these other materials, things

What Are the Issues for Information Managers?

*I*n today's information environment, many important issues compete for the attention of information services managers. Laura Gasaway identifies four that bear reflection:

1. We should be very concerned that fair use does not disappear in an electronic environment. Just because the technology allows you to count and track each and every use of a piece of intellectual property doesn't mean you should. The present trend in thinking about intellectual property, particularly in the United States, has serious implications for information services managers, for it could lead to closing down access to information without payment for every single use. This would change the whole image of public and free information.

2. We have to try to keep up with what's going on, particularly with respect to the laws having to do with electronic information. The pace of development is so fast, and of course it's almost impossible to keep up, but managers have a responsibility to their customers (and to their staffs) to know what's going on in these areas.

3. We must keep pushing those partnerships with IT staff, MIS managers, and others in our organizations who are involved in information delivery issues. Maybe this should be taken even beyond the firms or organizations where we work, moving the partnering out to include vendors, suppliers, and others who are equal information stakeholders in the process. There needs to be a much more collaborative "tone" to the work we do, and it's the information services managers who can set that tone.

4. We must give thought to how we bring along the, shall we say, "technologically challenged," the people who are uncomfortable with technology. As long as we have to do things two ways, that is, offer information in a paper-based format as well as in an electronic format, there are always going to be those who will delay learning how to use the technology. Here's one solution: in your organization, continue to offer any documentation or other information that comes from your office in two formats, but send out the paper-based version a day after the electronic version has been distributed. Once people realize that other people are acquiring information earlier because it is electronic, they'll want to get theirs first, too.

like materials in environmental law, say, or medicine, or science. These subject-specific searches will require a different kind of expertise that the lawyers don't have. But the librarians do.

"And all information will not be electronic. There is something about paper-based materials and finding them that—for lawyers— is important.

"Finally, though, there's the changing publishing structure. Much primary information is now being made available to the public without going through a publisher. Things like U.S. Supreme Court decisions, those of many federal circuit courts of appeal, state courts, and so forth are being mounted electronically and are available for free via the Internet, and librarians are going to be needed to find these materials for lawyers. Or to show lawyers how to access them efficiently."

But aren't the lawyers becoming more information literate?

"Yes," Gasaway says, "and as a teacher I'm very familiar with what the law students know about information and the use of information technology. Our recent survey of first year students showed that over 70% have their own computers. And some private law schools require them to have their own computers, but of course this can't be a requirement in some state-supported schools, at least not yet. But it will probably come. In any case, the students are more information literate, but that doesn't mean that they know all the various subjects, or the different levels of the different subjects. They're going to need librarians and information services practitioners to guide them through the maze of information that is available. We spend a lot of effort at the law library teaching E-mail and Internet usage to these students, but that doesn't mean they are going to know it all. Or use it when they go into practice.

"So I'm not worried about the future of information services, or the role of the information professional," Gasaway says. "It's not a problem, and the information profession is not becoming irrelevant. These people, the people who work in information services, will still be getting their training in graduate library/information services programs. Why? Because to succeed in the next century, organizations are going to need to have people who can look at the big picture, and that's what trained librarians do. While they are honored for their ability to deal with detail and understand the specifics of a situation, they also have an ability to think about information and information services from a 'big picture' perspective (well, many of them—those that don't will simply be left out). It's that understanding of the big picture that will keep them working."

In a conversation with Lolly Gasaway, one finds the subject returning again and again to teaching. It's obviously a great love of hers, but it isn't unusual for the directors of law libraries to teach. While many directors teach substantive law (e.g., not research), Gasaway goes a little farther afield, teaching subjects that combine intellectual stimulation with what we like to think of as the "real" world, things like intellectual property and gender-based legal issues, both of which she has taught successfully. She recently submitted a proposal for a new course on cyberspace law, and it's a course she's very excited about.

In fact, talking about cyberspace law, intellectual property, and similar issues provides a neat segue into the subject that Gasaway is most famous for. Although she is probably too modest to admit it, her name has become something of a by-word in the specialized libraries community, for she has long taken a strong position as an advocate for both copyright compliance and exercising fair use rights. As an active player in the "copyright wars," Gasaway has worked with the Special Libraries Association (where she long chaired that organization's Copyright Compliance Committee) and with the American Association of Law Libraries, which she served as President in 1986-87. With the American Association of Universities, Gasaway serves as the AAU representative in the current conferences on fair use, a singularly impressive assignment, for not many people have the expertise and the skill to handle such a difficult and—yes, volatile—role.

As the co-author (with Sarah K. Wiant, another Past-Chair of SLA's Copyright Compliance Committee) of *Libraries and Copyright: A Guide to Copyright Laws* in the 1990s (Washington, DC: SLA, 1994), Gasaway has become the information services field's "resident authority" in intellectual property matters, and while she enjoys the work associated with this subject, it does get a little overwhelming sometimes. Between teaching seminars for various associations, reacting to the (very pleasant, of course) success of the book, dealing with sudden fame as a result of a much-read article in *Library Journal*, and fielding all those telephone calls from librarians who want advice on this or that specific copyright problem, Gasaway finds that she has some difficulty getting "back" to being "just" a library director and law school teacher.

But it's worth the trouble, for Gasaway enjoys the intellectual give-and-take of the debate. Even in her own intellectual issues class, her goal is to raise the consciousness of the students with respect to these subjects, so she divides them up into three groups for debate and just lets them go at one another on issues such as the Texaco litigation. It's a challenging—and enlightening—exercise for them, and they all come out of the class exclaiming about how much more informed they are then when they went in. So she's succeeding in this effort, and she wants to continue in this vein.

"There's a long-standing tension in our society about intellectual property issues," she says, "and we have a responsibility to see that the citizenry understands these issues. And this tension isn't a bad thing. It's built right into the US Constitution, the rights of the copyright holder vs. the rights of the user. There is a long history of attempting to balance these rights, but part of learning to balance is to be informed, and that's what we do, as librarians, as teachers, as citizens."

Certainly Lolly Gasaway is doing her part. And her work has given her a particular expertise about these issues, an expertise that she's not shy about sharing with other information services managers. In fact, there are certain issues that all information services managers need to be thinking about—regardless of the environment in which they work —and Gasaway is quick to share her thoughts about these important matters.

In her current work, these interests continue. One project is contributing to a history of law librarianship. A recent president of AALL was concerned that there wasn't enough history about the profession, so Gasaway and Mike Chiorazzi, the Associate Director at Boston College, are editing the book, to be published by Rothman. Gasaway's section is on women as academic library directors, and it has already become a fascinating journey of exploration and discovery for her, simply because it is giving her the opportunity to learn about who some of the important women in law librarianship have been, and what their contributions were.

At the same time, Gasaway is involved in putting together a collection of articles on copyright issues that may appear as a triple issue of a library management journal, or as a monograph. It promises to become the definitive work on the subject. Under Lolly Gasaway's editorial leadership, it will have a mighty impact, indeed.

So it's a fine time Gasaway is having with her career, and it's turned out just as that college freshman meant for it to be. She likes what she's doing and she's making a serious contribution, both to information services management and to legal education. It kind of makes you wonder: Is there anything else she wants to be doing? Does she anticipate any changes in her career?

"Not really," Gasaway replies, and it's clear she has given this a lot of thought. "Although I do have to admit that I love to write. I love the process of writing, and I would enjoy doing more, perhaps even venturing into creative writing one day. And teaching is a great passion of mine, so I could see myself getting more heavily into teaching, perhaps after I retire from being a library director."

Until that time comes, the field of legal information and our society's current concerns with intellectual property issues are in good hands. With people like Lolly Gasaway leading the way, the horizon looks very promising indeed.

Meet Lolly Gasaway

Prior to coming to UNC, Laura Gasaway held a similar position at the University of Oklahoma, before which she had been Assistant Professor of Law and Associate Professor at the University of Houston. Well known as a educator, Gasaway regularly teaches courses in gender-based discrimination and intellectual property, and her teaching experience includes a stint as the director of the University of Oklahoma's College of Law Summer Program at Queen's College, Oxford, England. Much of her writing reflects the subjects she teaches, and in addition to the guide to copyright law she wrote with Sarah Wiant, among Gasaway's many published works which have brought her much recognition are "Scholarly Publication and Copyright in Networked Electronic Publishing," in *Library Trends* (43, 1995). Another important work, about to be published in a new book, is a chapter on "Universities, Libraries, and Fair Use in the Digital Age." In her personal life, Gasaway is interested in foreign travel. At home, which is in South Durham County, just 15 minutes from the University in Chapel Hill, she pursues other interests, including writing (both professionally and avocationally), reading mysteries by women authors, needlework, and spending time with Tulip Lee, her West Highland Terrier.

At America's new state-of-the-art specialist library, an optimistic
JOHN GANLY
says it's the content that provides a role for librarians

Wow! If there's any site that literally defines information delivery as it will be practiced in the 21st century, it's the new Science, Industry, and Business Library of The New York Public Library. As one of the components of The New York Public Library Research Libraries (as distinguished from the Branch Libraries, the administrative entity that supports the type of library service generally associated with public libraries in America), SIBL has come to represent—in the seven months it's been open for business—the epitome of the specialized library. If a "special library" is defined as a library which has "special" collections and services, SIBL not only qualifies in spades, it leads the pack. There are even people who refer to NYPL's Science, Industry, and Business Library as "the state-of-the-art specialist library for the new millennium."

"That might be going a little far," says John Ganly, SIBL's Assistant Director, "but there's no question that the information delivery structure we've put together represents a new paradigm in information services delivery."

For one thing, it becomes evident the minute one enters the building that the space is spectacular. Built into one of New York's most beloved buildings, SIBL from the outside is one of the several architectural treasures found in midtown Manhattan. Located at Thirty-Fourth Street, the library occupies the Madison Avenue side of the famous building erected in 1906 to house B. Altman & Company, one of the city's most cherished department stores (and closed, alas, in 1989). Designed by Trowbridge & Livingston, the dignified eight-story Renaissance Revival building is visually one of New York's most elegant buildings, and the decision to move NYPL's new specialist operation into the splendid space was an audacious

Originally published in *InfoManage : The International Management Newsletter for the Information Services Professional* 4 (1), December, 1996.

attempt to bridge the community's (and the library's) past with the information services demands of the future. It succeeded beautifully, and John Ganly is delighted to be part of this new challenge.

"What we're doing here," he says, "is actually the pursuit of an ideal. We have a concept of what SIBL is to be: we expect our organization to provide a seamless user interface for the people in our community—business people as well as lay people—to obtain the information they need. Now we have to recognize that what we're talking about here is, of course, a conceptual ideal. The reality is that you still need to have people in subdivisions (in patents, for example, and in various subject specialties), and in working with different people, the users are going to experience an information delivery that is not always necessarily 'seamless.' But we know what our conceptual ideal is, and we do what we can to move to that."

How the move toward that "seamless user interface" progresses is being watched attentively by information services managers throughout the world, for if anyone can make it happen, the people at SIBL can. And other information managers want to learn from them how it's done.

"One of the first things we learned," Ganly says, "is that a culture that supports change, that recognizes the value of change, doesn't happen overnight. And in fact, for some people it doesn't happen at all. But we had to do what we could to make it happen, to create a culture in which change and change management were not seen as something to be feared, but as something to be embraced, as something that would enable us to succeed in achieving our public service goals at SIBL."

Although the idea of developing the largest public information center in the world devoted solely to science and business had been in place since the late 1980s, the actual transition to SIBL took about three years, starting in 1993. And it was the move toward a changed culture that required a major expenditure of effort, for everyone associated with SIBL was determined that service—from the information customers' point of view—was going to be different at SIBL than in any other library or information services establishment.

Just how different has been described in these pages before, when William Walker, now Director of The NYPL Research Libraries, was interviewed in *InfoManage* (June, 1994). At that time, readers got an early taste of the excitement connected with the project—and the challenges

The Management Point of View

*O*n the June, 1994, issue of *InfoManage*, William D. Walker—as NYPL's Associate Director for SIBL—was the subject of that issue's "Information Interview." At the time, Walker was in the midst of putting together what is now commonly acknowledged to be one of the most important projects in library history. His comments then, about the value of customer service and the projected emphasis on staff development at the planned-for facility, were noticeably prophetic. For this special Third Anniversary Issue of *InfoManage*, Bill Walker, now Senior Vice President and Andrew W. Mellon Director of The New York Public Library Research Libraries, was asked to comment. "Over the past five years," Walker said, "as Library staff envisioned the new facility for The New York Public Library's $100 million Science, Industry, and Business Library (SIBL), everyone hoped that we would please users with the physical design, the re-engineered services and education programs, and state-of-the-art technology resources. Seven months after opening, both the Library staff and our users appear to be delighted with the result. The intensive staff planning effort has produced a mind-blowingly accurate product—few changes to program and layout have been made since the May, 1996, opening. It just keeps getting better and better, with the staff adding richer programs and content each week. What makes me most proud? The staff's leadership in developing and delivering a robust user-technology training program from scratch. These hands-on classes are always oversubscribed, and attendees give the instructors and the content A+ grades. SIBL has provided a prototype of resources and services for the other centers of The New York Public Library. The total Library community is very proud of the project."

that were built into its realization. Among the challenges was what Ganly refers to as a "merging" of staff cultures, for there were, in fact, three groups of people coming to work at SIBL. First there were the new employees, the people who had never worked at any of the administrative units of The New York Public Library and thus were new to the system as well as to SIBL. Then there were the employees, many long-term, who were transferred from The NYPL Research Libraries and who had been part of the established culture in such departments as the "old" library's Economic and Public Affairs Division, which Ganly himself had headed since 1985. And finally there were those employees who had transferred into SIBL from The NYPL Branch Libraries. Each of these groups had to be assimilated into the new SIBL management framework, and, at the same time, motivated to participate in and be part of the new SIBL culture.

"What we were interested in doing," Ganly says, " and I think we've succeeded, was to build a new culture, one in which the emphasis would be on customer service and on the subject specialties that are our focus at SIBL. To build a new culture, of course, meant rejecting—or at least putting aside—some of the characteristics of the former cultures that many of us came from, and to do that, we had to engage in some pretty serious retraining."

From the beginning, it wasn't simply an internal job, for Walker and Ganly and the others involved in the transition recognized early on that "outside input," as Ganly puts it, would be needed "to help existing staff adjust to changes." So SIBL's managers, long before they were anywhere near ready to move into the new facility, began to offer training courses in customer service and other programs to compliment the full line of services that SIBL would be offering to its customers.

And the key, as far as the customer service training was concerned, had to do with getting the staff together, getting them to work together as a single unit.

"It's critical," Ganly says. "When you are trying to create a service culture, a service perspective that will result in the highest levels of service for the users, you've got to get the staff sitting together, working as a team. It makes them more comfortable with each other, and if they're involved in creating service excellence, they will be the people who will promulgate and encourage excellence in its implementation.

"And it can't be postponed until some fantasy time, 'when we can get around to it,'" Ganly continues. "More than two thousand people use SIBL each day, and we serve the information needs of these information customers with a staff of about one hundred people, a ratio that takes some high-level teamwork to make it work. So when I say that we have this goal of providing an ideal level of services, part of the equation has to recognize that these ideal services will be provided in a highly pressured environment.

"So you can see why fostering a specific and appropriate culture is critical." So is there a place for librarians at SIBL? Librarians are the information workers who understand content, who understand the subjects. If SIBL is a state-of-the-art information center, aren't the people who come to work there specialists in information technology?

"No." Ganly responds so quickly that you realize he has heard this all before, and that this is not the first time he has answered the question. "You must understand that all this talk about the conflict between content and information technology is simply not a realistic way to look at what is going on in information services. The information environment today is one that I like to think of as a 'confluence of information industry and economics,' and as such, it means that the information customers get many different—and frequently conflicting—messages about how they can obtain the information they need.

"As it happens, end-users come in all shapes and sizes, and with much variety in experience, training, and even in their intellectual grasp of the information-gathering process. And it's these things, combined with the needs of the end-users, that determine the level of the services we provide, whether it is basic, intermediate, high-end, and so forth. But what we have to do, as librarians and information delivery practitioners, is determine from those end-users what their needs are and the level of services that they require, and then provide it. So it's always a balancing act, and always unique with each customer."

In John Ganly's opinion, there really isn't a conflict between information technology and content, but there is confusion.

"We ourselves," he says, "we librarians, have to be careful. We must understand both—information technology and intellectual content—but we must be careful because there is so much hype surrounding access mechanisms. It becomes very tempting to move off into the information technology realm and forget that it's in understanding, organizing, and advising about content that librarians have their real strength."

And as far as Ganly is concerned, it is not a real issue, this conflict between information technology and content, simply because we've all been there before.

"All this is not new to librarians and other information services practitioners," he says. "There has always been attention given to the access mechanisms, and to the number of them. And, as always happens, the wide range of access mechanisms will eventually narrow down, and then the role of the information professional will be recognized for the value it brings to the information transaction. Users will learn that they need to narrow the choices to get the answers they need, and will come back to the information professional to help narrow the choices."

. . . and the Management Perspective
from SIBL's New Director

*F*or many information services managers, NYPL's new Science, Industry, and Business Library represents an almost ideal paradigm for 21st-century information delivery. *InfoManage* asked Director Kristin McDonough to share some of her thoughts about SIBL.

"My first three months as director of NYPL's newest research center, the Science, Industry, and Business Library, have confirmed my expectation that it would be an exciting enterprise to manage. Lured to SIBL's world-class collection from an enormously satisfying twenty-five year career with the City University of New York—most recently as director of CUNY's brand new, high-tech library at Baruch College—I learned that although I'd left academe, I'd joined a dynamic educational institution.

"A critical part of SIBL's mission is to go beyond the serving up and doling out of discrete infobits, to equip library users with the apparatus, attitude, and expertise to navigate in today's complex information environment. Through various delivery modes—one-on-one consultations, hot links to websites via SIBL's homepage, an interactive kiosk, and a unique program of free public courses—SIBL's users are educated to become more independent information seekers, fed for a lifetime rather than for today.

"SIBL librarians also operate in a constant learning mode. With a generous grant from the Kellogg Foundation, SIBL's staff has, over the past three years, been trained in three key areas: technological innovation, organizational dynamics, and customer service, to graft on to their traditional role as organizers and interpreters of NYPL's incomparable collections the 21st-century role of global resource guide. As a new director, I'm privileged to have been thrust into an environment where re-tooled librarians have harnessed information technology to maximize efficiency, enhance service delivery, and encourage teamwork.

"For example, public service schedules are produced and stored electronically for instantaneous access; new policies and procedures are communicated immediately, too. Use of internal E-mail bulletin boards to explore various approaches to tough reference questions means that all staff—and our users—benefit from the right answer. Access to shared workfiles on the network facilitates collective input into documents, making the final product a group effort. And metering software, just now installed on the network, is generating usage data that is invaluable for enhancing customer satisfaction. In this period of rapid change, when members of some organizations view IT with frustration and distrust, the more enlightened staff at SIBL have exploited technology as a tool to deliver information services more effectively."

What's made the difference? Why is it that suddenly we have people who would have originally turned to a librarian to guide them to the information they needed, and now they are not, with the result that the librarians are worried about whether they are going to have a profession in the future?

"It's been the Web," Ganly says. "And it's all happened in the last two years. The World Wide Web was developed by CERN in Switzerland, and this easily manageable sub-network is today the fastest growing part of the Internet. But because it is easily manageable and growing so fast, it is also amazingly tempting to people who don't know better. They think they can—what's the phrase?—'find anything on the 'Net.' And of course they can, if they can find someone who can guide them through the morass of disorganized and, frankly, just plain bad information that gets transmitted back and forth on the Internet. And that's where librarians and other information services professionals come to the rescue. We know the content. We know what's good and what's not, and we can show the end-users how to get what they need. But for a while there will be some confusion, until the 'do-it-yourself' folks learn that it's to their advantage—both financially and intellectually—to consult with a librarian or other information services professional before they go off looking for what they need."

So it's the end-users who are really driving this move toward a new information millennium, and it's the end-users that the librarians and other information practitioners have to focus on?

"Absolutely," Ganly says. "In fact, there might be room for a little reinterpretation here. For a couple of decades now, special libraries have been characterized as those libraries where people go, as one writer put it, 'for the information, not to be shown how to find the information.' That may still be true in some organizations, and certainly it's true at certain levels of some organizations, but for most people seeking information today, that concept now has to be updated. Today's special librarian is very often giving the customer the information he needs to enable him to get the information, and that's something different. The role of the information provider is changing, and how it changes—and how the work we do changes—is going to depend on what the end-users need. Identifying that need—and meeting it—is what we expect to do at SIBL."

Meet John Ganly

John Ganly is Assistant Director for Science, Industry, and Business Library Collections, The New York Public Library Research Libraries, and Coadjutant Professor at Rutgers University. His undergraduate degree, in business administration, is from Baruch College. He also has earned an M.A. in political science from the New School for Social Research and an M.S.L.S. from Pratt Institute. Prior to moving to SIBL, Ganly had been Chief of the Economic and Public Affairs Division of NYPL since 1985. He is the author of numerous publications in the field of information services management, particularly in subjects having to do with business, demographics, and international business and management. His most recent publication is *Data Sources for Business and Market Analysis*, published by Scarecrow Press in 1993. Ganly has been a Board Member of the Public Affairs Information Service since 1984, and he becomes Chair of PAIS in 1997. He was awarded the Special Libraries Association DISCLOSURE Technology Award in 1992, and in 1993 he was given the SLA President's Award for his leadership in designing and implementing the information center for the Democratic National Convention in New York City in 1992. Ganly makes his home in New York City, and his personal interests include travel and going to the theater.

ALLAN FOSTER
At Keele University information convergence is the key concept for managing information

Forget your ideas about traditional library management in the academic community. Information convergence (as the British refer to what the Americans call "integrated information services") has come to Great Britain, and nowhere is the concept being more skillfully applied than at Keele University. Allan Foster is the University's Director of Information Studies (and University Librarian) and it is his responsibility to provide the university with the leadership, strategic direction, and management for computing, telecommunications, library, and media services that will,

Originally published in *InfoManage : The International Management Newsletter for the Information Services Professional* 4 (6), May, 1997.

as he puts it, "integrate these services into a coherent whole and build on the synergies generated by the process."

What a challenge!

And what a man to meet it!

The University of Keele is small, only 6,000 students (FTE, or about 9,000 people all told), and from day one, the university's pedagogical goal has been to integrate science and the arts (or, in the words describing the idea in the university's website: the university was founded "to promote interdisciplinary and multi-disciplinary scholarship . . . emphasizing the strength of a broad educational program.").

Lord Lindsey, the university's founder and a leader in the building of the "red brick universities" of the 1950s and 1960s, took seriously C.P. Snow's "two cultures," and the university as it exists today reflects that tradition. Students are consciously encouraged to integrate the study of science with humanities studies, and vice versa, and they are permitted to postpone making choices about which direction they want to go until they are ready to make those decisions. When the university was founded in 1949 (the first post-World War II university in the United Kingdom), this duality of emphasis was an idea ahead of its time, but it has been continued, and it continues today. As a result, the university produces graduates who are quite skillfully prepared for the integrated tasks (and values, some might say) required for success in the external, non-academic world.

So the integration of information services, in a culture built on the integration—the convergence—of ideas, subject areas, and philosophies, is not such a far reach after all.

"Of course not," Foster says. He goes on to point out that while the integration of information services is not moving forward in some countries and some societies, in the academic community in the U.K., it's pretty much a foregone conclusion that the merging of information services and the convergence of information-related functions is going to be the way information management is dealt with in the future.

It's a natural phenomenon, this convergence of information services, and it's interesting to see how it is being applied in different environments. In America, for example, the integration of information—particularly in the private sector—usually means combining some version of specialized librarianship, records management, archives management, and computer services into a unified, "holistic" (in Foster's terms) information services function. At some universities, the university's records management, archives, and library functions are operated under the auspices of the same information services management unit (in Atlanta, for example, at the Georgia Tech Library and Information Center). In other organizations, such as the American Museum of Natural History in New York, it is not uncommon for organizational archives to be included in the "special collections" of the organizational library, stretching that term to cover much more than the traditional rare books that were typically the artifacts handled by a Special Collections Department.

So convergence in its many forms is now a driving —and an accepted—operational framework in organizational management, and what Allan Foster and his team at the University of Keele are doing is not so unusual after all. Or it wouldn't be, except that at Keele, Foster has been able to put together an Information Services Department that successfully and—with considerable support from both the user community and senior management—quite naturally links library services, computing, media services, and communications (including telecommunications) services. At Keele, the structure doesn't include records management and university archives, but considering the enthusiasm that Foster and his management team demonstrate about their success with the convergence idea, and considering the impetus throughout higher education to move in this direction, no one will be surprised if those functions in some of the academic institutions are eventually incorporated into information services.

"It all goes back to how you define 'information,'" Foster says, "and to what the organization is interested in supporting. And it also has to do with the management interest, and the positioning of information management in the organizational chain of command."

That much is obvious at Keele, where Keele Information Services is part of a five-part Directorate (the others being Finance, Human Resources, Academic Affairs, and the University Secretariat) reporting directly to the Vice-Chancellor, the university's principle executive officer. The senior officers in these five management units, together with the deans of the university's four faculties (Humanities, Social Sciences, Natural Sciences, and Health and Medicine) work with the Vice-Chancellor in establishing policy for the university, and it will come as no surprise that positioning Information Services at such a high management level not only enables Foster and his team to move the university forward into a converged information structure, but also establishes the relative value of information management and information transfer in the institutional environment.

"It doesn't always work," Foster says, "and it is sometimes hard to get legitimacy, but we keep striving. For example, information skills are taught to students in the Social Sciences, and despite the fact that some people feel information skills are irrelevant to academic work, we've made it compulsory and the students do it. And find they're glad they did."

Foster left Manchester University in 1994 to take up the challenge at Keele, and while his generally modest nature leads him to describe what he's doing as something of a work-in-progress, it is clear during even the most casual visit that his influence has been felt, and that his success in coordinating the various "pieces" of information services management has been impressive.

"It's not just happening here," Foster protests, and he continues with just a certain level of pride as he speaks with his American visitor. "Already fifty percent of the institutions of higher education in England are actively reorganizing their information operations around the convergence model, and that ratio is going to increase dramatically in the next few years."

But what is being done at Keele, particularly in the three years since Foster has been the university's Director of University Services, cannot be dismissed lightly.

For one thing, with some 3,500 of those 6,000 FTE students living on campus, it has been necessary to develop an information infrastructure, to provide the residential students with an information architecture that is capable of handling the level of data connectivity that the university environment demands. And this is when Foster describes his holistic view, for it is his opinion that there has to be an over-arching institutional information policy that prepares students (and faculty) for dealing with what he calls "the real world."

And what he says makes sense, for (as he wrote in his regular column in a recent issue of *Information World Review*) "The new information markets are fundamentally different from those that came before. Information is now more disposable and transient. End-users are far more IT literate . . .Most schools now have good IT infrastructures and pupils tend to get their hands on information products at an early age." And these are the students, Foster contends, who have high expectations, for having been trained on fast networks—"free at the point of use"—throughout their university careers, they go into the workplace expecting the same high levels of information delivery. It's that university-level delivery that is Foster's responsibility, and as Director of Information Services, he must see to it that all of the components of that information-services "umbrella" are connected so that those enthusiastic and well-trained students don't lose their enthusiasm when they move into "the real world."

So by now it is obvious that Keele University is committed to the full integration of library, computing, and media services, and Foster's department, Keele Information Services, was created to be the management unit to handle this work. The first stage of the process was to move all Computer Centre staff and activities into the existing Library building, but in order to achieve the innovative integration of information services, the university was required to undertake a major capital project and to reorder the space in the building, which was renamed the Information Services Building. The reorganization included the development of an IT Suite, comprising two training PC labs with a total of 60 work stations, and an open-access, staffed IT Help Desk. Additionally, an integrated Computer Center and Library staff accommodation was included in the plans, which have gone forward and have now, in the main, been completed. The building also includes, in addition to the Library and the Computer Centre, the university's Media and Communications Centre, components of the Information Services Department.

Watching Foster move across his office to a large chalkboard is something of a heady experience, for he is quite comfortable describing the "matrix" which illustrates how the information services operation is organized, and how Keele Information Services functions. The division includes both the Computing Centre, with its emphasis on information technology (systems, applications, networks, PC management, and, particularly, in Keele's case, telecommunications), and the Library, where the emphasis is on customer services and 'front-of-house' issues: the help desks, training, document delivery, collection development and management, and, in a nod toward the insourcing of information services that is going on in many libraries today, liaison staff for all departments of the university.

"What we're trying to do," Foster says, "is to build a matrix that brings people across boundaries, to break up traditional ways of thinking about information products and information transfer."

And, yes, when asked, Foster can talk about the problems. Of course there are problems. For example, there have been management barriers, just as there are in any operation when innovation, risk-taking, and entrepreneurial management are applied.

"Despite the impression I might have given you earlier about the integration of the 'two cultures'," Foster says, "Keele is a traditional university—at least in the educational context—and especially in its support structure. So the university staff wanted to be told how this convergence of information services would work. They weren't sure that they had the skills and the capacities to make it work. But don't get me wrong. No one was really hostile, and those whose roles changed were usually pretty adaptable, but there have been some problems. Still, we weren't confronted with anything we couldn't handle."

Which probably has something to do with Foster's own management style. His part in this operation is very much that of leader, mentor, and guide, and when asked to characterize what he does, he laughs softly about the conflicts between information management at this level and the traditions inherent in the academic community, conflicts that academic information managers the world over are having to deal with.

"My role is very much an enabling, steering role," Foster says. "I really try to remove myself from the day-to-day work and give as much leeway as I can to the staff, particularly the senior staff. And I give them as much authority as possible,"

One of Foster's most successful new efforts has been getting someone appointed specifically to facilitate information technology studies in the humanities. It's important, he says, to get someone in the department to take ownership, because Information Services can only provide the framework, but with the new appointment, it has happened, and the Humanities Faculty is becoming as information literate—and as information comfortable—as the Natural Sciences, Health and Medicine, and Social Science faculties.

It's not always easy, for like any manager in an academic setting, Foster must spend a considerable amount of his time (25-30%) in work that is not related to information management, things like serving on the university's Budget Subcommittee or the Search Committee for a new University Secretary. These are important assignments, of course, and Foster would not want not to be doing them, but they also have the function of forcing him to concentrate less than he would want to on the work that he feels he was brought to Keele to do.

"All the time," he says, "there is a tension between the central role of Information Services and the overall academic framework, and I see the institution being driven by this."

And how will that tension be relieved?

"We don't know yet," Allan Foster says, and the look on his face makes it clear that this is a challenge he is not only up to meeting, but anxiously (and delightedly) looking forward to seeing through to its successful conclusion.

"We don't yet have a handle on innovation in teaching and learning about information services. It's fundamental to everything we do at Keele, but we are struggling to define a teaching/learning strategy, and the appropriate role of technology as an enabler of the learning process. This is a green field campus university. Students come here to join an intimate academic community, working and living in close proximity to internationally ranked faculty. On the whole they don't come here to substitute this human contact with working through computer-based materials on a PC. We have to work out a way of using the technology in a suitable, supportive fashion. This seems simple but it isn't. Faculty members are split on how much conventional teaching computer-based methods can and should replace.

"Until we have defined the direction of teaching and learning methods, then we can't really have an information strategy to support it. I suppose it has something to do with fitting IT into the 'traditional' academic mode, but it's more than that, too. So we'll keep working away at it, and we'll get there."

Of course they will. What is happening at Keele University and at Keele Information Services under Allan Foster's leadership is a remarkable transition into the future of information delivery. And the beauty of this particular iteration of information convergence is that it connects to the history (and tradition! we mustn't forget tradition!) of academic librarianship, to the role of information transfer in the pursuit of academic research, to the learning that is pursued by the students, and to the place of the university in the wider intellectual community. It's a splendid opportunity for today's information services managers, and Allan Foster (although he would probably be too modest to admit it) is a valuable guide and, yes, inspiration for the rest of us who are confronted with similar challenges. He's leading the way, and many, many other information services managers are going to be happy to follow what he's doing.

Meet Allan Foster

Allan Foster is Director of Information Services & University Librarian at Keele University in Staffordshire, UK. He has served as a member of the Vice-Chancellor's Committee, the university's management team, since 1994, and other committee appointments at Keele include the Keele MBA Review Group, and a recent appointment as Secretary to the University's Appointment Committee and Search Committee for University Secretary and Registrar. Prior to coming to Keele, Foster was Librarian and Information Services Manager at Manchester Business School (University of Manchester). He was named an Associate of the Library Association in 1972, and in 1993 he was elected a Fellow of the Institute of Information Scientists, nominated for his "contribution to the field of business information and electronic information services". Foster writes prolifically, and his many presentations, papers, articles, and columns (including a featured column in *Information World Review*) make him one of the most quoted information managers in Western Europe. His personal interests include sport (playing and watching), cinema, and walking in the "beautiful Lakeland hills." With his wife and their three children, Foster makes his home in Lytham St. Annes, in Lancashire.

TOM PELLIZZI
at InfoSpace Consultants in New York:
Showing information managers how to optimize space

Tom Pellizzi likes librarians. That much becomes clear when you first meet him.

"Long before I had decided on a career for myself," Pellizzi says, "I had worked in the art library at my college, and I knew then that I liked the whole idea of libraries and information transfer. I like what goes on in libraries. I'm just lucky to have a company that specializes in working with librarians. I like them and they like me. It seems to be a very workable relationship, this connection between what my company provides and what librarians need."

And if customer satisfaction is any indication, it is indeed a very workable relationship. Pellizzi founded InfoSpace Consultants eleven years ago, and in those eleven years, he has built a reputation that positions InfoSpace Consultants as a clear leader in the space planning and design industry. With its emphasis on space planning for libraries and information centers, InfoSpace Consultants has been able to land contracts with some of the major players in the business and finance, media, and advertising communities, and it's an emphasis that Pellizzi delights in talking about.

"On the whole, information managers are not trained in space planning and design," he says, "and in fact there's no reason why they should be. It's an entirely separate discipline." Having been in the business for seventeen years, Pellizzi has naturally formed some perceptions about how information managers deal with space issues.

"For one thing," he says, "most information managers—for a variety of reasons (and often external reasons that are totally out of their control)—wait until the last minute to figure out what their space require-

Originally published in *InfoManage : The International Management Newsletter for the Information Services Professional* 4 (3), February, 1998.

ments are, and this means that when the work is done, it's done in haste. And when they don't have the expertise that is called for, sometimes the work is not done as well as it should be."

To prevent such situations from arising, Pellizzi suggests a sort of ongoing study ("you might call it a space 'audit'," he says) a serious analysis from time to time of what the information unit's spatial requirements are, and what they should be. The idea is to go back to thinking about what the information facility is supposed to be, what its primary mission is.

"A good example," Pellizzi says, "is the training function. Most libraries—and certainly most specialist libraries—aren't planned as training centers, yet information managers are often required to offer training to their information customers, training in using specific databases, in working with CD-ROMs, in using particular resources for specific information. Yet even though training is required, the library does not have a training space, or even a place for the equipment required for working with the customers being trained. So it becomes the library manager's responsibility to look at the entire picture, the total mission that the library is chartered to achieve, and to provide the space for achieving those things. If training is part of the library's work, a training space should be provided.

"Ideally," Pellizzi continues, "information manaagers should know what their true space requirements are, regardless of how much space they actually have at present. As a manager, this information is vital, strategic knowledge. This information should be updated as needed and communicated to one's boss. In addition, if the organization is large enough to have a separate design/facilities department, this information should be communicated to an appropriate person in that area as well. In other words, the whole space/facilities/planning situation must be taken seriously, and thought about as a serious part of the library's operation. It shouldn't be an afterthought, or something that's given attention only when there's a problem, or an impending move, or a reduction in available space. It's a serious part of being an information manager, this thinking about the library's spatial requirements and making plans to meet them."

Pellizzi illustrates his point by talking about how information managers often find themselves working under what he calls a "deficit" situation, a facility in which there is already not enough space allocated for the work that has to be done.

"If that's the case in your operation," he says, "you need to communicate that to the decision makers, to those who have resource allocation authority. If, for example, you and your staff are already operating in a deficit situation (say you have a user-pc area that's too crowded) and you are short 350 square feet, you shouldn't go to management and say you need 350 square feet. That will only fix the deficit situation, without giving you any additional space. What you really want to do is ask for 700 square feet—or whatever the amount is—so you can cover the deficit and gain the additional space that you've already determined that you need. Most of us forget about the deficit situation we're already operating in when we go to look for new space."

Hearing Pellizzi talk about these things, it becomes easy to see why he gave his company the name it has.

"I thought up the name 'InfoSpace' back in 1987 when I started the company. To me the name embodied my activities as a consultant, dealing with the spatial aspects of libraries and information centers. Incidentally, I have a trademark on the name 'InfoSpace' and my company has nothing to do with the internet phonebook company that was started a couple of years ago. What the name does convey, though, is what we do: Our primary activity involves planning and designing special libraries and information centers, an effort that usually takes one of two forms. Either a client needs to determine how much space will be needed for a facility, based on a calculation of requirements, or the client merely wants to optimize the use of a given space that the facility is limited to already."

Much of his work, of course, is with architects, but they are not his clients. The client is the information manager, and Pellizzi's role is to work with the information manager to create a plan to take to the architect. It's a situation that grows out of the practical realities of the situation: the information manager has no control over the selection of the architect, but the information manager can make a case for hiring an information consultant.

"It's a communications function," he says. "I wear a lot of different hats, depending on the organization and the work to be done, but my primary job is to draw up the plan. Sometimes my role is to serve as a bridge, or a conduit of information, between the information manager and the architect or, in some cases, between the information manager and the manager's supervisor. But whatever form it takes, my job at InfoSpace is to develop a plan that incorporates the information manager's goals, and my role is a technical communications one. I work on the quantification of requirements, specific design goals, adjacencies of library elements, that sort of thing. And whatever the specific work entails, it is all built around one specific point of view: the best designs result from cooperative efforts between the information manager and the library consultant. It's my role to implement what I like to think of as my own work ethic, and it's pretty basic: functional efficiency.

"I try to make everybody happy." Pellizzi says. "Of course I try, but I can't always succeed. Nevertheless, I recognize that there are ways to achieve agreement with most of the parties involved, and that's what I focus on. Call it 'politics' if you like. Call it 'diplomacy.' It doesn't matter what you call it. My role is to establish a mood of cooperation, to be the go-between working to see that the efforts of the architect and senior management are brought in line with the requirements of the information management staff and their information customers' needs.

As part of this mediation effort, much of Pellizzi's work involves representing the information managers and their point of view—their interests—at meetings, planning sessions, and so forth.

"There are plenty of times," he says, "when I am present at project team meetings, meetings where just the consultants are present, with no department heads there, and that's when I serve as that conduit of information I mentioned earlier. My role is to carry information, both from the information manager to the project team, and from the project team to the information manager. The information manager could do it, but he or she doesn't have time, doesn't have the expertise, or, quite frankly, simply requires an external opinion. My role is to serve as a sort of buffer, an in-between representative who looks after and protects the interests of the information manager but at the same time understands and negotiates with the project team and the architect to see that corporate standards are applied and met. What I do saves the information manager time. I quantify information for the architect. It becomes a question of translating the information department's needs to the organization at large, and that's what I do."

Of course it is not always an ideal scenario, and there can be problems in designing a specialized library, particularly in the corporate world. When that happens, the pitfalls are not hard to determine, at least not hard for Tom Pellizzi.

"First of all," Pellizzi says. "there is the communications problem. What we see most often, either holding up a project or resulting in a badly designed project, is a lack of technical communication between the information manager and the design team. That situation has to be resolved right off the bat. The information manager and the design team have to be talking with one another about what the requirements for the library are, and they must work together to see that those requirements are calculated into the design for the facility. Another 'pitfall,' and one that we see a lot , comes into the picture when a designer is interested mainly in an aesthetic consideration, or has no previous experience designing a library or specialized information center. The information manager has the knowledge and the expertise about how the library or information center is going to be used, and that knowledge and expertise has to be incorporated into the plan."

There are, of course, other changes taking place in the information management field, and Pellizzi has to deal with these as well, simply because the specialist libraries he is designing for the twenty-first century are not going to be the same as those that companies put together as recently as eight or ten years ago. The whole subject of convergence/integrated information, for example, the combining of special libraries, records management facilities, and archives departments, is much talked about these days. Certainly it's a subject that people involved in space planning and design must deal with, but when asked about his take on this supposedly "hot" subject, Pellizzi is the very picture of calm, businesslike composure:

"We're just not seeing it happen," he says. "Certainly not on any grand scale. While it's a fascinating theory, and certainly the whole concept of convergence/integrated information flows quite naturally into the knowledge management information-delivery 'ideal' we hear so much about, I think in many respects it is still just that, an ideal, or a theory. Certainly in the special libraries community, in the industries in which our company works—industries like accounting, advertising, financial services, investment banking, and the like—there's a great deal of interest in the concepts attached to knowledge management and integrated information, but so far there's been no great change in the way we look at—and think about—space planning and design for these information facilities. That might change, but for the present, I'm not seeing a great deal of attention being given to space planning issues that relate specifically to a converged or integrated information-delivery function.

Pellizzi continues with the theme.

"A lot of it is going to have to do with how you define the terms, of course. In a hospital environment, for example, knowledge might represent something quite different from the way the term might be used in an investment management firm. Similarly, integrated information as a management concept might be applied in one industry and not work at all in another. It all depends on what the terms mean. Does everyone who's talking about knowledge management agree on what the term knowledge means? And what about integrated information? What information is being integrated? And what does convergence mean, in different settings? I'm afraid it's early days yet for some of us, especially in terms of space planning and design, the area in which my company works."

Having said that, though, Pellizzi is quick to point out that there is a definite—and observable—trend toward more digital sources of information. And there is a movement to less hard copy.

"Yes, certainly," Pellizzi says. "But any 'trend' definitely depends on the industry and the business clientele. For example, news organizations must still do research using historical information that is not available digitally. And media companies rely on advertising images and graphs from periodicals and magazines. Where these images have been captured electronically, well and good. But that does not—as far as I can tell—represent the vast majority of people working in these fields. But I think most library/information services managers know this already. They recognize that a fully digital library is a compromise."

Asked to talk about the critical issues affecting space planning and design in the modern up-to-date, state-of-the-art information center, Pellizzi smiles.

"Don't you think 'state-of-the-moment' is more like it?" he asks. "After all, it wasn't so long ago that we were looking at eighteen months as the typical 'generation' in electronic information systems. Now it's something like six months. So certainly one of the critical issues has to be adapting to change, being willing to work with what you've got until you can get upgraded or the system you have is replaced. But that leads to the other critical issue relating to all this: that your space needs have to be somewhat flexible. Of course you must recognize the movement toward automation, but you must also recognize that there are going to be people and books and paper reports and furniture and other things in your space, and that there's going to be a need for something more than an automated work environment. I think what all of us have to do, when we're speaking with management and designers and facilities people about libraries is to remind them what libraries are, and what their role is, in the organization in question."

Which is?

Pellizzi doesn't miss a beat: "I know what a library is. And so do you. You simply have to be able to tell the right people that a library is an organizational entity that holds information or sources of information not available on everyone's desktop. A library has resources for specialized research. That's the role that libraries have always played and will continue to play, and that role must be taken into consideration as organizations think about the spatial requirements for their employees and their work. Information managers themselves need to foster that idea. No one else is going to do it. Libraries have and will continue to have unique resources, and provide the staffs with the expertise to use those resources. Simply put, unless companies are willing to turn everybody, all their employees, into researchers—and how many companies do you think are going to do that?—libraries are not going away. And as long as we have specialized libraries and research centers, we're going to require specialist space planners and designers to make them work."

So of course Tom Pellizzi likes librarians. And librarians like Tom. Given the man's optimism about what librarians do (and will be doing), why not?

Meet Tom Pellizzi

Thomas Pellizzi established InfoSpace Consultants in 1987. The company provides a variety of consultation and project management services for special libraries and information centers, especially in the area of space planning and design. Pellizzi has designed special libraries and information centers for a prestigious group of clients in various industries, including accounting, advertising, corporate, financial services, investment banking, academic, and non-profit. He has achieved an outstanding record for designing comfortable and functionally efficient business libraries.

As a consultant, Pellizzi has more than 17 years of client project experience. Prior to establishing InfoSpace, he worked for eight years at The Document Management Group, Inc., where he worked primarily on special library projects.

A member of both the Special Libraries Association (SLA) and the American Society for Information Science (ASIS), Pellizzi is a graduate of Rutgers College, New Brunswick, New Jersey. He is married and resides in Manhattan. He enjoys skiing in Utah and travelling in general (especially Italy). He is an avid opera fan.

Team-based organizational management in the
research libraries environment:
CARLA STOFFLE, SHELLEY PHIPPS,
MICHAEL RAY, and CARRIE RUSSELL
describe the process at the University of Arizona
"You work with the organization to develop the organization."

Whether we call it "customer service" or something else, there's no doubt but that successful information delivery in the libraries of the future will be customer focused. And there are few places—either in the non-profit sector or the for-profit sector—where the focus on the customer is given the attention it is given at the University of Arizona Library. In fact, at this particular institution, customer focus is paramount (and yes, without apology, they call them "customers"). Even the library management org

Originally published in *InfoManage : The International Management Newsletter for the Information Services Professional* 5 (11), October, 1998.

chart is turned upside-down from the conventional charts we usually see in business and in academe. If you look closely (see chart below), you'll notice that the arrows all point up. The "Library Core Services and Teams" line develops from the "Library Governance and Support Teams," and that line is, quite literally, built on the foundation provided by the Library Cabinet. And supporting the whole organization is the Dean, at the bottom of the org chart. The customers are at the top.

Now *that* tells you something about the thinking that has gone into the massive reorganizational effort at the University of Arizona over the last few years. The entire information environment—undergraduate students, graduate students, faculty, community, and library staff—has thrown itself into the creation of the library of the future. And the success of the effort is remarkable.

The University of Arizona is not your traditional Ivy League or wannabe-Ivy League institution, and never intended to be. Established in

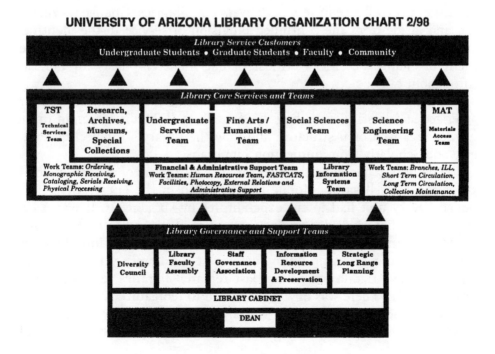

1885 with an appropriation from the 13th Arizona Territorial Legislature, the library began as a collection of agriculture, mining, and engineering books, and by 1893 had grown to 700 volumes. Today, with more than 4 million items, the library is "building on traditional strengths," according to one document handed to visitors. "The Library is moving into the information age . . . and provides electronic access to worldwide scholarly resources. You are invited," the statement continues, "to join us in building the Library of the future."

It's that library of the future that team-based management—in the information services environment—is all about. If the closing decade of the twentieth century has been about anything, it has been about preparing for life in the future, and those with administrative responsibility for libraries and other information services came to realize early in the decade that information delivery organizations would not—indeed, could not—operate in the twenty-first century as they had operated in the twentieth. Patrons were being offered—or were demanding—new and different service provision in every other service organization they encountered, and they soon began to expect the same service standards—including an attention to excellence in service delivery—in libraries. Change was called for, and (aside from the continued provision of service to the identified customer base, which can never be neglected) change and the management of change became a critical management emphasis for libraries throughout our society.

At the University of Arizona, the call for change could almost be characterized as "drastic," according to Carrie Russell, Media Librarian in the former organizational structure and now the library's Intellectual Property and Scholarly Communication Librarian.

"The library had gone through three or four years of continuing budget cuts," Russell says. "Morale was low, and in the latest university's budget, every unit had to cut expenditures by six percent. It was a bad time for the library, and everyone was aware of it. And to make matters worse, at a time when other research libraries were moving into the information age, there was no online catalog at the library yet, making the University of Arizona one of the last research libraries to not have an online catalog. There was obviously a need to reorganize."

Carla Stoffle, who was then working at the University of Michigan, was hired to be the Dean and Director of Libraries, and in coming to Arizona, Stoffle negotiated two critical funding issues, both required before the library could move forward. The first was funding for an online catalog, and the second was funding for staff and organizational development. More important than the funding, though, was the sense of opportunity that was equally critical. The library needed to move forward, and Stoffle found that within the library's community and its user base, there was a desire to move forward, so the first requirement for change was in place: the organization was ready for change.

In her first all-staff meeting, Stoffle made a presentation that is still being talked about at the university. She acknowledged that the library had suffered, but she also pledged to lead the library staff in proving to the university that "we're not going to fall down and die." It was just the inspiration that the library staff, including Russell, needed.

"The role of the library was changing," Stoffle says, "and we had to meet the challenges of that change. Traditionally, librarians have organized and stored knowledge, faculty created it. In this model, the university's research library has been an absorber of resources, the quality and rankings attained by how much the campus spent on the materials we stored. But that is not what we do now. The new vision at the University of Arizona is that the library is a partner in the scholarly communication process, and in this new vision the library is active, not passive. It is a role we have embraced with considerable enthusiasm, but it also meant a total rethinking as far as our own work is concerned."

On her arrival, Stoffle called for a volunteer group to plan a library-wide reorganization. It was a mixed bag, this planning group, and it included staff from all employee classifications. And the group didn't start out to recommend team-based management, or even to work as a team.

"It could have been anything," Russell says. "The only charge was to build a library of the future, using whatever means were necessary. Eventually many people were involved, and the group was to look at all the concepts they could come up with. Everything was subject to change."

And it became obvious, early on in the reorganization process, that the layers of hierarchy made operations unwieldy and bottlenecked many services. As the Librarians Council, consisting of the director, department heads, senior administrators (called Assistant or Associate University Librarians), met to make decisions, staff on the front lines were confronted with confused and upset customers. It was decided that these layers of hierarchy were not helping staff meet the needs of customers.

So after 18 months of staff and planning meetings, the reorganization group designed a new org chart that reduced 16 departments to 11 (now 9) teams. The AUL positions were eliminated, as were department heads, and these positions were replaced by team leaders, with the process for hiring team leaders intentionally structured so that hiring would be done from within (see Timeline, pp. 175–176). With a staff of about 190 people, reorganizing and redesigning the organizational structure was not a simple task, but once a decision had been made to go with a team-based organization ("You can call it 'team-based management' if you like," Russell says with a smile, "but we like to think of it as a 'team-based organization'."), there was no going back.

And as an aside, when she came to Arizona Stoffle developed her own organizational chart of how she thought the management function might be structured. She didn't show it to the group until after the changes had been made. At that point it was discovered that Stoffle's original chart had been, surprisingly, a "more traditional" org chart. Once again, the library was demonstrating its readiness for change.

As the work progressed, critical administrative support from the university stayed in place, a point that Michael Ray makes when he talks about the restructuring. Ray, who started at the university during the transition period supervising development and training activities in the Human Relations Department, was working with the university's president on a general program of quality improvement, looking at such things as process improvement, team building, etc. Having created formal training programs in such areas as Management by Planning, Effective Meetings, Training and Using Quality Tools, and similar programs for the university at large, Ray came to the library to work in its organizational transition. And while the university had started its own quality program, with principles much the same as those of the library's reorganization, the "quality" term wasn't being used in the work being done in the library.

"What we were attempting," Ray says, "required a huge culture shift, not just in preparing for the future, but in an historic sense. In the past, professionalism for librarians had traditionally included an assumption of autonomy. With the team-managed organization, with its emphasis on the customer, the librarian must think in terms of 'I have to demonstrate

Organizational Design Study and Restructuring
Timeline at The University of Arizona

BACKGROUND

Fall/Spring, 1990/1991: Task Force on Access Ownership (7 members—6 faculty, 1 staff) reports on their analysis of the change environment, after studying internal and external data. Key recommendation from Access/Ownership Report: "Work toward the creation of a 'Library of the Future' in which librarians are responsible for the creation and operation of a system which facilitates access and communication."

TIMELINE

Fall, 1991: Dean Carla Stoffle contracts with Association of Research Libraries, Office of Management Services, for a facilitated self-study in organizational design.

Mid-February, 1992: Organization Design Steering Committee is appointed from a list of library staff volunteers and nominees. The Steering Committee (7 members—1 department head, 4 faculty, 2 career staff). **Charge:** Create a new organization design for the future.

February 27/28: OMS Consultant holds All-Staff meeting, facilitates an Organizational Design Retreat for members of the Steering Committee and Librarian's Council.

March/April: Steering Committee conducts mini-retreats for Campus Library Council, Graduate Library School students, and Library staff and students.

April 6: All-Staff Open House.

April 7–June 7: The Basic Assumptions developed by expanded Steering Committee. Work begins on synthesizing all of the input gathered. Student Survey is conducted and the results analyzed. Steering Committee separates into two groups and develops two design models, Model A and Model B. Assumptions are reviewed by Librarian's Council and distributed to all staff members for their consideration.

June 8: Model A and Model B are presented at an All-Staff Open House for input.

June 9–21: Input is integrated into the Models. Members of the Steering Committee and Ad-Group select Model B (The Basket) for the basis for organizational structure.

June 22–23: OMS Consultant returns to work with the Steering Committee on developing the next stages.

continued

Organizational Design Study and Restructuring
Timeline at The University of Arizona
(continued)

July 16: The Steering Committee and Ad-Group select Design Teams from volunteers throughout the Library to develop the four areas identified in Model B.

July 22: Design Workshop is held to get the four teams started.

September 4: Design Teams present models at an All-Staff Open House and gather input.

September 9–October 7: The Operational Adjustment Team (OAT) works with the four models to create a unified Organizational Chart.

September 25: OAT shares its initial work on the organizational structure with members of the four Design Teams.

October–December: OAT meets with groups in Library for dialogue and University resource people to develop staff development plan.

December: Implementation Teams are appointed from a list of volunteers from all staff. OMS Consultant conducts team training.

December, 1992–April 31, 1993: The Implementation Teams do internal studies and report:
- Phase I: Amount/Level/Time for key work activities.
- Phase II: Threshold/Performance/Excitement priority ranking of activities and substructure of team organization.
- Phase III: Space and equipment needs, remaining issues, and final recommendations.

May–June 7, 1993: Selection Committee for Team Leader selection is elected (8 members—4 Library faculty, 4 classified staff). A consensus decision process is used to choose the new Team Leaders.

June 23–July 12: Assignment to teams takes place based on a checklist of Knowledge, Skills, and Abilities and an opportunity to list interests and choices of teams.

June 30–July 23: Remaining Team Leaders, Planning Librarian, Team Facilitation Librarian [positions] are filled, again using the consensus decision process.

Expectations of Team Leaders
at the University of Arizona Library

1. Understands and communicates the Library's mission, vision, values, goals, and while conveying the larger context in which the Library operates, exhibits personal commitment and takes leadership in creating team commitment to achieving them. Leads team in translating library and team strategic goals into action.

2. Promotes team commitment to a customer focus.

3. Works proactively and constructively to identify, define, and solve problems within their own team and between teams and other individuals and teams. Works with team members to develop coaching mechanisms to help individual team members who are having performance problems.

4. Facilitates and involves all team members in team planning, objectives setting, and problem solving, empowering and holding team members accountable for participation and results.

5. Works with team to define team and team leader roles and appropriate methodology for decision-making. Seeks and utilizes data and objective criteria for decision-making. Helps team recognize options and consequences of team decisions. Has final accountability for seeing that decisions get made and that there is appropriate follow through.

6. Fosters an environment that encourages risk taking and creativity.

7. Works proactively and constructively to develop and coach team members to be self-motivated; ensures professional, career, and skill development; ensures structure is in place for *all* team members to participate in the coaching and development of all staff.

8. Communicates and leads development of team understanding and support of library-wide decisions and priorities; helps the team communicate and create understanding of team issues library wide.

9. Helps promote and support diversity within the team and the Library.

10. Works with the team to build self-managing capabilities including effective delegation to sub-teams and individuals.

11. Champions cross-functional efforts to improve quality, service, and productivity.

12. Anticipates, initiates, and responds to changes in the environment to help the Library move forward.

13. Leads in management of budgets and fosters understanding of and responses to internal and external funding opportunities and constraints.

a greater depth of knowledge of who our customers are,' and librarians now have to put into the process an effort to build a relationship with the customer, in a sense, of being involved with the customer. It's a shift from a relationship with management to a relationship with the customer.

"Of course it creates discourse confusion," Ray continues, "as you try to figure out what you have to put forward to be eligible for promotion. But it can be done. But you don't really have any choice, since economic pressures and the implementation of technology in the library workplace means that you can't continue the old practices. And that brings us back to the relationship with the university's administration: Another important key, if we were going to be successful with team-based management at the university library, was the strong support that the new methodology had from the university provost, so that when some activity or program had to be embarked upon that was somewhat 'outside,' say, the established policy framework, or slightly 'beyond the scope' of what had been done in the past, an exception could be made and we could move ahead."

It's a point that both Stoffle and Russell refer to when they speak about the values that direct the services in the organization. Any management system must match principles, values, and laws already in place, but in a team-based organization, as Russell puts it, "greater flexibility is called for, and there has to be a strong emphasis on flexibility."

Stoffle agrees, and notes that among the values that the new structure built on was the flexibility "piece," the freedom to try new things.

For starters, the change management effort was based on several assumptions, which are evident as you think about the timeline for the redesign. Primary among these was talking with staff, surveying staff, going out into the library's community, identifying problems, seeking solutions, and—all the while—keeping at the forefront of everyone's thinking that this is a new endeavor, something that's never been tried before. Certainly such an effort had not been attempted in this environment, and to bring team-based management to its longed-for success required, probably more than anything else, a sincere and honest effort to bring all the library's stakeholders into the process.

They began with the problems, this group of information workers, and with a real desire to "fix things," to take problems that were causing distress among the identified customer base and to alleviate those problems.

Expectations of Workteam Leaders at The University of Arizona Library

Definition

The primary purpose of a Workteam Leader is to take leadership in facilitating processes within the scope of a specific workteam to enable the workteam to accomplish its work.

Assumptions

1. That the Performance Learning Project will result in each team developing work and behavioral expectations for all members and a mechanism for holding each other accountable.

2. Team will use these expectations as a basis for dialog about observable outcomes.

Expectations

1. Understands and communicates the Library's mission, vision, values, goals, and, while conveying the larger context in which the Library operates, exhibits personal commitment and takes leadership in creating workteam commitment to achieving them. Leads workteam in translating library and team strategic goals into action.

2. Promotes workteam commitment to a customer focus by modeling appropriate customer service behavior and responding appropriately to customer needs.

3. Works proactively and constructively to identify, define, and solve problems within their own workteam and between workteams and other individuals and teams.

4. Facilitates and involves all workteam members in workteam planning, objectives setting, defining expectations, and problem solving, empowering and holding workteam members accountable for participation and results.

5. Works with team to define team and workteam leader roles and how decisions are made. Helps workteam recognize options and consequences of workteam decisions. Is individually accountable for seeing that decisions get made and that there is appropriate follow through. It may be necessary for workteam leaders to make decisions for the workteam in limited circumstances such as the workteam being unable to reach a decision or during special circumstances.

6. Coordinates the gathering, analysis, and utilization of data and information to make decisions.

7. Models and encourages creativity and informed risk taking.

8. Works proactively and constructively to develop and coach workteam members to be self-motivated and to be lifelong learners.

9. Communicates and leads development of workteam understanding and support of library-wide decisions and priorities; helps the workteam communicate and create understanding of team issues library-wide.

continued

Expectations of Workteam Leaders
at The University of Arizona Library
(continued)

10. Demonstrates support for diversity as defined by the Library.

11. Works with the workteam to build self-managing capabilities including effective delegations to workteam members.

12. Champions process improvement and other cross-functional efforts to improve quality, service, and productivity.

13. Anticipates when possible, participates with an open mind, and responds appropriately to changes in the environment.

14. Understands the allocation of budget and resources process. Leads in management of budgets and resources.

15. Attends and actively participates in workteam meetings.

16. Models good communication skills by actively listening and giving and receiving constructive feedback.

17. Interprets, communicates, and applies relevant library policies.

18. Identifies and implements effective ways of making staff and students feel accepted and valued.

19. Leads and participates in the hiring process, primarily within the workteam.

20. Takes leadership in developing and implementing a training program for staff and students which may include customer service.

21. Schedules work to ensure that time is available for consultation with and coaching of staff and students. Maintains an open attitude to staff, students, and their ideas.

22. Develops facilitation skills, uses them, and supports workteam members in doing the same.

So they started with an early survey, asking faculty and staff what needed to be fixed.

The answers weren't long in coming, and it soon became clear that it would not be hard to determine what issues were perceived as the most urgent. Three were identified: shelving, reserves, and ILL management, and the first of these, the library's shelving situation, was almost out of control, to the extent that, as described in one document, "At the University of Arizona Library, complaints about the condition of book stacks were notorious. Library customers wrote letters of complaint to the Dean of Libraries; left messages on the Library's suggestion board; complained at our open forums for faculty; and even wrote letters to the local newspapers. The complaints were all similar: That the library had books thrown everywhere; books were difficult to locate at their proper location; and books on the floors and unshelved were a fire hazard."

A major problem indeed, but one that could not go unchallenged in the new environment. With the creation of a Performance Improvement Team created specifically to address the issue (they called themselves "The PITCrew"), change happened: By improving the shelving process, the PITCrew saved the library $40,000, by eliminating redundant steps in the shelving process. More important, from the customers' point of view, the average cycle time for reshelving books was reduced from 18 hours to 2.5 hours (and in one departmental library, from 81 hours to 1.5 hours!), with shelvers now scheduled on duty for every hour the building is open.

Was it worth the effort? Just ask any faculty member or student, and you'll get a resounding "Yes!" Or just ask the judges for the Arizona Governor's Award for Excellence, who gave the award to the university library's PITCrew in July, 1996.

Of course it was worth the effort. In any change process—and especially where services are going to be affected by the proposed change—acceptance by those involved is not always easy. As the situation with the shelving demonstrates, though, there was more acceptance as library staff moved into a serious process improvement 'mode' and could demonstrate that a team-managed organization can be successful.

But what about buy-in from the library staff members themselves? How was that achieved?

Stoffle doesn't mince words: "There are no magic answers," she says. "It's a continual process, and what we're dealing with here is a cultural change, a major culture shift. What we had in place prior to this was a culture that was built on a hierarchy, and it had been in place for a long time. 'Star' employees were rewarded, and others expected to be told what to do. You've got to recognize that it takes a while to get out of that."

And the best way to do that, Stoffle says, is to fix things so that the customers know what to expect, that they will find high standards of service delivery when they come to use the library.

"It's customer feedback,." she says. "As far as the staff is concerned, having happy customers helps a lot!"

But change management also requires keeping the staff involved, since, as Shelley Phipps puts it, "Involvement is key to success. People have to know that they have a chance to shape their future, in light of the environmental pressures to change." And while winning a governor's award for excellence is a rewarding recognition, that didn't come until 1996, nearly three years after the library had launched its new management structure—officially—in October, 1993. And it only involved one team although, it must be recognized, in team-based organizational management as practiced at the University of Arizona Library, one team's success is carefully (and enthusiastically) presented as *everyone's* success.

So other staff development efforts were required, and Phipps—who is Assistant Dean for Team and Organization Development and whose position was Assistant University Librarian for Branch Services in the former structure—knew well what the objective was:

"First of all," she says, "recognize what we were trying to do here: our goal was to work with the organization to develop the organization, and to do that, there were two givens as jobs were restructured: Everyone was guaranteed a job, and there would be no loss of salary. We understood that as we moved from the previous structure, as people were required to apply for new jobs, there would be personal and organizational stress. There would be a great deal of discomfort and, yes, some people would not want to be part of a team operation. But we also looked at what we were trying to do and we took that to the staff. We continued the 'involvement strategy,' asking for volunteers to work on the new micro-design scope and focus of new teams. Over 75 (of 200) staff were involved in this design phase and, as it turned out, when people applied for the new positions on the teams, 93% of the staff got their first choice.

"The strengths of the team-based structure are the broadening of expertise, the broadening of the employee's learning capacity, and expanding skills. This is accomplished by appointing a lot of cross-functional teams, empowered and trained to make decisions. This learning is carried forward and continues organizational learning. You can't do that under a hierarchical structure, or if you can, it's with great difficulty and on an ad hoc basis. In a team-managed organization, teams establish mission, they agree on the vision, and, significantly, they draw up performance measure projects that support and align competencies. And that's what we're trying to do with the staff here. We're looking for alignment, so we have people doing the things they do best. Instead of a simple concept of promotion, with respect to compensation and promotion issues, in a team-based environment we are trying to develop a structure based on the development of new competencies, moving away from the concept of 'expert leader' to one of the leader-as-facilitator, with its shared leadership role and so forth. And it works."

Stoffle agrees.

"We've managed not to lay people off," she says, "and that's the reward. Certainly you place them in new positions, and you retrain them, but you do everything you can to prevent the layoffs. From the beginning, we've worked very hard to realign positions, to see that the best people are in the best jobs. But we've also identified our established values, and they're all built around the customer: customer focus, continuous improvement, all those things we look for in a quality-focused organization, and we work with our staff to see that we're all in agreement about these values.

"As part of that process," Stoffle continues, "we've set up a compensation and reward system that builds on these values, and as far as the library's employees are concerned, we start with the assumption that you do a good job. Merit rewards come for adding value. We look at the employee, at his or her skills and competencies, and we ask: what kind of new work are we going to be doing that we need your skills for? And we have no problem that competency-based management is something we're using. Of course we recognize that much of this comes from industry but that's not a problem for us. There are plenty of times where we have to benchmark with industry, simply because the work just isn't being done in the research libraries community.

"And it's also based on trust," Stoffle adds, "this concept of team-based management, on building trust. This is not something that if you are smart enough, etc., people will fall in line. Too many people have been hurt in the past, and they are wary of too much change. You have to start from scratch, and you have to start with the administration, with the administration learning to trust the staff and the customers, and the staff has to be willing to be challenged, to make mistakes. There's a lot of challenging that has to go on. And we all have to be continually commit-ted to trying to meet those challenges every day."

It sounds as if there was some "downtime," some period during the restructuring when things didn't go as planned.

"Absolutely," Stoffle says. "There was a degradation of services for about six months, and we knew it would happen. We knew that there was going to be a period of time when we would not be good at what we were doing, but we operated from a very basic point of view: 'you have to trust the process.' In our case, we did, and we persuaded the university admin-istration and our customers to trust the process, and we got through those rough six months. We've been moving ahead ever since."

Totally?

"Of course not," Stoffle says. "We're not satisfied. And we may never be satisfied. We're not as far along as we had hoped to be, but we are bet-ter serving the user, and overall we're doing a better job of managing the library and its services than we ever did before. For example, the way the reserve lists are handled is a major accomplishment. It used to take three weeks to get reserve materials in place. Now they're in place within 24 hours. That's the kind of success we have to look for, and if it's not total success by any given time, we are still providing better service than we were providing before we became a team-based organization."

And there are other successes. Phipps and Ray both make it clear that communication is the key to any success that team-based management is going to bring to the university library, and open communication is a big part of the organizational redesign that the university library staff has put in place.

"Staff needs to know they're listened to," Phipps says, "and that action will be taken when problems arise. Of course you can negotiate. If, for example, you want people to learn by experimenting in other areas, then there's a fear of getting the 'work back home' done. But we tackled that problem by setting up a procedure by which individuals negotiated their work assignments with their teams and if 'critical' work could not get done, then the team could request additional one-time funds to fill-in behind the teammate assigned to a cross-functional team. Also, to sup-port staff taking on new learning we set up a policy that all staff could negotiate learning time with their teams, and we opened up what we call 'The Creativity Lab,' a purpose-built space where staff can go to learn new computer programs, practice computer skills, and do that sort of thing. It's just one more way of giving people signs that you are going to do what you've said you'll do."

Another innovation that demonstrates this is cross-team 'learning,' as it might be called.

"We know we are successful," Phipps says, "when what has been used in one project is successfully transferred into another project. For example, we recently had to put together a team to work on a new charge-for-printing process that was required. Everyone appointed to the team already had experience with process improvement teams, so the new team set up its own process, and was very proud to accomplish what they needed to accomplish in one-fourth of the time that other process teams had taken previously. It's that kind of success that makes the team-based organization exciting as a management methodology."

Still, there's work to be done, as Stoffle and the others in the group admit. There is no strong team reward system in place yet, and for Phipps that's a problem: "We still have to figure out how to handle that."

"But we are engaged in continued dialogue," Stoffle says, "and while we have a vision of what the library should be, as team members we have to make sure that the vision is carried out into the workplace. In the last three or four years, we've spent a lot of time bringing people along. Now, we're finished with that. The train has left the station, and we—as an organization—have to concentrate on the people on the train. Those people still in the station, well, we did what we could for them, and now we just have to move on. That's our mission, to be the library of the future, and we can't do that if we're held back."

It's highly unlikely that the team-based organization will be held back. At this point in the University of Arizona's history, what they're doing at that institution's library is remarkable for a number of reasons: better productivity, competency-based performance, staff interest and excitement, continuous process improvement, and any number of other deliverables that attest to the fact that things are just better than they used to be. Standing out above all these, though, is the one unassailable fact that defines the University of Arizona Library's mission and vision for all to see: service is excellent, and the customers are happy. That, in the final analysis, is what library management is all about.

ENTREPRENEURIAL MANAGEMENT

Entrepreneurial management in the information industry (or, as described in another context, "entrepreneurial librarianship") is an undisputed requirement for successful change management. In fact, the very people in the information environment who succeed in bringing change to their operations are the ones who are able to look at what happens in the "real" world (that is, the world beyond their professional sphere) and adopt—often quickly and often with little "adaptation"—the philosophies and management theories that drive entrepreneurial success.

It is not hard to see why. Entrepreneurs focus on one thing, and one thing only: determining (and providing) what the customers want. Yes, in the business world, it is provided at a profit, and in the information-delivery environment, it is (most often) provided as a service, but that is a distinction that is, in the final analysis, irrelevant and merely serves to confuse the very people who are to benefit from the information provided, the customers.

The qualities of entrepreneurial librarianship have been described, and they are evident in the interviews that make up this chapter. Two

187

librarians—one in America and one in Europe—demonstrate conclusively that entrepreneurial thinking can lead to successful information delivery. Mark Merrifield sees no contradiction in applying entrepreneurial values to the delivery of services in a public library and, in fact, in his interview Merrifield effectively demonstrates that the citizens who make up the user base for a public library expect entrepreneurial thinking in the provision of other services and they are, quite frankly, surprised when it isn't offered at their public library. In Berlin, Claudia Lux happily recognizes that successful change management in a large government information operation requires entrepreneurial management, including the very "entrepreneurial" recognition that political awareness and influence are as much a part of the management function as the more commonly recognized management essentials.

In Montréal, Judy Macfarlane picks up on the entrepreneurial theme and moves it into the *intrapreneurial* workplace, wherein the information center, which already exists to provide information services for a specifically identified customer base, expands that base (and, not coincidentally, brings additional revenue into the parent organization) to the wider information-seeking community. Certainly, to provide such services, and to provide them at a profit, requires a change in thinking and an operational change that must be planned for.

Three entrepreneurs in this chapter take the time to tell information managers how they—the information managers—can incorporate entrepreneurial techniques into the information delivery workplace. For Betty Eddison at Inmagic Inc., the secret is in adding value, and integrating information resources, for Eddison, is a perfect example of how specialist librarians can benefit from entrepreneurial thinking. For one thing, according to Eddison, integrating resources "is an opportunity for raising your visibility within the organization." For librarians and other information workers, that statement alone describes the value of the entrepreneurial philosophy and the value of developing a change management methodology that incorporates entrepreneurial thinking.

Taking that idea to a more formal level, Victor Rosenberg specifically teaches entrepreneurial thinking at the graduate level, seeking to inspire future information professionals to use entrepreneurial methods as they manage information facilities. Rosenberg, luckily, can link theory to practice, simply because in addition to his teaching, he manages an entrepreneurial enterprise that is very successful.

Michael Gruenberg, too, emphasizes the adoption of an entrepreneurial philosophy in the information delivery workplace, and he bases his contention on the fact that understanding customer requirements puts the information professional in the position (often unique in the information industry) of being better able to supply specific information products. It works in business, Gruenberg believes, and it can work in the information services field.

Inmagic's
BETTY EDDISON:
Adding value to information services

A recent profile in *The Boston Business Journal* called her a "Renaissance Woman," alluding, no doubt, to her highly varied (dare we say "checkered"?) career. Elizabeth Bole Eddison, Chairman of Inmagic Inc., has indeed been a busy person, and her career has, in fact, been several careers: wife, mother, world traveller, librarian, educator, and entrepreneur. And now she's a politician, having won a special election last September to the Board of Selectmen in Lexington, Massachusetts.

Its a new job she takes in stride, for she won the election because she knows how to handle information. When she campaigned, she figured out how to identify the voters by occupation and simply asked the librarians if they didn't want to vote for someone who understands libraries. She did the same with the people who work with computers, and she won the election. She knew how to do it.

Known simply to most of her colleagues as "Betty," Eddison received her M.S.L.S. from Simmons College, achieving membership in Beta Phi Mu for the excellence of her graduate studies. Today she is recognized and

Originally published in *InfoManage : The International Management Newsletter for the Information Services Professional* 1 (6), May, 1994.

admired throughout the information services field for her no-nonsense approach to information matters. She also is not shy about being a little "spiky," when the posturing gets to be too much, but don't let the seriousness put you off. Spend a few hours with the woman and you'll find yourself mightily impressed with her warmth, her interest in providing her customers with the best service she can provide, and most of all, you'll have a good time. Betty Eddison is a woman who has been very successful in the information services field, and through it all, the good times, the bad times, the scary times and the successes, she has maintained a sense of humor that can—and does—change a roomful of puffed-up academics or corporate executives into a gang of laughing kids, a personal characteristic that comes in very handy when you think about some of the surprises she finds when she goes in to do an information audit.

"When I help senior executives define their information needs," Eddison says, "an important part of what I am doing is exposing clients to the fact that information tools exist to meet their needs. It's as if I've become an information ombudsman. Sharing knowledge about information resources that can help meet their needs is almost like giving candy to a baby. They positively beam when they hear my good news."

Prior to her work in the information field, Eddison's life was an international one, a background that is, of course, now reflected in the international work that the company does. Her husband's work in economic development took the family all over the world, and Eddison credits much of her present success to the lessons she learned as an international gadfly.

"Having lived in a great many different cultures," Eddison says, "I know that you can find out how things work. We used to get off the plane running. We couldn't spend six months leisurely looking around—we were only going to be there two years."

She put those adaptability skills to work when she started Inmagic Inc. in 1983. With an earlier company—an information management consulting firm—she and her staff had developed a software product to help clients organize information, but they hadn't seen themselves as a software company. They were consultants, and the software just helped them help their clients, an admirable if somewhat altruistic attitude that was shortly put to the test.

As it turned out, the clients kept wanting more of the software, and by the early 1980s, when personal computers had come into widespread use and offices were buying them up, Eddison and her colleagues found themselves in a classic entrepreneurial situation. They had to have a PC product, or they had to stop selling software. When a client survey demonstrated that the customers were satisfied with their product, they decided to produce INMAGIC—the name means "information magic"— for the personal computer market.

And that's where they've been ever since, primarily because the client can do so much with the product. One important application is using the software for the integration of information resources, through the corporate or organizational library or other information services unit. To her clients, Eddison says, it's an opportunity for "raising your visibility" within the organization, and from her point of view, the integration of various information resources can play a critical role in making others in the organization—users, peers, and management—aware of the value of the information services unit. In fact, many information services managers are frequently surprised to discover how much more value their departments have, once they've incorporated information about other organizational operations into their own online system.

"Much information throughout an organization is underused," says Eddison, "and that's because there is no easy way for people to find or even know that these resources exist."

Eddison has identified a long list of information resources from different departments outside the information services section which can be integrated within that unit's database, adding value to the database. Many people within the organization would be delighted, she says, to have a central source for looking for such varied information as that contained in internal R&D reports, technical reports, conference proceedings, vendor catalogs, and a long list of other materials that are housed in separate offices throughout the company but which, if listed in the library or other information unit's database, would be much more accessible.

Ease of access is a big part of what she's trying to do, Eddison points out, and it's a point of view that can carry over into the delivery of any kind of information, regardless of format. "One of my philosophies," she says, "is that we must make sure that the customer expends the least amount of effort in order to use our products. In a two-step process, you lose at least half the people. We want to make it easier, not harder, to get to the information, so we go for the one-step process. Our goal is to remove the stumbling blocks for the clients, and we think we do that pretty well."

How well is pretty obvious, for in its ten years the company has established a strong reputation not only for the quality of the product but for the ease with which it's used. For one thing, the software stores large amounts of data in text form, as opposed to traditional software applications "biased," as Eddison puts it, "toward numerical data."

Eddison points out that the product doesn't require a program language, "so there's no need for fancy training," a fact not lost on the company's many international customers. Some 40% of the company's business is international, and the reasons are not hard to find. Companies throughout the world are increasingly standardizing their work, and the people who have the information send the disks back and forth among themselves, in order to exchange the data. Which means, Eddison adds almost parenthetically, that "the hugely enthusiastic users do most of the marketing for us. It's very much word of mouth."

The international market is growing for Inmagic Inc., and the company is now solidly entrenched in Canada, Australia, New Zealand, the United Kingdom, the Netherlands, Spain, Italy, and various African countries. In fact, a dealer in Spain has created a Spanish version, with Spanish screens, menus, and a Spanish HELP file, so there is even some movement toward a multi-lingual effort. Whether there will be more is still an unknown for Inmagic Inc. as well as for many other companies in the international marketplace, simply because English, as the current language for most business transactions, seems standard for the time being. Nevertheless, if there is demand for other languages, Eddison is not averse to the idea.

In fact, Eddison isn't—and has never been—particularly reticent about new ideas. Coming to grips with changing cultures, business practices, and organizational and management fads has been a lifelong characteristic. As a result, she has established herself among most of her peers as something of an entrepreneurial "change agent," and in this business of working with organizational managements in defining and actualizing the critical role of information services operations within the organization, Eddison has achieved notable success. One of her great strengths is her ability to advise librarians and other information services professionals about how to "sell" management on the value of the information services and products they provide. "The key," she says, "is added value, and it is a required, not optional, activity for justifying the information services operation within the organization."

Eddison adheres strongly to a point of view that information services professionals can be change agents for providing senior management with an awareness about the value of communication and of the information services unit within the organization or community that supports it.

In fact, as a presenter at a 1991 conference on progress and innovation in the library/information profession, Eddison made specific comments about the role of the librarian/information professional as change agent. Her remarks, it seems clear, can be valuable to any information services manager with information aspirations higher than the simplest level of information delivery:

"Perhaps being a change agent is part of the continuum of change," she said. "I am a change agent. I know I am. But it wasn't because I sat down and said, I will be a change agent. It's because opportunities keep sliding under the door, or in the window, or over the transom, and if you recognize them and they fit where you are that day, you can march forward. That makes for change."

As for the information services practitioners themselves, can they be change agents? After all, this is not a profession particularly known for its adaptability, but Eddison has no fears on this score.

"This a marvelous profession," she says with a friendly smile. "It's one of the most creative groups of people I have ever seen. The only limits that we have are because we haven't looked far enough around the next corner. We really can do anything we want."

There's no doubt that with folks like Betty Eddison showing us the way, we will.

MARK MERRIFIELD's
entreprenuerial approach to public librarianship

Think about a public library where forty percent of the operating revenue comes from contract services and ten percent from endowment income. That's the story at the Martin Memorial Library in York, Pennsylvania, where Mark Merrifield is Director of Marketing and Development, a position created in late 1992. When Merrifield moved into the job in January, 1993, his specific brief was to develop strategic new mission and vision statements for the library, to move it into a new era of public library services, and (as Merrifield says) to "position the future library for providing new methods of service."

For Merrifield, the only way to go about it was to move entrepreneurially, to take a look at the library's service community and its needs, to connect solutions to needs which could be identified in other environments, and to put together a package of services that combines private and public support to everyone's advantage. That's what Merrifield set out to do, and in only two years his success curve has shot up at a remarkable rate.

To achieve that success, Merrifield and the staff at the Martin Library have taken the basic entrepreneurial characteristics of risk-taking, innovation, and change management and moved them into the public library arena. In fact, at Martin Memorial Library, the pattern seems to fit comfortably with some of Peter Drucker's basic ideas about entrepreneurship. Drucker has described entrepreneurship as an operational process "founded on a theory of economy and society" that sees change as normal and, indeed, as healthy. And the major task in society, according to this concept of entrepreneurship, is (as Drucker puts it), "doing something different rather than doing better what is already being done." He could have been talking about the folks at the Martin Library.

Originally published in *InfoManage : The International Management Newsletter for the Information Services Professional* 2 (1), December, 1994.

Any re-thinking or re-structuring begins, of course, with the vision, and after much planning, many meetings, and what Merrifield describes as a "lengthy, complicated process" involving staff working simultaneously with members of Martin's Board of Directors, the Friends of the Library, and other stakeholders in the community's information services picture, "Martin's Vision" was announced: the library would be reinvented as a "more active supplier of knowledge and inspiration. . . ." It would "respond to customers. . . ." It would take "assertive action required by the rapidly changing marketplace. . . ." It would "build relationships through new products and delivery systems." And, as important as anything else said in the library's vision statement, "innovative thinking and flexibility" would be the hallmarks of the library and its services.

Part of that complicated scenario involved the creation of a business plan for the library, and this is where Merrifield brought his expertise to bear. The plan he and his colleagues designed is twofold, with the first cycle (now about to be brought to fruition) emphasizing a marketing goal, concentrating on the growth of marketing awareness within the institution itself or, as Merrifield puts it, having the staff agree on "how to serve the customers." The second goal, looking at how to pay for information services the community needs, is the development cycle, now being geared up for major concentrated effort by both library staff and the directors.

It's in the financial component that the "innovative thinking" piece of Martin's vision statement comes most notably into play, as the library increases its activities as service contractor and retailer, actively getting more seriously involved in the information "business." Although Martin has provided contract services, as a District Library Center, for some years, and more recently, as a service provider with the School District of the City of York, these services are now increasing, having been targeted as a specific function of the Martin Library.

Obviously the decision to take on such activities required putting aside preconceived ideas of what a traditional public library should be doing. There were, for example, identified needs in the school system for library assistants, classroom collections, and a summer reading program for elementary schools. The educational authorities could not provide these services, but they could, for a fee, acquire them through the Martin Library. Doing so meant reworking some of the usual relationships between the educational community and the public library community, and writing some rather specific contracts, but it was a do-able activity once all the parties involved got over their usual prejudices about what a school or public library "ought" or "ought not" do.

For Merrifield, though, it's the connection with the specialized library and information services community where truly innovative marketing will pay off, for the library has discovered that it can provide consultation services, information brokerage services, and similar information activities, for a fee, to the research and specialized libraries in its geographical area.

To date, the most spectacular customer has been a local hospital library. In a recent "right sizing" exercise, hospital administrators decided to close the hospital library because they couldn't afford to keep it going. By serendipitous coincidence, the president of the hospital serves on the Board of Directors at Martin Memorial Library, and he asked Executive Director William Schell if there were any way Martin could help the hospital continue to offer library services to its professional staff.

Schell and Merrifield went to work, and within a weekend, the hospital's president had a proposal in hand, a proposal that not only provided continued library service but offered improved library service for the hospital, and now the hospital contracts all its library services through Martin Memorial Library. Staff travels to the hospital for specifically defined onsite work, and is available for reference and consultation at Martin via telephone and fax. Even tangibles get into the picture, for in order to offer enhanced library services at the hospital, additional computer equipment was needed, and Martin was able to provide the machinery, for a fee. It all comes together to provide information services for the hospital that the hospital couldn't have on its own, and the end result is that the hospital administration is satisfied, the hospital's information customers are satisfied, and Martin Memorial Library creates revenue by doing what it has always done, that is, providing excellent information services, but to a different (and fee-paying) customer base. The success of the contracted effort has led Martin to market similar products and services to other specialized libraries in the community, and the public library is now a major information provider, on a contract basis, for businesses in York.

And the risks?

Merrifield smiles, and the confidence of the marketing and development manager comes through.

"I suppose you would call the kinds of risks we take 'calculated,' or 'educated,' risks," he says. "We aren't going to offer to do anything we'll lose our shirt on, but it's not difficult to look at some of the things we're doing on a fee basis and determine that we can do them easier and for less cost than the customer is currently paying.

"The hospital library, for example. When the idea came up, we looked at our internal resources. We had people on our staff who had experience in hospital librarianship, we could fit the new program into our usual operations without too much disruption, and we had people who were flexible in their approach to library work."

That flexibility, included in the library's vision statement, is of course a serious factor in reducing the risks, for Merrifield, Janice E. Herrold, the President of Martin's Board of Directors, and Executive Director William H. Schell have all committed to the creation of a very flexible organization, one in which, as Merrifield says, "the staff agrees to be flexible."

"There's a basic theme of cooperation between the library and its various constituent user groups," he says, "and it's the kind of cooperation that requires a high level of flexibility in all library staff."

Certainly the theme is played out in the relationship between the library and the local school authorities. Here is another group for whom the Martin Library provides special services, some for a fee, some not. For example, in addition to the contracted services referred to earlier, there is a "Homework Center" at the Martin Library, created specifically to support students of all ages with their assignments. Without question, this and other special services designed for and offered to specifically targeted segments of the library market position Martin as an entrepreneurial library of note in today's information services marketplace.

And the concepts of marketing, customer services, and the like? Are the people involved comfortable with these designations, these terms that are usually not connected with traditional library services?

"In the first place," Merrifield replies, "the Martin Library doesn't see itself as a 'traditional' library. If you want to characterize how we see ourselves, look at the vision statement. Or the intentions we announced in our last annual report, to 'turn our dreams into realities with sound financial planning, to step into the future with state-of-the-art technology.' Those aren't the planning concepts usually associated with a 'traditional' library.

"On the other hand, we have to recognize that everyone won't come on board at the same time. You asked about our comfort level with the entrepreneurial terminology. It's not a problem for many of us. Certainly the Board of Directors is comfortable using such terms as 'marketing,' 'customers,' and so forth. For some of the staff, it's been a little slower, a learning experience, but we work with them, we support them, and remember, we hire people for their flexibility. They agree to be flexible when they come to work for us. So we don't really have a problem with the terms."

And the relationships with the public authorities, with the funding authorities? With only fifty percent of its operating income coming from public funds, what kind of a message is the Martin Library sending to the funding authorities in its various jurisdictions?

"That we're not on the public dole," Mark Merrifield answers quickly, and with considerable assurance. "We're telling the people who make library funding decisions for the state of Pennsylvania, for the City of York, and for York and Adams Counties (which we also serve), that we recognize our own responsibility. We have to earn the support we obtain from the public authorities, and we're glad to do it."

What they're doing in York, Pennsylvania, is not just telling the authorities. They're telling the public, too, and the private sector as well, that library and information services are a valuable part of the community, valuable enough that they, the people who provide them, are willing to accept their share of funding them. It's a new look at public library service, but it's an approach that bodes well for library and information services in York. That can't be said about a lot of places.

Meet Mark Merrifield

When interviewed, Mark Merrifield had been Director of Marketing and Development at Martin Memorial Library, York, PA since 1993 . . . Previously, from April, 1988, Director of the Adams County Library System, Gettysburg, PA . . . Other career service as Business Reference Specialist for the Alexandria, Virginia, Public Library, preceded by other positions at Alexandria beginning in 1980. MLS from the University of Maryland, 1986. He is now Director, Nicolet Federated Library System in Green Bay, WI. Member, Information Futures Institute, American Library Association, Public Library Association, Pennsylvania Library Association. Personal interests include naval history, hiking, and cooking.

JUDY MACFARLANE
at the Price Waterhouse Business Information Center:
An intrapreneurial approach to providing information
for the Montréal business community

When Judy Macfarlane came to Price Waterhouse sixteen months ago, she had a specific job to do. She was to design and implement a Business Information Center for the firm's Montréal office, and she was to do it in three years. It would be a challenge—she knew that—for there had been no central information resource for the Montréal office until she appeared on the scene. But Judy Macfarlane is a person who seems to take special delight in working in challenging situations, and indeed, as one who relishes challenges (she is, after all, a ski instructor in her spare time!), Macfarlane was undaunted by the prospect of the task. It was something she knew she could do, and she knew she would do it well, so she threw herself into her work and the results, even at this early stage, are impressive.

"The mandate is clear," Macfarlane says. "Price Waterhouse is a client-centered organization, and building up a business information resource as one of the services the company can offer to its clients makes a lot of sense. The firm's clients need this information and we're already providing it for our internal customers, so it's only appropriate that we structure our business information operation so that we can offer these services to our clients as well."

So thanks to Judy Macfarlane, Price Waterhouse—at least in its Montréal practice—finds itself in an "intrapreneurial" situation.

"Oh, yes," laughs Macfarlane, recognizing the reference. "We've looked at the Gifford Pinchot book and all the other writings about 'intrapreneurial management' and we're putting the concepts to work for us. An information services operation is a natural for this kind of effort, and if you structure it right, there's a payoff from the very beginning."

Originally published in *InfoManage : The International Management Newsletter for the Information Services Professional* 2 (8), July, 1995.

There are specific steps to the intrapreneurial process, and Macfarlane slips comfortably into the subject when she describes how she and her staff moved into an intrapreneurial framework for their work at Price Waterhouse.

"Building the information infrastructure was our first step," she says. "Once we agreed that the offering of business information services was a viable goal for Price Waterhouse, we stepped right into planning and organizing the information operation so that it could be done. And to move in that direction, we had to first build the 'inside' infrastructure, to create a Business Information Center that would provide the information that the firm's staff needed in order to do its work."

Currently, however, the whole concept of 'building' has had a special meaning for Macfarlane, for the several days leading up to the *InfoManage* visit to her office had been remarkable, in every sense of the word. As a leader in the Special Libraries Association (Macfarlane, until June 14, was a Director and had additional responsibilities as Secretary to the Board of Directors), Macfarlane had, of course, been involved in preparations for the organization's 86th Annual Conference, held this year in Montréal, on June 10–15. Additionally, however, because her firm is located in the glamorous new IBM building in downtown Montréal, she and the Price Waterhouse partners had been even more involved, for the Association's first ever President's Reception, a fund-raiser for the SLA Research Fund, had been scheduled in the building's seemingly mile-high glass-and-stone atrium, and Macfarlane had been caught up in those preparations as well. And just to complete the picture, since it had been determined some time ago that a major reconstruction was required for the Business Information Center, Macfarlane and her colleagues had scheduled the packing, moving, and building work for the week of the conference, in order to keep the downtime to a minimum.

Did someone say something about challenges?

It doesn't seem to be a problematic situation for Macfarlane, for she is obviously a person who cares very much about her work, about the role of her unit within the organization, and about the information products, services, and consultations that she and her staff deliver.

"The success of the effort is built on commitment," she says, "commitment from the partners and commitment from the information staff. In fact, it's the commitment from the partners that is the second critical component of this operation. While, as I mentioned, we must first build up an internal information infrastructure, so that the partners and employees of Price Waterhouse have available to them the information services they need to do the work they must do, we must also have strong support from the partnership and that, I'm happy to say, is there.

"Of course," Macfarlane continues with a wry smile, "the proof will be in the success of the operation. You have to remember that any success in the accounting field relates to the basis of the organization. We're a firm that earns its revenue from hourly charges to the client, and my staff and I—just like other Price Waterhouse employees—are required to file a specified number of chargeable hours per client. With internal customers, we charge against the accounts they are working for, and with external clients, we bill directly. In either case, it is a structure for evaluating—with a monetary value—the work we do. It gives us financial figures—bottom line figures—to work with.

In those terms, is the Business Information Center successful yet?

"Absolutely," Macfarlane says, and you can hear the pleasure in her voice, for this is obviously a risk that was worth taking. It has paid off. "We are already recovering fifty percent of our operational costs, and we expect to double the number of external clients within another year, so we are on track and we are confident we are going to be successful."

The third component in this information picture is, of course, the commitment of the information staff, and that is where Macfarlane is particularly proud of the success of the operation. There are four of them in the Business Information Center (three information professionals and one support person). In addition to their work with external clients, they provide for the information needs of some 320 employees in the Montréal office and 75 or so at Quebec City. It's a big market, and the workload is a full one, but at this stage in the process, no one is complaining. All members of the information staff understand what their roles are, and the team approach to information delivery—the value of which is one of Macfarlane's strong beliefs—is implemented every day at the Business Information Center.

One of the key components in any modern information delivery program is, of course, an acknowledgment that end-user delivery is part of the information services picture, and Macfarlane and her staff are available to work as trainers and information navigators with end-users who come to them for advice. But they are moving cautiously into the "virtual library" environment, primarily because—with information services for so many customers—licensing costs would be prohibitive. Yet there are other reasons.

"End-user searching," Macfarlane says, "is not always necessary. What we have to be careful about is the easy assumption that our customers—who are not information specialists—want to be deeply involved in information work. That's not necessarily the case within our organization and, in fact, it's really very seldom the case. It's just not their role, and while we are happy to network certain CD products for certain groups, or even for everyone, if that's appropriate, it would be inappropriate to assume that everyone needs all of the available information resources all the time.

"And besides, that's what we're here for," she says. "I wouldn't presume to offer an audit opinion, and certainly the staff at Price Waterhouse wouldn't expect to be experts in information delivery. That's why they come to us."

In the final analysis, it's all relates to balance, and understanding that achieving a workable balance between customer expectations and the realities of information delivery in the partnership environment requires special skills in the information services staff. Finding people with those skills has been one of Macfarlane's goals, and in fact she is quick to redirect the conversation so that she isn't misunderstood.

"Of course the skills are important," she says, "but primarily what we have to have are information workers who have the competencies and attributes that are required for working in this kind of information environment. What we need in this work are people who are self-motivated and who have strong communication skills."

It's not a moot point with Macfarlane. In fact, she feels so strongly about some of these issues that she wrote, with Miriam Tees, an important article on the subject ("Special Library Education and Continuing Education in Canada," *Library Trends*, Fall, 1993). In the article, Macfarlane and Tees very specifically identified three "areas of competence" (as they called them) for success in special librarianship, and the first two are not hard to understand: information related/technological skills and management skills. For the former, being adept in the reference interview process and having in-depth knowledge of information sources and/or subject expertise are required. For the latter, information professionals must understand the planning process, organization methods, budgeting, marketing, and supervision, and they must have control of the information function in their organizations.

It's in the third category that Macfarlane and Tees make their real contribution, for they assert that successful special librarians must also have what they call "attitude" skills: the people who are going to be successful in today's information services environment must demonstrate "a professional attitude, commitment to service, enthusiasm, the ability to communicate, idealism, vision, flexibility, dedication, and motivation."

That's a very tall order for information services professionals. And the obvious question of course comes to mind: has Macfarlane been able to find those people for the Price Waterhouse Business Information Center?

Again, the smile, and this time it is a smile of pride.

"Let me tell you about two of our staff," Macfarlane says. "One of our people, Karen Bleakley, has developed her own clientele and she is definitely stronger in some areas of research than I am. She also is well known in the profession, and this year was the program planner for SLA's Information Technology Division as those people prepared to come to Montréal for the SLA Conference. I'm very proud of her development. I hired Karen before she graduated from McGill University and I've kept her with me. Her skills are complimentary to mine and, in fact, she has since acquired a Graduate Diploma in Management Information Systems from McGill, so we will continue to work together in a complimentary fashion.

"In another direction, the work I do with Linda McCallum is equally complimentary. She graduated last year, and I expect to have the same success with Linda that I had with Karen! Her undergraduate degree is in Translation, and while for some information services professionals that might seem to be an esoteric field for bringing one into a specialized library, you have to understand that everything we do, from routing slips to memos to shelf labels, must be in French and in English, so having someone like Linda to work with us is an enormous asset."

So what we are talking about here is, yet once again, the team approach to information delivery. With Macfarlane, obviously, it combines with the mentoring of quality people into the profession, but it is not simply an altruistic dreamy attempt to provide some sort of "idealistic" workplace.

"Of course not," Macfarlane says. "What we're doing is pretty simple when you get right down to it. We put together a staff that can work independently and interdependently. We're all different in certain ways. We have different skills and different approaches to our work. And that is just what the company needs. As you can see, the people who work for me certainly aren't clones of me, and I wouldn't want them to be!"

So it's teamwork, it's mentoring, it's understanding the value of information, and it's understanding the cost of providing that information. And more than anything else, perhaps, it's having the ability to link the information services operation to the company's goals and objectives, to the company's mission. When you can do that as clearly and as efficiently as Judy Macfarlane is doing it at the Price Waterhouse Business Information Center, you're well on the way to that success that information services executives are looking for. You know what your information customers need, and you have the information structure—with all its many parts—to provide it.

Meet Judy Macfarlane

Since 1993, Judy A. Macfarlane has been the Director of Business Information Services at Price Waterhouse in Montréal . . . Prior to that, she was for 13 years Senior Manager for Information Resources at KPMG Peat Marwick Thorne in Montréal. Earlier experience includes work in high school, public, and academic libraries (in the last of which she worked with government documents) . . . Active in the Special Libraries Association, an international association of some 15,000 information services professionals . . . Just finished a term as a member of the Association's Board of Directors, for which she served as Secretary, sitting on SLA's Association Office Operations Committee as well as on the SLA Finance Committee, with responsibility for a budget of some US$4 million . . . A past president of SLA's Eastern Canada Chapter, Macfarlane is well known as a co-instructor for two of the organization's most popular professional development programs, "Evaluating the Corporate Library" and "Rightsizing: Dealing with the New Economic Realities," both of which offer instruction to information services practitioners about the assessment of the value of corporate information services . . . Macfarlane is also an occasional lecturer at McGill University's Graduate School of Library and Information Studies . . . a frequent author of articles in both internal publications and professional journals and fluent in both written and spoken English and French, Macfarlane serves as an Editorial Advisor to *InfoManage* newsletter for the Information Services Executive . . . Married to entrepreneur Peter Macfarlane, the couple and their son Brendan spend their weekends at a country house far away from the city and, when the weather permits, look forward to skiing, their favorite sport.

VICTOR ROSENBERG
teaches information people who to be entrepreneurial.
He also runs his own company—it's a combination that works

Fourteen years ago, Victor Rosenberg started his own entrepreneurial venture. PBS, Inc. (also known as Personal Bibliographic Software, Inc.) was created so that Rosenberg and his colleagues could develop software to make it easier for scholars, librarians, scientists, and other researchers to access and manage information. It's a concept they called "Desktop Research," and it grew out of a desire to do something about the ever increasing volume of information. Researchers and librarians were spending inordinate amounts of time sifting through card catalogs, notes, journal articles, and reprint files to find the information they needed, and Rosenberg wanted to fix that. His ideas about desktop research led to the creation of a company that would assemble a number of products that make life easier for people who need to be moving information around. Among these were Pro Search, Biblio-Links, and Pro-Cite, all of which are now well known in the library and information services community.

It's a subject Rosenberg knew something about, this business of moving information around. He was (and still is) on the faculty of the University of Michigan School of Information and Library Studies at Ann Arbor, and as a scholar and an academic, he had had first-hand experience with the constraints of the usual methods of information delivery. PBS, Inc., which grew out Rosenberg's research at the university, was at first a purely separate operation.

"I was what is known as a 'faculty entrepreneur,'" he says, "meaning that I was expected to do research and also expected to do something with the results of my studies. For the first few years, it was something of a problem for me, for the faculty emphasis was pretty strong in my mind, and I was working pretty hard to keep the entrepreneurial part of my life

Originally published in *InfoManage : The International Management Newsletter for the Information Services Professional* 2 (10), September, 1995.

separate from the university. In those days, I never felt comfortable linking the two."

That changed, of course, as Rosenberg continued his research and began to realize that the same skill sets that make for a good faculty member are the same skill sets that make for a good entrepreneur. And vice versa. In fact, it wasn't long before Rosenberg had figured out that the entrepreneurial experience in the information services field was an experience that would be useful to him as he worked with his students.

"Not that I would say that entrepreneurial skills can be applied across the board in the university setting," Rosenberg says. "When I say that the same skill sets are applicable in both the academic and business setting, I'm talking about the skills that enable an entrepreneur—or a faculty member—to start up a company or a project. When we get to talking about the skills necessary for running a company, I think the two groups diverge."

It isn't the relationship with the other faculty and the university that claim the lion's share of Rosenberg's attention, though. In his work at the university, it's the teaching that has him excited, and he has achieved a certain fame for his course in "Entrepreneurial Librarianship," taught at Ann Arbor. He himself teaches the course, as would be expected, but he brings in various colleagues—entrepreneurs in their own right—to work with him in putting across certain points. The combination seems to be working, for the course continues to be popular, and it is offered every year. And its focus is exactly what its title says it is: Rosenberg is attempting to impress on librarians and other information services professionals just beginning their careers that the same attributes that make for success in the business community can result in successful library/information services management.

"In the very first lecture," Rosenberg says, "I try to make it clear that even if the students aren't interested in starting a business, the skills they would need for business success—budgeting, a willingness to take risks, customer focus, marketing—all lend themselves to success in library and information work."

Even offering such a course is something of a departure for many graduate education programs in information studies. In many institutions—although it's not the case at Michigan—it's something of a given that adjunct faculty teach the "real" management subjects (if they're offered at all). Tenured faculty are often not available, since they are busy teaching other subjects, often subjects more related to library and information services as a discipline of its own. So to have an on-site, real-live entrepreneur on the faculty and teaching a course about entrepreneurial skills for librarians is unusual, to say the least. And in library schools, like everywhere else, change comes slowly and not without some resistance.

"Certainly when we started the course there was some resistance," Rosenberg says, and you can almost hear the smile in his voice as he recalls his early efforts to get the course accepted. This man obviously has a little rebellious streak, and he takes just the littlest bit of pleasure in rebutting the accepted conventional wisdom.

"When the curriculum committee had to look at the proposed course," he says, "there was some reluctance to accept it because there was no 'theory' behind the concept of entrepreneurial librarianship. But how could there be? The entire entrepreneurial perspective is, by definition, an avoidance of theory."

The course did get accepted, but it is interesting to note that the entrepreneurial concept wasn't what the curriculum committee was willing to buy. After all, Rosenberg points out, "despite all the talk about innovation, universities are not necessarily the most entrepreneurial of organizations."

Yet it wasn't that the curriculum committee was in any way against a course in entrepreneurial librarianship. There just wasn't any experience or framework to which the committee could attach the concept.

"When they asked me about this lack of a theory, and as we discussed it and I was telling the committee about some of the subjects that would be included in the course, it was the marketing piece that saved the day," Rosenberg says. "Of course. There are all sorts of theories about marketing, and if marketing is included as part of entrepreneurial librarianship, then it makes sense. So the course was approved, and we're still teaching it today."

Even so, other resistance sometimes comes from the students themselves, for they are often—especially the ones coming from a strictly humanities background—worried about the idea of linking entrepreneurial thinking with information delivery.

"For some reason," Rosenberg says, "these students come to us with ideas about the role of the library which don't match what is going on in the real world. They seem to think that the library is a kind of last refuge for a socialized community, and they can't understand how people involved in librarianship can 'sell out' to entrepreneurial thinking. I'm troubled by that.

"It's not that I am a crass capitalist," Rosenberg says, warming to his theme, "for I'm not. I believe very strongly that a purpose of government is the redistribution of income, to provide for those who are in need. In fact, I'm known as something of a 'socialistic entrepreneur,' because I'm not prepared to accept the extremes, the divisions, that an entrepreneurial society, strictly interpreted, calls forth. For example, one of the things we've seen since the collapse of communism and socialism is that those points of view now have a bad name, that they're seen as the opposite extreme from what is 'good.' That's not what we need. What we need is a blend. Otherwise you get situations like I had when I lived in Brazil, where you find yourself sending your children to school with a bodyguard to look after them."

Then what is it that brings students to graduate work in library and information studies with such an antipathy toward entrepreneurial librarianship? Why are they attracted to a field in which they are predisposed to resist innovation?

"There are no easy answers," Rosenberg says, "but some of it might have to do with the way librarianship and the library establishment seem to have been characterized as a helping profession, a nurturing profession. Those are the fields in which much is expected of the practitioners, and yet there is very little money to support them. In fact, at the risk of being crass about it, I often joke that the difference between a librarian and an information professional is about $25,000 a year."

And that is just about as neat a way as we can find to segue into a discussion of PBS's products and Rosenberg's company, for products like Pro-Cite and Biblio-Links have been created to help librarians and others involved in the delivery of information add value to the work they do. As such, not only do librarians benefit from the presence of these products in their libraries or information centers, but the very way in which the products come to their attention can be linked to the way information services people are marketing their own services.

"Why we're here, basically," Rosenberg notes, "is to provide help for people to do their jobs, and that's what librarians do for their users. It has much to do with the way librarianship and information services are being defined today. If, for example, the information customers are able to do much of the searching themselves as end-users then the librarian becomes in effect the person that end-user goes to when he or she wants guidance. The users want to know what to read, what to do, and the librarian's role is now more than ever one of guiding, of making value judgments about what the users can use."

Before the point is made, however, Rosenberg is quick to assure his listener that he recognizes that this is not the usual way of looking at these subjects in traditional librarianship.

"No, it's not censorship, and I prefer to look at this entire phenomenon from a positivist point of view. Librarians try to be 'objective,' providing information but never selecting it for the user. The librarian equates selection with censorship. But the librarian is there to tell the user what is important, to augment the users' own skills. That's what I mean when I say, for example, that Pro-Cite is a tool that enables librarians to add value to the information function. In the past, librarians and libraries have been seen as carrying out a more-or-less 'find-and-fetch' function, with the user making the value judgment. If that is all librarians do, they can be replaced easily by machines. Now there's too much information for the user to do that, no matter how sophisticated he or she is about information matters. What the librarian does now is enable the user to use the information. The user doesn't have to spend time gathering the information."

In talking about this new role for librarianship, this new status which requires the librarian to take a more proactive role, Rosenberg has, of course, brought the conversation back to where it was supposed to be, for it is through the application of entrepreneurial skills, the risk-taking, the innovative thinking, the customer focus, and the marketing, that the "new" librarian can provide those value-added services that the users now require. Rosenberg illustrates his point with a story.

"I was with another librarian not too long ago, and in our conversation, he made the point that the access problem has been solved. Now, he asked me, what do we do? Meaning, what is it that librarians will do now that their customers can find their own information?"

But it's not that easy yet. Rosenberg makes it clear that all the problems have not been solved, for there is a long tradition of "find-and-fetch" that is going to be with us for many years to come. But as his colleague's remark illustrates, there is also a willingness in librarianship today to recognize that the information retrieval function is not necessarily the only way to operate. In fact, before too long it may very well be a thing of the past, simply because there are other information providers and practitioners who—probably sooner rather than later—will be able to "find-and-fetch" better than librarians can. And if the librarians have not moved on to the value-added role, there won't be a place for librarianship.

Is it such a bleak scenario? Not at all, for one of the impressions that Vic Rosenberg leaves you with is that the entrepreneurial approach to librarianship, things like the adding of value, the marketing, the customer focus, all come together to enable the librarian to do a better job of helping people distinguish between what's important and what's not. It's obvious, of course, that using tools like those created by PBS, Inc. is a step in that direction, and it's a good direction. If librarians are willing to move in that direction, if they're willing to be the entrepreneurs that their users need, they don't have anything to worry about.

Meet Victor Rosenberg

Victor Rosenberg is Chairman and C.E.O. of Personal Bibliographic Software, Inc., in Ann Arbor, Michigan. He is also Associate Professor of Information and Library Studies at The University of Michigan . . .

Dr. Rosenberg is the author of numerous papers, films, and software packages. He is a member of the American Library Association and the American Society of Information Science, and he has just completed his tenure as Chairman of the Nominating Committee of ALA's Library and Information Technology Association . . . Prior to coming to Ann Arbor, Dr. Rosenberg taught at the University of California at Berkeley after getting his doctorate in Library Science from the University of Chicago and a Masters degree in Information Science from Lehigh University . . . In 1976, he spent a sabbatical year teaching in Brazil . . . Dr. Rosenberg , who is married and the father of two children, lives in Ann Arbor.

▮▮

The "entrepreneur" in "entrepreneurial librarianship": perhaps
MIKE GRUENBERG
at Disclosure can provide some tips

Entrepreneurial librarianship. We're hearing it a lot these days. Whether it's just a fashionable buzzword in library and information services management, or whether an "entrepreneurial" perspective is truly a reasonable and appropriate approach to information delivery, today's information managers are hearing more and more about how enterprising and businesslike practices pay off in the information workplace. Not only do information customers get better service, but those who manage the information services operation have a framework that's built on customer satisfaction.

It's an appropriate model, according to Michael Gruenberg, Vice President for Public Sector Sales at Disclosure, Incorporated.

"The whole object is to get close to the customer," Gruenberg says, and his career with Disclosure is testimony to the value of making friends with the people you're selling to. It's a sales philosophy that he learned from his dad, who was also in sales, and it's a point of view that Mike Gruenberg has carried with him as long as he's been in business.

"If your customers like you," he says, "they'll buy from you. If they don't, they probably won't."

Certainly it's a point of view that's not about to be disputed by anyone who has ever watched Gruenberg and the Disclosure team in action. If you catch up with them at, say, the annual conferences of the Special Libraries Association, you soon realize that this is a sales team that makes friends. And it makes friends in numbers that leave other vendors back at the starting gate. Of course there's the product (Disclosure continues to be one of the major players in what is, to put it mildly, just about the toughest market in the information industry), but what really brings

Originally published in *InfoManage : The International Management Newsletter for the Information Services Professional* 3 (7), June, 1996.

home the bacon for Disclosure is the personal approach that Gruenberg exemplifies. These are people who like their customers and who take great pleasure in the interactions that grow up between them and the librarians and other information services managers they market to.

Gruenberg, who is well known in the library and information services community for his cheerful and fun-loving (dare we say "boisterous"?) personality, belies that shallow image with his seriousness of purpose. For him, providing a quality product that helps information providers do their work better is connected with knowing and caring about the people who are his customers.

"Relationships and friendships between clients and providers are an important part of it," Gruenberg says. "Sales to the library and information services community only work when we get to know our customers, and get to know them so well that we understand what they are looking for and can provide them with exactly what they need in order to do their jobs. One of my colleagues used to talk about how librarians are 'so grateful'—he used to say—to us for the work we do, but that just tells us that we're doing what we're supposed to be doing: we're giving the librarians the tools they need to help them service their internal customers."

It's an idea that has a place in information delivery these days, for it doesn't really matter whether the provider is a vendor selling a service to a library, or a librarian or other information provider offering services to an identified and specific user constituency. In both cases, understanding the needs of the "customer" is key to the success of the transaction. And when that transaction can include a friendly demeanor that links the provider with the customer, the success of the transaction is assured. It's the foundation of entrepreneurial management, and it works in libraries as well as it works in the marketplace.

Not that anybody should be surprised. For years Disclosure has been listening to its customers, and as new products have been developed, the success of those products has literally grown out of the relationships that the Disclosure people have developed with practitioners in the information industry. Disclosure Select, for example, one of the company's newest products (launched in February of this year) permits customers to view or print exact images of company documents from the PC desktop, a key priority which librarians and other information providers had made clear to Disclosure product developers and sales reps. As a result, the many applications that Disclosure Select can be used for, from competitive analysis, investor relations, client prospecting, joint venture research, all the way through to business school case studies, position the product as a very important one for people who are providing information products and services for their information customers.

Similar claims can be made for Disclosure's newest product, Global Access, which Gruenberg is particularly excited about.

"This is the kind of product we want to provide," he says, "because it is exactly what special librarians and others who deal with their own information customers have been asking for. When we ask librarians what they need, this is the kind of thing they tell us they want, and we worked hard to put this product together."

It's easy to see why Global Access is a product that Gruenberg is pleased with, and one he is happy to bring to his customers. Advertised as a "one-of-a-kind electronic index and on-line ordering system," the product's breadth of coverage is pretty spectacular, offering desktop access to financial and business information on more than 27,000 public companies worldwide, going back to 1968. It's a product that librarians need, and Disclosure has once again responded to its market.

Gruenberg's pride in what the company is doing goes a little beyond the good salesmanship, though, and the company's good products (although he would be the first to recognize the importance of those criteria). And it's sometimes a little sad for him to describe the context, for his history with the company relates to a personal connection as well, to his great friendship with Steven Goldspiel, the late President of Disclosure who died in 1992. Long-time friends, the two men had both been schoolteachers together, but both had left teaching in the early 70s. The change had been particularly ironic for Gruenberg, as he had received his layoff notice on the same day that his New York State Principal's license arrived in the mail.

So the two men went in different directions, with Gruenberg moving into the music industry as a record producer ("There were a few good years and then there were a few bad years"). Goldspiel had gone to Disclosure, owned then by Reliance Insurance, and then by Snyder-Hixon. When the "few bad years" got to be too many bad years, Gruenberg found himself looking for work and called his friend, who suggested that he come to work for him in sales at Disclosure.

It was a good fit, but one that was not apparent at first because it looked just too easy. Having been given the Northeast U.S. for his territory, Gruenberg hadn't been with the company long before he realized that while the big banks, other large privately held companies, and similar institutions were strong customers, there were major gaps in the public sector. Much to his surprise, he discovered that the universities, the graduate business schools, large public libraries, and similar public sector organizations were not customers, and they should have been. That gap in the market didn't make sense, and once Gruenberg began to investigate, he determined to fix things. He wanted to figure out how to get the public sector institutions as customers, and he set out to do so.

The first thing he learned came as no surprise.

"In sales," he says, "the goal is to move fast, make the deal, and close the deal. The private sector can handle this, and it's accepted as part of doing business. But this is not the case in the public sector, and with the built-in bureaucracies, there is not the incentive for the salesperson. The deal takes too long."

So, in typical Gruenberg fashion, he took a look at these public sector "prospects" and determined to call on them, to let them know what products and services Disclosure could offer them. The connections were made, and soon he had the public sector accounts he wanted. But it wasn't easy, and it took a lot of hard work, a lot of footwork, a lot of being out in the territory.

And—the kiss of death for most sales people—he had to deal with the bureaucratic timelag. How did he do it?

Gruenberg grins, and you can tell he likes telling the story.

"Volume," he says. "You call on lots and lots of prospects. It's a basic rule of sales: You throw enough possibilities into the air and eventually some of them come back as orders."

As a result of the volume of sales (and—let's not forget—all the footwork that went into getting that volume), Gruenberg became the company's leading sales representative. He had brought the public sector clients in, and kept the clients that were already on board from the for-profit sector, so his taking on the Northeast territory turned out to be a good fit after all. It was a neat piece of salesmanship, and it worked for Gruenberg and, obviously, for Disclosure as well. Together they've never looked back.

And reduced funding, that old public service bugaboo?

"Don't believe it," Gruenberg says. "If the customer tells me that funding has been cut, it's usually a situation in which the customer is just looking for an excuse to buy. It's time then for creative ways to help them buy."

When that happens, Gruenberg doesn't make any excuses of his own, for that's when it's his job—and what he trains his people to do—to make the product attractive to the customer. Once again, what might have been a problem for someone else becomes an opportunity for Mike Gruenberg. He goes to work on it, and if he does it right—and he usually does—that customer with the "lost" funding finds a way to get the Disclosure products back in place. It's a technique, but it's a technique that works to everyone's satisfaction, Disclosure's and the customer's.

So now it's been nineteen years that Gruenberg has been with the company, and although there is often a sense of personal loss since his friend is gone, the pleasure and excitement of selling a product that is needed and anticipated continue to be fulfilling.

And the industry itself? And library and information services? From Gruenberg's perspective, future prospects for the industry are good, which is just where he wants things to be.

"The companies that are succeeding," he says, "are the ones that are staying ahead with technology. So the industry looks good from a business point of view, and also from the view of the information provider, as long as the provider is willing to change to keep up with all that is going on."

So is it "entrepreneurial"? Is it "proactive"? "Creative"? "Market-focused"? Of course it is. And is it a climate in which the successes of the marketplace can be "transferred" to such service applications as librarianship and information delivery? Of course, as long as the basic tenets of entrepreneurialism can be incorporated into the service workplace. Things like innovation, risk-taking, understanding what the customers are looking for, taking on the burdens of the customers, they're all the hallmarks of quality salesmanship—as Mike Gruenberg has proven—and they can be the hallmarks of quality information delivery as well.

And it doesn't hurt—as Gruenberg and his librarian pals will be the first to admit—if we become friends and have some fun along the way.

Meet Mike Gruenberg

Michael L. Gruenberg was Vice President, Public Sector Sales, for Disclosure, Incorporated, when this interview was written. With direct responsibility for leading the Disclosure Sales Force in selling all subscription products offered by the company to the public sector, and for selling Primark company products to the public sector as well, Gruenberg's career with Disclosure has included several highlights. Since 1985, he has participated as the senior sales executive in the development, planning, and introduction of six new database products and five new document imaging products, and in 1988 he created and implemented the company's Telesales Department, now registering annual sales of $9 million. In February, 1998, Gruenberg became Vice-President, Sales and Marketing/North America, for Oxford Analytica, Ltd.

Prior to coming to Disclosure, Gruenberg had a seven-year career as a teacher in New York City schools, and was later President and Founder of Audio Talents, Inc., a musical management and production company. His undergraduate degree, with a political science major, is from Long Island University, and his graduate degree, M.S. in Educational Administration and Supervision, is from St. John's University. An avid tennis player, Gruenberg is also known for his delight in attending baseball games. He has a large record collection (which he describes as including "all kinds of music"), and he enjoys having his own jukebox at his home in Plainview, NY. Particular pleasures include spending time with his daughter Erica, a first-year student at SUNY, Buffalo.

CLAUDIA LUX
at the Senatsbibliothek Berlin:
Looking at information services with a political eye

That heart Frau Dr. Claudia Lux is drawing for her visitor is not a mis-dated valentine, and it's not a cute little attempt to make him think about information services the way he thinks about buying chocolates. That heart is the symbol Dr. Lux has chosen for demonstrating to her staff and to her library's customers—but especially to the political authorities who control the management of information at the Berlin Senat—that information is the core product of the Senat's work. It's the foundation on which all decisions are made, the framework on which all operations are structured, the very heart of the organization's functioning.

It's a good symbol, this heart, for Dr. Lux has been brought to the Senatsbibliothek to make change happen and to oversee a course of change management that is going to result in better services for all comers. And the list of information customers is pretty daunting, for it includes not only city agencies and administrative managers within the Berlin city government, but information users from throughout the country and, in some cases, from other countries of the European Union as well. In the long run, Dr. Lux is going to find out that connecting "heart" to the information delivery process is a very smart idea, for without it, without the, shall we say, "human" connection, the task of putting together a changed information operation for the Berlin Senat would be a bleak one indeed.

There's no question that change is needed. The facility Dr. Lux manages is part of the Berlin city government and up to now has been very much a "historical" collection. In the governmental hierarchy, the Senatsbibliothek comes under the supervision of the Ministry of Science, Research, and Culture, also responsible (as is typical in many European municipalities) for the supervision of the city's public libraries. Thus

Originally published in *InfoManage : The International Management Newsletter for the Information Services Professional* 3 (10), August, 1996.

there was for many years a focus on a very traditional, very collection-oriented type of library management within government agencies, and the Senatsbibliothek was part of this picture. Previous directors were very much librarians, very concerned with buying books, with building up a collection of materials (including antiquarian books) that would be available just in case anyone ever asked for them. Money was spent only on collections, only on buying more books (never on office furniture or decoration, for example), and little attention was paid to getting the information in those books—the content—to the people who needed it.

"Sadly," Dr. Lux says (and her voice tells you things are changing), "only those people who already knew about the special collections of the library got a very good, special service."

So the Senatsbibliothek was strongly associated with collecting, especially collecting everything that was published about Berlin, so much so that the library's primary function—to serve as an information support operation for city government—somehow got lost in all the paperwork and red tape. For example, one of the products the Senatsbibliothek provided was the "Berlin Bibliography," the all-inclusive catalog of everything published about the city. As Dr. Lux surveyed the library's products and services, the catalog obviously fell into that category of "nice-to-have" products we all like to be associated with, but which are hardly germane to the function of sophisticated information delivery to city agencies, the task for which the Senatsbibliothek had been created. Needless to say, the publication of the Berlin Bibliography is no longer a function of the Senatsbibliothek.

The Senat is Berlin's city government, and Dr. Lux is quick to point out that some distinction should be made about the kind of library the Senatsbibliothek is.

"It is not a parliamentary library," she says. "It is an information service that focuses on the function of government. The heart of the operation"—there's that word again—"is the service we provide. We are here to meet the information needs of a variety of clients. Our primary customers, and the people we give most attention to, are the administrative staffs of the fifty or so chapters or departments of the Berlin city government. Some of these have small libraries of their own, and the Senatsbibliothek provides back-up services, as these are frequently one-person libraries."

Dr. Lux continues describing the customer base for her operation. "The Senatsbibliothek also supports the information needs—relating to city government and the issues connected with that work—of the 23 Berlin 'boroughs,' I think you would call them. Each of these has its own administrative operation, courts, and laws, but there needs to be a central information agency related to the work of government, and that's what we provide."

The collection is not small, some 450,000 volumes, but as can be imagined, much of the material in the collection is not in standard book form, so a typical count by volume number is not, strictly speaking, the most accurate way to describe the library. There are many reports, documents, and other representations of the so-called "gray" literature, and much of what is collected comes into the Senatsbibliothek through its connection with the city government.

"We are a depository collection for everything published under the authority of Berlin city, and approximately 70% of the collection comes to us as donations," Dr. Lux says. "As for the library's subject specialty, there is a well-formed collection about local government subjects for the entire German-speaking community, including Switzerland and Austria, and we collect—and provide information for studies in—all the subjects having to do with city government. The development of parking zones, regulations for children's playgrounds, town planning, housing, all of these come into our subject sphere. We even focus some attention in the area of health studies, as we took over the Berlin Medical Library in 1983 and literature in that area is collected here as well. So this core collection—this 'heart' material—is then used to provide whatever administrators and other officials need."

Dr. Lux pauses in her description to give an example. "Recently," she said, "a senator was seeking to find all the financial plans for all of the federal states. He needed to compare figures, but nobody else had all of these documents. Of course they were found here, and that is a pretty typical situation. So in effect the Senatsbibliothek now functions as a special library—we might even say the premier special library—for all of Germany in the area of community studies."

About thirty people make up the staff at the Senatsbibliothek, and Dr. Lux is enthusiastic about the level of services they provide. Half of them have attained professional qualification and thus work at different levels of librarianship, a mix which provides a useful combination of talent that enables Dr. Lux to move forward with her program of change.

"Certainly the service focus is not on students," she says, "although they use the collections of the Senatsbibliothek in pursuing their studies in city-planning and architecture. For us, the focus is now on city administration, which is appropriate, as that is what is needed in Germany at the present time."

To that end, Dr. Lux describes how the library has shifted from serving as an interlibrary loan agency to a more direct service, of lending its own materials to the customers in the administration. At the same time, there is much more focus on providing the specific information the customer is seeking. So fax, mail, and e-mail are now utilized strongly as information delivery mechanisms, and while the staff is perfectly willing to provide the book and let the customer find the information for himself, if it is only the specific piece of information that is needed, the staff will provide that as well.

With its connections with government, it is not surprising that politics plays a role in Dr. Lux's management style.

"Of course," she says with a laugh. "My task is to move the Senatsbibliothek from a library into an information center. Our services need to be better known, and we need to process more, to do more. We can do that with the technology that is now available, but getting approval from the authorities to acquire that technology—and the people to set it up—is difficult. So we have to be political."

Just how political she must be becomes apparent when Dr. Lux tells of some of her recent "battles." In one situation, for example, she needed two new people for work in information technology, but from 1991 on, there was no money for additional staff. In fact, a 30% staff cut had been enacted, simply because with unification there were just too many people for the jobs that were available. She sought to outsource the work, but her administration was opposed to that, so she was left to her own devices. Coincidentally, however, she had identified an important new market for the Senatsbibliothek's services in the new administrative units that were opening up in the former Eastern sector of the city. For example, a contract between the Ministry of Science, Research, and Culture and the Institute of Urbanistic Studies obligated the Senatsbibliothek to provide special services, but meeting the terms of the contract required utilizing an information technology system Dr. Lux hadn't been able to get. By the spring of 1992, Dr. Lux was discussing the situation with the Minister of Culture, as well as with other people who could be useful in her cause, people she identified as "most influential, and who themselves would benefit."

It seemed to be the right approach, for she had positive responses, and she wrote up a formal document, a special draft to the Senat of Berlin, "but it somehow got stuck in the bureaucracy." Undaunted, Dr. Lux pressed forward, putting together a one-page document ("legislators won't read more than one page," she says) and having discussions with legislators. And at a special meeting of a decision group of the Berlin parliament, she was in the audience, but there was a problem.

"It looked as if my proposal wasn't going to be discussed," she remembers, "so I just went to the stage."

And there, in front of the amazed legislators, she made her case. In doing so, she was able to obtain approval of at least the "idea" of the proposal, but there wasn't money for the feasibility study. Aha! There again the "political" Dr. Lux had a response. Through her contacts, she could pull in funds from another project for which she had responsibility, in the amount of DM100,000. Now, since she already had approval for the "idea" and she herself could come up with the funds for the study, she was on her way.

Did it work?

"We have the study," she says, "and we have the funding for a five-year project of outsourcing the technical and many organizational problems associated with moving the Senatsbibliothek to an electronic environment. The contract is done, we have the hardware and software in place, and we've just started using the system as a first step."

And once the decisions had been made, things started moving fast.

"In April we were connected to the Berlin government's high-speed metropolitan area network," Dr. Lux notes, "giving us new possibilities for special services for our clients. Our alphabetical and systematic catalogs are being scanned, so we no longer produce catalog cards, and with the network in place, we're moving ahead with the CD-ROM and multimedia installations."

The entire effort involves much technical planning, but when asked about how involved she has been with the information technology, Dr. Lux has a quick response.

"I don't care about that," she says with a wry smile. "I just want the system that will do the work. What I do care about is the input/retrieval of the content. That's what our customers are interested in."

It's certainly a novel approach, this lack of interest in "controlling" the technical side, but Dr. Lux does not see it as such.

"Oh, no," she says, again with a smile that tells you she is probably very relieved not to have to deal with technology issues. "I don't have the control. I don't want it."

What she does control, of course, is the new "tone" that these changes have brought to the Senatsbibliothek, particularly in terms of the staff and its work.

"With the new system," Dr. Lux says, "the staff is already using in-house e-mail and the change has been incredible. And this movement forward is going on and on. The eighteen-day training program has had much to do with this, for as the entire staff went through the training, much of the earlier anxiety was calmed down."

And what about new hires? With the new system, will Dr. Lux and the Senatsbibliothek be seeking any special skills? Will she be looking for, say, traditional library skills in the people who come to work at the Senatsbibliothek?

"In the first place," she replies, "for a while—at least for the time being—there's no chance of hiring new staff, simply because of the general financial situation. If a position becomes free, we might be able to look for new hires. When that happens, we'll look for people who are flexible, creative, and without fear, because they will have to work a lot with bureaucracy, government employees, and a very wide range of different problems and situations.

"As for 'library skills,' we may want some of this, at least along the lines of 'information management methods,' but what we really need is flexibility and an ability to work well with other people, someone who can think about the 'big picture,' who cares about the future development of services, and is," she stops for emphasis, "practical!"

"What we really must have," she says, "are people who not only have ideas, but who talk about their ideas, who like working with clients and with their colleagues, who have fun in their work, and who don't fear responsibility."

That, in brief, might be the formula for the information worker of the future, if change is, as we're told, the hallmark of the future, and if the progress being made at the Berlin Senatsbibliothek is any indication. With all the change taking place, Dr. Lux says, "it's like being on an Achterbahn, like being on a rollercoaster that makes sudden curves, then speeds up going down, then slowly climbs back up again. You feel high when you're on the top, coming up with good solutions to the many problems that come along, driving forward. And our staff is doing it so well, giving in all their energies to move this process along."

What all this means, of course, is simply that Dr. Lux understands her role—and that of her staff—in the community of which they are a part, in the Berlin city government. She and they are there to work with the customers from the customers' point of view, to understand what those customers' needs are and what content the customers are concerned with. As for the mechanisms for getting that content to the customers, well, that is not her primary focus. Other people do that well, and she doesn't need to. And she's happy to make the distinction.

Meet Claudia Lux

Since 1991, Frau Dr. Claudia Lux has been Direktorin of the Senatsbibliothek Berlin, the official library and information center for the Berlin city government. Prior to coming there, however, her career path had been anything but information focused. Her early studies were in social science, and she obtained her doctorate in Sinology, specializing in Chinese politics and economics, a field in which she expected to have her career. While working on her dissertation at the Staatsbibliothek, she was recruited to study librarianship, which she did during a two year training program which she undertook in the mid-1980s. When she completed her studies, she was appointed, at first part-time, to a position in the East Asian Department of the Staatsbibliothek, while at the same time she was working, also part-time, with the Deutsches Bibliotheksinstitut, where she was involved in establishing standards for fees in libraries and for retroconversion projects. She returned to the Staatsbibliothek full time in 1989, when she was employed as Specialist in the Chinese Collection, the largest such collection in Germany. It was from the Staatsbibliothek that Dr. Lux moved to the Senatsbibliothek. She is a native of Ruhrgebiet, in the industrial center of the Western part of Germany.

Dr. Lux spends her leisure time with her family and, as a special interest, she enjoys adding to her large collection of paperweights, the popular Schneekugeln ("snowballs"), many of which are displayed in her office.

5

MANAGEMENT PRACTICES IN
INFORMATION SERVICES—PLANNING

f conceptualizing, organizing, and thinking entrepreneurially are the foundation on which successful change management is built, planning change and implementing change are the obligatory next layer. And it is a layer (if we want to think about successful change management as a pyramid with four levels) that is equally matched by one that follows, for two important layers build on the conceptualization/organization/entrepreneurial thinking base.

The first of these layers, or levels, has to do with planning for change management. Obviously, as described in the interviews in which industry leaders talked about how they conceptualize change, once the conceptualization has been created, it must be planned for and implemented. The planning is the tricky part, for no sooner has one set of ideas and plans been agreed upon, than circumstances change, or political and/or fiscal influences intervene, and the change leader in the organization must look for new approaches or, more likely, be willing to adapt what has been agreed upon to the specifics of the particular situation.

Mary Park knows this, and in the discussion in her interview in this chapter, she recognizes that the whole concept of "partnering," so much discussed in information services, is perfectly valid, but for success in planning for change management, it must include the organization's senior management as a key player in the partnering effort. Otherwise, the proposed change will have little chance of success, simply because—lay persons all—senior management must be brought "up to speed" if these people are to be recruited into a supportive and committed role in the organization's information delivery activities. Park makes these points in the interview, and she later built on them, and made others, in a valuable book of her own on the subject.

Such partnering is not to be taken lightly, as Tom Lutgen and his staff at *The Los Angeles Times* Editorial Library make clear. When Lutgen talks about planning for change management at his place, the role of senior management—and the cooperative environment in which the commitment to excellence in information delivery is simply expected—becomes clear.

Planning, as a management methodology in and of itself, and not necessarily as a part of the change management process, is commonly recognized as essential in any successful operation. What often happens, as Mary Dickerson demonstrates when she describes *directional* planning as practiced at the Ontario Legislative Library, is that a new management tool becomes a change management tool as well. At her place, when it became evident that change was going to come, whether the library and its staff were ready for it or not, Dickerson determined to be ready, insisting, for example, that all senior managers in the library agree on priorities. She was, in effect, planning for change at the most fundamental level, and it worked. And in the process, it created a new "slant" on the management experience, one that Dickerson and her staff could characterize with a name, *directional management*.

Planning as a critical "essential" is the key to the work that Ethel Himmel and Bill Wilson describe, as they talk about the planning and transformation process that is now required in the American library management environment. For Himmel and Wilson, libraries are now required to be in a "continuous transformation process," because, as they enthusiastically proclaim in their book on the subject, "libraries that plan are more likely to achieve positive results; and results are what it's all about!"

And results are what Lucy Lettis is all about. At Arthur Andersen's New York Business Information Center, Lettis has taken up the change management challenge and is very nearly, well, *relentless* in her pursuit of excellence for the operation she manages. Lettis is not satisfied to provide ordinary information delivery, and she works hard to establish an information presence for herself and her staff at the parent organization, noting that her role, as she sees it, is to accomplish three "rewards," three measures of success that will indicate to her that the operation she manages is an information operation that *works*. It is a formula for any manager with information delivery responsibility who aspires to success: "Of course we do it for the customers," Lettis says, "and of course we do it so our organizations can succeed, but we also do it because we're good at what we do, and there is satisfaction in that." When planning for change management in information services includes that three-part recognition, successful change management is not far off.

MARY PARK
thinks "partnering" is a good idea—
if the partner is senior management

Mary Park's experience in providing high-level business executives with information has led her in many different directions. None has been as important as the growing realization that the way executives use information does not necessarily match what information providers think they understand about how these executives use information. It's a disparity that most of us don't think much about.

In fact, these two groups of workers are often so far apart in their thinking about information that Park has taken it upon herself to bring them together. It is a formidable task, but one Park has undertaken with considerable enthusiasm and determination, both characteristics that one discovers—after only a few meetings with her—that are part and parcel of her approach to her work. It's this combination of enthusiasm and determination that has made her company, The Information Consultancy, one of the major players in the information brokerage community, and it's this same combination that is launching Mary Park into a role as

Originally published in *InfoManage : The International Management Newsletter for the Information Services Professional* 3 (2), January, 1996.

"philosopher-thinker" in a profession that is not particularly distinguished for its philosophic inclination.

"Oh, no," she laughs. "Don't make too much out of the 'information/philosopher' part. It's not something that I set out to do, and I'm not sure anything is going to come of it."

She pauses in her conversation, and it's clear she is thinking about how she wants to characterize what it is she is doing. "I'm just talking about things I've observed," she says, "and some of the conclusions I've come to."

But isn't that what philosophy is? And besides, Mary Park is moving in some very specific leadership directions within the information services field, and if her own modesty prevents her from making "too much" of her contributions, her activities speak for themselves, especially with regard to those issues having to do with the value of information, the role of the information worker, and the ways information is used to contribute to a company or organization's success.

In October, for example, Park co-sponsored an important seminar put together by the Greater Baltimore Committee's Technology Council (of which she is a member) on the subject of "The Information Literate Executive." She also led an impressive discussion at the seminar, the title of which was "Key Information Issues and Developments in the 1990s: The Role of Information Literacy in the World of Business." That presentation, combined with a book she has just finished about how executives use information, can certainly put to rest any qualms she might have about her role as a thinker in the information services field.

For Park, it all grew out of her career as an information provider in a field in which information is critical to success but isn't always recognized as being so. That field is business, of course, and she comes to business information work from an investment and finance background, so she well understands the value of information in the corporate environment. In fact, she understands it so well that she long ago came up with her own metaphor to depict the information scene as she sees it. She calls it "The Sisyphus Dilemma."

"Sisyphus, of Greek mythology, knew all too well how it felt to be overloaded, overworked, and overwhelmed," she says. "He was condemned by the gods to eternal labor by pushing a heavy stone up a mountain, only to have it roll back on him. As our information overload increases—and it will become more burdensome in the future—information professionals and information users need to understand and practice core information competencies if they expect to succeed in the work they do."

If there's any question about just how burdensome that information overload is becoming, Mary Park—like so many of us who deal with information on a daily basis—has her own technique for dealing with what we're talking about here. She's quick to admit that it isn't original with her, but it works nevertheless.

"Of course I quote [Peter] Drucker all the time," she says with a laugh, "just like the rest of us. And his comment about data being what *was*, information being what *is*, and knowledge being what *could be* is a neat way for compartmentalizing this information overload we information professionals must deal with."

The problem, of course, then becomes one of dealing with it for others as well, for "information"—as a concept in our society and from the lay person's point of view—has come to mean just about anything that anybody wants it to mean. Information professionals, whether they're management personnel with information services responsibilities or the information providers themselves, are the people who have to clear the air, so to speak, to cut through the layers of information overload and show information customers how to handle the problem.

For Park, it isn't such a large step to finding the solution, and she reckons that it is emphasizing the content in the information transaction that will bring both the information professionals and their information customers the success they are hoping to achieve.

"The point is to raise the awareness of executives—and of IT people—about content and what it means for their success. The objective is to get to knowledge. It's knowledge that creates productivity and wealth. What's keeping us from getting there is a lack of core information competencies, what we call 'information literacy.' This includes technology—as the conduit that carries the information—and the content. In today's information environment, one cannot exist without the other."

Those competencies, those basic skills and experiences and abilities that enable us "to access the information and to use that information in a manner that creates knowledge" (as Mary Park puts it) have been discussed and argued about in the information services field for a long time. Of course each practitioner seems to have his or her own list—most of whose items, fortunately, seem to overlap—and Park is no exception. The

difference for Park, though, is that it's the understanding of these competencies, on the part of both the information customer and the information provider, that makes the information transaction work. And for this
to happen, Park moves the concept up the management ladder one more
step. Not only do both the people who provide information and the people who use it have to understand these competencies, those who make
decisions about information within the organization must get involved as
well. It's here that the present information services management process
seems to break down.

"What we're really talking about here is connecting, or linking up, two
different groups of people," Park says. "The people we should really be
focusing on are the decision makers, the people who buy the technology,
who start libraries, who have research and development teams in their
organizations, and the second group, what we call the 'information
providers,' the librarians, the information professionals, and the brokers.
It's these two groups that have to come together, and unfortunately it's a
little too early yet to know where this is going to go. Over the last couple
of decades or so, we've had a tendency to get lost in the technology and in
the management layers, and that has caused much of the confusion. And,
not coincidentally, that's why so many CIOs only think of the technology
when they think about 'information.' No one has worked with them on
the content, and that's the 'piece' of it that leads to acquiring that knowledge we were talking about.

"In fact," Park continues with some enthusiasm (and it soon becomes
obvious that this is a subject she's pretty excited about), "the decision
maker doesn't even have to know about the process. He or she doesn't
have to look under the hood. But that person does have to go directly to
the information provider, or the information will get lost in the process,
either in the 'conduit,' in the 'information technology' structure, or in the
different layers of management that exist within the organization. So the
direct link has to be between the decision makers and the information
providers. All the rest is just the mechanism that makes that link happen."

How do you make it happen, this link that Mary Park is talking about,
this connection between the information provider and the organizational
decision makers?

"It's not easy," she says, and for the first time you see a look of concern that clouds what has been, so far, a delightfully optimistic and positive conversation. "It's especially not easy for information services

executives, who are themselves attempting to deal with these misunder-standings about conduit and content, these 'gaps' in the information con-text. And this is compounded by the difficulty in trying to identify executives who use information.

"I believe that it is critical for providers of information services to edu-cate decision makers about the 'benefits' of their services that speak directly to the interests of the decision makers. Providers must 'change the metaphor' so that they are no longer perceived as those who 'point to the information' but as those who can not only help define a problem, but can get the information that solves that problem."

Park cites the example of how the information staff in a multi-national company offered to become the "information" component of the various teams that were dealing with specific problems. They worked directly with the teams—with no interference from other levels of man-agement—and they are now considered an integral part of the company's operation. They documented their work and the outcomes so that they have real-life "case studies" that provide proof of the contributions their information made to the company, and senior management has recog-nized their work and compensated them for it.

Park also says that if a connection can be made with the decision mak-ers, they must be the ones made to think about the issues.

So how do you get them to do that?

"You ask them," Park says, and the cheerful smile, the optimism, returns. "You want to find out from them what the information function means to them, so you ask these executives a few questions."

In fact, the questions are right at hand, for in an article about Mary Park in a recent issue of *The Baltimore Business Journal*, she was quite open in sharing with the newspaper's readers what they need to be think-ing about. So for any information services manager, when you have the ear of those decision makers, here are your questions:

- If you or someone in your company needs information on a new competitor in your industry, where do you get the information? What do you do with the information once you get it?

- How do you know if the information you retrieve from electronic sources is reliable? Could you make a decision with the informa-tion? Where would you go for additional resources?

- Is there someone in your organization who is responsible for infor-mation retrieval? Does your organization have an information policy?

It's questions like these—and using the answers to put together an information services program for the organization—that enable the organization to move forward into a successful information arrangement. It's an arrangement that works, and it works because it has brought all elements of the company together to think about information services. And an important consideration is that it has emanated—with a little prodding from the information services staff—from the top down.

So the "partnering" has to happen, and of course it has to take place between all the various information-connected units in the organization, the libraries, the records management units, the MIS departments (particularly the MIS departments, for they provide the physical link—the conduit—that we all have to have).

Mary Park is on to something here, something that could very well revolutionize how information practitioners and information services managers think about their work. It's the realization that it is the connection between the information providers and the organization's senior managers—those decision makers—that makes the difference. And it takes that stone to the top of the mountain once and for all.

Meet Mary Park

Owner and principal information provider, The Information Consultancy,Baltimore, MD . . . Began her library career in the public and academic fields, but quickly moved into corporate information work as Corporate Librarian for the Delaware Management Company, Philadelphia, PA . . . Following a five-year foray into the investment consulting business, moved back into information services by founding The Information Consultancy in 1985 . . . Long list of professional activities, including The White House Conference on Libraries and Information Services in 1991, service on the (Maryland) Governor's Information Technology Board, the Presidency of the Baltimore Chapter of the Special Libraries Association in 1991-1992, and membership in the Greater Baltimore Committee Information Technology Council . . . Author of numerous articles on libraries and information delivery to the business community . . . Publishes *InfoProse: The Newsletter from the Information Professionals* . . . Editorial Advisor to *InfoManage* . . . Lives in Baltimore and (in the summers) in a remote cabin in Montana with her husband, a Johns Hopkins psychiatrist and researcher . . . Personal interests include her two sons and her two stepsons and their families, hiking and trout fishing in Montana, and traveling.

Ⅲ

"Determined"? "Driven"? Perhaps Even "Relentless"?
At Arthur Anderson in New York, success in the company's
Business Information Center connects to
LUCY LETTIS's
own career path

There aren't many information professionals who wear the change management "hat" comfortably, but Lucy Lettis obviously thrives on the challenges that managing change brings to her professional life. At Arthur Andersen's Metro New York Business Information Center, Lettis has taken a relatively moribund information services operation and turned it into an information powerhouse for the company. And she's done it in just seven months.

Surely there's some discernible characteristic that explains how she did it?

Lettis laughs at the question. "Self-discipline might be an answer," she says, and then a shy sort of look crosses her face, giving away her own charming self-deprecation. "Or perhaps self-discipline to the point of being relentless. I grew up determined to achieve what I set out to do, and I learned how to push myself so I could realize those achievements."

The statement is not an empty remark, for Lettis has always been something of an achiever. As a child prodigy, she had a spectacular career as an organist and choir director (beginning at age 11!), and although her career path seemed to be set in that musical direction, she discovered while attending Westminster Choir College that she didn't want to "live, eat, and breathe" music. Of course she didn't give it up completely, and music continues to give her much personal pleasure (she's an avid and regular supporter of the annual Tanglewood Festival), but as a career, she decided she wanted to do something else. She tried business for a while, as an office manager for a travel agency, and then discovered that her true

Originally published in *InfoManage : The International Management Newsletter for the Information Services Professional* 3 (5), April, 1996.

métier is libraries and information management. Having a mother who was a school librarian helped ("At least I knew what an M.L.S. was," she says with a grin).

Librarianship wasn't her first choice, though. After moving away from a career in music, she had embarked on the pursuit of studies in comparative literature (at Columbia University), but that field soon lost its attraction for her.

"Simply put," Lettis says, "at that time—and we're talking about the early 1980s here—fewer than 50% of the Ph.D. candidates in literature, even from the Ivy League institutions, were gainfully employed. That bothered me. So I decided to pursue librarianship and I was lucky to be able to work, almost from the beginning, in positions that combined information delivery with management."

Yes, "relentless" and "self-determination" seem to be the operative words here. Lettis has what she calls "a 4.0 personality" (she achieved no grade below "A" in her undergraduate and graduate work). She defines this as "less an indicator of brilliance than of tenacity and focus." And just as she understands the role of change and adaptability in her own life, Lettis understands the role of change in organizational success, and it's those very attributes that have enabled her to bring success to the information operation for which she has management responsibility at Arthur Andersen.

"I quickly figured out what I needed to do here," she says, "for it had actually became clear in my first meeting with the people who eventually hired me. Perhaps they didn't realize I saw it this way, but in fact the challenge confronting me was very obvious right from the beginning: with respect to information services management, I was to turn non-believers into believers. It's what I was hired to do, and I think we're being successful."

With such a challenge, how do you determine success? For Lettis at Arthur Andersen, you begin with usage. You analyze what the information customers need, you figure out how to provide the services that meet those needs, and then you measure. One of the first steps was to provide staff to do the work, but the staff had to be competent to provide the level of quality services that were required, so building the staff was critical.

"I came to work on September 11th," Lettis says, "and we began by hiring the people we needed—three people in three weeks, as a matter of fact. Then we initiated a very focused program of marketing the services

Lucy Lettis on Successful Information Services Management

InfoManage asked Lucy Lettis what she would say if someone came along and asked her the secret of a successful information services operation.

Find supportive management. It is key. But working with management is also a two-way street. Yes, management has to be interested in what is going on in the library or information center, but the information practitioners must also recognize what senior management's information needs are. And how they can be served. Catering to the decision makers is not a choice, it's a requirement.

Build a top-notch staff. No matter how good a manager you are, you can't do it all yourself. You simply must find the best people, see that they are trained (and that they continue to be trained), compensate them properly, and let them do their work. Trust them and they won't let you down.

Keep up. As the manager, you yourself must keep up, by reading, by participating in professional organizations, by going to conferences, by doing all you can to learn all you need to know. And you don't limit yourself to information issues. You're a manager, and you have to keep up with what's going on in management as well.

Understand marketing. And recognize that you're not just marketing a department or an organizational unit, but you're marketing yourself and your staff as well. Don't hide your light under a bushel. If you've reached a management level of responsibility, your talents are too good to be hidden away. And so are those of your staff and your department.

Work hard—and be fascinated by the work. Being the manager of a successful information services unit is not easy. Long hours are required, and while an obsessive/compulsive personality is not necessarily called for, having some tendencies in that direction can provide serious motivation. More important, however, is the requirement that you be really excited by the situation. Not necessarily the content of the information being delivered or the subject specialty of the organization, but the process of managing an information unit. It's that fascination that spurs you on to try newer and better things, to look for even more demanding challenges.

we provided. We looked at what the operation had been in the past, and we decided that the customers' perceptions about our services had to be changed. What had originally been the tax library had at one point been merged with the auditing library, but those subjects were only a part of what we worked with. So we created the Business Information Center, complete with a new focus, new signage, and—something we're particularly proud of—a new brochure. There had never been a brochure describing the information services available, so we pulled out all the stops."

It is an impressive piece of marketing literature, this handsome brochure that describes the services of the Business Information Center. Lettis wrote the text in its entirety; the company's graphics department came up with the eye-catching design. Staff is listed, with individual telephone numbers, and the list of services provided by the BIC reads like a veritable state-of-the-art catalog of what an effective information services operation should have on offer. In addition, though, and equally important, is the brochure's other descriptions, of BIC personnel, of its programs, and, in true marketing fashion, a list of "benefits and advantages" for the center's information customers. The people who read this brochure are told right up front why it is good for them to contact the Business Information Center.

And do they? That's where the measurement comes in. For among the management techniques Lettis had learned in one of her other positions (when she had been Manager of Library Services at the Pall Corporation in East Hills, NY), was the development of a keen appreciation of the value of collecting "certain statistics."

At Arthur Andersen, what needed to be measured early on was usage, and Lettis isn't shy about pulling out the graphs. In the first two months that the new operation was being organized, usage tripled, and once the Business Information Center had services and staff in place, that growth continued, an impressive 570% during the BIC's first five months of operation as a new information entity. So the numbers are good, and there is every reason for Lettis and her staff to be pleased.

But the numbers are only a beginning, and much else contributes to success in any information operation. Staff, of course, is critical, and Lettis is very happy that she was able to bring in such highly qualified people to work with her in creating this operation for the company's information customers. The other essential ingredient, of course, is the support of senior management, and here again, Lettis could read the runes when she met with the five people who would decide on hiring her.

"What was needed," she says (and it's obvious she is not shy or reticent about admitting the importance of this fact), "was someone to stir things up. They got that."

Prior to the reorganization of the unit, the library was not a popular place, and it had not been attracting the number of users it should have been attracting.

"People were staying away in droves," Lettis says, "and we had to fix that. So our marketing efforts had to combine several discrete components. Of course, the signage, reorganized space, and the brochure were key, but we had to do more. For example, in January we produced an open house and vendor exhibition for our customers. We had seven major information vendors give demonstrations for our customers, and at the same time, we provided a party atmosphere to lighten things up. This was tremendously successful, and many new faces turned up in the BIC.

"Shortly after the open house, we began to go into different departments with 'special topic' seminars or discussions of new research products. Although I enjoy presentations and am considered fairly adept at doing them, this wasn't going to be just my show. Two of our professional staff went with me so that we could provide a complete picture of what we were attempting to present. And we were successful, so much so that we are now being asked to do more of these. We don't have to sell other departments on the idea of research presentations. They now come to us and invite us to come in and work with their staff on these matters. It's a winning combination, this teamwork between the customers and the BIC staff."

Teamwork is not an alien concept for Lettis. In fact, it was in her previous position, as Manager of the Corporate Information Center for the American International Group, that she realized just how valuable the concept is in the management of an information operation. While she had enjoyed her work at the Pall Corporation—a position which had provided her with a fine opportunity to master the management component of information services—when she was recruited for the position at AIG she at once saw the potential for career growth.

"It was a move up," Lettis says, "not so much in the work to be done, but in the level, you might say, of the work. It was a notch up, for example, in management sophistication, in technology and technology products, that sort of thing. There were many different products to be working with, many different databases, and so forth, and moving to AIG provided an opportunity for me to be working in the technology forefront, to be on the cutting edge, and I liked that."

Going to AIG also gave Lettis the opportunity to build that information team she had been wanting to build (and when linked to her work in this same connection at Arthur Andersen, it's obvious that team building is one of Lettis's great management strengths). She's quite proud of what she did at AIG, for she likes to talk about the team there, people she refers to as "some of Manhattan's finest information professionals." It's a talent she has, and the strong information services team is certainly going to be an important focus at Andersen.

So was it a good move for Lettis to come to Arthur Andersen? The question is anything but rhetorical, for when asked, Lucy Lettis's face lights up with enthusiasm.

"It was one of the best decisions I've ever made," she says, and you know she means it. "I'm happier than I've ever been, and the rewards and the challenges of building what we're building here all come together to create an information services operation that—as far as I'm concerned— is providing benefits to everyone involved."

And the benefits for Lucy Lettis?

"Let's not be too self-effacing about this," she says. "Of course there are rewards, and it would be slightly disingenuous for me to pretend that I'm not pleased. In the kind of work we information services managers do—especially at this level—there is a certain amount of ego satisfaction involved. Of course we do it for the customers, and of course we do it so our organizations can succeed, but we also do it because we're good at what we do, and there is satisfaction in that."

It's the way the world works, quite frankly, and when there are information practitioners (especially at the management level) who can recognize that three-way success, there are benefits all around. Lucy Lettis is giving the information customers what they need, the Arthur Andersen Metro New York Business Information Center is contributing to the company's success, and Lettis herself—as a manager—is happy. This "success" combination is what a lot of people are looking for, and she's very lucky (which she readily admits) to have found it. It's what makes being an information services manager the rewarding profession it is.

Meet Lucy Lettis

Lucy Bara Lettis is Director of the Metro New York Business Information Center at Arthur Andersen and Co. SC in New York City. Prior to coming to Arthur Andersen, Lettis was Manager of the Corporate Information Center for American International Group in New York, and prior to that Manager of Library Services and, later, Marketing Research Manager at the Pall Corporation in East Hills, NY. From 1983 to 1985, she was Automation Technologist at Adelphi University Library, where she supervised a staff of 30 and managed the conversion of the library's 600,000-title catalog. She was the Facilitator for the National Information Policies Group at The White House Conference on Library and Information Services in 1991. Lettis has both her undergraduate (B.A., English Literature *summa cum laude*) and graduate (M.S.L.S.) degrees from Long Island University. An active member of several professional organizations, Lettis is incoming President of SLA's New York Chapter, the organizations' largest with some 1,500 members. Her personal interests include music, reading, theater, fine dining, and travel. She lives in Port Washington, NY, with her husband Richard Lettis, a writer and Dickens scholar. Now retired, he served at C.W. Post College as Professor of English Literature and Dean of the College of Arts and Sciences.

A high-visibility focus at *The Los Angeles Times*.
In the Editorial Library
TOM LUTGEN
and his staff have put it all together.

News libraries have long been regarded as the movers and shakers in the information delivery industry, and the history of news libraries has been bright with major successes. Those who know about these things often speak about how newspaper, magazine, and broadcasting libraries—representing a kind of "best-case" scenario for the journalism profession—are valuable adjuncts to the news gathering process. Of course there have

Originally published in *InfoManage : The International Management Newsletter for the Information Services Professional* 3 (11), February, 1997.

been sad exceptions, but by and large, news libraries are generally recognized as leading the way in the specialist library field.

Practical and utilitarian information delivery defines a special library, and in a news library the practical, utilitarian role of the library must take precedence over all other considerations. News libraries cannot afford the "just-in-case" framework that some other information delivery operations might claim. In fact, for news libraries—as exemplified in spades by The Los Angeles Times Editorial Library where Tom Lutgen has managerial responsibility—even "just-in-time"isn't good enough. At *The LA Times*, much of the Editorial Library's success is directly related to anticipating need as well as meeting clearly established and defined need. It's a management philosophy that's been in place for a long time, and it continues to characterize the information delivery process that takes place there.

Like libraries in other fields (museum libraries come to mind), there has been a long tradition of news libraries, and it is not surprising to learn that a newspaper or a magazine has had a library in place for many decades. At *The LA Times*, there has been an Editorial Library since 1935 or so. As he describes the history of his operation, Lutgen notes that the library's primary activities in those days—and continuing on for another couple of generations—were clipping articles and saving photos. There was a "librarian," but there was no professionally educated and trained librarian until Cecily Surace was hired in 1979.

When Surace came to *The LA Times* (she retired in 1993), the collection in the library was pretty limited—with things like *World Almanac* going back to the 1880s, and some California history materials—but there wasn't much of what would be called a "research" collection. There were about 12 people ("doing everything," Lutgen says), and the staff of the Editorial Library spent a lot of time with reporters, primarily helping them find *LA Times* articles, to see what, if anything, had been written previously in the newspaper about a particular subject. All the searching was done from the clipping files, and there were no authority files, so there was much tracing and retracing of steps. This particular situation, incidentally, is being rectified, for the library staff started working on a thesaurus for full-text searching in 1991-1992, and when completed, the thesaurus will have three sections (Photo Research, Research and Reference, and Indexing), enabling the newspaper's writers, reporters, and researchers to find what they need.

Lutgen was hired as head of Reference and Research in 1980, and immediately he and Surace set out to put together a research team that would be fully supportive of the newspaper's efforts to provide their reporters with the information they need for their work. Surace's strengths had been in developing staff (and with providing competent research, whether searching for internal or external information); she made it clear that she wanted the two of them to work together to develop the team the newspaper needed.

"She had no trouble making decisions," Lutgen says, and she delegated to him responsibility for hiring and developing staff, together with developing the collection needed to support the work of the reporters. It was a big responsibility, for the reference staff, which had been seven people when Lutgen came on board, eventually grew to 12-13 people, with the Editorial Library as a whole employing 54 people at one point in the transition.

In 1993, Lutgen became head of the operation, in reaction to organizational changes at the newspaper. There was significant downsizing throughout the company, and management had known all along that—as far as information delivery is concerned—technology would eventually drive the service, so Lutgen and the staff went forward at full speed.

One of their first projects was the microfilming of the newspaper's clippings files, an urgent priority since so many of the clippings—as has been the case in all journalism libraries—were in danger of disintegration. To date, the years from 1935 to 1972 have been completed, and the 1973-1984 section was started, but only got about half done. By the mid-80s it had been determined that the microfilming of the clippings files was not critical to the successful achievement of the corporate mission, so the project was dropped.

Not mission-critical? Why not?

"Simply because," Lutgen says, "the development of the full-text database began in 1985, so the 'finding aids' for searching the newspaper existed and could be used to locate subjects that have been written about."

The downsizing continued into the mid-1990s, and there were some hard choices, for the library (and the newspaper at large) lost people with experience, commitment to the work of the newspaper library, corporate memory, etc. In the library itself, six people chose to leave (and they were, unfortunately, "the best and the brightest" of the library staff, Lutgen comments with a tone of regret in his voice). The loss of these good people continues to be a problem "throughout the paper," and morale—to some extent—is still suffering.

But Lutgen is working hard to reverse the situation, and when asked how he is able to keep the enthusiasm up, for himself and his staff, he has some answers.

"One of the things we've done," he says, "is that we have established high visibility in the newsroom. For example, all the Reference and Research staff work with a particular departments on a project or assignment. As a result, the library is recognized and often our researchers' work is acknowledged through a credit line."

But the high-visibility isn't confined to the newsroom, for the library staff look for other opportunities as well. There is now, for example, a library employee at a separate work station at the metropolitan desk, and it wasn't so long ago, in the midst of the historic trial, that the Editorial Library put up its own "OJ Home Page." It was an example of what Lutgen likes to call "enterprise librarianship."

"Our OJ 'specialist' created an internal Home Page on our intranet to provide background for the staff reporting on the case. She also left the confines of the library and worked for about a year in the newsroom at the City Desk." A similar effort is currently under way, as the library staff is working with the political desk to develop strategies for "developing information services for the elections," an activity that is "a pretty typical situation at our place."

It all relates, it would seem, to the company's major commitment to supporting information literacy and the development of information-gathering skills among all staff, an organizational perspective that naturally carries over into the Editorial Library. There, Lutgen says, "all the Reference and Research staff are trained to use the Internet, and they use it extensively. In fact, I think it is fair to say that the library's Research Section took the initiative and introduced the Internet to the newsroom. By now more than 800 reporters and editors have been trained to use the Internet through the Lynx text-based browser. This new instructional relationship with reporters and editors has also helped changed perceptions for the better."

In addition to the high visibility (or perhaps as a part of it), Lutgen and his staff have taken a creative and proactive approach to working with end users. In some cases it's not necessary, for as with all news libraries, some of the reporting and writing staff are library users, and some are not. It's a situation Lutgen and his staff have learned to live with, and when asked if the reporters use the library, Lutgen's answer is typically realistic.

"I would like to say that all the reporters want to come to us for their information needs, but that isn't necessarily the case. Political writers, for some reason, tend to be information aggressive, but many others, like the people doing research and writing articles on entertainment, the arts, and so forth, are not so aggressive."

As in other industries, there is naturally a great deal of apprehension in the information-gathering behavior of the Editorial Library's information customers. Some editors, for example, don't want reporters using the Internet for complex research, for they see that as a function of the library staff. On the other hand, Lutgen and his team are trying to exercise their influence where they can, and as they meet new staff at the newspaper, they look for opportunities to make them aware of the Editorial Library and how the library can support their work.

"We always offer invitations to new hires," Lutgen says, "but the hiring units are not always too interested in participating. Nevertheless, the opportunities are there, and they do pay off from time to time, for young reporters are anxious to be information literate, and they often want their own passwords so they can continue to gather their own information, just as they did as they were being trained and educated."

Another factor in the visibility effort is, of course, the information itself, what is provided to the reporters, writers, and researchers who come to use the Editorial Library.

"We use every database conceivable," Lutgen says with a laugh. "All the usual ones, of course, plus specialized databases for business, demographics, etc. And with respect to the training for end-users, we do our own public relations, so the reporters and others on the editorial staff know to come to us."

Part of what might be called Lutgen's "high-visibility effort" connects with the staff he hires to work in the Editorial Library, for the jobs are various and, as noted, very team-oriented.

"So we look for skills to match needs," Lutgen says, "and we also look for experience in finding information in particular subject fields that are important to our work, things like health and medicine, law, and so forth.

And we're pretty open-minded about the resources we use, for we long ago learned that we don't have everything here and right at hand. For example, we have a deposit account with MCLS [the Metropolitan Cooperative Library System, the local public library system] and use it as a back-up resource and, like any major information operation, we even use external information brokers for database searching when necessary."

As with many information services operations these days, the relationship with end users looms large in management planning, and serious progress is being made, as Tom Lutgen points out: "We've recently switched to our new photo archive system, Cascade Systems' MediaSphere. With all our online systems we hope to design them in such a way as to make for easy access by end-users, our reporters and editors. Both TimesOnline and MediaSphere are popular with the news staff, and to the extent we can migrate simple searches to the end users, this allows us to focus on more complex research projects and to spend our time archiving additional kinds of images."

And does the high-visibility effort go beyond the inhouse work, beyond the reporters and editors and other newspapers employees? Of course, for there is always the public's insatiable desire for information, for facts and stories that people remember they "read in *The LA Times*." The Editorial Library and its team are meeting those demands as well, a fact which Lutgen is happy to point out.

"*The Times* offers a fee-based research service, Times on Demand," he says, "available through an 800, toll-free number. There are three researchers whose job is basically searching only for *Times* articles, including those going back to 1881 through our microfilm resources. Our text archives from 1990 to date are available on the Times Web site (latimes.com), and we will begin charging for this soon. Searching and viewing headlines will be free, but viewing entire articles will cost."

It's an impressive story, and the operation of the Editorial Library at *The LA Times* is—by any measure—a success. But we can't go too far in this description without coming up against Tom Lutgen's own natural reserve. He's a modest person, and he takes special care to see that full credit is given to the many other people who participate in and contribute to that success. Lutgen is quick to point out how valuable the various library staff members are, how hard they work, and how their commitment to teamwork all combine to permit the Editorial Library to achieve its success in information delivery.

Lutgen is also quick to give credit to his predecessor: "Management sees the library as successful because of Cecily's vision," he says. "Before she came here, Cecily Surace has been Library Director at RAND Corporation. She was the guiding force behind the creation of a top-notch news library, for integrating a strong research unit with a photo archiving section and a professional indexing staff to construct the electronic text archive for internal and external use."

It's that ability to visualize what kind of information service the Editorial Library can be offering, how good it can be, that positions the Editorial Library and its team of information workers for success in the company. And it's a vision that pays off, as Lutgen notes, for it is also a vision that recognizes that the library's role is not just information delivery.

"Top management recognizes the value of having a professional library team," Lutgen says, "a team that is able to contribute both to the quality of the newspaper's content and to the company's bottom line through the distribution of a high quality archive."

So what is in place at *The LA Times* Editorial Library is, in fact, just what Cecily Surace—and after her, Tom Lutgen and his team of information professionals—set out to achieve: an information operation that is a "top-notch" news library, one that works for both internal and external information customers, and one which contributes to the newspaper's financial success. It's a formula that has been shown to work, and it's one that other libraries, whether in the news field or not, can follow with considerable assurance of success.

Meet Tom Lutgen

Tom Lutgen is Editorial Library Director for *The Los Angeles Times*, a position he has held since April, 1993. He has been with *The Times* since January, 1980, when he was hired as Head of Reference and Research Services in the Editorial Library. Prior to that, he had been, since 1990, an Information Specialist with *The Times*, with specific responsibility to provide complete research support for a new weekly section of the newspaper called "World Report," which focused on international events and trends. Before joining *The Times*, Lutgen had been Adult Services Supervisor at the Commerce (California) Public Library, from 1971 to 1980, and before that he had been the business specialist at the Santa Ana (California) Public Library, from 1970 to 1971. While he was working on his graduate degree at the University of Southern California (M.S.L.S., 1970), Lutgen worked at the Riverside (California) City and County Public Library. His B.A. degree is from the University of California, Riverside.

A native of Waukegan, Illinois, Tom Lutgen grew up in Riverside, California. He now lives in Pasadena. When he has leisure time—which isn't very often!—Lutgen's private interests include gardening ("though you couldn't tell it from my gardens," he says, which is probably because of that lack of leisure time). His reading for pleasure includes *The New Yorker*, and the museums and wonderful Old Town of Pasadena are "great to lose time in." He is also the owner of a condominium in Maui," so whenever I have some time I run over there to check on it."

MARY DICKERSON:
At the Ontario Legislative Library,
change management calls for directional planning.

Like many information services managers today, Mary Dickerson is continually confronted with managerial challenges that call for innovative and original solutions. For her, the challenges are simply part of the job, and whatever challenges she faces in running the Ontario Legislative Library, this innovative manager seeks a team-oriented solution rather than simply imposing her own views on the library's staff.

But "team-oriented" could be a misleading characterization, for if there is any one quality that marks her management philosophy, it's Mary Dickerson's commitment to flexibility. And that commitment is even evident in the way she organizes the library's staff, for although there's a team-management "flavor" to the way staff gets things done, if a team approach is not the best one, another approach will be substituted. As the library's visioning statement in 1995 put it, "The Ontario Legislative Library uses different methods of organizing staff—teams, hierarchies, temporary work groups, matrices—to suit specific tasks. Many staff members work with others with different skills and functions on work teams whose responsibility is to produce and deliver a product or service. Managers and supervisors spend much of their time coaching work teams."

The obvious connection is to the information customer. And that's where Mary Dickerson excels as an information services manager, for at the Ontario Legislative Library, customized information delivery is already a primary focus in the library's operation. In fact, if there is any core philosophy of service that drives the delivery of information products, services, and consultations, it's the library's commitment to the information customer and obtaining for that customer what he or she needs.

Originally published in *InfoManage : The International Management Newsletter for the Information Services Professional* 4 (9), August, 1997.

Dickerson, who has been at the library since 1978, worked for many years under another innovative and resourceful leader, Brian Land, and during Land's tenure the library experienced major growth (which, Mary Dickerson is quick to admit, as a budding information services manager she was happy to be part of). All of this was well and good, as long as it lasted, but in the real world of information services management, such periods of exciting growth can't be expected to last forever, and this one didn't either. By the time Dickerson took on the job of Executive Director in 1993, times had changed, and it was time to review the many services that were being offered. And although she didn't know it at the time, looming on the horizon would be tremendous challenges in terms of staff reductions, service cuts, operations funding, and a variety of other management setbacks that would test her skills for providing the highest levels of information delivery under conditions that would prove to be far from ideal.

But she would not cave in to the challenges, and allow herself and her institution to lower their standards. Not Mary Dickerson. That's not the way she works. In fact, Dickerson had reserves—personal resources within herself and experiences from her professional management career—that she was able to call forth when she needed them, and the happy result is that, even with diminished resources and fewer staff, the Ontario Legislative Library is today continuing to provide the key information products, services, and consultations that its customers require.

The Ontario Legislative Library

The mandate of the Ontario Legislative Library is to provide non-partisan research and information services to meet the needs of the Members of the Legislative Assembly. These services include a range of information services and products customized to meet the diverse and ever-changing requirements of the primary client group as individuals and as members of legislative committees. In addition to enhanced reference services, the Ontario Legislative Library has a team of research officers—subject specialists ranging from lawyers to urban planners to environmentalists—who provide analytical reports, briefing notes, and background papers on a wide range of topics. The library also has a press monitoring service. The management infrastructure for the library is similar to that of an academic library while its services are those of a highly focused service-oriented special library.

The library has a permanent staff of 70, of whom 39 are professionals (librarians and research officers).

The first of Dickerson's assets (as you might call them) was, in a broader sense, her work in the information services profession at large, and with that, her ability to scrutinize the information industry and pick out those situations and those criteria that could be adapted successfully for the Ontario Legislative Library.

A long-time and active participant in professional activities, Mary Dickerson is known for her contributions to the information services profession, and she has been particularly active in the Special Libraries Association. She is best known, perhaps, for what has so far turned out to be her most impressive work for SLA, chairing the association's Presidential Commission on Professional Recruitment, Ethics, and Professional Standards, popularly known as "The PREPS Commission" (1991-1993). With the creation of the commission, specialist librarians were for the first time thinking about how they are different from other practitioners in the information services field (and from other branches of librarianship) as they explored issues, as Dickerson described them, "relating to recruitment into special librarianship, ethics, and standards, as well as the necessary basic competencies for special librarians."

"It was an important period in my professional growth," Dickerson says, "for it helped me to focus on my work, on what we are supposed to be doing, and to think about things in my organization in a different way. Perhaps because growth at my place had been so rapid, I needed to step back and think about the standards that we would be using to measure our work, and the competencies required for our staff members to succeed in that work."

It was a major challenge for Dickerson when she took on responsibility for running the library. Some administrative units within the institution had not had as effective a relationship as they might have had, or had not been working as effectively as they needed to be working in the new environment, and although much work had been done in each department, a culture of separation had built up over the years. There was a real need, by the time Dickerson came, to pull the library's staff together, to find some way of encouraging them to see themselves as all part of the same operation, and not as separate, stand-alone units, each working in its own little vacuum. It was a tall order, but Dickerson felt she had to tackle it.

Why?

The look of disbelief on Dickerson's face makes it clear that—to her—the answer is obvious:

"We don't have a choice," she says. "We can't operate a series of little fiefdoms, not if we want to survive in the future. That's why we took as one of our concepts, 'If we don't think about the future, we won't have one.' In this day and age, a library has to be proactive, and its staff members must all work as a unit. Otherwise, the users will go elsewhere and we won't have a future.

"So one thing we wanted to do," she continues, "was to get rid of the little turf battles, to determine how we could set up an organizational structure in which different staff members and the different units were thinking of themselves as part of the overall organizational team, rather than thinking only of themselves. For example, we become very skilled at what I like to call 'cross-branch' management, in which we took a look at issues across departmental lines, looking at how those issues were affecting—or might affect—the bigger organization. As a result, we found ourselves—as managers—thinking about management issues across departmental lines within the library and within the legislature at large."

Thinking about these issues ultimately led to the development of something the staff at the Ontario Legislative Library calls "directional" planning, a new approach to looking at what needed to be done—with respect to the management of the library—in terms of where the library was attempting to go, rather than just in terms of finding the strategies to get there.

Within the library, Dickerson had often spoken with various staff about the need for change, about some of the challenges that she knew the Ontario Legislative Library would be facing. At the same time, through her involvement with the work of the PREPS Commission and the Professional Development Committee in SLA, she knew that change in the information industry could be managed, but part of managing that change has to do with making the change palatable to the people who will be affected by it. So one of the steps Dickerson took was to hire a team of consultants who were experienced in working with staff in change management, to get the staff thinking the same way. It was an important first step, for it did, indeed, "level the playing field" for all staff at the library, and they were, for the first time in many years, speaking the same "language" in terms of services, customers, and the library's role in the legislative process.

Then in October, 1995, came a real wake-up call, and suddenly the move toward directional planning made a great deal of sense: the Government mandated a 20% budget cut, and Dickerson was required to eliminate 22 positions.

"When we saw that this was going to happen, we weren't about to take it sitting down," Dickerson says. "We knew that we would need to conform to this, but we wanted to be leading the change rather than having it imposed on us, and when we got the news in October that we would have to make these cuts by April, 1996, we knew that we would have to rethink some of our ideas about how we were going to manage the library. Of course it was difficult, because we had not be able to plan for these changes. The timing was just too sudden. But we knew that there were things we could do, and as we had already been thinking some about change and change management, we had some options open to us.

"For one thing, it became very important that all senior managers in the library agree on what the priorities would be: we had to consolidate the technology levels, for example, so we set up a committee to implement this. And at about this time we decided to push forward with our new directional plan. The reality of the situation was that we were going to be short 22 people. There would be no new funding, and we had to live with this fact, so we did a lot of brainstorming, looking at where there were areas of duplication and overlap, so that we could eliminate these. We got heavily into reviewing collection policies and plans, and we worked on communication, both within the library itself and then, when it was time, with how we would take the news to the customers.

"So it was time to go to work with our directional plan. And while senior staff had drafted it, that is, provided the framework for the plan, the action plan that made it work was actually developed through total staff involvement. It was a cooperative effort, and we knew we had a good product, so we took it, and decided that we would operate with the plan. And we've been doing so since October, 1996."

The directional plan which Dickerson alludes to is, in fact, a real plan, a document put together in order to, as is stated in the document, clearly define "what our purpose is and what steps we have to take to meet that purpose." And while strategies are built in (those "steps we have to take"), the directional plan is a little different from the usual strategic plan because—again quoting from the Ontario document—"it provides the means of keeping track of what needs to be done, assists us in setting priorities, and helps to ensure that we are not trying to do too much at once and that we are not duplicating efforts." And one of the most important points made with the directional plan—with its emphasis on direction rather than on strategy—is the philosophy built into its implementation. "It is a guide, not a rule book."

One of the beauties of directional planning, as used by Mary Dickerson and her staff, is its provision for ownership, for having staff take responsibility for getting the job done. Being a guide rather than a rule book, a directional plan enables staff to ask the questions that relate to doing good work: What are we doing? Why is it necessary? What is my role? What does it mean for me?

Additionally, directional planning is built on communication strengths, and in fact much of the emphasis in directional planning has to do with supervisors and management staff understanding the role of communication, the need to be honest, the value of communicating exactly what is going on to the people who report to them. In this case, that emphasis was taken even further, for as it became clear that communication work needed to be done, a committee of staff members, representing all parts of the organization, drafted and arranged a series of communications workshops that, not surprisingly, was discovered to have paid off handsomely when it came time for staff and management to review the success of their directional plan.

An important theme running throughout the directional plan—along with the previously mentioned flexibility that has become almost a byword for Dickerson and her operation—is an emphasis on realism: Phrases like setting "realistic priorities" and adopting "realistic and progressive" strategies pop up throughout the plan, and the emphasis is clearly on encouraging staff (all staff, not just managers and supervisors) to think about what they are doing, to establish a clear list of priorities so they don't become "discouraged and bogged down with trying to do too many things at once." In very specific terms, directional planning recognizes that "without consciously planning to do so, over the past few years we have added more and more things to our 'to do' list." Directional planning, appropriately, leads to review, looking at that list and determining to focus on only those things that should be done and which can be managed.

It's that review, together with staff ownership, management agreement on priorities, and a commitment to customer values that make directional planning work, and Mary Dickerson and her staff and customers at the Ontario Legislative Library are having a high old time watching it progress. It's not always fun—this directional process—for some well-loved traditional services and practices have to be eliminated, and doing that is not always an easy (or pleasant) task. But it's pretty exciting, from a management point of view, and it's stimulating and definitely motivating from the staff's perspective. So they practice directional management at the Ontario Legislative Library, and the result, just as Mary Dickerson and her staff and her customers desire, is better service for the customers, which is what they're supposed to be providing anyway. Good for them.

Meet Mary Dickerson

Mary E. Dickerson is Executive Director of the Ontario Legislative Library in Toronto, a position she has held since 1993. Prior to her current appointment, Dickerson was Deputy Executive Director and Director, Information and Reference Services (1986-1993) and Head, Information and Reference Services (1978-1986). Other positions held during her career are that of Serials Librarian at the Ontario Legislative Library, Life Sciences Book Selector, University of Toronto Libraries, and Collections Librarian, Health Sciences Library, University of Western Ontario. Her B.A. degree is from the University of Western Ontario, and her B.L.S. and M.L.S. were awarded by the University of Toronto. An active leader in the profession, Dickerson belongs to several professional associations, including the Canadian Library Association, and she has served as a Director (1992-1994) of the Ontario Government Library Council. In 1996, she was a member of the review team for the Information Reference Services Review organized by the Ontario Government's Internal Administration Project.

Mary Dickerson's primary professional membership is the Special Libraries Association, which elected her a Fellow (F.S.L.A.) in 1993. She was a member of the SLA Board of Directors from 1988-1992, serving special assignments as a member of both the Finance Committee and the Nominating Committee, and serving as Chair of the SLA Presidential Commission on Professional Recruitment, Ethics, and Professional Standards ("The PREPS Commission") from 1991-1993. Dickerson has also served SLA as a member of the association's Conference Planning Committee for its 1984 Annual Conference, as a member of the Professional Development Committee, 1992-1997 (Committee Chair, 1994-1997), and as a member of the Special Libraries Advisory Board, 1993-1996.

Mary Dickerson and her husband Dennis, a businessman, live in Toronto. In their spare time, they indulge their enthusiasm for golf.

Planning: it's the critical "essential"
in the library transformation process and
ETHEL HIMMEL and **BILL WILSON**
are the planning and transformation experts.

Transformational librarianship. It's a concept that's been written about in these pages before, and now transformational librarianship, as a management concept for moving public libraries into a "planned," "imagined," "invented," and "assembled" future, is the tool that is going to make it happen. For transformational librarianship is exactly what Ethel Himmel and Bill Wilson are using as they work with librarians, library administrators, government authorities, state library agencies, and similar clients to plan for the future of public library service in America.

Not that they would necessarily call it that, for the term—that "transformational librarianship" that seems to pop up frequently in the literature of specialist librarianship—has not yet totally insinuated itself into the language of public library management, but it's coming. It's a term that—as readers of *InfoManage* well know—sneaks in from time to time into the literature of change management, and library managers like Stephen Abram and Jane Dysart use it frequently to describe how librarianship—when it works—makes a difference. And that's the key to the planning models Ethel Himmel and Bill Wilson put forward as they work with customers.

Read what they say in their latest book, *Planning for Results: A Public Library Transformation Process*, described in the press as "a unique, results-driven program that empowers public librarians to meet community needs and to develop strategies to anticipate future demands." Writing about the future of public libraries and how public library management can be structured to meet that future, Himmel and Wilson have this to say:

Originally published in *InfoManage : The International Management Newsletter for the Information Services Professional* 5 (10), September, 1998.

"Libraries need to be involved in a continuous transformation process. They have to change constantly and adjust as their communities change. Our motivation for planning shouldn't be the preservation in amber of a revered institution. We should plan because we want the library to contribute to the success of the community and its people. . . . Why plan? Because libraries that plan are more likely to achieve positive results; and results are what it's all about!"

Change! Continuous transformation! Planning! Or, as Himmel and Wilson put it at another point in the book: inventing the future, envisioning what the ideal state of public librarianship can be, identifying who will benefit if the ideal state is achieved, what benefit they will receive, and what will result from the benefit. Describing nothing less than the difference the library intends to make in its community . . . .

Now that is transformational librarianship at its best. And the quotation proves, once again, that despite all our arguments to the contrary, our basic premise is wrong. Despite all our assertions that what works in one branch of the information industry won't work anywhere else, it is a false assumption, and Ethel Himmel and Bill Wilson are proving that. What works in public library management can work in specialist librarianship, can work in records management, can work in publishing, in telecommunications, in information technology, and in any other branch of information services in which excellence in the delivery of information is the primary objective.

For Himmel and Wilson, transformational librarianship connects into transformational planning, to something that they (and Dysart and Abram) and other management theorists might characterize as transformational leadership, which builds on trust through positioning, communication of meaning, the deployment of self, a widely shared commitment and enthusiasm, and, as important as anything else, optimism about the desired outcome. Transformational librarianship is a form of information delivery in which the focus is through the vision, and for information services practitioners (and those who manage them or advise them), that "transforming" of information delivery is what provides—for the library patron—a changed relationship with the original problem that he or she came into the library to solve. As Abram put it on one occasion: "You have added value," he said, "when your client is 'different' for having used your service—when that person is more knowledgeable and decision-empowered." The same can be said about planning for library services.

When the community is changed as a result of the success of the planning, when the library makes a difference in the community and that difference can be articulated and codified, transformational planning and transformational librarianship has taken place.

It works for Ethel Himmel and Bill Wilson because this is a couple that has taken the basic concepts of teamwork—as they apply in the workplace and in the community—and put them to work for their company. Both of them are very positive about their careers, and about the contributions they are making to the library systems and agencies that hire them for their advice. And both Himmel and Wilson are eager to talk about what it is about library consulting that they like.

Wilson, for example, likes the problem, likes the opportunity to look at a library management situation and think about how Himmel & Wilson Library Consultants can come in and "make things work" for the library's planners. And he enjoys working with the library's contract officers to see if they can come up with a project plan that will (of course!) enable Himmel & Wilson to win the contract but, in a slightly more altruistic vein, enable the library to position itself for providing excellent library services in the future.

"It's the marketing that makes it happen," Wilson says, and it soon becomes obvious that this is the part of the challenge that appeals to him. "We do proposals that are good. In fact, they are often better than other proposals because we make a real attempt to get into the heads of the people who write the RFPs. Some require preparations, some more elaborate than others, but we do a good job for our prospective clients, and they like the way we pitch our product to them."

And they are successful, having moved themselves into a leadership position in the market, to the point that they are now winning about half the jobs they propose, up from about one in three just a few years ago.

Himmel knows why: "Bill is very good with the hook," she says with a laugh.

Himmel, too, has a part of consulting that she likes, and that's the fact that their work provides them with an "outward focus," as she puts it.

"I'm interested in trends," she says, "and being a planning consultant enables us to get out into the community, to learn what the neighborhoods and the different districts are looking for in library services. And that's why we are comfortable advising our clients about change, about how to deal with change and how to plan for it. Change is happening in the community, and the library administrators need to know what those things are and what they mean for the kinds of library service they'll be expected to provide."

The tool Himmel and Wilson use—and which they describe quite usefully in their new book—is a variation on the environmental scan. A basic management methodology for several decades now, the environmental scan assumes that change is both inevitable and desirable and produces a picture of the several environments in which libraries operate and then details what changes libraries can expect from their constituent communities. But Himmel and Wilson add scenario planning to the process, attempting to project—with their clients—what the changes will be.

They describe the process—their "community scan"—this way (again quoting from their book):

> "The data gathered in the community scan should
> (1) describe reality or what currently is,
> (2) identify trends, the direction things seem to be going, and
> (3) describe what reality will probably be three to five years out."

And it's the Himmel/Wilson spin that makes so much sense for the library manager who wants to keep libraries relevant for the 21st century: "Remember that what you're trying to conduct is a discovery process, not an autopsy! The job . . . isn't to dissect the community; it's to know and understand the community in order to design library services that are responsive to its needs."

Well said. And that phraseology also permits a glimpse into another of the reasons Himmel and Wilson are so successful at what they do. They're excited by the work, and they enjoy being able to work with clients who can then—using their advice and following their procedures—bring the transforming process into the library's planning.

Certainly that enthusiasm becomes clear when you meet with Ethel Himmel and Bill Wilson and then connect your observations with the work they did with the Public Library Association. *Planning for Results* was written for the PLA ReVision Committee, appointed in 1996 and charged with revising and updating an earlier PLA planning document. As Sandra Nelson, the ReVision Committee Chair, wrote in her Foreword, the book "continues the philosophy and work done previously by PLA in this area . . . to help public library directors, staff, and board members manage the future rather than merely react to the present."

And that philosophy clearly comes through in the guidelines published in the book. The planning process, condensed into six "manageable steps," reflects the underlying methodology that Bill Wilson and Ethel Himmel bring to their consulting practice.

For them, those six planning steps (Prepare-Envision-Design-Build-Implement-Communicate) provide the critical framework for how libraries will be successful in the future. And for these two positive and optimistic consultants, they also provide an opportunity for doing good work.

"It's always exciting and fun," Himmel says, and her listener can quickly pick up on the fact that she and Wilson are enjoying this. "We love going into new situations, and we haven't yet had a bad experience. In fact, it's usually the case that at the end of a consultancy, the people we've worked with are sorry to see us leave."

"That's true," Wilson interjects. "They're always asking us to come back as friends. And when we can, we do."

But there is a caveat to Himmel and Wilson's success, and they are not shy about alluding to it.

"It's not always easy," Wilson says. "There are plenty of situations where it doesn't come easy, and we have to work very hard with our clients to get them—or their staffs, or their boards—to be open to change. Certainly, nowadays, technology adds a layer of stress."

Still, Ethel Himmel and Bill Wilson don't shy away from the challenges of their work, and just recognizing that the "layer of stress" is there is part of what they do. That recognition, ultimately, gives them yet another tool to use in bringing change into the public libraries where they work.

And it is a line of work that is, ultimately and for a great variety of reasons, very rewarding. When asked, for example, if they have favorite library "types," the kinds of libraries where they most like to work, both of them laugh. After all, it is kind of an unfair question, for with their planning skills, and their reputation for excellence, Himmel and Wilson can make an important contribution wherever they're hired to work.

"But since you asked," Himmel says, and the quasi-smile indicates that she is a little embarrassed by the question, "I like the more literary types of places. I like to think about readers' advisors services, and how people get to the materials they want to read."

"And I go for the social work," Wilson says (and that's not a surprise, since was Senior Citizen Coordinator, planning library services for the aging, at the Buffalo and Erie County (NY) Public Library, from 1971-1976). "I like going out into the community, and I like seeing how the library works with the community."

Is there, then, a secret to their success? These are two modest people, and probably either or both of them would be embarrassed to be asked that specific question, so the question isn't asked. But without meaning to, Himmel provides the answer.

"You always connect with the positives," she says. "Users don't go to libraries with losers. And our job is to go in there and do what we can to change things, to see that the library isn't in a position where there are losers. It's the only way to go."

And that—it must be said—explains why Ethel Himmel and Bill Wilson, and the company they run, are not only a very workable combination, but a winning one as well. With their positive outlook on the work they do, their planning expertise, and their transformational focus, these are two people who are making a very important contribution to the library profession as it moves into a challenging and changing new century.

Meet Ethel Himmel and Bill Wilson

Himmel & Wilson is a consulting firm that helps all types of libraries with their planning, technology, management, and building needs. Both Ethel E. Himmel and William J. Wilson have worked with libraries, library systems, and state library agencies in twenty-five states since the company started in 1987. Their most recent published collaboration is *Planning for Results: A Public Library Transformation Process* (Chicago: American Library Association, 1998).

Ethel Himmel has been consulting full-time since 1991. Her bachelor's degree (in political science) is from the University of Illinois and her M.S.L.S. if from the University of Wisconsin. Before returning to UW for her Ph.D. in Library Science, Ethel served as Deputy Director of the La Crosse (WI) Public Library. She has chaired the Wisconsin Association of Public Librarians, and in 1994 Ethel was President of the Wisconsin Library Association.

Bill Wilson has been a full-time consultant since 1987. Before that, he was Wisconsin's State Librarian. His bachelor's degree is from Gordon College (MA), and his M.S.L.S. is from the State University of New York—Buffalo. Additional graduate studies, in library science, social work, and urban and regional planning, were completed at the University of Wisconsin—Madison. In 1987, Bill was President of the Wisconsin Library Association.

Ethel Himmel and Bill Wilson make their home in "America's Most Livable City," Madison, Wisconsin, where the company is located.

6

MANAGEMENT PRACTICES IN INFORMATION SERVICES— IMPLEMENTING CHANGE

*T*here are two critical requirements that must be in place before change can be successfully implemented in the information workplace: new roles and new responsibilities must be identified and accepted by all information stakeholders, and the information "culture" must be expanded beyond the department or facility whose mission it is to provide information delivery.

The first of these "implementations" begins with the information workers themselves, a point John Wilson makes in his discussion of the information provider as internal consultant. He teaches the subject at professional conferences, in programs he calls "awareness seminars" because, as he puts it, "the people who attend them are being prepared to bring to their managements a new level of understanding about the value of information." Implementing change, for Wilson, includes establishing the value of information within the company or other parent organization and then, almost as a side product, positioning the information operation as a key resource in the company.

It's a point that is not lost in another of the information disciplines, in the records management field, and Peter Emmerson at Barclay's Bank

makes much of the role of management in implementing change by training staff for providing value-added services. As society in general (and
internal information customers in particular) seek more and better
responses from information providers, Emmerson's enthusiasm for training information staff in the basics of the information function and its role
in the workplace make a great deal of sense.

At J.P. Morgan in New York, Ellen Miller may no longer be providing
"library" services herself (she was once a very successful specialist librarian), but information is very much a part of what she does, and her previous work has positioned Miller for success as Chief Administrative
Officer in Global Equities at J.P. Morgan. As she and her team look at the
implementation of change in their operation, the bottom line is not difficult to discern: "We came up with what I call our 'guiding force' for information services. . . . Our standard is simply this: *Is this the information
that people in this institution need to do the business of this institution?*"

Certainly such thinking influences the implementation of change at
the opposite end of the "subject" spectrum, as two interviews demonstrate. At the Victoria and Albert Museum's National Art Library, Keeper
and Chief Librarian Jan Floris van der Wateren is able to combine museology, research librarianship, and organizational management with a skill
and unique style that encourages the acceptance of change from a vast
body of information stakeholders. And at the University Club of New
York, Library Director and Curator of Collections Andrew Berner has for
several years delightfully refuted the contention that standard management practices don't work in "traditional" libraries. In both institutions,
change and the implementation of successful change management are a
constant and ongoing element, and both van der Wateren and Berner
make it clear that implementing change is simply a matter of identifying
and understanding what change needs to be made and positioning themselves to make the change.

Much of the success in this area involves cultural change, of course,
and if van der Wateren and Berner are influential in bringing both management change and cultural change into the humanities, they have a
compatriot in Lany McDonald's success in the editorial/corporate world.
At Time Warner, McDonald was brought in to bring cultural change to
both the information-delivery side of the operation and to the editorial/
corporate operation, and she was uniquely successful. Starting with the

information staff and making sure that staff members understood their role in the change operation ("You share the vision"), McDonald moved to the organization at large, targeting the information clients in order to change their perceptions about information and information delivery in today's editorial climate.

JOHN WILSON
at JMW Mosaic talks about internal consultants

John Wilson caused quite a stir at EBIC'94, the European Business Information Conference held in Paris in March. Having come to the meeting to present a workshop entitled "Life After Downsizing: How to be an Internal Consultant," Wilson had little idea his subject would be so popular. Many attendees at the meeting wanted to hear what he had to say, as they themselves were groping with these very issues. For these information services managers, the emotional upheavals connected with the downsizing process—and their attempts to present themselves and their staffs as valuable information providers within the very organizations that were questioning their worth—made Wilson's subject a very "hot topic" indeed.

A few months after EBIC, *InfoManage* caught up with Wilson in London. His firm, JMW Mosaic, Ltd., had just landed a couple of important contracts to bring his ideas about in-house consulting to a wider audience. Needless to say, this is a prospect that makes Wilson happy, and he was in a very confident mood as he talked about his company and its work.

"What we're doing at this point is raising awareness about information and information services, which is why I refer to these programs as 'awareness seminars.' The people who attend them are being prepared to bring to their managements a new level of understanding about the value of information.

Originally published in *InfoManage : The International Management Newsletter for the Information Services Professional* 1 (10), August, 1994.

"In many cases, what we have with senior management is a complete lack of awareness about what they're missing. They just don't know what a proper information services operation can do for them."

Wilson's ideas about information management and about establishing the value of information services have much to do with his entrepreneurial approach to libraries and information work in general.

"I'm a great believer in 'cheek,'" he says, and despite the grin on his face you know he means it, for his skill at bringing entrepreneurial thinking into the information workplace enabled him to have several successful information positions before he went into business for himself.

But the "cheek" must be based on solid value, and Wilson makes it clear that in each of his positions, he has been required to match his performance with management expectations.

"In the information field," Wilson says, "you learn to back up your strengths with good, solid contributions. You learn to differentiate your information market so that you can demonstrate, immediately if necessary, the business benefit of whatever it is you're trying to do."

It was while working as the Assistant Librarian at the Geological Society of London that Wilson decided to pursue an entrepreneurial direction for his career. With a special interest in science, exploration and, particularly, map librarianship, and having targeted the oil industry, Wilson soon found himself employed as the first professional librarian in the Technical Library at Esso Exploration Europe Africa's UK office. It was at Esso that Wilson realized the scope—and power—of automation in the information delivery process.

"I'm interested in increased access to information," he says. "That's what drives me, motivates me, and if I can use electronic media to get better information—faster information—to those who want it, then I'm going to do so."

And the newest buzzword in information management, the "integration" of internal and external information?

"It's an artificial distinction," Wilson says, "an artificial distinction created by librarians. Most people who are looking for information don't care about whether the information is internal or external. They are more interested in what I call its 'provenance:' Can it be trusted? How accurate is it? How quickly can I get it? And how much is it going to cost?"

That philosophy, Wilson suggests, evolved for him after he left Esso, for it was while he headed up the Technical Library at BP Exploration (after a brief stint at BP Minerals) that he began to realize the power that's built into a recognized quality program of information delivery. At BP Exploration, the library operation had just been computerized, and Wilson recognized that he had an entrepreneurial role to play there.

"First of all," he says, "all the grunt work having to do with setting up the system had been done, so I didn't need to worry about that."

Wilson continues, and the sly smile tells you he's about to tell you something about himself.

"But more important," he says, "the system wasn't yet so far along that John Wilson couldn't influence it. So that's what I set out to do." Over the following six years, under Wilson's direction, the system was developed and became the standard library application in all six of BP Exploration's European offices, with over one million records indexed on the London database alone. Last year the application was successfully migrated to a UNIX-based system and is still in use in BP Exploration's London and Aberdeen offices.

In fact, it was at BP Exploration that Wilson first began to think in terms of internal consultancy. By the end of the last decade, there was much pressure at BP, as with many other organizations, to downsize, For Wilson, this pressure provided the opportunity to put his ideas to practical use. The internal consultant, in his terms, is the employee (in this case, a professional information practitioner) who can bring to the company expertise and specific problem-solving ability. If obtained externally, these skills would be prohibitively expensive or, at the very least, difficult to justify. By training selected internal information professionals to refocus their efforts into a "consultancy mode," both the information operation and the parent organization benefit.

As Wilson explains the concept of internal consultancy, it becomes clear that one of the first requirements is an understanding—on the part of the managers—involved of the distinctions between various types of consultancy. He has identified three:

- The direct purchase of information or expertise, in which the client has correctly diagnosed the problem, but does not have the skills, resources, or desire to provide a solution from within the organization.

- The doctor-patient model, which Wilson characterizes as something like this from the client: "I know that there is something wrong and I would like to find out what it is and I want you to either tell me what to do or fix it."

- The process consultation model, in which the client is aware of the problem, but not of its precise nature, or in which the client does not know what type of help is needed or what is available, or in which the client could benefit from being involved in the diagnosis of the problem.

In all three of these scenarios, as described by Wilson, the running theme is that the information services staff—having information expertise—can serve as consultants for solving the clients' problems. At the same time, management can see the justification, in terms of resource management, for using the information staff as internal consultants, which Wilson demonstrates by patiently picking up a pencil and drawing a functional "ladder" for the information services unit.

"The organization," he explains, "already has a 'consultancy' structure in place. It has a commodity—the information provided by the information services unit—and if the unit is being properly managed, value added services and products are provided as well. By establishing themselves as internal consultants, the information services staff merely follows through on the 'information challenge,' if you want to call it that, that already exists."

A primary goal for in-house consultants, according to Wilson, is an understanding of the role of senior management in the organization, especially in terms of information consultancy.

"Managers are often not aware of what they are missing," he says, "and until the consultant recognizes this, and comes to an agreement with management about the value of the consultant's work, the effort is not particularly productive. Agreement comes, of course, when the consultant can demonstrate credibility. People don't employ or engage consultants—whether internal or external—unless they can see business benefits or ways to alleviate pain. And when these can be demonstrated to management, the consultant can get on with the work."

Again the pencil comes out, and Wilson makes his point with another drawing.

"Unfortunately," he says, "for most people trained as librarians there is a very strong belief that the success comes because they know they can find what they need. The real success, however, comes when the consultant can work with the person who knows he or she doesn't know, and, more important, can demonstrate real information value to the person who doesn't know that he doesn't know. That's where the internal consultant can excel."

Wilson is quick to describe the positive side of using an internal consultant. One important advantage, for example, is the built-in continuity with the clients. Also important are the internal consultant's knowledge of the organization, his or her personal networks, the trust and teamwork that come from successful internal relationships, an understanding of the corporate or organizational culture and, of course, the fact that the internal consultant is, from management's point of view, a "free" service.

But each of these positive characteristics has a negative side, and the information services executive seeking to serve, or to have specific staff serve, as internal consultants must recognize these built-in limitations: there is, in any organization, historical "baggage" that the employee has been carrying around, and he or she may simply be too close to the client to be objective. Also, there is necessarily a lack of experience in dealing with similar situations in other organizations, and the employee/consultant might be too closely associated with a former role or service within the organization, and thus might not be able to be objective about the conditions he or she is attempting to correct. And while limited consultancy skills might be a problem, another potential problem is the situation that occurs when unpopular, but necessary, recommendations have to be made, recommendations which could even be career damaging for an employee/consultant. These are less of a problem to the more independent external consultant.

And of course there is that old adage about value: if the internal consultant is "free," do the results of the consultancy have any value? Wilson raises an honest question: "Is the consultant's advice worth anything, if management and the clients perceive that they didn't pay anything for it? Of course it is, and you and I know that it is, but for many in the corporate world, solutions aren't really solutions until they've been paid for."

So it would seem that the negatives equal or perhaps even outweigh the positives. If that's the case, why even consider internal consultancy as an option? Why not always go for the external consultant?

"Because management—even management within the information services unit itself—will not provide the resources for all the problems a consultant is needed for. By offering the members of the information team as internal consultants, the work of the information operation itself is enhanced. So much so, in fact, that the work provided by the information staff becomes part of the framework of the organization and, as such, becomes indispensable to the success of the parent organization."

To talk with John Wilson about using the information staff as internal consultants, and training them to operate as consultants, is to talk about entrepreneurial thinking in the information workplace. What happens with internal consultancies—if they're done right—is simply job security. At the same time, however, the information services unit is integrated into organizational operations at a level far beyond that usually associated with information work, and the value of the products and services provided by the information staff is properly recognized. At that point, the provision of information—in management terms—becomes a required function within the parent organization and, happily for the professionals who supply the information, is perceived as such.

Meet John Wilson

John Wilson describes his company: "JMW Mosaic was created to assist organizations to realize maximum value from their investment in information and documentation.

"Consultancy is provided for all or part of the information management 'life cycle,' from preliminary feasibility studies, through requirements analysis and business justification to the selection and implementation of solutions and their integration with working practices and procedures. Training is also an important consideration. Not only the 'hands-on' training of those individuals who will be directly involved in utilizing new tools and techniques, but also the education and awareness of others, who will be impacted by the changes taking place. This includes senior management who may not be aware of the possibilities for significant business enhancements opened up by information and document management 'beyond the paper paradigm.'"

PETER EMMERSON
at Barclay's Bank: Training records managers
for value-added service

When you're in charge of records management for one of the largest banks in the world, training and education for practitioners is not an abstract concept. According to Peter Emmerson, Head of Barclays Records Services, it's the training process that enables the bank to provide the highest level services and products to its information customers. And it doesn't matter whether those information seekers are the internal staff who use corporate information to provide their customers with the information they need, or the bank's customers who need information to know how the bank is performing. Whether internal or external, the information that passes through Barclays Records Services is critical for the people who need it, and it's the training that the bank's records management employees receive that enables Barclays to provide that information at a level that matches customer expectations.

"Customer care is taken seriously at Barclays," Emmerson says. "Our job is to provide value-added services for our customers. That means we work with them to minimize the time they spend looking for things. Our records management system must be easy to use, as simple as possible. In fact, what we are trying to do is to create an information system that the user can use without interpretation from the provider. That's what we need, in order to be effective."

Effectiveness is the order of the day for Peter Emmerson. For almost thirty years, he has worked in records and information related activities, both in government and business, and in both developing and developed countries. His commitment to maintaining and promoting the highest professional and technical standards in the workplace has won much

Originally published in *InfoManage : The International Management Newsletter for the Information Services Professional* 2 (2), January, 1995.

admiration, and his determination to encourage the highest levels of expertise and skill among his fellow professionals is well known.

Professional training is, of course, one of the avenues for achieving these goals and it is certainly in the training field that Emmerson has excelled. Indeed, throughout his career, one of Emmerson's main aims has been to ensure that there is a "pool of qualified professionals" available, with skills that match the continuing and changing needs of the marketplace. He has done this by developing training programs and sharing his experience and expertise by every possible means, including writing, presenting, training, and one-to-one encounters. His list of published articles and presentations is impressive, and as the editor and co-author of *How to Manage Your Records* (Cambridge, 1989), Emmerson is recognized as the compiler of a standard work for teaching purposes in graduate programs both in the UK and throughout the world.

At Barclays, where Emmerson has been employed since 1987, he has been involved in the full scale development of a records and information management program, and he is now heavily involved in the development of a corporate strategy for the management of all recorded information in all media, to take the company into the 21st century. As part of this effort, Emmerson and his team have had to recognize that the entire records management field is going through a change process.

"At first," he says, "Barclays was resistant to change, but following a successful pilot project, we have been working on the development of integrated departmental and business unit based systems which provide approaches to the media-independent control of recorded information. The essence of this approach has been the application of what is now a unique method of analyzing business processes by function, activity and transaction, and whether they are substantive or facilitative, and the design of new systems which mirror that analysis."

"The design is structured so that it can be applied to electronic as well as hardcopy records, and it is also 'organization proof,' allowing information to migrate comfortably with functions which change their position in the corporate hierarchy. The design is supported by comprehensive retention management based on real corporate and business needs, rather than mythical assumptions about statutory or regulatory requirements."

"The main framework of the methodology," Emmerson notes, "has been included in a set of standards for records and document management which have been adopted by the bank's senior management, meaning we ensure that all managers are aware of, and understand, their level of accountability and responsibility for ensuring that the company's interests are protected."

"It's hard to influence what people do," he says, "so we must take our records management processes down to the business level . . . That means we must take a look at what customers are looking for when they are seeking information, that we must in effect train records management staff to understand that for customers, a record is what I like to call, 'evidence of what you did.' When that customer comes looking for information, the record must be complete. The 'footprints' of the data, so to speak, must stay in place even though you may be working with only one or two components of that record. It is in the 'depth' of that 'footprint' where the record has value. We mustn't break it up, or the record loses its value."

Training for records management goes beyond the issue of value, however. When discussing qualifications for a career in records management, for example, Emmerson agrees that basic skills are needed, but he feels strongly that there is also a need for a more general understanding of the information function and its role in the workplace.

"When employees come to us with these qualifications," he says, "it's the bag of tools we help them unpack. It positions them, we think, for the kind of in-house training that will then incorporate a philosophy of service and customer care that will do what we want to do for our information customers."

One technique which Emmerson uses is to recruit employees to work for a year before they go to university for their graduate training. There is a need to instill what he calls "right attitudes" about information services before these would-be practitioners have their formal education, and working with these people—the "seed corn," he calls them—accomplishes this.

Other training issues that Emmerson thinks about include a number of concerns that all information services managers recognize, for there is apparently a universal interest in such subjects as the need for a distinction between formal education and what we generally refer to as "training," and for the right level of training for entry-level employees. And regardless of whether you're talking about records management or some other area of information services management, certainly there is concern about certification. Emmerson does not equivocate about this hot topic.

"Certification is ultimately an essential path down which you have to go," he says, noting that certification, when combined with a body of sound, theoretical literature and an enforceable code of ethics, enables information services providers to then meet the standard list of requirements that all professional service practitioners must meet if they are to be recognized as such.

Another of the training issues that seems to come up with some frequency is the need for information services training to be more focused, and more integrated, relating various kinds of information services to one another. For example, as part of his responsibility Emmerson manages the bank's corporate records center, the largest in the UK, and it is a position which gives him the opportunity to look at the entire information spectrum at Barclays. From this perspective, he can track how the company uses both internal and external information, and being in charge of Records Services permits him to see how the two types of information are connected (or not, as the case may be).

"There is some concern about integrated information," Emmerson says, "but I'm not sure all our information staff understand the value of integrated information services. Information 'warehousing' is built on a myth that all information is equally valuable, so it becomes difficult to train staff to understand what should be retained and what should not. Internal information, of course, is more specific, more 'at home,' but it is often only part of a larger information need that includes external information gathered from a specialized library or other information source. Staff need to be taught that the customer's needs might incorporate both."

Teaching the staff. That's where Peter Emmerson concentrates his efforts, and it pays off. By positioning his department and the information it provides as an essential resource within the company, and by working with his staff to ensure that they are trained with customer care values in place, with that "right attitude" instilled, Emmerson and Barclays Records Services make a contribution that is recognized—and valued—throughout the bank. It is a recognition that is well deserved.

Meet Peter Emmerson

Since 1987, Head of Barclays Records Services, Barclays Bank PLC, London. Prior to that, Regional Manager, Records Services, British Steel Corporation from 1976 to 1987, with previous employment at the National Archives of Rhodesia (now Zimbabwe) from 1965 to 1975. Chairman of the Records Management Group of the Society of Archivists from 1984 to 1988, Executive Vice President, President of the International Records Management Council from 1988 to 1992, and a Founder Member (1983) of the Records Manage- ment Society of Great Britain. Mr. Emmerson is the author of numerous publications about records management and has taught at the Roehampton Institution of Education, London, and served as an external examiner at the Manchester Metropolitan University, Manchester. As a leader in the records management field, he has striven constantly ("evangelically perhaps," he says) to promote records and information management as a discrete discipline and to widen its base.

Does "moving up" mean "moving out" for information professionals? Not necessarily.
ELLEN MILLER
at J.P. Morgan is no longer a "practicing" librarian. But information management is still very much part of her work.

Career advancement. It's a big topic with library and information services professionals these days, because lots of people are discovering—the hard way—that they aren't able to move up in the corporate or organizational management structure. It's not that they aren't qualified. It's that senior management thinks of them as "librarians." Or "information specialists." And what they're looking for, they say, is "managers." "Organizational

Originally published in *InfoManage : The International Management Newsletter for the Information Services Professional* 2 (12), November, 1995.

types" is one of the phrases used. And "generalists" is another. But not "librarians." Not "information professionals." That's too specific. And besides (the most common reaction), "You're doing a very good job as librarian (information manager/records manager/archivist/information technology manager)." "You're good at what you do." "You wouldn't like working out of your area of expertise."

Ellen Miller, Vice-President and Chief Administrative Officer of the Global Equities Division of J.P. Morgan doesn't like that kind of talk. In fact, she wouldn't have the job she has today if she or her managers thought that way. She's working for a company and with a team of corporate executives who wouldn't pay attention to that kind of talk even if someone tried to foist it on them. It's not part of the corporate culture at J.P. Morgan. The bank, located on Wall Street in the heart of New York's famous financial district, has long had a reputation for the teamwork approach to management, for the emphasis on being part of the Morgan "family," so it's only natural for the company to encourage people to move up, regardless of their "specialties" or professional expertise. With some 16,000 employees worldwide and ranking as the sixth largest bank in the United States, the company has long had a reputation for believing in the value of team spirit among its employees, and the bank rewards that team spirit. It all connects back to the bank's commitment to client service, and to, as Miller puts it, "doing what's best for the client—that's what's paramount at Morgan." If you're good at what you do, and if it relates to doing a good job for the client, you're a candidate for promotion.

Miller's move to the administrative world is not so unusual when you think about some of the directions her career has taken. Having pursued her undergraduate degree at Chestnut Hill College, she graduated expecting to have a career "in business," but librarianship—as a career—was not part of the picture. Miller comes from a family of white-collar workers. Office work in one form or another has long been part of their lives, and she had just assumed that her work would be in that field in one capacity or another. As it turned out, following her graduation from college, she began to look for a job but didn't find anything that really seemed to grab her interest. Then, after some time, as the kids say, "just hanging out," someone in her mother's office told her about a relative of his who was pretty important at The First Boston Corporation, and that there was an opening in the library. As a courtesy to this family friend, Miller went along for the interview and was surprised to find herself being seriously considered for the job of Assistant Librarian. (At the time she was pretty naïve about it, but now she wonders just how much influence that "friend of a friend" had in the decision.) In any case, she got the job, and thus began what seemed destined to be a pretty straightforward career as a librarian in the financial community. She earned her graduate degree while she worked for First Boston, and then became Head Librarian at White, Weld and Company, an investment banking firm. This was followed by an eight-year stint as Director of Research Services at Booz, Allen & Hamilton, which she left to become Vice-President of a library space planning firm, Designs for Information.

It was while working on a consulting assignment for this company that Miller came to the Mergers and Acquisitions Department at Morgan Guaranty. After she had developed an information strategy for the unit, the bank hired her in 1989 as Vice President and Manager of the Information Resource Center. In 1991 she added managerial responsibility for the bank's Presentation Services Group to her duties, and she continued in this dual role until January of this year, when she, as she says, "left the library community" to accept the position she now holds. And although taking the job was, indeed, a move away from librarianship—that is, librarianship as practiced on a "day-to-day" basis—it was a move that would permit Miller to continue to maintain her ties with specialized librarianship and with the library community, which she felt (and still feels) is an important part of her work.

As she got started in the new job, a newly created position in the Global Equities Division, she found it was not easy to categorize exactly what she was supposed to be doing. And the position still doesn't have a job description.

"There's a reason for that," Miller says, and her easy smile lets you know that the lack of a formal job description is not something that worries her and her managers very much.

"The work is very broad based, meaning that my authority and my responsibility move all around the equities side of the bank. Theoretically, there are two primary areas of responsibility, my supervision of the research editorial group, nine people who work with equities research and edit and publish the reports we produce, and what I call 'the events and road show desk,' which is a sort of 'hospitality' job, for the four people in that section plan events, entertainments for clients, execute client road shows when the bankers go on the road, that kind of thing."

While that part of the job might seem sufficiently codified, Miller laughs when she is asked to describe some of her other responsibilities.

"I don't know if it's a word or not," she says, "but a big part of my work is a sort of 'liaison-y' kind of function for the non-officer staff, working with Human Resources on performance appraisals, raises, working with the different managers to determine what is appropriate and what is not appropriate in the compensation picture at any given time. It can get complicated, and it involves negotiation, there's no doubt about that."

So it looks as if Miller has chosen the right phrase to describe her job change, for she has, in a way, "left" the library community.

"But not the information services field," she is quick to remark. "As we talked about this position, and as it began to take shape here in the division, I felt very strongly that there was an information services component linked to it. Although I was going to be leaving the Information Resource Center and the Presentation Services Group—if this thing came through—I felt that there was still a strong information element that I needed to be involved with. We are in the business of buying real-time information as it comes in and repackaging it for our staff, and that's where I felt I could make a good contribution. The systems and technology people are usually very involved in IT, as they should be, but there has to be input from the content side, and that's where my experience comes in.

"Most librarians," Miller points out, "are dealing with historical information. Even if it's only fifteen minutes old, it's 'historical,' in the strict sense of the word. What we do, by dealing with real-time information, is to handle information differently, but we still need someone who understands the content side of it, who understands how people use information. That's where I come in, and that's where my experience as a librarian supports what I do in this position."

It hasn't, of course, been without its bumps. No major change is, and one of the biggest jobs Miller had to do in the course of her work was to rethink some of the information "mission" at the bank, particularly once the bank's traditional research-type library had been subsumed into the Information Resource Center, a change that took place while Miller was managing that facility.

"We had to come up with a retention plan," she says. "We were buying too much and keeping too much, and all the while our focus in the delivery of information was changing. So we came up with what I call our 'guiding force' for the Information Resource Center, and I've transferred that over to the work I'm doing in Global Equities. Our standard became simply this: 'Is this information that the people in this institution need now to do the business of the institution?' When the mission statement is that clear-cut, it isn't difficult to make some of the decisions that have to be made."

Surely those decisions have involved some risk. What kind of chances did Miller feel she was taking, when she headed up the combined Information Resource Center and the Presentation Services Group? What about the chances she's taking as Chief Administrative Officer in Global Equities?

It is not a problem, she says. It all relates back, as Miller tells it, to the culture that is in place in the organization. It is a culture of empowerment, of innovation. The bank wants its staff to be forward thinking. It wants to be close to the cutting edge, if not on it. And in terms of what she was doing in the previous job, where she had to take the staff from 65 people to 122, in order to do the work that had to be done, it was clear that she was empowered. She was expected to take risks.

"Here at the bank, when you're given something to run, they let you run it. I was working with two vital support areas, and when we had to do something, I would make my presentation, and before I left the room I had a decision. It's that kind of place. Any innovation, any plan is entertained seriously. We continue to do it. For example, we now have published three equities reports on the Internet. They're free, and they enable our clients to access—with a minimum of effort—information that we've put together for them. In another area, related to the internal operations of the bank, we have a new group at the bank called Vendor Management, and I represent equities with the group. My job is to look at the relationships we have with vendors and then, working with other members of the group, come up with new methods and new ways for managing those relationships. It's all part of the innovative package we have in place in our management scenario here."

So is there a drill, then, for librarians and other information services professionals who want to move up in the managerial hierarchy? Is there a procedure, a plan? If there is one, Ellen Miller has probably come closest to formulating it than anyone else, and it's clear that it involves a number of components that have to work together. The person herself has to be innovative, to be a risk-taker and be excited by change and the change management process. As important as anything else, she has to work in a milieu in which innovation is respected and encouraged. There has to be, as there is at Morgan, a culture of innovation. But there has to be more, too, and Miller's innate modesty holds her back from speaking about this one, but it's there nonetheless. It's that clear understanding of who you are and what you are supposed to be doing within the company or other enterprise that employs you. Miller has it. In her case, it's that thing that so many librarians bring to the information delivery process without even knowing they're doing it, that connection between the "content" of the information, of how the users will use it, and the mechanisms for delivering it. In most cases, of course, nowadays this latter has to do with IT, but it doesn't really matter what the mechanism is. The thing that's important is that the librarian/information specialist knows how to link it with the content and what the users need. That linking, that connection-making, so to speak, can carry you anywhere in the organizational management you want to go, as long as you're willing to let senior management know what you know. And what you can do with it. Making that connection is, without question, an ability that Ellen Miller has in spades.

Meet Ellen Miller

Ellen L. Miller is Vice President and Chief Administrative Officer in the Global Equities Division of J.P. Morgan . . . Prior career as a librarian, financial services information manager, and consultant to librarians and information services practitioners . . . Active member of the Special Libraries Association, for which she served twice as President of the New York Chapter, the organization's largest with some 1,500 members . . . Has taught seminars at SLA Annual Conferences on space planning for special libraries, planning techniques for special libraries, and corporate library excellence . . . Served a four-year term on SLA's Finance Committee . . . Frequent speaker at SLA Annual Conferences, as well as before other information organizations such as ASIS, IIA, NENON, and graduate schools of library/information services in New York and Boston . . . In her spare time, Ellen Miller enjoys travelling and considers herself fortunate to have had an opportunity to visit most of Western Europe, Asia, Australia, and Africa, as well as the breadth of Canada from British Columbia and the Yukon to the Maritime Provinces. Miller is also an avid mystery reader and theatre goer.

At London's V&A,
JAN VAN DER WATEREN
is enthusiastic about moving Britain's National Art Library into
its new space—and about the managerial challenges the move provides

Excitement abounds in London's South Kensington these days. The Victoria and Albert Museum is moving rapidly toward the 21st century—Full Steam Ahead!—and those who would impede the museum's progress are hereby warned to prepare themselves for defeat. The future will happen, and change will come to the V&A, Britain's National Museum of Art and Design.

In fact, change and change management are already subjects of much interest among managers at this great institution, and the V&A is shrewdly positioning itself to retain its designation as the world's greatest museum of the decorative arts. As the world changes around it, the V&A, too, will change. Managing that change process, an activity which is already in the implementation stage, is the responsibility of a group of highly skilled and well-organized managers led by Dr. Alan Borg, the V&A's level-headed and foresightful director.

Among the managers—and perhaps (according to some who know about these things) even leading the charge—is Jan van der Wateren, Keeper and Chief Librarian of the National Art Library, located at the V&A. Van der Wateren himself is part of the excitement in South Kensington, for he is preparing the NAL for a move to a new facility, and as a leader in the international art research community, he has managerial responsibility for preparing the museum's curators, staff, and researchers for the digitized electronic environment that is going to literally transform the way information in the field of art, design, and the decorative arts is delivered.

Originally published in *InfoManage : The International Management Newsletter for the Information Services Professional* 4 (5), April, 1997.

It's not an easy job, certainly, but it is interesting managerially, which becomes clear in any conversation with van der Wateren about his work. It's a broad-ranging discussion, to say the least, and as the topics wander among such subjects as the planned move into a new library facility, the V&A's automation management projects, the political issues that surface in a library that provides information services for both a specialist clientele (the Museum's staff) and the art and design research community at large, there's no question that van der Wateren's busy schedule these days is one that includes a considerable amount of juggling.

Managing the various collections [see sidebar on next page] and ensuring that the NAL's many clients, with their differing information needs, get the specific information they are seeking calls for an emphasis on quality information services management, and for van der Wateren, quality service is directly related to the excellence of the NAL staff. As a result, he has, in his nine years as Keeper and Chief Librarian, focused much of his attention in building up that staff, in determining that the people who come to work at the National Art Library understand that their role is an information delivery role. They're not there to "warehouse" the books. Although, naturally, in a collection as extensive and as varied as this, preservation and storage issues are important considerations, almost as soon as they come to work at the Library, new employees become aware that at the NAL, information is paramount. It's a service culture that is unique among the many libraries that make up the art and design research community.

"We do it by concentrating on excellence in our staff," van der Wateren says. "There are currently about 65 staff, of which 50 are professionals. That wasn't always the case. Previously, three of the 40 or so staff were professionally trained, qualified librarians. The others were here in various positions that were connected with working at the Museum, but their primary emphasis was not necessarily library- or information-oriented. For many years, jobs in the library were used as an easy way to get on the museum staff, and there was a sort of tradition of dilettante librarianship, people working in the library as a stepping stone to other Museum work. That's not the case now. In fact, the NAL is a very professional operation, and working at the National Art Library is recognized, both by the museum community and the workers themselves, as a very serious, information-focused activity."

The National Art Library

The National Art Library was created originally as the Library of the Schools of Design at Somerset House, which had been founded in 1837 following parliamentary concern about the nature of instruction in design. Over the years, the collection continued to grow, and when the V&A was built in South Kensington, it was moved into purpose-built rooms at the Museum, rooms in which it is still largely housed (but not for long, as it will move in the future to the building that formerly housed the Public Records Office).

Subjects covered in the NAL's collections include those central to the work of the Victoria and Albert Museum: prints, drawings, and paintings; furniture and woodwork; textiles and dress; ceramics and glass; metalwork; sculpture; and the art and design of the Far East, of India, and of South East Asia. Particularly relevant to the Library's collection area are its holdings in the history of the art, craft, and design of the book. All of this core material is supplemented by literature from a much broader subject field including, for example, a strong collection of documentation about architecture. Materials are acquired in most Western European languages, and some Asian language materials are acquired as well. A wide range of formats is collected, from manuscript material to videodisk publications.

Major strengths of the Library's collections are the holdings of 18th and 19th century sales catalogs and 19th century exhibition catalogs. Interestingly, though (thanks to the eclectic collecting habits of some of the Museum's donors), the NAL collection also includes medieval manuscripts, artists' books, comics and graphics novels, trade literature (including a major collection of material issued by Liberty & Co.), and an outstanding collection of 19th century periodicals. Among the special collections are two significant 19th century libraries, that of the Rev. Alexander Dyce (1798-1869), which includes a major collection of Shakespeare's works, most notably the First Folio of 1623, and the collec-

tion of John Forster (1812-1876), which includes the manuscripts and first editions of many of Charles Dickens' novels and three Leonardo da Vinci notebooks.

In 1977, the foundation of the Archive of Art and Design widened NAL collecting responsibilities to include archives. More than 170 archive groups representative of the activity of individuals, businesses, and societies involved in the production, marketing, promotion, and study of art and design have been collected. The Library also manages the Victoria and Albert Museum Archive and Registry.

The work of the National Art Library is three-fold: it is a curatorial department in its own right; a research and reference library; and the library of the Victoria and Albert Museum and its staff. As a curatorial department, the NAL has a specific responsibility to contribute to the understanding and enjoyment of the history and design of the book by collecting, conserving, and making available published and unpublished examples ranging from the illuminated manuscript to the artist's book.

As a public research and reference library of last resort, the NAL provides seats for 85 readers and its information service answers approximately 66,000 personal enquiries and 11,000 telephone enquiries annually (as well as 4,000 enquiries by letter).

As the Library of the V&A Museum, the NAL also provides a service which supports the work of the Museum staff, including access to a wide range of international online databases and to the interlibrary loan network via the British Library Document Supply Centre. To make the Library collections more accessible, the NAL automated catalog is networked throughout the Museum and the holdings of departmental libraries can be identified through the central NAL catalog. Library liaison representatives work with their opposite numbers in the Museum Collections to ensure effective communications about acquisitions, and to assist with the induction of new Collections staff.

Just how focused becomes evident when van der Wateren describes the multiple collections that make up what is known as the National Art Library. There are a variety of different collections, all organized at different times in the Museum's history, and even the various finding aids, the many different catalogs, weren't coordinated until recently. As a result, without a single classification system and with materials shelved in many different locations, there was what van der Wateren refers to as the Library's "hybrid collection." With Museum staff having free access to the collection, it was an administrative nightmare.

The problem was solved by assigning a permanent location for each book: now with the new sequential location marking, reshelving time has drastically improved, taking only two minutes for each book. And every morning, materials used during the previous day are reshelved, with the shelving done by the people who must be most familiar with the materials. "Every junior professional shelves," van der Wateren says. "You can't be a librarian if you don't. It's the only way you know the collection." And it makes a certain amount of sense, for since each Library staff member has some specialty, knowing the collection becomes intricately linked with that staff member's success in delivering the materials connected with that speciality.

With respect to automation, it was the Library that led the way for the Museum at large, for the Library had started using OCLC in 1985, and by 1988 the automation was complete. The Previous Keeper and Chief Librarian, Elizabeth Esteve-Coll, who later became Director of the Museum [and who is now Dame Elizabeth Esteve-Coll, Vice Chancellor of the University of East Anglia], set up unified systems in order to build an automated environment, coordinating eight different units in the museum. The Library's Collection Management Librarian became the Head of Records of the Museum, with the task of developing automation for managing the Museum's collections, numbering more than 4 million objects. Despite the reluctance of some of the Museum staff, it was a natural step for someone with knowledge of library systems to be employed to do this job.

"After all," van der Wateren says, "libraries have had experience with handling large masses of data for a long time, and while there was some reticence—you know how they say 'museums are different'—the project was a success."

Perhaps too much of a success, in fact, for there are now some problems of a different nature, as there is a move within the Museum to centralize everything having to do with automation, and the Library's management doesn't want to give up the NAL's internal automation staff. Will it happen? And will the Library's automation expertise be folded into the Museum's centralized automation program? Perhaps, but with van der Wateren in charge of the NAL, don't count on it!

But whether in the development of automated services, or in efforts to develop more direct staff involvement, the move toward excellence in staff performance continued, and accountability and responsibility—those two elusive criteria in library employee management—were introduced. More formal staff training was pursued, and as each staff member has a speciality, much attention is now given to staff training, networking, and similar activities (every Monday, for example, is Training Day). People are sent off to library school, if that's the direction they want to pursue, and if it's a study program that is not necessarily a "library" program but one that relates to the employee's particular speciality, that staff member is given the time and the resources to pursue further study, either formally or through participation in continuing education programs.

It's not always a painless process, of course, for one of the problems van der Wateren discovered as he attempted to put in place the new automated catalog, or to reorganize the way materials are shelved, is that the Museum's curators and staff want to use the old system, to do things the old way. They don't want to use the database, for example, so they require intermediaries, which they don't always like. But when they complain about using intermediaries, Borg, the V&A's Director, responds by telling them that "they've got to become altruistic for future generations."

It's a phrase that van der Wateren likes, for it matches his philosophy and point of view about information delivery. In the intermediation process, the Library sets up training sessions: "We'll come in as partners," van der Wateren says, "and we'll set up a liaison arrangement with each of the departments. Sometimes it works and sometimes it doesn't, depending on the liaison person the department chooses. And it certainly doesn't work when the person is uninterested or not qualified, and no matter how well-intentioned the effort, appointing a secretary, for example, to liaise on research matters with the NAL staff is not going to result in a useful outcome."

Yet for those departments that have appointed "appropriate" liaisons to work with Library staff, the results have been remarkably good, and the information that goes back and forth between the departmental liaison and the Library staff liaison turns out to be invaluable as the NAL seeks to enhance deliverables to information customers from that department.

Certainly related to this interest in better information delivery, and one of the NAL's challenges that must be confronted head-on, is the political challenge. One of the many issues that van der Wateren must tackle in connection with the move is the political situation, the fears (and sometimes the complaints) of this or that curator or reader about the perceived difficulties of using the collection, about how the NAL's materials will be harder to use ("harder" being a casual synonym, perhaps, for "inconvenient," or "requiring some planning and less spontaneity.") So a considerable amount of van der Wateren's management time is spent reassuring the Museum's internal users (who in fact constitute a very small percentage of the NAL's usage) that their information needs will continue to be provided for. It will simply be done on a more efficient, more cost effective, and, yes, more generous basis than has been possible before. And it will require that certain level of altruism for future generations. It's not possible, in this day and age, to think only of our own generation's information needs. In today's library management environment, especially in terms of a responsible approach to information delivery and the stewardship role that is required in the management and preservation of such precious materials as those housed at the NAL, a certain amount of perceived inconvenience by the current users is a small price to pay for ensuring that these important materials are available for future users.

In very practical terms, the move to the building that formerly housed the Public Records Office is one of the best things that could have happened to the National Art Library. In one fell swoop, without constructing an entirely new building, the collections can move into a space that is virtually fireproof and one that was designed for the preservation and security of important materials.

"Security is our hottest issue," van der Wateren says. "The material that we collect at the National Art Library is by and large and will remain—or become—historical documents. This present facility was built in 1883, when people were honest. It was not designed for the kinds of security issues we are confronted with today. The beauty of the new facility is that not only can we build in the protection we need for working with modern researchers, the building itself is divided into storage 'cells' that can be individually secured, and any major physical disaster, such as a fire or a water leak, is confined to that specific 'cell'."

What we have here, in effect, is a thinking that reflects a special kind of attitude that is sometimes associated with the "green" movement in Europe, and perhaps elsewhere in the world, but it is not an attitude that is usually reflected in management thinking when a facility, such as a library, has outgrown its space and must move to another site. Built around the concept of "Using What You Have," this thinking makes eminent practical sense, for it encourages administrators, managers, and others with facilities-management responsibility to find well-built and well-maintained spaces that already exist, and to adapt them rather than build new structures. Of course the "old" spaces must be up-dated, and there are those times when cabling, rewiring, adding atmospheric controls, and similar requirements will cost more than a new facility, but in most cases, adapting an older building is far more cost effective than building a new one. When Director Borg asked van der Wateren to accompany him to have a look at the Public Record Office as it was being emptied, it immediately became apparent that this was a space that with certain adaptations, and with the addition of a new wing to house readers' services facilities (seating for over 200 readers, state-of-the-art connections, etc.), it would be an ideal setting for the National Art Library. It would not, of course, be physically connected with the Victoria & Albert Museum in South Kensington but it would, better yet, enable the National Art Library to function as a national resource. When the new facility is completed in 2002, it will be, as Jan van der Wateren puts it, "an art library for the nation." With van der Wateren leading the way, and with the support of his information-oriented staff, this seems certain to be the outcome.

Meet Jan van der Wateren

Jan van der Wateren is well known in the art libraries field, both for his affiliation with the National Art Library at the Victoria and Albert Museum, where he has been Keeper and Chief Librarian since 1988, and for his leadership in the art libraries community at large. Prior to coming to the NAL, he was Director and Sir Banister Fletcher Librarian of the British Architectural Library at the Royal Institute of British Architects (and he was elected an Honorary Fellow of the Royal Institute of British Architects in 1995).

Van der Wateren currently chairs IFLA's Art Libraries Section, and from 1991 he has served on the Committee for Literature and Art Archives of the International Council of Archives. From 1994 through 1996, van der Wateren served on the British Film Institute Governors' Sub-Committee on Library and Information Services, and since 1993 he has been a member of the British Library Standing Committee on Art Documentation. Also since 1993, van der Wateren has served on the Executive Committee and the Steering Committee of the Visual Arts Library and Information Plan (VALIP).

Van der Wateren has been a member of the Art Libraries Society/UK & Ireland since 1971, and he was elected a Fellow of the Royal Society of Arts in 1994. In 1995, the same year he was elected an Honorary Fellow of the Royal Institute of British Architects, van der Wateren was elected a Fellow of the Library Association, of which he had been a member since 1967.

Van der Wateren makes his home in London's Notting Hill Gate, "a great center for the artistic demi-monde, as well as for the Great and the Good." His apartment, the top floor of a Victorian house, resembles a gallery, with more than 60 paintings on the walls. His friends have dubbed it "The Florianium" (from his second name, which his close friends use when addressing him). Van der Wateren's personal interests include the study of the Japanese language. Having "always pursued a double career," he is also a trained and registered psychotherapist," maintaining a very small practice "to keep my hand in."

ANDREW BERNER
at the University Club of New York:
Library management includes customer service, a team focus—
and library promotion, done subtly.

Visitors to the splendid University Club Library in New York are frequently surprised. After all, if any library/information delivery environment were to encapsulate what most people mean when they think of
"traditional" librarianship, it would be a place like this: a 125-year history, a collection and a facility within an institution organized specifically
for "the promotion of Literature and Art," several floors of books, an
extensive rare books collection, an on-site conservator and conservation
facility, and a massive reading room designed by one of the world's greatest architects to emulate the Pinturicchio rooms of the Vatican. Yes, most
people expect to be stepping back into some sort of quieter, gentler world
when they come to the University Club Library.

And they do, for the space is impressive, the collections are exceptional (some 100,000 volumes, at last count), and the organization itself,
one of America's preeminent private institutions, simply reeks of gentility and restraint.

But don't be fooled. Step aside from the 900-square-foot Library Foyer
(Imagine! In midtown Manhattan! 900 square feet used as a foyer!) and
you find yourself in the busy "Library Office," as it's called. And that step
is a step into another world, for inside the Library Office, Andrew Berner
and the club's hard-working library staff are busy, busy, busy. Telephones
are ringing, the fax machine is spewing forth documents, Associate
Librarian Jane Reed, in charge of reference, is working with another staff
member to solve a trick enquiry, and other staff members are at their terminals or otherwise occupied taking care of some of those "backstage"
activities required for the successful functioning of any library or information center.

Originally published in *InfoManage : The International Management Newsletter for the Information Services Professional* 4 (12), November, 1997.

Hardly what those visitors expect to find when they visit the club's "traditional" library.

That is what makes Andrew Berner's work so fascinating, for him and for the people who know him. In fact, Berner, whose official title is Library Director and Curator of Collections, finds himself wryly amused from time to time, as professional colleagues come up to him and tell him of their envy of his "cushy" job. It's not cushy. There's a great deal of responsibility, there are any number of management issues being resolved at any one time, there's institutional politics to be dealt with, and there's the constant quest for resources (despite income from an endowment fund that provides the basics, supplemented by the Club's own annual support). So it's not always easy, and Berner, like any other conscientious information services manager these days, has his share of sleepless nights. Still, the pleasures built into his work so far outweigh the problems that he long ago learned to smile at his envious colleagues, thank them for noticing, and then move the conversation on to something else. It's all part of being a gracious manager in an environment that requires— literally—that the management of the facility and the "backstage" work be as unobtrusive as possible. It's what's up front that's emphasized, library services delivered to the library's customers (in this case, the members of the University Club, their guests, and serious scholars upon written application).

Juggling several management balls at once is something of an acquired art, and most information services managers will attest to that fact. For Berner, there are a few added challenges, all of which, as far as he's concerned, just make his professional life a little more interesting and, as he says, "a little complicated" from time to time.

For example, that title of "Curator of Collections" means that not only are Berner and his staff responsible for the management of the world's largest private club library, with a sizable rare books collection and special collections in subjects as varied as 20th-century fine printing and antebellum Southern history, they are also responsible for the club's fine arts collection and the organization's archives.

And not to be dismissed lightly are Berner's responsibilities as a sort of social planner and arbiter, for as Library Director he works closely with the University Club Library Associates, a sort of self-selected friends group created in the early 1980s to bring in additional support to the library and to give people who choose to participate a special reason for attaching themselves to the library.

"That special reason is important," Berner says, "for although the Associates as a group is a source of financial contributions, it is primarily, I would say, a vehicle for people to become involved in the library in a serious way. For most people, visiting a library and using its services is a singular experience, a one-on-one activity in which the user, if he or she interacts with anyone (and many don't), interacts with only the library staff member. What we do with the Associates is to provide them with a reason for being interested in the library."

How they do it at the University Club is an accomplishment of some note, for it's no secret in the New York library/information community that Andrew Berner is greatly admired for the way in which he deftly balances his users' interest in the library with the services that the library provides for them. A side product of this activity, and one that explains his colleagues' admiration for his work, is the sort of "cultural loyalty" that results. The people who use the library at the University Club soon become—literally—friends of the library and participate in its activities and, not to be ignored, contribute to its support.

"But let's be careful here," he says, with just a touch of caution in his voice so his listener will not jump to conclusions.

"Of course we want people to contribute to the support of the library. Any cultural institution wants its audience to contribute, and at our place we do a great many things to encourage them to do that. But the first purpose of the Associates—its primary reason for existence—is to provide a forum, a vehicle through which people can come to the library for meetings, for programs, for receptions, in fact for all kinds of activities. In doing so, they have the opportunity to express their pride in this facility, not just by giving money (which some do and some don't) but by participating. It's a key concept, if you're going to be successful in this game."

Game? How is it a game?

The answer to that question comes more from observation than from asking Berner directly. If you watch him in action, you can see that this is a man who just loves what he's doing, whether it's rounding up Stephen Sondheim to be the speaker for the Associates' Annual Dinner in 1996 (which he did) or organizing a rare books tour for Associates to such places as England (twice), Scotland, Ireland, Germany, Italy, or, stateside, to Chicago, Philadelphia, or Boston. Berner is also responsible for putting together as many as fifteen "meetings" at the club each year, events at which experts in numerous fields, a variety of authors, and bibliophiles and art specialists talk about their work to the members of the Associates, and here again, watching him operate is in itself an object lesson in how to get people enthusiastic about what you're doing. He loves his work, and people want to work with him, so they cooperate, and they say "yes" when he asks them to do something.

So while Berner carefully observes all the rules of good management, and as a library director operates a functional unit that provides the services his identified customers expect, he also brings something else to the management experience, a friendliness and a pleasant "tone" that sets him aside from the "dog-eat-dog" or "swimming-with-the-sharks" management fads that get popular from time to time. It's not hard to see why: This is a man whose work connects directly with his personal life, and his many friends at the University Club attest to that, for his relationship with many of the members of the club long ago evolved from that of a manager of one of the club's many facilities to that of colleague, fellow scholar, fellow raconteur, and friend of many of the people he comes into contact with. It's a very happy ambiance, this management operation that Berner is responsible for, and it can be so characterized because Berner, as a manager, isn't afraid to put his own personal stamp on the work he does.

It all falls into place in the way Berner connects what some might consider a "fringe" group, the University Club Library Associates, with the work that the library itself accomplishes. As he sees it, guiding the Associates is not a fund-raising operation. It's a planning activity, a mechanism for giving people who are affiliated with the University Club Library the opportunity be part of the library. And it all has to do with public relations, as Berner freely admits.

"Everything we do in a library or information center has to be done with an eye to how it will be perceived," he says, "and our work at the University Club is no exception. If there is some aspect of the collection or services that is not a potential public relations tool, you have to ask yourself why you have it or why you do it."

"Of course there are exceptions. For example, the technical services function is not an activity that is exploitable from a public relations point of view. But generally speaking, such things as the specialties in the general collection or the rare books collection, etc. can provide promotional opportunities"

Asked for an example, Berner is quick to respond.

"In a library like this, there is certainly much that is considered 'classic' material that any good library would have, and naturally that material is used. But there are always materials—what we like to call 'second-tier classics'—that were purchased long ago and sit on the shelves. Now no library manager worth his salt wants to take up shelf space with unread materials. Some do just that, while others discard the materials. But there's another alternative. You can see those unread materials as an asset to be exploited. A couple of years ago, we published a brochure called, 'Awaiting Re-Discovery at the University Club Library.' The point was to get people to read these 'second-tier classics' before, for example, they turn up as Masterpiece Theater productions (which is, of course, when these things are called for big time!). Authors like F. Marion Crawford, Edward Everett Hale, Charles Lever, Charles Reade, R.S. Surtees are too good to be ignored, so we thought we might see if we could get them read. And we decided to do it by taking a slightly different slant, and we published this brochure telling people to take a look at these materials. 'Be a trend-setter,' it said. 'Read these things before they show up on PBS.' Well, it worked, and we had great success with getting these materials read. It worked because people like the members of the University Club want to be out in front, even if it involves looking to the past to be so."

And incidentally, although Berner is reluctant to make too much of the connection, the 'promote-the-classics' effort coincided with a very impressive gift to replace and/or restore the volumes in those very same collections that were not in very good shape. It all pays off, if you plan it right.

Still, Berner wants to make sure that the people he speaks with about these things (and he is in great demand as a speaker at conferences, study groups, and so forth) don't think it's all about promotional work, fundraising, etc.

"It's not just fund raising," he says. "You can't just get money out of people. It has to be an enjoyable experience, and that's why we put together so many different programs. We've created a sort of 'University-Club-Library-Family' here, and if some of those family members want to make donations, so be it. But our primary effort, as I keep repeating over and over, is not to raise money. It's to provide a library and information services program for our customers that is organic, alive, and relates to their lives. We've gone beyond just providing books for people to take elsewhere to read, or answers to reference questions, or instruction in using reference materials, that sort of thing. We do those things, and we do them well, but what we really provide is an organic, living library for our customers. That's what they want, and that's what we give them."

And in the long run, in Berner's opinion, it all comes down to service: "Certainly we can establish all sorts of activities to get people to the library," he says. "We can design programs, trips, meetings, whatever you want, and it all falls into the category of 'promoting the library.' But no amount of promotion can substitute for quality service. Promotion can enhance quality but it can't replace it, and it's quality service that we have to provide. It's no more complicated than that."

Isn't that a pretty tall order, providing traditional library services, doing them well, and at the same time supervising all these, well, social activities? Doesn't it sometimes get just a little frantic?

"Of course," Berner says with a laugh, "but even when it gets frantic, you realize that you've got two things going for you: first, you have a staff that's been chosen because they're comfortable working in this environment and because they have a commitment to quality. There's no law that says that traditional library services must be second-rate, or bureaucratic, or full of nonsensical rules and regulations. Those rules and regulations are usually created for the convenience of the staff and not for the users, and that's not the way we do things at the University Club Library. We choose people to work in our library who love libraries, who love books and reading and all those 'traditional' ideas associated with libraries. But there's one more thing they have to have. They have to be people who are committed to delivering quality service to their users.

"And the second thing you've got, that makes it work, is the staff working together as a team. We're not all hung up here on job descriptions and the like. Of course we have job descriptions, and each of us has specific responsibilities, so we have a reference 'specialist' and a 'technical services librarian' and so forth, but we all work together. We talk about our work, we share assignments, and we concentrate on providing the best services we can, regardless of which one of us is handling the task. Management is taken seriously here, as is the service we deliver, so seriously that our daily staff meeting often becomes something like a team-building exercise, with all of us working together to figure out the best, the very best, way to deal with a request or a task. It's an approach that works, and in an environment like this, it's the only approach that works, as far as I can tell."

The service aspect affects relationships too, not only with staff and between staff and the library's customers, but Berner's role as a manager.

"We don't have a choice," he says. "Service must be quality service, and staff must know this, simply because there is so much competition for the kinds of services we provide. To take a very simple example, much of the usage at the University Club Library is for recreational reading, and let's face it: in that area, our customers can get much (if not most) of what they get from us at many different places. But they can't get our level of service anywhere else. We provide them with something that simply doesn't exist at any of the other libraries, bookstores, and similar places that they might go for these materials. We're in the business of adding value. It's what we do. It's why we exist."

That added value (and not just in recreational reading, but in all the services offered by the University Club Library) is what makes the library succeed, and Berner and his people know it. There are also others who know it as well, people who sit on the club's management committees, the club's professional management staff, interested users, the club's Library and Art Committee (with which Berner works closely on policy matters), the Associates' leaders, even visitors. They're all stakeholders in that glorious entity called "The University Club Library," and it's a system of library services and information delivery that brings with it not only considerable responsibility but considerable influence as well.

"Let's go easy there," Berner says, obviously uncomfortable with the suggestion. "I suppose there is a certain amount of influence, and, yes, the library is an influential part of the club's functioning, but these are not activities that stand alone, permitting me to 'call the shots,' as it were, with the organization dutifully falling into line. Not at all. We're running a service operation here, and our information customers, our users, know what they want and expect us to provide it. If we influence them somewhat in their interests, if the library staff and the Library and Art Committee and I in fact have some influence in the operations of the club with respect to the library, that influence is incidental. Power and influence can't be based on an illusion. They must be backed up with substantive reality, and the substantive reality is that we provide library service that is designed specifically for our identified customer base. It's what they want, and it's what we give them. And we do it well."

Customer service. Promotion. Influence. Power. They all come together at that magnificent library operation in midtown Manhattan and it's a pretty obvious that they come together because the library's manager understands the environment in which he operates and knows how to match the library's products and services to that environment. It's a combination that—at the University Club of New York—works and works well, thanks to Andrew Berner and his management skills.

Meet Andrew Berner

Andrew J. Berner is Library Director and Curator of Collections at the University Club of New York, where he has been employed since 1982, first as Assistant Director (1982-1984), and then as Associate Director (1984-1987). Educated at Herbert H. Lehman College, New York, NY, Berner was awarded his B.A. (History) in 1974, the M.A. (History) in 1979. In 1982, he received the M.S.L.I.S. degree from Pratt Institute in Brooklyn, NY.

Recognized internationally as a leader in the specialist library community, Berner was a Co-Founder and Director of OPL Resources, Ltd., serving as Managing Editor of *The One-Person Library: A Newsletter for Librarians and Management*, published by OPL Resources. Berner is also an Editorial Consultant for *InfoManage*, for which he contributes frequent articles on management issues, particularly in the field of human resources management. He has served in numerous positions for the Special Libraries Association, including Chair of the Museums, Arts, and Humanities Division and President of the New York Chapter. In 1991-1993, he was a member of SLA's Presidential Commission on Professional Ethics, Standards, and Professional Recruitment ("The PREPS Commission"). Berner is considered an expert in time management for special libraries, having written several articles and authored the only computer-assisted self-study course in the subject. Awarded the SLA/New York Chapter Distinguished Service Award in 1997, Berner is also a member of Beta Phi Mu, the international library science honor society.

Berner's writings also include his work as editor and primary contributor to *The Illuminator*, the occasional publication of the University Club Library, for which he has written studies of the Medicis of Florence, the voyages of Captain James Cook, illustrator and painter George Cruikshank, Mark Twain, John James Audubon, Samuel Pepys, Sir Winston Churchill, Bret Harte, the fine printing of Bruce Rogers, English romantic poetry, John Charles Fremont, and an informal history of Greenwich Village, 1609-1918. Additionally, his annual "Librarian's Lectures" at The University Club, on subjects as diverse as a history of book illustration to "The Civil War Era Through the Eyes of Harper's Weekly," are a much-anticipated event in the organization's events calendar.

In his personal life, Berner enjoys the New York cultural scene, particularly the ballet and opera, and quiet evenings—when he can find time for them—with his family and friends. Andrew Berner makes his home in New York City.

W

LANY McDONALD (I)
at Time Warner changing the culture in the editorial/corporate environment: you start with information staff, and, "you share the vision."

Assumptions are always difficult to refute, and assumptions associated with change management are particularly worrisome. In the information services field, when managers start thinking about change management, two well-entrenched assumptions seem to come into play. One is that resistance is a given, that the people who work in the organization will automatically assume that change is bad and will do their level best to prevent the change from succeeding. The second assumption has it that simply by changing the processes the organization will change the culture.

But it doesn't always happen that way. While some people will resist change — and resist mightily — change management can be undertaken successfully and those who resist can be brought around. At the same time, though, changing the processes won't necessarily insure that the culture will change, and that particular goal will, most likely, require special efforts in order to be achieved.

Lany McDonald is an information services manager who has been successful on both fronts. At The Research Center at Time Inc. in New York, McDonald has led a major change management process at one of the most important research facilities in the journalism profession. In the five years she has been with Time Warner, McDonald has achieved, rather dramatically, a level of staff loyalty and pride that is totally surprising to the various nay-sayers who doubt that change management can succeed. And to top it off, this change management process she's led has resulted in an impressive cultural change within the organization itself, not only in The Research Center—which is McDonald's specific responsibility—but in the center's client community as well. The journalist/correspon-

Originally published in *InfoManage : The International Management Newsletter for the Information Services Professional* 5 (6), May, 1998.

dents (and everyone else at Time Inc.) will now tell you that information delivery is an established part of the quality workplace, that research now truly "informs the story" from beginning to end.

That was not always the case.

McDonald's domain—The Research Center at Time Inc.—began its existence as an editorial library, a resource for the many magazine fact-checkers whose job it was to ensure that every statement published in *Time* was indisputably accurate. It was a noble aspiration, and for many, many years (and not only at *Time* but in the journalism world at large), the "editorial-library-as-fact-checker" was the established norm: you hired many, many people, you collected as many hard-copy reference materials as you could possibly cram into your space, your staff clipped newspapers and magazine articles and anything else that could possible be thought to contain a fact worth saving, and hours and hours of staff time were spent in organizing, filing, and retrieving the jillions of clip-pings that accumulated.

Of course the coming of electronic information delivery changed things, but not all at once and not at all comfortably. And it was especially difficult for those organizations with a tradition of fact-checking that required the journalists/correspondents to supply their own story research and then rely on magazine fact-checkers to provide or verify their facts after the story was written. The magazine fact-checkers turned to their editorial library and librarians to supply these facts in a rush just before each issue went to press.

McDonald's first job was the change that scenario, to reorganize the department so that the librarians—the people who were specialists in information management as well as in information delivery—would be repositioned to be part of the editorial process. After all, they are the infor-mation experts, and it certainly didn't make sense to wait until a story or a project was nearing completion to call them in.

"These people knew about information," McDonald says, "but they weren't being used to their best advantage. My job was to take this oper-ation and give these people the work they were supposed to do."

It wasn't a simple task, and it was a job that required of her some seri-ous thinking about the true function—the true role—of her staff. And it was a job that had some almost built-in perils.

"For one thing," McDonald admits with a bit of irony in her voice, "we were organizing our work to operate differently, to go beyond the tried-and-true Time Inc. way. In fact, there was one very important thing I had to remember all along: the magazine had been very successful without me, thank you very much, and it was sometimes a little humbling to recall that. But, on the other hand, management had asked me to make the information process more efficient. And then I found out we could make it more effective as well, and I knew that we could do that if we emphasized the information management skills that our librarians have. In the past we had been spending resources storing information, not doing research to provide information. The librarians were not doing the main thing librarians are trained to do, so one of my first goals was to redirect our focus. We needed to be doing what we could do best—providing information to all areas of our corporation."

But changing that focus wasn't going to come easy. And while this is not a story about downsizing, that particular management methodology was immediately established as a major element in the process [see pp. 300-301]. And the effect of such massive downsizing certainly could not be ignored: there had to be a way to work with the reduced staff in such a way that the effectiveness of The Research Center was enhanced and noticed.

"We did it," Lany McDonald says, "by putting the emphasis on the staff, on our exceptional information management expertise, and on the important return on investment that the company at large would realize by having this team of information experts available to them. For example, in the master plan that I was required to produce for corporate management, the staff emphasis was more on the professionalism of the staff, and less on the clippings, routine fact-checking, that sort of thing. We also brought in strong people. We used ABC and Newsday as models for the type of culture we should have, and we hired a consultant who had been a news librarian.

"And," McDonald says with emphasis, "we spent much time on the so-called 'vision thing.' It was so important to us that everyone in the Research Center participate, and we spent many hours in my office talking about our vision of a department of information specialists who would operate in an anticipatory mode, and not in a reacting mode.

"The plan was to provide better information services to all editorial departments and to the corporate side of the company as well," McDonald says, and you can hear a certain level of pride in her voice. "And part of the plan was to create a group of business information specialists who could provide very high level business and financial research to our corporate departments as well as supporting the editorial research needs of *Fortune* and *Money*. This idea works, and it works well.

"We also created a virtual information center in Time's editorial department and staffed it with librarians we call news researchers. They attend group editorial meetings and work directly with the journalists through the story development."

For these news researchers, it's more than subject specialization, McDonald says.

"Of course it is. It's a style specialty, a way of thinking with the journalists. The news researcher must think like an investigative reporter. It's the same rationale, the same approach to the story. In this context, the News Division of SLA has been especially helpful for us."

"What we're really talking about here," McDonald continues, "is a style change. In the past, our research librarians didn't gather background material, they didn't select it, didn't try to anticipate what was going to be needed. Basically they waited to see the journalist's finished product, and when they got it, it was their job to check the facts, even when they had no idea how the information got there.

"Now it's a totally different process, at least in our operation. Our people now conduct research to inform the story. That's the phrase I use over and over again— 'research informs the story'—and I say it often because it's what I strongly believe: the information—as much as possible — should come first."

Certainly, such an emphasis meant a complete turnaround in staff thinking, and changing the culture within The Research Center itself was not a simple task, but McDonald and her senior staff have done it. It wasn't simple, and it wasn't easy. In fact, it was a very impressive undertaking, characterized if for nothing else by its sheer size. But they did it, and it worked.

Their initial effort, as Lany McDonald will be the first to admit, was to debunk the assumption that everyone will interpret change as bad. The assumption is not necessarily a particularly productive one, and it can clearly get in the way of progress in any change management situation. But there are steps managers can take to ensure that the change management process doesn't get derailed by such preconceived notions, and McDonald took them.

"Despite the downsizing," she says, "which in itself was a very troubling experience, what we were able to do was to create a productive and positive environment, one in which staff members were not dictated to, not commanded, but were, in fact, encouraged to participate in the change. For example, as I said in the speech I gave on downsizing, the company I work for is not only a compassionate company in terms of human resources, but in terms of management needs as well. We are provided with excellent support. Remember that Time Warner is a huge operation—there are 5,000 employees at Time Inc. alone. And when I was brought in, the first thing I had to do was think about my own role, and I was quite frankly a little concerned that the resources would be there to do what we needed to do.

"Well, I shouldn't have worried. I realized that the culture wasn't going to change unless I forced it. I had been brought in to do that, and that was my job. There wasn't room for any equivocation in this matter. I had been hired to bring change to the information delivery process at Time Warner. So accepting that, I moved on to my first step, and that was to create a master plan. I worked with the people I report to on this, and what we came up with was a master plan that had one single underlying foundation or commitment: with respect to change management we would always be positive. What we're talking about here—what we were creating—was an enabling change. For even less money than was spent in the past, we were promising to give you more and better resources and more and better information. And, as I found out very quickly, thankfully I had supportive management that was willing to give me the resources to implement that change."

The second "piece" in this process relates to those resources, and to the assumption that changing the processes will change the culture. Of course the processes had to change (after all, these people were now going to be news researchers and business information specialists anticipating information needs, not librarians managing clipping files), but changing the processes alone will not necessarily change the culture. For that, leadership is required, and McDonald and her management team—and the

Hot Topics in Information Management:
When Change Management Calls for Downsizing

*W*hen Lany McDonald was brought to Time Inc., her brief was, as she put it, to change the library. Just what form that change would take was—at that time—not known. What was known was that the company's traditional, hard-copy based library, although beloved, was less and less easy to cost justify, and frankly, less and less effective when compared with electronic information research centers. Part of the process would, of course, require downsizing. It's a tough spot for an information services manager. In June, 1997, Lany McDonald described some of her ideas about the subject of downsizing in a presentation to the Library Management Division of the Special Libraries Association at SLA's Annual Conference. Here is some of what she said:

In October, 1993, we announced that the Library would be downsized from 81 to 48 staff members. It is a measure of how rare this RIF was for Time Inc. that it made the pages of *The New York Times*. On the other hand, Time Inc. is a very generous company, and I quickly learned that the best part about working at Time Inc. is that the company provides its managers with expert support—the days of the do-it-all-yourself world in my previous work were definitely behind me. . . . And for the staff, Time Inc. is a compassionate company, and a first requirement was that we must put as much money as possible into retraining. That became our first priority for dealing with downsizing. Are there other downsizing tips? Here are a few:

1. Never shirk the responsibility for what you're doing, and try to blame 'the management.' Remember, you are the management, and if you cannot accept the weight of this responsibility, you should probably step aside and let someone else handle it.

2. Find a professional colleague to talk to. For most of the first year I was at Time Inc. I couldn't bring in anyone new from the outside. Also with a few exceptions, the professional librarians within the company were working for me, so finding such a colleague was difficult.

3. Get out of town often. Find people who know a different side of you, not just the corporate role you must play.

4. Develop a personal mantra—preferably one that makes you laugh. For me, it became 'Sufficient unto the day is the evil thereof.' When I realized that I was grinning, it helped me through many a dark hour. Don't ask me why.

5. Keep your eye on the long-term goal and know that it will be attained—that the department and its staff will rise from the devastation of downsizing to be far better than ever before.

Remember that downsizing is frequently the result of postponing sorely needed changes. Since change is truly inevitable—it will happen whether you want it to or not—the continued refusal to introduce purposeful change can make downsizing inevitable. So don't postpone needed changes, and as you prepare to make changes, ensure that you have expert support methods in place for dealing with staff.

continued

Hot Topics in Information Management (continued)

As managers dealing with change, we must:

1. keep our focus on the future, even while we're working overtime doing today's work.

2. learn as much as possible about the political and financial climate of the company, so we can train our focus and direct our staff members toward goals that match those of the company.

3. not assume that just because others have loftier titles that they are adequately informed to make the smartest decisions about the company's information needs. It is our professional responsibility to help keep our companies informed, even at the risk of sounding like prophets in the information wilderness and delivering unpopular messages about both information needs and opportunities.

4. not worry about why downsizing comes about. It's like worrying about a random act of nature—it's pointless because these things can happen to anyone anywhere. Our responsibility to prevent downsizing cannot extend beyond our sphere of control.

5. in the long run, better manage what we do control: the vision, the direction, the training, the skills, and the intelligent application of our department's staff and resources for the betterment of our company's current and long-term goals.

senior management she reports to—all agreed that training would be the key to success in this particular environment.

"No question about it," McDonald says. "You spend so much money on training. You spend whatever it takes. In our case, during the downsizing phase of this process, we were obligated, through our guild contracts, to provide training, and we jumped at this opportunity. We trained those being laid off and we trained those being kept on. It had to be done. We could not change the culture if we weren't willing to train our staff to do the different type of work that they would now be doing. We couldn't ask them to be news researchers if they didn't know how, and we knew they already had a level of information expertise. We just needed to train them to be better at what they were already good at."

But we have to be careful here, for we don't want to oversimplify. At Time Warner—thanks to McDonald and her master plan—the training is not limited to staff. In fact, the training function has become one of services that The Research Center has come to excel at, and Pam Brooks, who heads up the operation's training function, sees to it that the training is passed on. She and McDonald (and, to be fair, the rest of the research center staff as well) are quite open about their role as corporate information gurus. They say to management and to company's editorial staff: "We will help train your staff to be smarter, better end-users. We'll train, we'll create resources, we'll help you create resources, whatever it takes."

For this energetic information staff, the emphasis is on creative specialization, and the people from The Research Center are happy to train corporate staff at whatever level they want ("but only," as McDonald is quick to say with a laugh, "where it makes sense—we don't just offer training to give the people something to do. It has to relate to their work and their information needs.").

Still, there's a level of openness and shared knowledge that is bound to have a positive effect on the relationship between the research center staff and their clientele throughout the company.

"Of course there is," McDonald says. "We get them started, and we leave them with the understanding that information delivery is something we're happy to work with them on. What we're primarily interested in doing is just letting them know that there's lots more. It's a good way to use these relationships we already have in place with the editorial staff. They begin to partner a little with us. And one of the techniques we use helps to strengthen that partnering, for we encourage everybody in editorial to take training, to know what information is there. If we can get them all doing the training, we avoid the pecking order mentality, the 'I'm too good to do that' sort of thinking. And we've been pleasantly surprised to see that it works. Those with open minds react best, and we love it, because we have them saying things like: 'These people in The Research Center really do know something we need to know'."

And with respect to training for the corporate staff, the editorial goal at Time Inc. is pretty clear, as McDonald describes.

"I think the day will come," she says, "when the magazines won't need many research librarians. We've already reduced the number of our staff doing editorial research, but that doesn't mean our department will need fewer people. We'll always need people who can stay on top of the information world, who know about the latest information resources, who know how to create information products, and who can train and consult with others about the best information resources for their needs. What we've become, in the process, is information consultants and information trainers.

"For most of us, for the majority of the staff, we can handle being information consultants. Although some librarians have not been trained to think of themselves this way, we remind them they're the information experts and that their expertise is needed. Once we establish their professionalism and honor their pride, they become very good information consultants."

And that has to be the secret of a successful change management operation: If you're going to do it, you start with the staff, you bring them along with their expertise intact, you help them enhance that expertise, and you focus their energies in directions of greatest value to your company. In the long run, of course, the assumptions are still in place, and that's not very pleasant to admit. On the other hand, when people like Lany McDonald can take a massive information services operation like the one she runs at The Research Center at Time, Inc. and change the culture and contradict the assumptions at the same time, the future for change management in the information services field looks very promising indeed.

Meet Lany McDonald

Lany Walden McDonald is Director of The Research Center of Time Inc. in New York, NY. She came to Time Inc. in January, 1993, after working over twelve years for the Raleigh, NC, *News & Observer*, a daily newspaper, where she was Director of News Research. At *The News & Observer*, she worked with editorial to establish an extensive computer-assisted reporting center that became a model within the newspaper industry. Before becoming a news librarian, she was an academic librarian specializing in bibliographic instruction and reference services.

Lany McDonald has been an active member of the Special Libraries Association's News Division since becoming a special librarian in 1980. She served as the News Division's chairman in 1990-1991, was editor of the News Division's professional bulletin, *News Library News*, served on the News Division's board as Director of Publications, and was program chairman for the SLA Annual Conference in Pittsburgh in 1990. As Chairman of the News Division's Automation/Technology Committee in 1985-1986, she initiated a nationwide survey on the use of online services in newspaper libraries and presented the results at the SLA Annual Conference in New York and in Paris for IFRA, an international newspaper research organization.

McDonald has been a guest speaker at numerous library conferences, seminars, education courses, and computer-assisted reporting/journalism conferences. One of her favorite talks—given to a group of corporate librarians— was on the necessity of laughter in library management.

McDonald has an M.S.L.S. from North Carolina Central University in Durham, NC, with her undergraduate degree (English) from The University of North Carolina at Greensboro.

She lives happily in the Chelsea area of New York City with two cats, Lacy J. and Bad Bob, but returns to North Carolina often enough to keep her Southern accent. Her two grown daughters, Puckette, a graphic designer for the Durham (NC) *Herald-Sun* newspaper, and Liz, who's in theater production and travels throughout the U.S., drop in from time to time to liven things up. Her favorite hour of the week in spent in lessons with a voice teacher who teaches 'real Broadway singers.' McDonald says she hopes to retire someday to the stage (way off-Broadway).

▌▌

LANY McDONALD (II)
Changing the culture in the editorial/corporate environment:
now you target the information customers
"research informs the story"

There are management operations in which trust and teamwork—the cornerstones of any quality improvement program—are built into the change management process, and efforts are made (sometimes by choice, sometimes simply serendipitously) to ensure that change is not limited to staff and staff functions. Customers, too, will benefit from the changes being put in place, and the smart organization will see to it that the customers are included in the holistic effort being made.

Certainly that's what Lany McDonald had in mind when she took on the major responsibility for bringing change to the information delivery function at Time Warner. Brought to the company in 1993 to reorganize a traditional editorial library into a functioning research center, McDonald build into her master plan an agenda that acknowledged the role of the client in the information transaction. While she concentrated much of her planning energy into assuring that the culture of the library was changed, she also never allowed herself to forget that the information function exists for the information customers.

"I thought I was brought in to change the library," she says, "but what I realized was that if the library's working culture changed, it naturally followed that there would be changes in the way we worked with our clients. This in turn would affect the information gathering culture of our clients. In other words, my department was one part of an information system, and as we all know, changing one part of a system is bound to require adjustments by the others."

At Time Inc., as at most magazines in the past, the library and library staff existed primarily as a fact-checking resource, not as a source to

Originally published in *InfoManage : The International Management Newsletter for the Information Services Professional* 5 (7), June, 1997.

provide editorial departments with background information throughout the story development. The library staff frequently did little in the way of research until after all the stories were written.

"Indeed," McDonald acknowledges with a pained look on her face, "sometimes in the old days, as an issue would be going to press, my staff would spend all week-end fact-checking hundreds and hundreds of separate items—some very complicated and terribly difficult to prove in the wee hours of the morning. This last-minute fact-checking method frequently held up the magazine closes—a costly as well as time-consuming way to operate. It was obvious to me that this was an inefficient use of an excellent information resource, and no longer made sense in an age when information could be gathered and delivered electronically anywhere in the world. So I realized that my primary job was to demonstrate to editorial management how our research skills and resources could be integrated into the editorial process from the beginning through the end as opposed to just being a fact-checking force at the end."

First, it would be necessary to change the current perceptions about the library and its role. McDonald knew she had management support for efforts to raise the awareness of the greater research value her staff could offer the company, but there was still a somewhat resistant existing customer base to deal with. It was important to change the current perceptions of their editorial clients about when and how to include research into the flow of editorial information. Without realizing just how entrenched the fact-checking culture was with the editorial staff members, the first thing McDonald and her staff discovered was how very difficult the adjustment was going to be for these clients. They couldn't imagine the value of this kind of information delivery because they had not worked this way before.

That, for McDonald, made the effort even more of a challenge. But she believed that once the journalists were provided high-quality information with fast turnaround delivery, plus additional resources they could access directly themselves, they were bound to be impressed with how useful this could be.

"We took a two-part approach—we'd make information specialists available to provide preliminary information to inform the story idea and development and then gather information as requested when stories were being developed, and we'd also provide more information resources for the journalists to use themselves at their desktops or at research stations."

McDonald says, "I determined that we would need two new groups of information specialists—news and business. Our general information researchers would continue to support the non-subject specific clients."

In 1994, the then Executive Editor of *Time* magazine agreed to help create a space within their editorial floor for a virtual research center that would be an extension of the main Research Center.

"So we hired a seasoned news librarian—Lynn Dombek—who was working for the ABC Research Center, to lead the effort on Time's floor. (Lynn has now been promoted to Assistant Director of The Research Center.) As the *Time* magazine research coordinator, Lynn would go to editorial meetings and pretty soon you had an information specialist working with editorial staff members as they think about ideas and deal with ways of handling stories. She'd make sure the editorial staff members were aware of the many resources available to help develop a story. Frequently that meant just going ahead and giving it to them so they could see for themselves."

Having someone like Dombek on the staff makes a major different, as McDonald is quick to point out.

"Lynn comes from a news background, and she understands the news process. She helped others on our staff learn to be news researchers. Until she came, there was little understanding of this role here. New researchers have to think ahead of the articles, and have to be aggressive researchers, thinking of stories the way journalists do. When an event happens, the *Time* magazine research specialists hop into action gathering information to help move the editorial process forward. An example of how we work in these situations was during the horrible Oklahoma bombing. Our staff knew this occurred on the anniversary of the Waco fire, so in addition to gathering information on the agencies and occupants of the building that had been bombed, we pulled up the information on the Waco event, gathered information on various militant right-wing groups, and created electronic files of all kinds of relevant information. The research staff then let the editorial staff know the data was gathered and ready to go. We continued to add data into organized files as more information poured in.

"The main point is that this research staff did not wait until the stories were written and the calls came in as they would have in the past.

Instead, the anticipated many of the journalists' information needs from the very start."

Obviously such aggressive information delivery has its value, and it's a value that many editorial staff members began to appreciate. After all, if they could begin their work with background information and accurate facts in hand, they were that far ahead of the curve. Also, with more electronic information resources available for the journalists to use themselves, the magazine staff members could do as much of their own research as they wished.

According to McDonald, this combination of research by specialists and end-user seems to be working well for many of the magazines.

"For example," she says, "with *Time* magazine, the news research specialists attend section news meetings and work closely with all editorial staff to provide research and resources, but also to help train the editorial staff members to use information resources on their own. This has resulted in more relevant research throughout the story process, and a huge reduction in the number of fact-checking questions The Research Center or anyone has to answer at the end of the editorial process."

In addition to developing a group of editorial news research specialists, McDonald developed a group of business information specialists to serve their business and financial clients, *Fortune* and *Money*. She believed that with the proliferation of the specialized financial information products, it was essential that her staff be experts in their field. This group would also be positioned to handle research needed by various corporate financial and strategic planning groups.

Fortune magazine was actually the first of the Time Inc. magazines to change their working relationship with The Research Center.

"Because of their need for deep background information, and because we had developed a group of business information specialists who could do the job they needed, the editors of *Fortune* led the way in helping all their editorial staff members use The Research Center's information specialists smartly."

McDonald notes that their business information specialists now attend editorial meetings at *Fortune* and *Money* magazines, and she proudly points out the Research Center's business information manager, Mary Danehy, is called on by both magazines and corporate clients for advice and assistance with various new financial information products and project guidance.

Other changes were made to strengthen The Research Center's role within their client community. Important new roles are that of magazine database development and intranet content development.

"By creating a team to develop a centralized electronic database of the Time Inc. magazines that is delivered within the company and to external information vendors, by having the research staff review, select, and organize subject Web sites, by creating special databases to meet various information needs, we have extended the range of our information services beyond traditional research.

"Changes in information technology have allowed us to reach out in ways we never could before. Unless you're in this information management business, you can't keep up with what's going on in information delivery. Everyone knows that it's just impossible to keep up. But that's our business. That's what we librarians and information specialists do, and the sooner we could convey that to the Time Warner community at large, the more we were going to be perceived as valued members of the corporate team. I think our strong presence on the corporate intranet, coupled with our end-user training initiatives, has helped change the perception of our role within the company."

According to McDonald, The Research Center has become known as one of the main sources within the company for help in creating various kinds of databases and new media information products. She sees this as an area where the information specialists will make even greater contributions in the future.

What's next at The Research Center?

"It's not an easy question to answer," McDonald says. "For one thing, there is just so much going on now that is exciting and stimulating. Just coming in to work every day is a real challenge—which is exactly what I like. But since you asked, I think what we're doing now is to move on, to go beyond what we've accomplished so far.

"We have changed our information culture," she says, "and we do have a staff of information professionals who have rewarding jobs, and there are journalists and corporate staff members whose information needs are better served than they ever expected, but there is so much more that we can do."

And then she reveals that product development might be the next big "wave" at The Research Center at Time Inc.

"It's a whole new avenue for us, and it's exciting. It is, right here in our own industry, applied research: you find the data, decide how to sort it and present it, put it in a database or organized file all neatly packaged, and you've got an information product. We are already negotiating with potential vendors and have some new Web products on the drawing board."

And that, in brief, tells you what Lany McDonald and her information team at The Research Center at Time Inc. are all about. They've worked hard to change the culture of their own unit, to provide services and products that meet—as exactly as they can predict— the requirements of their information customers. And at the same time they've tackled the very ambitious challenge—and they're succeeding—of influencing the information culture of the company so that their role is better seen for the value it brings. It's a phenomenon that is rare in any industry, but particularly in information services.

For Lany McDonald, it doesn't seem to be all that remarkable.

"Oh, don't misunderstand me," she says. "I would never diminish the success of our achievement here, but isn't it all just thinking in a very encompassing way about information, about anything having to do with information? I think that's just doing our jobs."

Of course it is, and for people like Lany McDonald, that's when it's fun.

Meet Lany McDonald

Lany Walden McDonald is Director of The Research Center of Time Inc. in New York, NY. She came to Time Inc. in January, 1993, after working over twelve years for the Raleigh, NC, *News & Observer*, a daily newspaper, where she was Director of News Research. Before becoming a news librarian, she was an academic librarian specializing in bibliographic instruction and reference services.

Lany McDonald has been an active member of the Special Libraries Association's News Division since becoming a special librarian in 1980, chairing the division in 1990-1991, and prior to that, contributing to the division in a variety of other positions (including Program Chairman for the SLA Annual Conference in 1990). In 1998, Lany McDonald is being honored with the News Division's Kwapil Award. Named for Joseph F. Kwapil, who founded the division, the award is the organization's highest recognition, given for major achievement in the field of news librarianship and outstanding and prolonged service to the News Division.

McDonald has an M.S.L.S. from North Carolina Central University in Durham, NC, with her undergraduate degree (English) from The University of North Carolina at Greensboro. She lives in the Chelsea area of New York City.

CUSTOMER CARE
IN THE INFORMATION ENVIRONMENT

*T*he next level in that "Successful-Change-Management-in-Information-Services" pyramid is also composed of two important building blocks: customer service and total quality management (or, as we describe it in the information industry, QIM—quality information management). The first of these is given attention in the interviews recorded in this chapter. Called different things in different service environments ("customer service" in much of the for-profit sector, "customer care" in some European locations, "service excellence" in the public sector), the management function that gives attention to the people who will *receive* the products, services, and consultations emanating from the information-delivery operation becomes, in well-managed information units, a *primary* management function.

Certainly that was Carol Ginsburg's thinking when she brought her bold approach to the Bankers Trust Company. Not content simply to provide information delivery to walk-in or 'phone-in clients, Ginsburg began to think about those information users who might be gathering their own information. While she laughingly characterized her concepts—described in the first issue of *InfoManage*—as possibly putting herself "out of a job,"

311

the reality, of course, is that the information "independent" customer actually ends up requiring considerable guidance from the information staff. Of course he or she will get the final information "piece" independently—if it is available independently—but to get to that stage, to know *how* to get that information, means learning how to get it or, when stuck, knowing where to go for help. That's where the information specialist comes into the picture, and managing the change that positions the information staff for providing such different approaches to service delivery is change management in its purest form.

On the other side of the globe, Meg Paul made the valuable discovery that in information services work, the satisfied customer can become—under the appropriate and subtle tutelage of the conscientious information staff—an advocate for the work of the information unit and a useful spokesperson in the effort for the continuous improvement of information services. Jane Dysart, then president of the Special Libraries Association, made a similar observation as she studied the frequently subtle elements that link service excellence, effective and efficient management, and organizational leadership. In the Meg Paul/Jane Dysart information management paradigm, there is no surprise in discovering that the best information delivery is that in which the information customers are well satisfied and the organizational function that manages information delivery is well managed by an organizational leader.

For some organizations, though, the need for new service models requires a specifically different—and new—way of looking at how customers are to be thought about in the change management process. At Coopers and Lybrand, Trish Foy had responsibility for literally "reinventing" information services for the company, and in some cases, some of the company's operational units were required to take a hard and serious look at what their information needs are. Foy's charge was to match corporate information services with corporate information need, and reinventing information services was the only way to do it, to ensure that information customers would be provided with exactly what they needed, and would be guaranteed the highest levels of information delivery quality.

That level of quality is a universal goal, of course (or should be), in any information delivery function, and when it comes to understanding change management in information services with respect to reference delivery, the acknowledged expert is Anne Lipow. Known for her incisive understanding of the customer point of view, Lipow works hard to establish that the reference staff has the same commitment to excellence in reference delivery in the digital age that it was recognized for having in previous periods in information history. The interview with Lipow—outlining as it does a veritable formula for excellence in reference delivery—provides insight and planning tools that all information managers can rely upon. As the information customer comes to accept (and seek out) the wide variety of possibilities available for the pursuit of information, customer service processes change, and Lipow's comments, and those of the other industry leaders interviewed in this chapter, provide viable and useful techniques for bringing success to the information interaction between information customer and information provider.

The information independent organization:
CAROL GINSBURG's
bold approach

Last winter, a group of senior information managers in New York got together to talk about their future. Carol Ginsburg, Vice-President, Bankers Trust Company, was one of the group who put the informal meeting together. As discussion began to focus on the specifics, on just what information providers would be doing in future jobs, Ginsburg startled some of her colleagues.

"I might be working myself out of a job," Carol Ginsburg said, "but at our place we are moving toward an information independent organization."

"The information independent organization." The phrase certainly has a ring to it, and it seems to make a lot of sense these days, this idea of encouraging information users to be on their own. Of course the corporate library and other information providers in the company are going to con-

Originally published in *InfoManage : The International Management Newsletter for the Information Services Professional* 1 (1), November, 1993.

tinue in place, to help when they're needed. But whenever possible in an information independent organization, end-users are taught to use the system themselves, to go their own way in tracking down what they want to know.

Speaking with the easy confidence of someone who knows she's on the right track, Ginsburg explained that at Bankers Trust the idea isn't threatening, and the concept of an information independent organization hasn't come about to downsize, save resources, cut staff or for any of those other usual reasons that an information services unit takes off in a new direction. At Bankers Trust, information independence is seen as the way to go because it's the best way to move information through the organization.

Several months after meeting with her peers, Ginsburg elaborated on the concept of the information independent organization at a quiet lunch in midtown Manhattan. The idea came about, she told *InfoManage*, through a combined interest in information within the organization. It was an interest that Ginsburg, who manages the Information Center at Bankers Trust's Park Avenue office, shared with several of the information technology people in the company, and with senior management. Among them, the concept just seemed to fall into place, since they were all trying to manage information in the bank.

"It's an organization-wide policy," Ginsburg explained. "It isn't formulated into a written 'plan' as such, and there's certainly no document at this point providing strict guidelines. Presently the concept is more of an 'attitude' or an 'ambiance' within the bank, to move toward a more effective delivery of information."

Certainly it's an attitude that matches the present information needs within the company, for with more and better technology continually becoming available, and with a reputation for "leading edge" service for its clients, it is only natural for Bankers Trust to look to information independence as an information "philosophy" for its operations. The concept drives much of the thinking about information provision and undoubtedly affects how certain decisions are made.

One major initiative, for example, has been the Magellan Project, an integrated information system within the bank, now implemented not only in the New York offices but throughout the company, including the London and Mexico City offices. A similar effort has been the bank's heavy involvement in the utilization of Hoover, Sandpoint Corporation's successful "information agent" (as it's called in the literature) for pulling together the many—some would say the "overwhelming"—chunks of information available from online services, CD-ROMs and news feeds. Bankers Trust is now Hoover's largest customer, with a 1,000-user license and about 750 people online at the present time. So there's no question about it. The folks at Bankers Trust are serious about moving toward information independence!

How does it go down, this idea of information independence? Do the users like it? And what kind of entrepreneurial efforts had to be put into getting it accepted? How do the information workers on staff feel about it, this new approach to the delivery of information? Are they frightened that an information independent organization might put them out of work?

"Not at all," Ginsburg replies. "There's been remarkable staff acceptance. In fact, the work load seems to grow rather than shrink, but staff buys into the concept because it means the information center can offer more services and a broader range of resources. And users like it because they can do their work better and easier than with mediated queries. Of course with some of the users, success depends on age and rank. The 22-year-old whiz kids of 20 years ago are now in senior management positions, and they appreciate the value of the information we've been providing that helped to make them successful. So of course they are going to support what we're doing."

Ginsburg notes that the 20-plus staff take pride in their work and have no problems with the fact that their roles are changing, from the traditional providers of information to information "navigators," or "counselors," or "consultants" for the other bank employees. It's not a problem for them, for they expect to provide the services the users need, and if guidance is needed for something other than traditional book answers, they'll be provided with that guidance.

Of course some answers still come from books, but in fact "about 85% of the information provided comes from online or other automated sources," Ginsburg points out. On-site users are asked to do book-type research themselves. If they're off-site, "depending on the query and the time estimated for the job," staff will provide the answer.

Still, the Corporate Information Center is there to provide service. Staffed 72 hours a week, with evening hours until 9:00 PM, most users who work at the Park Avenue building can get the information they need pretty much when they want it. And of course there are the late night faxes and E-mail messages from the Tokyo and Sydney offices, both of which are supported by Ginsburg's facility in New York.

From Europe, Ginsburg works closely with Una Byrne, who heads up the London office, with the two of them sharing in a number of cooperative ventures. In Canada, the Toronto office, too, benefits from the expertise and resources that Ginsburg and her staff provide.

In fact, international information cooperation is something of a trademark for Ginsburg. She seems to be taking a special pride in the work that is going on at the Australian facility. "There is a very strong information presence in Sydney," she notes, "and the librarian there, Joanne Bottcher, is a good manager and very committed to providing the kinds of services the bank needs in that location." At the present time Ginsburg has no plans to go to Sydney to offer hands-on advice, but she doesn't rule out the possibility. And with the frequent E-mail conversations she has with Bottcher, the two of them have already established a good professional rapport that has to be good for the bank.

Continuing the international effort, Ginsburg and Byrne are preparing a program on global information resource sharing, for presentation next June. And in yet another international engagement, Ginsburg—a speaker at the 1993 European Business Information Conference in Barcelona—has been invited back for another presentation in 1994, in March in Paris.

Ginsburg was brought to Bankers Trust 12 years ago, specifically to set up the Corporate Information Center. It's a task she takes great pride in, and well she should, for it's obvious that she was the right person at the right time. In those 12 years, the list of information products and services offered to the bank has grown considerably, and as Bankers Trust—as a company—found itself moving to a more technical information environment, Ginsburg was clearly motivated to see that the information she and her staff provided kept up with the quality that the technology could support. It was a combination that worked. And continues to work.

Yes, Ginsburg is welcome to attribute the success of her operation to an "attitude" or an "ambiance" within the bank. And certainly that idea is not to be discounted. If the stakeholders at the bank hadn't had an encouraging attitude about information in the first place, Ginsburg wouldn't have been able to move things along as she has. But in addition to her professional managerial and information skills, Ginsburg has brought along something else, an information vision perhaps, about what the bank—and she and her staff—could be doing for their customers and their information needs. So much of the credit goes to her for recognizing the potential of the technology to do what it can for information, and for doing her part to put it in place. If, in fact, it leads to an information independent organization at Bankers Trust, Ginsburg will have done a very good job indeed.

MEG PAUL
talks about information in Australia, and about the satisfied customer as advocate

Two themes emerge when you talk with Meg Paul about information services. One is that she has a clearly detailed understanding of the information services picture in Australia. The second, equally important, is that she and her colleagues in the specialized libraries community in Australia have a notable commitment to the promotion of customer service excellence in information management.

Paul is co-director, with Jenn Evans, of FLIS Pty. Ltd., a personnel placement and consulting firm located in a suburb of Melbourne. Long established as a major player in the Australian information arena, the company has provided Paul with a variety of experiences in the information marketplace. As a result, hers has been a refreshing and provocative voice in the information community in that huge country.

The Australian information picture, like many others, is driven by economics, and Paul points out that Australia is coming out of a recession with a continuing string of positive economic indicators. "But," she says "as our economy is strongly dependent on both the US and Japan, the success of their economic growth impacts strongly on ours."

Because of these limitations, it has been difficult for Australians to get involved in a "connected" information environment. There is certainly a

Originally published in *InfoManage : The International Management Newsletter for the Information Services Professional* 1 (5), April, 1994.

sense that it will happen, thought, which becomes obvious when Paul describes the current situation.

"We have no information superhighway, as such, specific to Australia," she says. "Universities and other academic institutions and large research organizations use AARNET, the Australian Academic and Research Network, a non-commercial co-operative network which acts as a linkage and also as a gateway to enable them to access the Internet. The public library sector has some access as well, by hooking into a service offered by the State Library of New South Wales, but for everybody else, including business users, access to the Internet is limited to connections with a few commercial organizations."

Nevertheless, even without the level of information interaction found in some other countries, Australians are—after the US—the second largest user base for the Internet. So once the gateways are opened, so to speak, connectivity can be expected to increase in major and impressive increments.

Yet because Australia is a vast land mass with a small population, most of the telecommunications infrastructure is government funded, and Paul notes that at present the federal government is looking at taking optical fiber to homes for pay television. Since this would also provide a means of connecting home computers (estimated to grow by some 80% in 1994 alone), this activity has major implications for the creation of an Australian superhighway. But it doesn't exist yet.

Along with concerns about what the country's information infrastructure is going to be, a parallel issue is the relationship between librarians and the people who manage information technology. Paul notes that the Internet is forcing librarians to rethink the services they provide and the ways in which they provide them, which requires, of course, that they work with IT managers.

"For example, information services could be delivered to the individual user's terminal via E-mail. The problem is that IT managers know about the technology but very few of them understand how the accessible information is put to use. On the other hand, the librarians know the scope, availability, and costs of the databases, but they don't fully understand the IT side of the picture, especially the evaluation of commercial information services packages."

To solve the problem, information services providers—the librarians, records managers and so forth—need to understand IT, and they're taking steps to do that. "In the past," Paul says, "they've wanted to wait for the products to be tested, but now, with the continuous changes in information services management, they can't wait. The librarians are taking the initiative and looking for additional training in information technology for themselves."

Another piece of the information scene in Australia, and a characteristic that ensures that for specialized libraries, at least, the connections will be made, is that special librarians in Australia are good at what they do, according to Paul, "certainly up to the standards of special librarians in the US and the UK."

"Special librarians are well educated. They do a lot of professional reading, and they're committed to performing well." She points out that the Specials, as they're called, represent the strongest section of the Australian Library and Information Association, and they're all great friends. "Everyone knows everyone else and they ring one another up when they need to discuss these information issues."

Which explains, perhaps, why Paul and her colleagues have begun to focus on a strong customer service commitment for information services professionals. Because they all know one another and have shared experiences in the workplace, they are aware, for example, that the job picture for information workers is different than it was even a few years ago. With these changing employment trends, Paul notes, "employees are realizing for the first time that no one has a secure job. Unsettling as this is, it also has the beneficial effect of motivating people to perform."

But haven't information professionals been performing all along?

"Not as well as they could have been," she says. "Many good libraries have been closed because the organizations they were part of did not have the information proving how the work of the library made other employees more productive or their decisions more relevant."

As in many other countries, librarians and other information services professionals in Australia have usually avoided issues having to do with performance standards and accountability, but in the present economic climate they cannot be avoided any longer. In fact, Meg Paul asserts that the information providers themselves are not exactly innocent of blame, and at ALIA's 1993 Conference she spoke bluntly about the subject.

"Some of the closures are the fault of the library staff," she said, and then she asked what she called the $64 question.

"Why have special libraries closed or downsized in these days of information overload, when it appears logical to us that a professional librarian is the person in an organization with the particular attributes, skills and training to sift through the information mass, extract what is important, package it and deliver it to the appropriate person? Why are these libraries closing, especially when the information sector is the sector of largest growth in the Australian economy?"

The answer, Paul feels, lies in the qualifications and training of the managers to whom special librarians and other information providers report, managers who are generalists, who do not know what a library does, and who see library budgets as an easy item to cut. "The library," she says, "is seen as overhead."

So why aren't information professionals seen as the gatherers and disseminators of information?

"It's our own fault," Paul says. "We have been working so hard delivering the service that we have not educated advocates to speak on our behalf. We have not been political enough within our own organizations, and we have not been involved in listening and observing the information needs of our clients. We've been giving them what we think they need, not what they know they need."

In her pleas for increased attention to the real needs of information customers, Paul looks to the information services staff: "An important part of motivating staff is appropriate training, recognition of a job well done, and the delegation of responsibility with designated areas of responsibility."

"Most important," she continues, "a quality service ethos must be set and owned by the staff with management backing and approval. Staff must understand how quality service benefits them with more fulfilling employment, better interpersonal relations, and the approbation and approval of others within the organization."

Survival also contributes to this emphasis on excellence of service. "If a library does not meet the needs of its clients, the value and integrity of the information it provides is not recognized, and the library is not able to prove its cost effectiveness," And at this point, Paul doesn't mince words: "The library will cease to exist as clients withdraw their support.

The clients are the stakeholders and those librarians who do not heed their needs and listen to them will face extinction or radical upheaval."

It's a frightening prospect, but there is, according to Paul, a way for preventing this radical upheaval: "An astute librarian should realize that even an excellent service needs advocates within the organization. . . . There are always occasions when you will need advocates to lend support in internal political situations and these will usually be clients who value your services. Your clients become your insurance policy."

The service must be sold to the clients, Paul contends, "but you cannot sell an effective service unless you are delivering one. If libraries are to survive tough economic times, they must have a fully paid up insurance policy in the form of an educated and satisfied clientele who know that the library provides an excellent service. These are the people who will support the library. They are users who understand the value of the information you supply."

"They also understand," Paul continues, "the value of what you do. For this alone they must be cultivated."

Advocacy, customer service, and accountability. They're basic requirements for the successful delivery of information, and smart information managers are recognizing that. If information services professionals in Australia will hear what Meg Paul is saying, they'll be ready to get on that information superhighway when it's ready for them. In the meantime, they'll be developing some very satisfied information clients, which is, of course, good insurance for all of them.

Matching corporate information services to
corporate information needs: At Coopers & Lybrand
TRISH FOY
is reinventing information services

Yes, that's the word she uses: "re-inventing." In June, at the Special Libraries Association Conference in Montréal, Trish Foy presented a paper that had her listeners excited and stimulated at the same time. It was full of good ideas, some radical and some simply so logical that you wondered why no one else had thought of them before, and the entire tone of the paper was one of re-invention and re-modelling. In fact, she called her paper "The Re-Invention of the Corporate Information Model." When you spend some time with Trish Foy you understand why. This is an information executive who recognizes that information—in today's business environment—must be tailored to match the information needs of the information customers.

Those needs are changing, and have been changing for a couple of decades now. And they will continue to change. Change is the name of the game here, and information services in the corporate environment must change as well, must go along with whatever changes are taking place in the environment itself. Trish Foy is clearly on to something, and "re-inventing" the corporate information model is not just some trendy management fad. The requirements for change in corporate information services are very real, and Foy is determined to see that the products and services that are her responsibility measure up to the needs of the employees of Coopers & Lybrand. It's not "change for change sake," certainly, and it's not simply managerial posturing. It's keeping up, no, leading the way in the very real world of corporate information delivery. Nothing less than a re-invention is called for.

It begins, Foy says, with a recognition that the traditional library model, even the traditional corporate library model, doesn't work in busi-

Originally published in *InfoManage : The International Management Newsletter for the Information Services Professional* 2 (11), October, 1995.

ness anymore. This is not to say that libraries are no longer appropriate, or that traditional librarianship is bad and that business information provision is good. Not at all. It simply recognizes that they are different, and proceeds to build on that recognition.

"The perspective is different," Foy says. "In the public library community—which is what most librarians are trained for—the perspective is not geared to supporting a business clientele. I serve on the Board of Trustees of my public library, and I understand very well what that library is supposed to be doing. I support it and I am happy to be a part of it. But it is not what we do in a business environment. The concerns are not the same, and we have to think about those differences.

"The concept of traditional librarianship, with its broader-based constituency and its wide range of services, just doesn't fit in the business environment. In corporate information work, we're dealing with a variety of users, the majority of whom do not necessarily know where to go for their information. They might come asking for one thing, for example, and we have to work with them, guide them along, to find out what it is that they are really looking for. It's our job to let them know that many different 'pieces' of information are available that might be applicable for what they need, and if they are focusing on just one of those pieces, they might not be getting the quality of content that they need."

The re-invention of information services came to C&L because, quite simply, it was time. It's a big operation, this partnership, and it is one of the famous "Big Six" public accounting firms, with some 16,000 employees working in 119 offices in the U.S. And although it is known as an accounting firm, C&L identifies itself as a "professional services" firm. In the fiscal year ending September 30, 1994, its global revenue increased to $5.5 billion. So we're not talking about an information services operation that is "nice to have." In this company, every function and every service must be justified and that, in fact, is what led to the innovative initiative that Foy now directs.

"In any company this size, ongoing financial review is part of the picture, and as library and information services were looked at here, it became clear that some change in direction was called for. But in fact that was not a bad thing, for by looking at the information services role in the organization, the company is giving attention to information, and to the value of information. It sets the stage, so to speak, for moving beyond what isn't working."

What wasn't working, they found out, was an information services operation that was based on traditional library concepts, resulting in wide variations in the levels of services that were provided. There had even grown up, awkwardly, a mixture of "have" and "have not" offices with regard to information delivery. It was not a system that worked very well, and Foy and the partner she works with—Mik Chwalek, responsible for Market Research and Analysis—saw that their work was cut out for them. It would be their job to design a process that establishes a responsibility for information throughout the company.

Fortunately, C&L is the kind of company where there isn't a great deal of "holding back," and Foy did not have to be too concerned ("Well," she says with a smile, "within reason.") about her authority to move ahead with her innovative planning.

"At Coopers & Lybrand," she says, "There is an expectation that if you step up to the responsibility of the job, you get to do it," and that's what has been happening over the past few years with the information services operation.

"Of course we work hard at justifying ourselves. There is always financial pressure, but what we've done is to establish an information services program that works for the C&L information customers, and as long as we are providing them with the services they need at reasonable cost, we can innovate. And besides, we're firm believers in the 'it's-better-to-ask forgiveness-than-to-ask-permission' school of management, and if we've come up with something particularly good, it can be 'sold'."

The re-invented information services operation at Coopers & Lybrand has a number of specific features that characterize it, and among these is a remarkable attention to the role of communication in the information services effort. Not only is the information staff required to understand the value of communication, public relations, and customer service, the marketing and promotion of information services is built into the success of the operation.

"Communication is the key," Foy says, and it is a point she emphasizes several times during the conversation. As she talks about how she gets the word out to customers ("If we need to, we put a marketing piece in the envelope with their paychecks. Then we know they'll see it."), about what she expects from new hires, about how the operation is identified ("Not 'libraries.' We are restructuring library operations into something else and we'll call them something else. We are changing expectation levels, and we can't call them 'libraries' if we're going to do that."), it becomes clear that communication is essential to the success of what she is doing at C&L.

"This is a different kind of operation, and any kind of change of this magnitude must rely on a successful communications effort. It is something we concentrate on all the time, and it pays off."

Just how "different" is this information services operation? There are several defining characteristics, and each of them provides particular insight into how Foy and her colleagues at Coopers & Lybrand are re-inventing the corporate information model. In the first place, aside from the emphasis on communication, the role of information services is a different one.

"We are charged to take information responsibility," Foy says, "to evaluate content and quality and to restructure library operations. We have recognized that in the last 25 years, as the structure of the corporation has changed, the enabling role of technology is having a tremendous effect on how information can be accessed and delivered. And on what customer expectations can be."

Foy herself comes to this work with an information technology background, and although she has an M.L.S. degree, she has spent much of her career in information technology implementation and information analysis. For the past two years she has directed strategy planning for the C&L libraries, and for five years prior to that she headed C&L's Technology Intelligence group. So the place of information technology in this re-invented information agenda is a critical one, for which she must take much of the credit. And it is that IT connection that leads to the second major characteristic of this re-invented model, the structure of the service.

Described in detail in her paper at Montréal and received with much enthusiasm, the work at C&L builds on three information "layers." A desktop layer helps, as Foy puts it, "to build the information-independent user," for the information the customer needs is retrieved from desktop tools or from a specialized information kiosk, and both external and internal information is identifiable and accessible in this format. The kiosk piece of this concept, now being tested in parts of the company, will meet the demands of what Foy calls "high-voltage" and vertical industry specific groups, and is self-contained and interactive.

The information fulfillment center is used for simple factual reference, for directing users to specific product/service providers, gathering and transmitting research materials, controlling the C&L Catalog, and basically eliminates the duplicative sources and expenditures that now occur throughout the firm. Its backbone is a firm-wide internal information hotline, inaugurated in 1993, that operates from 8:00 AM to 8:00 PM daily, staffed by knowledgeable professionals. They do not do administrative or secretarial work, and their brief is information analysis, pure and simple. When staff at C&L ring up 1-800-KNOWHOW, they are confident that they will get "true" information delivery. And linked to the information fulfillment center is a new fax-on-demand service for frequently requested internal and external reports. Now operating far in excess of original expectations, the fax-on-demand service just might turn out to be the most successful of all of these new information products.

The third layer is a network of C&L information specialists, planned to include internal industry group experts, information center and library professionals, market analysts, and C&L line-of-business experts, all interfacing closely with the information fulfillment center and there to synthesize and evaluate information available. As many of the information specialists will have a thorough knowledge of a specific subject, they will also have quick access to other subject experts, thus compounding and dramatically increasing the potential for success in the information quest.

Of course the entire operation is based on the people who are part of it, and it is this "people" component that moves Foy's work into the winner's circle. It's not always been easy, of course, and there has been turnover, because, quite frankly, what is taking place here is a sea-change in the information delivery system.

"It's not just different careers that these people are moving into," she says. "It's a different operation, and what we require are information professionals who can sell 'specialist' skills. As one of my colleagues says, we're not providing 'baby' information anymore, and so we're working very hard with our information staff to help them. With librarians, we need to show them how to see themselves in different, other roles. And when it's necessary, we look elsewhere in the organization—beyond the usual 'library'-type activities—and we bring over people who are skilled at gathering particular types of information."

Is it difficult to find the people to do this work?

"You must understand," Foy says with some emphasis, "that this is a totally different operation. We are asking people to work in an entirely different way, to interpret, to consult, to add value, and the new job descriptions—with the new salary structures—that we have in place require a way of thinking that fits into this 'different' picture. Of course communication is basic, as I've been saying, but we also have to have people who are comfortable with technology, who are creative, who are team players, and, as much as anything else, who are willing to take risks. These are the people who will make this new model of information services work."

So re-inventing information pulls a lot of things together, and what Trish Foy is doing at Coopers & Lybrand makes a lot of sense. Of course those characteristics described here—the enabling role of technology, the structure, and the staffing—are all critical, and probably equally critical, in the success of the new model. But riding above all else, from a management point of view, is that understanding that information delivery today is not the information delivery of the past (of even, in fact, of the very recent past) and, equally significant, that information delivery as practiced in traditional librarianship is not the same as information delivery in the corporate environment. Of course they are all part of the same information spectrum—that information services "umbrella" we all hear so much about—but they are, truth to tell, in very different places in that spectrum. Trish Foy has discovered that, and now she's making it work for her company and for her information customers. By re-inventing the corporate information model for Coopers & Lybrand, Foy is positioning information services where it belongs: at the very heart of the company. Good for her.

Meet Trish Foy

When this interview was published, Patricia S. Foy was Director of Libraries and Technology Research at Coopers & Lybrand. She has extensive background in library and information center operations and strategy. Prior to coming to C&L, Foy was Director of Systems Applications and Development for a major New York county government. Earlier in her career she performed systems and management analysis for a large West Coast bank, participated in planning and controlling supply systems for the Federal government, and worked in systems measurement and design for a large insurance firm. Foy has a B.A. from Allegheny College in Meadville, PA, and an M.L.S. (with distinction) from Pratt Institute, Brooklyn, NY. She is a member of the Chappaqua (NY) Library Board of Trustees, of the Special Libraries Association, and of Beta Phi Mu. She has had articles published in *Computerworld* and other trade and professional journals. She is the author of "The Re-Invention of the Corporate Information Model-The Information Professional's Role in Empowering Today's Workforce," an invitational paper delivered at the 86th Annual Conference of the Special Libraries Association and published in *The Power of Information: Transforming The World* (Washington, DC: Special Libraries Association, 1995). Foy lives in Westchester County, New York.

The service / management / leadership continuum: Is SLA's
JANE DYSART
the model for specialized librarianship?

Some people need models, someone to look to as an example. For energetic practitioners in specialized librarianship, it's now becoming clear that Jane Dysart's career could be an ideal prototype. It's a career that has been—and continues to be—rewarding, satisfying, and delightfully professional in its focus.

And it's that delight that pulls it all together, for being in Jane Dysart's presence—if only briefly—clearly demonstrates that this is an information services professional whose success is built on enthusiasm, on a

Originally published in *InfoManage : The International Management Newsletter for the Information Services Professional* 3 (6), May, 1996.

foundation that matches that enthusiasm with a real pride in her work. Add to that a commitment to the highest standards of information delivery and an attention to quality management that permits no deviation from "the best," and you have an information leader who is indeed delighted to be doing what she is doing.

Certainly that enthusiasm has been evident in each of her presentations as President of the Special Libraries Association. Dysart has headed this 15,000-member organization—now positioned as the preeminent international professional organization in the information services field— since June of last year. For those who are employed in what is referred to as the "non-traditional" side of librarianship, SLA provides a perfect framework for their organizational needs. During a recent presidential visit to SLA's Texas Chapter, held in Austin, Jane Dysart once again demonstrated that she is the ideal person to be carrying the "enthusiastically professional" banner of information services into the 21st century.

"The future is what we are about," Dysart told some three hundred Texans. "The skill of end-users is increasing and special libraries are starting to shift from physical place into virtual space." It's a concept Dysart has spoken about many times, including the presentation in Austin, and she's even been identified in an important Canadian business magazine as a person who is looking ahead to "future success" in information delivery.

In the January, 1996, issue of *Quill and Quire*, Susan Merry talked about Dysart's unique SLA presidency: "Because Jane looks ahead," Merry said, "she is recognized for her ability to identify barriers to information success," and she has been making "every effort" to help librarians get beyond those barriers. "This is going to be Dysart's presidential legacy," Merry says, and she could well be right in her appraisal of Dysart's skill in working with other information practitioners.

Looking to the future isn't out of character when you think about Dysart's career. She went from being a bank librarian—seventeen years as the Royal Bank of Canada's information resources manager—to opening her own business as an independent consultant. All the while she was performing in a volunteer capacity with a great variety of professional organizations, including SLA, where she served in a number of volunteer leadership positions.

A regular seminar leader at SLA's continuing education programs, Dysart became well known throughout the Association as one of its most dynamic presenters, so it was no surprise when, after serving twice on SLA's Board of Directors, SLA's members chose her to be its President-Elect in 1994. Her innovative career continues, however, for as she leads SLA during this presidential year, she and her partner Rebecca Jones maintain a grueling schedule of training and consultancy assignments, including a successful new venture in conference planning and organization. It all adds up to a very demanding and (yes, there's that word again) satisfying professional life for Dysart.

There are, of course, those who ask how she does it all, how she accomplishes all that she seems to be accomplishing. The answer for Dysart—as for many information services consultants these days—has to do with the role of what is called "strategic partnering" in the information consulting field (some use the term "strategic alliances"). Taking a cue from the management community at large, many consultants now engage in this kind of shared involvement in projects. By working with strategic partners, they are able to provide high levels of service while keeping the business overhead low (and, not to put too fine a point on it, they can also tap into expertise that they themselves might not have at a marketable level).

In Dysart's business, the strategic partnering is not limited to only the consulting work. Since Dysart & Jones Associates has now moved so heavily into training and conference organizing, the partnering includes bringing colleagues into that activity as well, and Dysart talks about it easily.

"One of the key precepts of leadership is to know your strengths and weaknesses," she says. "That's a lesson I learned many years ago when I first started working with Stephen Abram, owning and running an information conference (Canada Online) and later in presenting workshops together. Even though Stephen is outgoing, he had real difficulty calling people he didn't know on the telephone. On the other hand, I had no problem calling people and enlisting them in various activities, but I did not do so well on the details of moving something forward. In my current business, Rebecca Jones, my partner since 1993, is a whiz at process management and ensuring that all the steps are in place for moving ahead. I am much better focusing down the road, looking at the future, putting together pieces from different places to create an 'opportunity'."

Dysart pauses, and the sound of the futurist comes into her voice again. "Although putting together core competencies and strengths may be called 'strategic partnering' now," she says, "I believe it will be a natural way of doing business in the future. Individuals and companies will come together to form a virtual company, whether it's for a specific project or for a long-term endeavor."

So it's consulting, training, strategic partnering, and probably a number of other "pieces" as well. In the final analysis, of course, and at this particular point in her career, much of her attention must be given to the information services profession at large, and specifically to work of the Special Libraries Association. As she ends her presidency (she will step down at SLA's 87th Annual Conference, to be held in Boston in June), she is very aware that the organization is struggling with its own future, and she easily moves into her presidential "mode" to discuss some of the issues relating to the Association and its role in the profession.

"SLA's vision is to be leading organization in the information industry, a catalyst in the development of the information economy, and a strategic partner in the emerging information society. It is moving ahead to support its members in the 21st century—strengthening its global network, creating more electronic opportunities for members in all corners of the globe, and further developing its web site."

Dysart pauses, and as the image comes to her, she smiles. Jane Dysart likes being President and thinking about what SLA can do.

"SLA is building on the foundation of its members," she says. "It's the members who are at the center of what I call the four pillars of SLA: information, technology, service, and people. This is the launching pad, or catalyst, that will allow SLA to position itself as a leader in the information industry."

But everyone in the information services field is not so optimistic. There are some who assert that an organization like SLA can play only a limited role in serving the needs of the information professional. For example, the great variety in the job descriptions of the members of SLA makes it difficult for the organization to focus on which "niche" of the SLA membership should be served, and how they should be served. Dysart has obviously given this issue much thought, and she has her views on the matter:

"I believe that SLA is very responsive to its members," Dysart says. "The Association is creatively increasing the diverse methodology of delivery of its programs. As an example of what I mean, look at the Professional Development Program, which provides continuing education programs not only at annual and winter conferences, but regionally. In addition, the program promotes further learning at many levels and via video, distance learning and soon to be tried, web-based courses."

Diversity, whether in the SLA programs or in its membership, is an important issue for Dysart. "Our organization needs to have more professional diversity," she says. "It needs to attract information professionals from many different backgrounds. Diversity brings enrichment, and we need to enrich our knowledge and experience in the information industry as we approach the 21st century. We need more creative ideas and strategies to meet the challenges of the information age and the speed with which the platforms and cultures around us are changing.

"What brings SLA members totally together are our values," Dysart continues, and she then proceeds to list some of these values and how they are represented in the Association: "Our belief in continuous learning and professional development, for example, or the leadership role of SLA and its efforts to help members become information leaders in our organizations and communities. The use of technology to enhance our jobs, our organizations, and society. Our ability to add value to information services and products. Our role in the development of information policies. New opportunities for information service and delivery in the information economy. And most certainly, our networking and collaborative culture. Within SLA, we have a high degree of congruence from our members, even if they have different job titles and roles. They operate as highly effective information professionals who are focused on information, technology, service and people, coming together in SLA."

On the other hand, from an outsider's perspective, that is, for library and information services practitioners who are not part of the leadership team at SLA, it sometimes seems that the Association is not very concerned about its members. By becoming as "institutionalized" as it has become, SLA is sometimes perceived as being primarily focused on continuing its own organizational role. Rather than changing to meet the demands of the information marketplace, especially in terms of member needs, SLA is seen by some as existing to ensure its own continuity as an institution, and not to meet the needs of a membership that is increasingly diverse in their professional interests.

To be fair, the same charges are hurled at almost any other professional organization in the library/information services field, but that fact does not make the idea any more palatable for Dysart. For the first time, her face clouds over, and you can tell she's angry. Still, she recognizes that an dispassionate response is called for, and while the first few phrases she mutters might be unprintable, she continues with her thought. Dysart is an articulate leader, and she makes her point very clearly indeed.

"SLA has just gone through a dues increase and maintained its level of membership. In fact, membership has actually increased! Our 15,000 members are a reality, and they obviously gain value through their membership in SLA."

Dysart rises to her subject "What is powerful about SLA is not the institution," she says, "it's the members' energetic volunteerism. It is that volunteer interest that keeps us flexible, keeps us growing, and changing. Look at the creative programming our chapters do. The recent Northwest Regional SLA Conference was a highly successful intranet-focused meeting held in Seattle. Leading-edge speakers and members already involved in this new phenomenon proved that SLA members are leaders in the information industry. SLA's organization chart and the staff of 30 do not reflect the heart and soul of the organization, its members do. SLA is its members, and it is not an institution. Of course there are rules for running such a large organization, but most of those rules are based in guidelines that are flexible and ready for change when the need arises. And the guidelines are created by volunteer members to meet membership needs. SLA exists because of its members and for its members."

Those are strong words, but not unexpected, coming from someone who is as committed as Jane Dysart is to the success of the Association. SLA has a firm place in the information services profession, and she is quick to defend its place.

But connected to the role of SLA, and organizations like it, is the ongoing concern with what the workers are to be called. For any leader in a non-traditional library field these days, the issue is a "hot topic," with the very descriptors we use coming under fire. It's not a problem for Dysart, and when asked about the term, about the use of the word "librarianship," she had a ready answer. Not surprisingly, she puts her response in terms of SLA itself, and the ongoing controversy within the organization over whether it should change its name or not.

"I agree," Dysart says, "with those who say that the title 'librarian' more accurately reflects our past and not our future. We have many roles and many titles, and these 'non-traditional' opportunities are increasing: cybrarian, navigator, evaluator, analyst, trainer, guide, product developer, webmaster, facilitator, consultant, marketing manager, president, publisher, director. I certainly recognize the power, history and pride in SLA as a name and I would like to see us retain the letters 'SLA.' But I think we should enhance it with a subphrase or tagline—something like 'the Association for information professionals.' It's a hybrid name, I admit, and only an intermediate step for the Association, but I think it's something we can live with, and it reflects who we are at this point in history. And, in fact, we'll have more information about this soon anyway, for SLA's supersurvey this spring will let us know if our members are ready to change the name of their organization."

So there's a lot going on in Jane Dysart's professional life these days, and whether it will all really come together in a cohesive whole that can serve as a model for other specialized librarians remains to be seen. But whatever the future brings, Dysart and the strong-minded, independent information professionals who think like her are having a tremendous impact on the way information services practitioners see themselves these days. They are showing us all that the library and information services profession is one that can be as exciting and as energizing as we want it to be. What they are really demonstrating, in fact, is that the profession can be just as exciting as we are willing to allow it to be.

Meet Jane Dysart

Jane Dysart is a principal with Dysart & Jones Associates, a consulting company specializing in information management and services solutions, including direction planning, change management, and conference planning. Dysart served as President of the Special Libraries Association 1995-1996 and is widely recognized as a futurist in exploring matters having to do with information services. The author is many articles on the subject, she was Guest Editor in 1993 for a special issue of Special Libraries entitled "Standing in the Future." A popular seminar leader and presenter, Dysart delivered the Lazerow Lecture at the University of Toronto in 1995, and she will be Program Chair for Computers in Libraries '97. She is a resident of Toronto and has worked since 1985 in assisting the Quetico Foundation in the set-up and development of the John B. Ridley Library, located in a wilderness park in Quetico.

Quality reference delivery is critical—
and as society moves into the digital age,
ANNE LIPOW
has some provocative ideas on the subject

Enthusiasm—as a requirement for success in the library/information services industry—is often neglected. Or even disallowed. But those who would discount enthusiasm in the successful achievement of the librarian's goals simply haven't yet run across Anne Lipow. And when they meet her, they'll change their minds, for Lipow represents just the kind of customer-focused, service-oriented librarian who takes the profession's primary challenge and runs with it.

Few people—once they've got to know Anne Lipow—would deny that she is anything but the best in getting the library/information unit's customers what they want. That's why we all went into the information business in the first place, and for Lipow, that challenge—providing her information customers with the information they need—has been the key to success throughout her career. In fact, Lipow hasn't been at all shy about describing what it is she likes about being a librarian, and even though her career has passed through a variety of stages, at this point she is still happily describing—in absolutely glowing terms—what she does and the profession of which she is a part. As here, when she wrote in the latest issue of *Reference and User Services Quarterly*:

> "What do we do that's unique and needed?" Lipow asks. "To me, the answer is easy. We're the only profession in this complex information industry whose mission is to provide an evaluated collection of resources to a defined clientele at no charge. That's the key: relevant, quality information at no charge. No other profession is so tied to principles of democracy: we have a code of work principles that guarantees open, equitable access; we are thought of as a

Originally published in *InfoManage : The International Management Newsletter for the Information Services Professional* 5 (9), August 1998.

lifelong learning center; we provide a range of viewpoints for our users to be able to make informed choices. And best of all, we offer a world of information that began before the World Wide Web."

That, in a nutshell, describes why Anne Lipow is so good at what she does. It's enthusiasm, pure and simple, and it is a love for information, for delivering information or for helping information customers get it for themselves, that has got her to where she is today.

Lipow has most recently been in the news as the moderator for the Library of Congress Institute, "Reference Service in a Digital Age," held in late June in Washington, DC. With some 170 participants, the institute was convened to grapple with some of the major issues affecting reference service and to consider how librarians can shape the future of reference to ensure high quality service. Organized for reference librarians and managers concerned with the impact of technology on the future of reference services, the institute had a simple aim: to provide effective local and/or national leadership as libraries undergo change.

It couldn't have been a more auspicious goal, this determination to provide library managers with the tools for leading their organizations into providing better service in a dramatically changing society. And it's a place Anne Lipow has been before, for although she is now managing a company that specializes in providing services to the library profession, her earlier career was spent working in libraries. Employed for 30 years at the University of California, Berkeley, Library, Lipow advanced through her career at the UCB Library to the position of director of library instructional services and staff development. That experience, and the work she does now, managing Library Solutions Institute and Press and travelling the world giving workshops in Internet training for librarians, is a natural "lead-in" to moderating an institute on reference service in the digital age.

Lipow's career has been, it's safe to say, a lively one, and if there is any one thread that runs through her career (or links to her personality, for that matter), it's that she's always been a person who wants to, as she puts it, "fix things." She herself recognizes that character trait, and credits it with empowering her to have the career she's had.

"I wasn't at all sure it was going to be like it turned out," she says a little wistfully. "As it was with all women, my career choices were limited when I was thinking about what I wanted to do. In those days, you could become a teacher, or a secretary, or a librarian, or a telephone operator, or go into one of about six other careers that were considered 'appropriate' for women. Well, I didn't want to be a secretary, and I didn't want to be a teacher. I was working as a manuscripts editor in the Psychology Department at Berkeley, and a friend told me about the graduate library program. I investigated, decided to enroll, got my degree, and when I finished I got a job in the library's Acquisitions Department.

"And that was the only job I ever had that already existed," Lipow continues. "I never had a position for more than three years, and every job I got was a job that was created, a job that someone in authority and I were able to put together because I saw something that needed attention, or needed to be fixed, and I wanted to do it. So after my first job, my career was built on finding things that needed to be done, and doing them."

Certainly the record of her work at the UCB Library reflects that idea. While she had many exciting and innovative jobs there, Lipow speaks about two of them with special fervor, and hearing her describe them connects directly with that thread of "fixing things." It also provides a good picture of how she created this career combining her interest in reference services with her involvement in training and instruction.

"My involvement in reference work came about through a very circuitous route. For example, one of my early jobs was with John Knapp, who had been brought in to run the Systems Office. I was the first person he hired to do systems analysis, and for me, it was the most marvelous thing. I'm very good at systems organization, and working with John enabled me to put it all in place, to see how the work we did in the library fit with the work that was being done throughout the university."

It was not far from systems analysis to other work at the UCB Library: working in the serials unit, creating and managing a departmental order division, that sort of thing. These and similar jobs kept Lipow busy, and—as you would expect if you knew her—kept the enthusiasm and the entrepreneurial juices flowing. In fact, it was her ability to think entrepreneurially that led to one of the jobs she most loves to talk about.

"Richard Dougherty was the University Librarian, and he wanted a document delivery system for the university. Such a thing had never been done before, but we knew that in this environment, the faculty and students often simply didn't have time to go get something. So we created a service that would do it for them, and we had great fun putting it together. We knew that our users did not always understand the library system, and they knew they didn't understand it. And as we worked on this, as we did our market research, we also discovered that people would pay to get something sent to them that they couldn't get for themselves. So it was a fee-based service. It became known as 'The Baker Service'—BAKER being the letters for the five-digit campus telephone number we were assigned, and we got into the whole idea of 'Baker Street,' and sleuthing, and Sherlock Holmes. It was tremendously successful, and in fact we found ourselves getting a great deal of attention in the profession for this work. I even delivered a paper on it at the first ACRL (ALA's Association of College and Research Libraries) Conference, a paper I still find referred to from time to time."

Naturally Lipow's work with the Baker Service pulled her into doing something else and that something else, in this case, was destined to be her first venture into the line of work that would eventually define her as a librarian and teacher. Recognizing that the faculty and students at Berkeley needed more than just document delivery, she began to put together workshops and seminars to help them learn how to find the information and the materials they needed.

"But the seminars wasn't necessarily all library-oriented," Lipow says with a laugh. "We started with a first series of classes for the faculty, one of which was called, 'Where Did I Put That Paper?—Organizing Your Personal Information Files.' It was the most popular course in the series. From there we went to offering these seminars annually. Now many of us at the library wondered how these classes would be received, for there were plenty of people saying that faculty would never admit that they didn't know how to use the library. But that didn't turn out to be the case. They were delighted to have the programs we were offering.

"And by that time, we weren't surprised," Lipow continues, "for we were discovering that when people got in touch with the Baker Service, they were asking for things after they had looked for them. We wrote to them and asked them if they would like to know how to look for things— how to use the library—more efficiently. And the response was far beyond what we expected. In fact the response was so good that our first offering had to be seven classes, and we had 40 people in each one."

So it isn't hard to see why Anne Lipow has become so interested in quality reference services, and in the prospects for reference service as society enters the digital age. Certainly hers has been—and continues to be—a career that focuses on determining what people want from libraries, and on figuring out how to get them what they want, on fixing things. At ALA's Midwinter Conference, in January, Lipow facilitated a hearing on these new reference services, and between January and June she worked with LC staff to organize the national institute referred to earlier, which she also moderated.

The reaction to the institute has been—to put it mildly—overwhelmingly positive. First of all, there is the subject. "Reference Service in a Digital Age" is a subject that every library manager must deal with [see sidebar below], and we're all looking for help, trying to figure out what the next steps are going to be.

More impressive, however, is what happened at the institute.

"The key concepts are things like collaboration, and partnering with the users," Lipow says. "We have to recognize that the reference environment is changing, and that we are finding ourselves working with new kinds of information seekers, people who are comfortable with technology. But they can also find much of what they need for themselves, from their offices and homes, but when they have a question, they are not going to come to us unless we are much more conveniently accessible than we are now—until we are a click away. Using interactive video technology, that's a realistic goal for us. Those are the kinds of challenges reference librarians are confronting these days.

Reference Services:
Why We Should be Worried

On *Reference & User Services Quarterly* (37, 2, Winter, 1997), Anne Lipow offers "eight observations that, by themselves, may not seem bad news, but taken together I believe amount to early signs of a decline in our (not our client's) perceived importance of reference service." Here is Lipow's list:

1. Declining circulation statistics
2. Fewer walk-in users
3. Staff can't keep up
4. Reference Desk eliminated
5. Outsourcing on the rise

6. Reduced reference service hours
7. Search engines: automated reference librarians?
8. Need for large building and staff not clear

"But that's good—that we're so challenged—for that's where the collaborative idea kicks in. It was David Lankes, at the ERIC Clearinghouse on Information Technology, who put it in perspective for us when he said that with electronic information delivery, the reference librarian has the opportunity to move to center stage. With digitized information, our 'library' is now an infinite, disorganized, and unevaluated collection, and we're the ones who can help the user make sense of it all."

And connected to those new resources is the new attention to how we think about our customers.

"Absolutely," Lipow says. "We're partnering with our users, and when users come to us nowadays, what we're working with is, as Lankes put it, 'a problem looking for a solution, not a question looking for an answer.' We librarians can now pull from this infinite collection, and we become, in effect, the quality assurance person in the information transaction."

The other part of all this, Lipow is quick to admit, is that we don't have a choice.

"If we don't do this," she says, "we run the risk of becoming one-dimensional, of being able to focus on only one type of information, or one type of question, or subject. But as the curator of this infinite collection, the reference librarian gets to be involved in all the media, and all the subjects. It's a thrilling prospect."

Indeed it is, and with people like Anne Lipow guiding us as we move to meeting these challenges, the role of the reference librarian in the future delivery of information will be one that links directly to what we've always done well, leading that information customer to the information he or she needs, and being proud of being part of the process.

Meet Anne Lipow

Anne Grodzins Lipow is Founder and Director of the Library Solutions Institute and Press, which offers library consulting services, Internet training and library skills workshops and seminars, and think-tank institutes for information professionals throughout the world. Library Solutions' trainers are acknowledged as outstanding and the workshops models of practical instruction. Among its publications, the company is best known for its Internet Workshop Series (for which Lipow is the Coordinating Editor), some of which are the only self-paced tutorials on Internet topics available in print form.

Lipow is a frequent consultant, speaker, author, and classroom teacher. She manages long-term educational programs, such as one with the California State Library's InFoPeople Project, which provides sustained Internet training to public libraries that are members of the Project, and another with the Library of Congress, which is seeking to identify its special role in working with libraries to ensure the relevance of their information services into the 21st century. Non-library clients include organizations such as Caltrans, the California State agency overseeing state transportation regulations, and which, because it is no longer producing its documents in printed form, is committed to teaching city transportation engineers throughout California how to access and use those materials on the World Wide Web. Among her many publications, Lipow is co-author with Roy Tennant and John Ober of the popular Crossing the Internet Threshold. She is also a co-editor of Staff Development: A Practical Guide,

published by the American Library Association. With Sheila Creth, she edited the proceedings of the Library Solutions Institute "Building Partnerships Between Computing and Library Professionals," and her chapter describing the work of Library Solutions Institute and Press has been included in a new book, published by Neal-Schuman, entitled What Else You Can Do with a Library Degree? Lipow is currently working on a book with John Ober, I low to Teach the Internet. In 1994, Lipow was the recipient of the American Library Association's Isadore Gilbert Mudge/R.R. Bowker award for "a distinguished contribution to reference librarianship." The award recognizes, among other achievements, her role in organizing "Rethinking Reference" institutes throughout the country. These institutes have been sowing new ideas among library reference managers nationwide, who in turn are forces for constructive change in librarianship. (Lipow is also the editor of the Proceedings of these "Rethinking Reference" institutes.) Lipow may be the world's only manufacturer of a hand-made wooden dreidel (a 4-sided top used for celebrating Chanukkah). From 1974 to 1995, she was so-owner of The Dreidel Factory, and armed with a street vendor's license, sold her redwood dreidels on Berkeley's famed Telegraph Avenue during the holiday season. She says that the high she gets from seeing people enjoy something she has created is the same, whether it's dreidels or her consulting services, or the publications produced by Library Solutions Institute and Press.

8

QUALITY MANAGEMENT

Quality Information Management—QIM—begins with values, the values of the information customers, the values of the information staff providing information products, services, and consultations to those customers, and the parent organization or community's values. They all mix and link together into the happy brew that information managers strive to produce: a level of information delivery that matches the needs of all information stakeholders. In the change management process, it is that move toward quality information delivery that drives the actions of those who have responsibility for information management.

During his tenure at *Newsweek*, Ted Slate became well known in both the specialist library profession and in the journalism community for his commitment to quality information management (although it wasn't called that in those days). When Slate retired from the company after 29 years of service, he was able to look back with considerable satisfaction at the changes he and his staff had been responsible for, and among the change management efforts that brought the *Newsweek* editorial library particularly pleasing recognition was Slate's effort at initiating an information-services thrust to the business side of the magazine. For Slate, change meant doing as *much* (not as *little*) for the parent organization as he could do. It was a change that had far-reaching impact at *Newsweek*, as Slate describes in the interview.

Rich Willner, too, is an information manager who understands the value of quality management in the information arena. At Lehman Brothers, Willner took a long, hard look at how information services are measured in the company, and by concentrating on real dollar expenditures (and by quantifying savings when they occur), Willner and his people provide management with financial information that reflects accurately what it costs to provide information services.

At the Amateur Athletic Foundation in Los Angeles, Vice President for Research Wayne Wilson runs an operation that literally requires a quality approach to management, simply because the tremendous effort in administering such an operation cannot be made without attention to customer service, accurate measurement, continuous improvement, and trust and teamwork among all information stakeholders. The Paul Ziffren Sports Resource Center at the Foundation("Otherwise known as 'the library'," Wilson says with a laugh) is a serious research institution, a library, an information delivery operation, *and* an organization that creates information products.

But quality isn't something that is limited to the management of information services, and for many executives in the field, quality information management includes going into the identified customer base and working with the users to ensure that they understand the value of information and the value of information services in their organizations. And what better group of users to teach than those who are learning to be managers? At Ashridge Management College in the United Kingdom, Andrew Ettinger has responsibility for delivering information for students enrolled at the college, but his larger role, as he sees it, is to work with future managers on the information services function in their work, or in the work that they will be doing. Ann Wolpert, too, when she was in charge of information services at the Harvard Business School (she is now Director of Information Services at the Massachusetts Institute of Technology), saw as a primary mission introducing the new generation of business managers to the relevance and usefulness of information in a successful career. In these interviews, both Ettinger and Wolpert make it clear that quality in information services means defining your student users as customers, regardless of what their other academic or professional pursuits might be.

For Barbara Spiegelman the quality information management focus had to be taken to a new level of management involvement at Westinghouse Energy Systems. For several years, total quality management was successfully implemented and, appropriately, charted at Westinghouse. What eventually evolved, however, was interestingly enough a move toward a slightly different management methodology, competency-based management, a new management approach that became a sort of synergistic "partner" with TQM (and one which has critical service delivery implications in the broader information services management field). Spiegelman was later able to incorporate her work with competency-based management into the study that SLA's Special Committee on Competencies for Special Librarians was doing, and into the book she edited on the subject, *Competencies for Special Librarians of the 21st Century*. Now established as one of the most important contributions SLA has made to the information industry, Spiegelman's experience in this area, which she describes in the interview from the perspective of the work she does at Westinghouse (and which is detailed in the chapter she wrote on using competencies as a performance appraisal and compensation tool in the book) is a practical case study for information executives who want to think about quality information management as it connects to what else is used in the workplace.

TED SLATE

At *Newsweek*: he likes the look of what he's leaving . . .
and where he's going

There's an Edward Lear story that ends with the line, "And he ran away in all directions."

Could that line have been Ted Slate's inspiration?

Slate is retiring in October as Director of Research Services at *Newsweek*, one of America's legendary news organizations. Having been with the company for nearly 29 years, with a top-notch staff and a research facility that is the envy of many who work in information services, Slate's early retirement has come as something of a shock to the information community. Most of his colleagues just aren't ready for him to retire.

Yet when questioned about the subject, specifically in terms of why he's retiring, Slate is characteristically straight forward with his response.

"I just don't want to continue doing what I've been doing," he says. "I've been here a long time, and I've been responsible for the factual accuracy of the magazine for years. As I see it, I've got about seven more years of work ahead of me before I really retire, and there are many things that interest me that I would love to pursue. And, unlike Shirley MacLaine, I have only one shot at things in this life and I know I'd have regrets if I didn't go for it now. I want to go on to something different."

And what is that "something different"?

Slate laughs, and that's when you get the Edward Lear quote.

"There are a lot of things happening," he continues, and as he begins to describe some of his upcoming activities, you realize that the company press release, stating that he is leaving "in order to pursue teaching and consulting opportunities," is something of a genteel copout. This man is going out on his own because he has new roads to travel, new adventures

Originally published in *InfoManage : The International Management Newsletter for the Information Services Professional* 1 (12), October, 1994.

to experience, and, not to put too fine a point on it, because he wants to test himself, to see just how much he can do in the working years he's allotted himself.

Information services is part of it, of course, and Slate is deep in negotiations with a variety of organizations in the information business. He'll continue his longtime "side" career as a tour director, he expects to get involved in fund raising for the library community, and after six months, he'll be back at *Newsweek* on a part-time consulting basis to "provide whatever input I can" to a technological update that is in the works.

And, yes, there's the teaching. Several graduate schools have called, and he obviously enjoys being tempted to influence up-and-coming information services practitioners. Yet there is also talk about teaching at a journalism school, a course on "The Elements of Research," so it's not all focused on information.

Slate would be a good teacher, there's no doubt about that. In fact, just to sit and listen to some of his war stories would be an education in itself. His work, his particular outlook on life, and the various interactions that come into play throughout one's life combine to make him one of the best raconteurs around. If his graduate students will listen to what he has to say, they'll learn a lot.

So this is a man who is going to be very busy for the next few years. For him, the idea of "retirement" (if we must use the word) is something of an anachronism. This man is definitely not retiring.

Nor should he. Ted Slate's career has been one of innovation, breaking molds, start-ups, creative energy, and even political upheaval. He is not a child of the '60s for nothing. Who among us remembers (who can forget?) the Librarians' Anti-Defamation League? There they were, the members of the profession, demonstrating because a major corporation had an advertising campaign depicting happy, energetic, athletic people consuming its product, but also including, as contrast, a lone, lorn frumpy soul, the "town librarian." Make your blood boil? Absolutely. And Ted Slate was leading the march.

Back at *Newsweek*, Slate was presiding over a growing, increasingly complex, and increasingly productive research organization. Having been brought in as Library Director in 1966, Slate was responsible for transforming a sleepy clipping and filing department into a major information/research facility. Prior to his appearance on the scene, the library had not been one of the shining stars of the magazine's operation. The youngest staff were assigned throughout the various departments to clip magazines and newspapers, and the twelve people in the library were busy assigning subject headings to the clippings. Throughout the magazine, the general orientation about the library had been one of "Don't bother the librarians—They're busy clipping and assigning subject headings." It wasn't a very impressive sight, for there was no defined budget, there were no routines, and no one could find anything.

Slate was determined to create a news library that worked, and he went at it with his typical enthusiasm. He took two approaches, either of which would have provided satisfactory results. Combined, they made Slate's name at the magazine.

First, he began to put out feelers to the movers and shakers in the company. By the time he got to Osborn Elliott, the famous *Newsweek* editor who eventually became Dean at Columbia University's School of Journalism, Elliott was ready for him.

"How much will it cost," he asked Slate, "to put the library in shape?"

Ted Slate admits that he didn't have an immediate answer, but he was not shy about saying he would bring in the figures. To arrive at those figures, Slate looked at the model of service "levels" that Ed Strable had put forth in his book on special libraries, published some years before. By the time he reported back to Elliott, Slate was prepared to offer the editor a choice: he could have a news library that was "passive," one that was "moderately active," or one that was "active."

Elliott didn't hesitate. The magazine went for the highest, most active, most productive level, and that's where the *Newsweek* library has been ever since.

So the next question has to be: how long? What kind of time frame was involved in turning this big ship around?

"About a year and a half," Slate answers, and he's almost a little glib about it. He knew what he was doing and he was confident that it was the right thing to do. And that he was doing it right. "In fact, within about two years the staff had grown from 12 to 26, and those six clip desks, scattered throughout the editorial departments, had been reduced to two people, working in the library. The subject headings reflected what people asked for, and they could now find things."

It was that "turning around" of the editorial side that convinced Slate that the magazine needed a library that was broader in focus, and that was his second smart move: to initiate an information-services thrust directed to the business side of the magazine. He knew that management, sales, and the other financial entities at *Newsweek* required information, and he also knew that his library's staying power would have something to do with how executives on the business side perceived the services the library was providing. So he extended the library's services to the business people as well as the editorial staff, going to annual sales meetings, doing presentations, and, in general, offering the management side of the company an information resource it had not had before. Of course it worked, and today the library's support of corporate activities represents a significant proportion of the work generated in the library.

It's a big operation and, as Director of Research Services (a title he was given in 1990), Slate has some 80 people in five departments reporting to him. These include the library, the reporter/researchers, the copy desk, the proofreaders, and the letters department. He has had a major impact at the company, and *Newsweek* Editor Maynard Parker said no less when he announced Slate's retirement.

"Ted's achievements are legendary," Parker said. "He has built a research library that is second to none in our business and managed a research staff with energy, efficiency, and a keen eye for up-and-coming talent."

It's that keen eye, not just for the talent, but for the quality of the work as well, that perhaps most characterizes Ted Slate. Certainly it was that keen eye—and his own professional craftiness—that enabled him to pull off the coup of his career. It's his favorite story, and the event in his career that he seems to be most proud of.

Oddly enough, it didn't happen at *Newsweek*. Prior to coming to the magazine, he had worked at a couple of other jobs, at the Library of Congress and at *The New York Times* Washington bureau. They were good jobs, fulfilling, exciting, and there was certainly much pleasure in working at the *Times* with people like James Reston, Anthony Lewis, Arthur Krock, Russell Baker, David Halberstam, Max Frankel and the like.

But Slate's finest hour, he says, came about when an effort of his led to a change in governmental policy, and it is, indeed, a remarkable story. By the time the United States was involved in the Vietnam War, the nation had evolved two foreign "policies." There was, of course, the accepted policy that was carried out by our Ambassador, Henry Cabot Lodge. At the same time, however, there was a clandestine C.I.A. "policy" that involved the skullduggery, secret assassinations, mysterious disappearances, and the like that came to be associated with this particularly unsavory part of American history. No one could figure out who was behind this clandestine activity in Saigon, and in a staff meeting, Reston, then heading up the *Times* Washington bureau, said he wanted to nail the culprit and, hopefully, expose this duplicitous policy.

Slate went back to his staff, and they put together a listing of everyone connected with the embassy in Saigon. In the Biographical Register that the State Department used to make available, they found a listing for a man who was the chief of intelligence at the embassy, with a job ostensibly confined to the gathering and analysis of intelligence information. Was this man working as the C.I.A.'s chief in Saigon, carrying out his own "policies" that reflected a C.I.A. focus? If he was, it was a job that didn't match the usual job description for a "chief of intelligence" in an embassy.

What Slate and his staff discovered was that the man in question had attended the University of California, knew several of the languages of Southeast Asia, and had had several postings in Asia. As the coincidences piled up, Slate called the University of California Club, pretending to be a friend who was trying to find the man, and he learned that the fellow (of course) was not there. He was told, however, that there was someone in Washington who was a close friend, and that Slate might call that person. Slate called, identified himself as a friend who was visiting in Washington and wanted to look the man up, but the other person said he wasn't there. He was in Saigon, working at the embassy in some "intelligence" position, "probably with the C.I.A. or the N.S.A.," and wouldn't be returning to Washington for a couple of years.

That was all Slate needed. He took the information to Max Frankel, who cabled it to David Halberstam in Saigon. There, Halberstam did his own investigation and blew the embassy employee's cover, as well as the policies he conducted. He had, indeed, turned out to be the C.I.A.'s man in Saigon, and thanks to Ted Slate, the library staff at the *Times* Washington bureau, and the courage that Reston, Frankel, Halberstam, and the rest of the staff had in pursuing the lead, the story was told and the "secret" policy was out.

"Was it librarianship?" Slate asks. "Isn't it the librarian's job to use all the sources, use all the media, including the telephone? I guess some librarians might be uncomfortable asking some of these questions.

"But we got our reporters the information they needed. That's what the news librarian is supposed to do. That's what is required, if the news librarian is integral to the news process."

But it requires taking some chances, this being "integral to the process," not just for news librarians, but for any librarian, any information services professional. Slate has taken some chances, both at *Newsweek* and before he went there, and now he's getting ready to take some more.

How will it all turn out? Slate has no idea, and that's part of the fun of it, the curious unpredictability of moving in these many directions.

"Quite frankly," he says, and you can almost hear the pleasure of anticipation in his voice, "with so many balls in the air, I'm anxious to know how it will all play out."

So are the rest of us.

Meet Ted Slate

Since April, 1990, Director of Research Services, *Newsweek*, New York, NY . . . Library Director, *Newsweek*, 1966-1990 . . . Assistant Head and Chief Bibliographer, Arms Control and Disarmament Bibliography Section, Library of Congress, Washington, DC, 1964-1966 . . . Assistant Librarian, Librarian, *The New York Times* Washington, DC, Bureau, 1962-1964 . . . A native of New York City . . . B.A., History, Rutgers, The State University of New Jersey, 1957 . . . M.A., History, M.S.L.S., Library Science, University of Michigan . . . Named Distinguished Alumnus, University of Michigan, 1988 . . . Past President, Mercantile Library Association, New York, NY . . . Member, Board of Trustees, Metropolitan Reference and Research Library Agency (METRO) . . . Member, Advisory Board, The Center for the Book in the Library of Congress . . . Member, The New York State Commissioner of Education's Committee on Statewide Library Development . . . Professional memberships include the Special Libraries Association, the National Micrographics Association, the New York Library Club, the American Library Association, and the American Society for Information Science . . . Home in Cliffside Park, NJ.

ANDREW ETTINGER
At Ashridge Management College: Total quality learning for managers

If you're going to visit Andrew Ettinger, the first thing you become aware of is the place. It's just too beautiful, and it's just too easy to be charmed by the lush gorgeousness of the physical surroundings. Yes, we all recognize how blasé the English are about their stately homes, and we try to fall into step, but the drive from the station is pretty overwhelming, and you start looking about for the Merchant/Ivory film crew.

Then there's that drive up to the house. And wow! There's the house itself. "Try to keep things under control," you say to yourself. "This is a visit to a management college, not a stop on some guided tour. Try not to be too impressed."

But it's not easy, for the site is truly magnificent. Ashridge Management College is set in 150 acres of parkland in rural Hertfordshire, housed in a building that has been at one time or another a monastery, a royal residence, the mansion of dukes and earls, and, from 1928 until it became a management college in 1949, a training college for the Conservative Party. Now the primary facility and headquarters building for one of the most prestigious training centers in Europe (there are also facilities on the Swiss-French border, in Hong Kong, and in London), Ashridge House is the central architectural feature of a 170-bedroomed college that is used year round for management education. Characterizing itself as an independent, self-financing management and organization development centre, Ashridge Management College exists to improve the practice of management and organizational effectiveness throughout the world, through the provision of research, executive development, and consultancy services.

Andrew Ettinger manages the college's learning resources, in a separate facility housed in a purpose-built learning center (but using the walls

Originally published in *InfoManage : The International Management Newsletter for the Information Services Professional* 2 (4), March, 1995.

of a 17th-century barn!). It is his job is to see to it that state-of-the-art information management and training are provided for several thousand participants in Ashridge programs (4,626 participants in 1993 alone). Of course not nearly that many people use the Learning Resource Centre, simply because many of these participants are involved in other Ashridge programs at different sites, but the numbers are still impressive and with information support responsibility for some 350 internal customers as well (the Ashridge faculty, staff, and so forth), the operation of the center is an important component in the college's administrative program.

A major effort has been to establish that the facility is an "information and learning center," not a "library," and much attention is given to delivering information products and services that relate to customer needs.

"We're not shy about moving 'beyond' the traditional library orientation in the profession," Ettinger says, and his emphasis makes it clear that this is a subject that has commanded much of his attention for some time. "Most managers," he says, "do not think very highly of their corporate libraries, and they assume service will be poor. It's our job to change that kind of thinking."

It becomes clear as you tour the place that Ettinger and his staff accomplish this change by linking what they do with the major trends in executive training that are being incorporated into the college's teaching programs. If, for example, the college is going to be creating modular programs for educating its students and clients (since many of the college's clients—perhaps 15% at any given time—are consultancy clients), the Learning Resource Centre will be matching its services to the program. Such packaged information products as the "corporate library" with data on more than 3,000 companies, the information files on every country in the world, and the market research and forecasting collection are designed to be folded into the teaching programs that are in place. In addition, there are over 300 packaged information files on industries, management techniques, and topical business issues, and the popular multimedia "Learning Guides," put together in collaboration with the participation of the teaching faculty, are created as part of this effort. It all comes together to establish and maintain a level of information credibility that Ettinger expects the resource center's customers to carry over into their work in the management community.

In fact, credibility is at the top of the list of "key principles" that Ettinger has identified. He has put himself and his facility squarely in the middle of the move to the concept of the learning organization, and for Ettinger, the crucial link between information services management and the learning organization (as he has said in public and in print, as well as in his conversations on the subject) is "a commitment to and an understanding of" the customer.

"It's that simple," he says. "You look at what the customer requirements are and you arrange to meet them. But it also means that you aren't just delivering information or data. You're not there just to order, collect, organize, and disseminate. You're there to connect that information to learning and knowledge. That's when learning becomes total quality."

It's that transition from information to total quality learning that drives Ettinger's philosophy of information services management, and the required credibility is essential. Such credibility doesn't come easily, particularly for traditionally trained information services practitioners, and an understanding of the strategic direction and mission of the organization is built into the process. In fact, he says, referring to librarians and other information providers, "one needs to almost lose ownership of the information resource and pay attention to the benefits the organization derives from it." When that happens, the credibility of the information services operation is established, for it is now perceived as truly a part of the organization and not as a stand-alone facility that sometimes is and sometimes isn't relevant to what is really happening.

Ettinger's other 'key principles' come into play in his management of the Learning Resource Centre at Ashridge, and certainly involvement in the organization is easily recognized when you hear him talk about the various parts of the college that connect to the center. Serious efforts are being made to incorporate integrated information services throughout the college, and Ettinger and his staff play an important role in this activity as they move the delivery of information into the knowledge-based learning arena. An important part of this effort, of course, is the way Ettinger works with the various other members of the teaching faculty, and with his being responsible for media services, graphics design, and some computer operations as well as library and information services, it is obvious that organizational involvement is taken seriously by Ettinger and his staff.

This involvement demonstrates another of Ettinger's "key principles," his insistence on a proactive stance and attitude in the delivery of information and his efforts to build a team approach in the delivery of information products and services. For example, while there are specialist staff at the Learning Resource Centre, future plans call for an emphasis on multi-skilling. In what might turn out to be a whole new approach to information services delivery, multi-skilling is to be put in place so that, as Ettinger says, "the customer can be helped and satisfied more often." It's certainly not an easy process, and Ettinger is quick to point out that it must be handled subtly, but in a facility such as the one he has responsibility for, multi-skilling is critical.

"We are open twenty-four hours a day, seven days a week, and we have staff at the Centre for ninety-one hours a week," he says. "If we are going to offer these hours of service, we can't have staff ask customers to come back another time when someone will be there to help them with their particular needs. We need to do it all, or as much of it as is practical."

So is he trying to achieve at Ashridge something like the "one-stop shopping" so many information services managers are talking about these days?

"Absolutely," Ettinger says. "In these days of management change—the flatter organization, de-layering, business process reengineering, and more emphasis on flexibility—we must do the same in delivering information services and products. And that requires that our staff be qualified to do many different 'types' of information delivery and help managers learn to utilize a variety of media and technologies."

And as you move about the spacious and open Learning Resource Centre at Ashridge and observe staff members interacting with their customers, it becomes perfectly obvious that a high level of success is being achieved in the delivery of information services and products in this environment. There is much end-user training, and it pays off, for you can see any number of Ashridge residents simply walk up to a computer, pop in a CD-ROM disk or open an online database, and go to work looking for the information they need. Others go straight to the industry files or similar products (all displayed openly and easily accessible), and it is clear that they have incorporated the information-seeking part of their work into the larger picture. It isn't a big deal, and these people are absolutely comfortable looking for information however it is captured, regardless of format.

In fact, from a visitor's perspective, sometimes it can't help but look too easy. Certainly moving information services management to a customer-focused and total quality learning level of delivery isn't as easy as it looks, and when asked, Ettinger's smile is quick to appear. He's been waiting for you to ask.

"Of course there are problems," he says. "With all this openness, security is bound to be a problem, and while some parts of the collection are locked up when it's necessary for them to be locked up, we budget for a 4% loss each year. It's just our way of dealing with reality."

And management problems? What prevents total success?

"The usual," Ettinger says. "There are often problems with customer expectations. We just can't do everything that everybody wants, and some people go away disappointed. Other customers tend to take advantage of us, and we have to be on guard about that sort of thing, but we try to address that early on in our student orientation programs. We have a fairly sophisticated program for introducing the Learning Resource Centre to new students, and we try to 'inspire' them about their work here."

Another clear success—at least from a visitor's point of view—has to do with the attitude of the staff. They are businesslike, there's no doubt about it, but they have managed to combine a pleasant demeanor and a friendly approach to the customers with their businesslike manner. The result is a very positive information ambience. Not surprisingly, it reflects Andrew Ettinger's ideas about staff training and development.

"First of all," he says, "we try very hard to train staff that the way you treat people is the way they treat you, so if we're dealing with customers, we have the opportunity to set the stage, so to speak, in how the transaction will go. It's also important that the place look good. It can't be boring and dull, with illegible signs falling down, out-of-date notices and inaccessible staff. That won't work, and we put a lot of effort into making our customers—who are, after all, managers in training—comfortable in the Learning Resource Centre. We put ourselves in the users' shoes. And it works."

Of course it works, because what Andrew Ettinger and his staff are doing is taking the total quality management paradigm and moving it—

not easily, not boldly, not drastically, but certainly confidently—into the information services management field. There will be times when the model doesn't fit, and there will be times when total quality learning isn't exactly what the customer wanted, or expected. But when it does work—which is, of course, most of the time—information services customers at Ashridge Management College come away satisfied. And that's the whole point.

Meet Andrew Ettinger

Manager, Learning Resources Centre at Ashridge Management College in Hertfordshire, England, where he is responsible for the multi-media information services program . . . Teaches information services management and is currently researching quality information provision . . . Has worked on consultancy assignments in India and Poland and previously worked in information services at the London Business School . . . Educated at London University, where he was awarded his BSc, DipLib . . . Early education in London and New York . . . Frequent lecturer in UK and Europe on information services management subjects, visiting lecturer for several graduate and postgraduate library/information studies programs . . . Author of professional articles in professional journals, most recently, "From Information to Total Quality Learning" in *The Value of Information to the Intelligent Organisation* (Hatfield, Herts.: University of Hertsfordshire Press Key Issues in the Information Business Series, 1994) . . . Often speaks to professional organizations about information services management and the implications of new technology in the delivery of information services and products . . . Personal interests include the Tottenham/Hotspur Football Club, collecting penguins, and his girlfriend Ceris . . . Makes his home in London.

Defining the corporate library:
RICHARD A. WILLNER
at Lehman Brothers

Take a look at the equipment, the services offered, the files, the staff. Despite an offhand comment that things are a little disorganized and the promise of a reorganized space in the near future, the 15th Floor of the American Express Tower at the World Financial Center is impressively put together. Investment banking is serious, and this is a place where people take information services seriously.

At the same time, though, there is a positively cheerful atmosphere in this large space, and while many of the thirty-three staff at the Corporate Library are obviously very busy juggling any number of queries and projects, the tone of the place is one of teamwork and mutual support in delivering the information products and services that the library's customers need for their work. "The Lehman professionals," the firm calls its employees, and they come to the Corporate Library and its affiliated information operations for an amazing variety of services, services organized and managed by Rich Willner and the team of specialist managers he has reporting to him.

At Lehman Brothers, however, the complete information services picture includes more than the Corporate Library, and although that unit is the focus of much of the firm's information activity, Willner's full responsibility takes in the firm's overall research services organization—Business Information Services (BIS)—as well.

One unit of BIS, for example, Financial Data Services, supports the firm's major initiative in end-user database searching. Long established as a primary information function at the company, FDS and its end-user training and support efforts have been in place for so long that most Lehman employees just accept FDS, and its analysts with their financial backgrounds, as part of the standard information picture. Surprisingly for

Originally published in *InfoManage : The International Management Newsletter for the Information Services Professional* 1 (8), July, 1994.

them, they have to leave and go to work somewhere else before they realize just how much data they had available at their desks when they worked for Lehman Brothers.

Business Information Services also includes other specialist units. Legal Research, for example, exists to support the firm's attorneys in their work, and with Records Management rounds out the on-site BIS team. Also part of the BIS group, however, is the firm's London Library, Lehman's center for European business information, where Director Mark Jewell and his staff of seven work closely with the New York office to provide trans-Atlantic cooperation for BIS customers. Altogether, the several units of Lehman's Business Information Services, created to be a client driven, cost effective research organization to serve the worldwide Lehman community, employs fifty-five people.

It's a strong information operation, and with such a wide-ranging "marketplace" for information services and products, it begins to look as if the firm's Business Information Services operation might take on a broader international role. Asked if he is envisioning a global information system, Willner takes his time in responding.

"Lehman Brothers is a fairly centralized company," he replies. "Much of the work is concentrated in one place, so perhaps instead of a global information service, what we're really looking at is a different kind of support. I believe in giving the person on the scene the tools, systems, and so forth. Perhaps that is the way we provide that service."

Such a perspective makes a certain kind of sense at Lehman Brothers. Although information services are extended to Lehman professionals worldwide, the concentration of the effort is in New York, where the investment banking side of the company is located. With that part of the firm's activity accounting for some 70% of the information services units' usage, it seems reasonable to assume that the concentration will remain in New York.

As far as his work at Lehman Brothers is concerned, Willner describes it as managing "a late 20th-century information services operation," an information program built around a "relatively ambitious" corporate library. When discussing what such a program might entail, certain themes come into play and Willner, with his easy manner, is happy to elaborate. The measurement and evaluation of services, for example, is a primary component.

Like many information services executives, Rich Willner understands the importance of measurement, and while effectiveness measures are appropriate for many information operations, at Lehman Brothers Willner "watches the cash register." The simplest measurement tool—and most useful, for Willner—is data expense, the cost of the information, which at Lehman is "many times staff expense and occupancy expense." Unlike the situation in many other information services organizations, Willner can put his finger on the real costs of providing the information, and he can provide quantifiable figures, for himself and his planning staff, and for his senior management when such figures are needed.

Such attention to hard data is what makes information services management work in the organization. Willner's not interested in some "idea" about information services costs; he wants to know specifics, just as his managers do. When he arrived at Lehman Brothers four years ago, there were some 30-40 lines for charging back costs. Now there are over 300, counting some of the service agreements that have been included in the various reorganizations and sales that have taken place in that time. By concentrating on real dollar expenditures (and by quantifying savings when they occur), Willner and his people are able to provide management with financial information that reflects accurately what it costs to provide information services. And that accuracy is paramount, at least in this operation.

It comes, Willner says, in understanding what he refers to as the "landscape of the place." Here he's not talking about the usual concepts of corporate or organizational culture, those now almost overworked ideas about "fitting in" in order to be successful. For Willner, the "landscape" in a company is more an understanding of where you work, of what the information services operation does.

"It's understanding what you are going to tell your manager about the operation," he says, "of determining what your managers need to know about information services." And then, of course, conveying it to them. It's obvious that Willner has strong feelings about the kind of place the firm is. In fact, he likes it there very much, a fact which comes through as he talks about the company.

"It's a great pleasure," he says, "to work with such intelligent people, people who understand the value of the information they get from the

Corporate Library. At the same time, we all like each other. There's not a stuffed shirt in the place."

So understanding the environment is important, as is using that understanding to be able to convey to your managers what they need to know about the work you do. Equally important is a concern with the people, with the staff who will deliver the information products and services that the Lehman professionals need. When you talk about staffing, of course, you're touching on other subjects that Willner is interested in these days, including several that were given serious attention in his recent article in *Library Trends* ("Education for Library and Information Management Careers in Business and Financial Services," 42, 2, Fall, 1993, pp. 232-48). In conversation, Willner is not reticent about sharing some of his ideas about staffing issues.

"I'm very involved in hiring," he says, "because there are certain values, certain work values," he emphasizes, "that we must have in our employees. Of course I don't talk with them about the specifics of the job. I don't need to know whether they know how to use this or that type of reference tool. The people who report to me do those interviews, and they do them very well. In fact, to work here requires five interviews, and all along the way we are trying to establish how the prospective employee feels about work values."

Elaborating on this idea, Willner points out that he and his staff have to be very upfront, very honest with one another in their work relationships. So he looks for things like good judgment, responsibility, people who are comfortable talking with one another. He looks for, as he puts it, people "who have the maturity to ask for help."

"In an organization of specialists," he says, "all must approach the work with the same 'heart,' with the same respect for the work environment. We all work together to achieve customer satisfaction, and there are times when one person can't meet a deadline or do everything that's been asked for, so we have to see ourselves as a team, willing to talk with one another and ask for help when we need it."

If it sounds as if Rich Willner puts into practice the guidelines he put forth in the *Library Trends* article, that's very much the case. For example, one of the basic requirements, "for every library job," is analytical ability, which Willner defines very much in terms of meeting the user's needs: "the application of fundamental learning to solve what is essentially a single macro-level problem—managing client expectations with reference to the strengths and weaknesses of sources and delivery systems as well as their associated costs." That task, managing client expectations, is part and parcel of the information services operation that Willner and the people who report to him have created.

Part of the success in the Corporate Library has certainly been tied to the success of the Financial Data Services and its commitment to end-user database searching, as mentioned earlier. A great deal of energy and effort is devoted to training, and one of the successes of the training is that most of the Lehman professionals can get themselves up and running in their search for quantifiable data just by following simple printed directions that are readily available. Willner refers to it as the staff's "quantify/qualify" approach, for by becoming adept at doing their own searching for quantifiable data, the employees are then prepared seek mediated assistance when they need qualifiable (as opposed to quantifiable) information. It's not a complicated concept or approach, but it works. And it pays handsome dividends when users come to the Corporate Library in the "right frame of mind," so to speak, for their mediated research.

It's a busy place, the Lehman Brothers Corporate Library/Business Information Services, and the numbers are impressive. And despite the emphasis on the cost of the data, other measures are incorporated into the organizational work patterns. There are, for example, some 70,000 reference requests completed annually, and a typical monthly statistic might include 2,700 end-user database searches and 850 or so research projects.

With so much going on, it's no surprise that Rich Willner likes what he is doing. He is a man who is obviously stimulated and challenged—and not threatened—by change, and he has chosen to work in an industry in which change is part of the package.

"The financial services industry changes a lot because the markets change," he says, "and it's an industry in which we librarians can watch information content, the knowledge, and the technology coming closer together. In the entire history of libraries and librarianship, there has never been a comparable period of change like the one we're living in today."

For information services at Lehman Brothers, whether the information is delivered through the Corporate Library or through one of the other units of the firm's BIS operation, meeting the challenges of change management—in the financial industry or in information management—is fundamental. No one knows that better than Rich Willner, and no one seems better positioned to guide it along.

Meet Rich Willner

Since 1990, First Vice-President and Director, Business Information Services, Lehman Brothers, New York . . . Began career as a Systems Analyst for UNIVAC . . . Graduate degree in library and information services from Columbia University . . .

Grew up wanting to be a history teacher . . . Lives in Brooklyn Heights, NY . . . Married to an artist, and has two sons, Dave and Jake . . . Personal interests: "enjoying the city with my family."

ANN WOLPERT
at the Harvard Business School:
Introducing new managers to information values

Of course you're impressed when you go to visit Ann Wolpert. After all, the Harvard Business School is by tacit agreement the epitome of graduate business schools, and while society accords due respect to the many (and frequently very fine) business schools connected with various other universities and educational institutions, it is the reference to HBS that brings forth the smile of recognition, the quick catch in the breath, the comfortable confidence that reflects the attitude "of course—Harvard Business School—that's the way it should be."

Not that Wolpert herself conveys any such attitude. Modest, with a good sense of humor, and very businesslike (which—in her environment—is only to be expected), Ann Wolpert has come to the Harvard Business School with the "modest" goal of helping the School redefine the traditional academic business library. At the same time, she expects to

Originally published in *InfoManage : The International Management Newsletter for the Information Services Professional* 2 (7), June, 1995.

introduce a new generation of general business managers to the relevance and usefulness of information in a successful career.

Wolpert's conversations about her approach to her work, her faith in the information delivery process, and, especially, her enthusiasm about the future of information all combine to position her as a leader in the information services field at large, a position which brings her a great deal of respect and admiration from the many professional colleagues with whom she comes in contact. In the two years she's been on the job, it's become very clear that, with respect to HBS and what the institution is trying to achieve, Ann Wolpert is the right person to be the School's Executive Director for Library and Information Services. In fact, there really isn't anyone else who could be doing this job right now, and certainly there isn't anyone who would be doing it as well as she is doing it.

What's the secret? For those who have known Wolpert through the years, who've worked with her on various projects in the different professional associations with which she's been affiliated or who knew her through her previous work, as Manager of the Cambridge Information Center for Arthur D. Little, there's no mystery. They are quick to come up with an answer, and when her colleagues talk about Ann Wolpert, three characteristics are frequently mentioned. It's not too far a reach to put them together to come to some conclusions as to why Ann Wolpert is good at what she does.

In the first place, she's simply a nice person. That's not such a big deal when you're talking about librarians and information services people because, in the common perception, librarians are by definition "nice" people. In fact, some of them are perceived as being too nice for their own good, and that's why they don't get anywhere with their managers and find themselves scrounging for resources just to be able to do the work they're supposed to do.

With Wolpert, though, the "nice person" characterization connects with an assurance, a self-confidence, that moves things forward, that makes things happen, and that is good for the information services program at HBS. It all falls into place with something a man named John Nathan once said, that successful people in the management community are people who are insulated against self-doubt. These people, Nathan asserted (and obviously he's right about this), have a highly articulated vision of the world they inhabit and of how they want it to be. At the same time, they have the energy and the self-confidence to bring that vision to realization. Nathan called it—this combination of vision and energy and self-confidence—a great "empowerer" and that, if anything, characterizes Ann Wolpert. She is empowered. She has empowered herself, through her "niceness," through her self-confidence, and through her vision, to be able to do for HBS what HBS needs done with respect to information services.

It's a pretty big job, for not only does Wolpert have management responsibility for Baker Library, the largest business library in the world, she must also work with HBS faculty and management to organize and plan information services for the twenty-first century, for people who will be—without question—the most demanding and the most affluent (with all the expectations that that entails) information customers in our society. It's a constant challenge, and a convenient analogy might be made between what is being done as far as the school itself is concerned and what is going on with—or anticipated for—information services.

In the handsome brochure that's put out to describe the HBS campus, the point is made that "while the stately beauty of the HBS campus is a constant reminder of its distinguished past, the School takes pride in its history of change and its willingness to adapt to the evolving needs of its students." That is what Ann Wolpert is dealing with, and while the handsome HBS campus, with its McKim, Mead & White buildings occupying some 60 acres on the Boston side of the Charles River might represent the "distinguished past," what she and her staff are delivering and creating for future delivery, in terms of information services, represent in very clear terms the future of the institution.

"Our goal for Baker Library," Wolpert says, "is to retain the best of its extraordinary past, while working with faculty to define the business library of the future—whatever that may mean. Networked environments and electronic information resources are already transforming the way many companies do business. The business managers who will have responsibility for such companies must be informed information consumers."

Which brings us to the third of those characteristics her colleagues attribute to Ann Wolpert, for they seldom stop by talking only about her niceness or her self-assurance. They also—almost always—comment that they appreciate the fact that she is a good listener, that she hears what they are saying and thinks about what her response will be before she gives it. It's not surprising then that one very noticeable quality in staff attitudes has to do with staff loyalty, not only to the organization for which they are employed, but to Wolpert as a supervisor. There are approximately 100 staff members at the Baker Library, and Wolpert herself has seven direct reports. Even so, she makes it her business to get to know each of her staff as well as she can. For example, it is her practice, after a new professional employee has been on staff for a while, to take the person to lunch.

"Part of my job," she says, "is to offer encouragement, and to show how everyone plays a role in supporting our vision. Going to lunch with a new professional staff member gives me that opportunity. There is some mentoring, and it helps to give the employee a 'feel' about his/her role in the organization."

Wolpert's office is located in Baker Library, named for the chairman of the First National Bank of New York who, when asked in 1924 for a donation to help start the construction for the HBS campus, gave enough money to build the entire campus. He gave $5 million, so of course the library—which with its white columns and gilded bell tower is the central focus on the campus—is named for him. It only makes sense. And the collections available there are equally impressive: 570,000 volumes, 800,000 microforms, and over 6,000 active serial titles covering most aspects of management plus such specialties as banking, labor relations, and management education. HBS is, indeed, the exemplar of business management education, and its library's collections reflect that.

Information Services at HBS are usually described in five categories, each of which represents a significant market for the services that Wolpert and her staff provide. In fact, her job title, which was created when she was recruited for the position, was deliberately chosen to emphasize that the position is not a "librarian" position. The HBS Executive Director for Library and Information Services is a job much like that of a chief executive/operations officer in a corporate environment and Wolpert performs more as a CIO than as an academic librarian, certainly more so than in the traditional university community. One of the reasons for this is the School's focus on research support.

"Faculty are our primary market," Wolpert says, "because research support is, indeed, one of the defining strengths of the school. HBS would have little need for the tremendous resources of a facility like Baker Library were it not for the School's world-class research program."

Certainly this perspective makes sense, when you think about the kind of work that is currently being done—and projected for the future—at the School. To meet these needs, the Research Services Group in Baker Library is comprised of professional researchers from a variety of disciplines (including many MLSs) whose sole purpose is to support faculty research in a manner that is, as Wolpert describes it, "more typical of a professional services firm—that is, with the emphasis on the consultant/client relationship—than that of a traditional library."

This does not mean that what might be called "academic" services are neglected, only that—in terms of overall importance—research support is given serious attention at Baker Library. In fact, service to the various student constituencies represents the library's highest use by volume, which is not surprising when you learn that those constituencies are made up of some 1,200 MBA students, 200+ doctoral students, and a variety of other program participants, some 2,200 or so who come annually to Cambridge for the Executive Education Program or other management programs lasting from three days to twelve weeks. In terms of the library's overall service picture, however, research support has been and will continue to be a primary focus. And in another step in this direction, HBS Publishing was recently incorporated into a wholly-owned nonprofit subsidiary of the School (it was formerly an HBS departmental business unit). That work , too (e.g., the production of *The Harvard Business Review*, for example, and the publications of the HBS Press and of HBS Management Productions), will bring new research demands to the information operation since, as Wolpert says, "The Publishing Corporation does look to a stronger working relationship with Baker Library as part of its overall business plan."

There is one very traditional service that is part of the Baker Library. While most management scholarship concentrates on recent (or relatively recent) information, the Business History special collections of the Harvard Business School are world renowned for their rare books, manuscripts, and collected papers. Of these, the Medici Family Papers are probably the most unusual. Other special collections include archival records of more than 1,400 firms and the Kress Library of 40,000 rare European books, journals, and pamphlets from 1470.

As in all information settings, general information services play a big role in the HBS information picture, for Harvard undergraduates, graduate students in other Harvard programs, HBS administrative personnel, and a variety of other information customers use the services, and the number of telephone and letter queries, information requests via E-mail and the Internet, the query line on HOLLIS (the Harvard Online Library Information System), etc. bring in large numbers of information transactions. And not to be overlooked are the walk-in customers—some 84,000 in 1994. These, combined with what are referred to as "client services," the intrapreneurial, fee-based efforts, make up a significant part of the work that gets done through the HBS information services program, and of course it is this vast number of information transactions that enables Wolpert and her staff to understand the market they are trying to reach.

"We track everything," Wolpert says, "and it is in the tracking that we determine not only usage patterns, but anticipated needs as well." It's a movement toward a more customer-focused environment, obviously, and Wolpert is quick to describe some of the work being done in this area.

"There is a lot of emphasis on understanding and meeting customer needs in Baker Library these days," she says, "That philosophy applies to both faculty and student requirements. At the same time, we are investing heavily in training and skill-enhancement for our staff at all levels. The availability of information resources in a networked environment is already redefining reference service, and we want our staff to be prepared to work in the information future."

Wolpert and her staff face a variety of challenges in the next academic year. The MBA program will be changing from a traditional two-semester program to a "trimester" program. At the same time, faculty are introducing new courses and new approaches to teaching MBA students. Wolpert looks forward to these changes, even though there will some adjustment in the organizational culture. For example, Baker Library will no longer enjoy the luxury of reduced hours (now 44/week in the summer vs. 92/week during the academic year) and "dress down" summers. It is an important change, for it reflects the move toward a more realistic environment in terms of the corporate world. Business doesn't operate according to the academic year, and Baker Library won't either.

It all fits together, as far as Wolpert is concerned, and she is enthusiastic when she talks about the challenges: "I see the academic library—and I've felt this way throughout my career—as the place where special library users and management learn about libraries, about how to use them, about information values. Faculty are very interested in using relevant new technology in the MBA and executive education programs. They also understand the importance of published information in the early stages of a business manager's career. We have been delighted to work with faculty in new curriculum initiatives aimed at introducing students to the value of information resources in an applied environment. This approach to information resources makes their relevance real, rather than 'good' in the abstract."

It's that "real" relevance, of course, that business managers need when they begin their careers in the "real" world. And it's thanks to people like Ann Wolpert and the information staff at HBS's Baker Library that their understanding of the uses for—and value of—information resources is clearly established. Certainly it makes their emergence into the real world easier, and that, in today's business environment, is no small matter.

Meet Ann Wolpert

When this interview was published, Ann Wolpert (now Library Director at the Massachusetts Institute of Technology) was Executive Director of Library and Information Services for the Graduate School of Business Administration of Harvard University, where she was responsible for the general management and development of Baker Library and related information services. Prior to joining the Business School in the fall of 1992, Wolpert was Manager of the Cambridge Information Center of Arthur D. Little, Inc., an international management and technology consulting firm. She is active in the professional library community. In 1993-1994, she served as a member of the Search Committee for a Dean of the Simmons College Graduate School of Library and Information Science. She is immediate Past-President of the Alumni Council of Simmons College Graduate School of Library and Information Science. From 1990 to 1993, she served on the Research Committee of the Special Libraries Association, and other activities with that organization have included a term with the Long-Range Planning Committee of the Boston Chapter. Wolpert chaired the NELINET, Inc. Board of Directors in FY1988 and served as Treasurer in FY1989, and she has been a member of the OCLC Board of Trustees since 1990 (currently chairing the Personnel and Compensation Committee). She is a member of the Massachusetts Board of Library Commissioners Strategic Planning Committee and serves on the editorial advisory boards of both *Library and Information Research: An International Journal* and *Info-Manage: The International Management Newsletter for the Information Services Professional*. A graduate of Boston University (BA) and Simmons College (MSLS), Wolbert has long lived in Cambridge, where she continues to reside, together with Sam Otis, her understanding husband, and "Blaze, the Wonder Dog."

WAYNE WILSON
at the Amateur Athletic Foundation: Olympic-class management for an Olympic-class sports information facility

When you read this story, don't call Wayne Wilson on the telephone. He won't be there.

Wilson is the Vice President for Research at the Amateur Athletic Foundation of Los Angeles, but for the next few weeks, you won't find him at his office. Indeed, he won't even be in town, because he's headed for Atlanta. It's time for the Olympics, and that's where Wayne Wilson is going to be.

He's not going to Atlanta to watch the events, though. Wilson, who is one of the most knowledgeable people currently working in the field of sports information, will be helping NBC Sports with its Olympic coverage. It seems the powers that be at NBC Sports needed someone to respond to producers' and reporters' questions, and it just so happens that Wilson knows the NBC Senior Vice-President for Olympic Programming. So it's off to Atlanta for Wilson.

But before you get too envious and too excited, keep in mind that it's a labor of love (literally—for there are few people who are as committed to the sports information field as Wayne Wilson is). He's giving up his vacation to be one of NBC's sports-information providers, and he'll be away from his home, his family, and his job for thirty days. This is it for Wilson. When he gets through working at the Olympics, he goes back to his regular job.

But still: he'll be in Atlanta for the Olympics! For a lot of folks, that's like dying and going to heaven. For Wayne Wilson, it's but one more opportunity to do what he does best, to bring state-of-the-art information delivery to the sports field, and to do it as effectively and as efficiently as he can.

Originally published in *InfoManage : The International Management Newsletter for the Information Services Professional* 3 (7), July, 1996.

He's a rare bird, Wayne Wilson. He's one of those people who loves sports with a passion, but he's also an educated and authoritative scholar who spends his professional life (not to put too fine a point on it) pursuing knowledge and meaning in the complicated and highly specialized relationships that exist between sport and society. At the AAF, Wilson is able to keep his career moving in this direction by managing one of the finest research facilities in the sports community.

"There are other libraries doing some of what we're doing," he says, and it is clear from his tone that he's rather proud of the level of sophistication that his operation provides. "The International Olympic Committee has a research facility at its headquarters in Lausanne, Switzerland, but it tends to serve only a small number of scholars who must apply in advance. In Colorado Springs, the United States Olympic Committee has a very good library devoted primarily to serving Olympic coaches and elite athletes.

"As for ourselves," Wilson continues, "we view our mission as being more broad. We will serve anyone who needs our service on a first-come, first-serve basis. Unlike the IOC and the USOC, we don't turn away users because we don't approve of their points of view about particular issues."

What it probably boils down to—as quickly becomes apparent to anyone who visits Wilson at the Foundation—is the seriousness of purpose at the Paul Ziffren Sports Resource Center ("Otherwise known as 'the library,'" Wilson says with a laugh). It is an educational and research center for sport, and in beautiful and very charming surroundings, that seriousness of purpose is very clear. With a collection that includes interactive CD-ROM materials, books, journals and magazines, some 90,000 photographs dating back to the turn of the century, and other research materials, the center is open to students, athletes, coaches, academic researchers, journalists, and the public by appointment. With its amazing core of resources, and with the services that emanate from the Resource Center, it is, indeed, the central core for the services and programs that are produced under the auspices of the Foundation.

The Amateur Athletic Foundation came into existence after the XXIIIrd Olympic Games, held in Los Angeles in 1984, when it was determined that part of the surplus realized from hosting the Games would be dedicated to the young people of Southern California. The total surplus was about US$225 million, and according to a prior agreement involving

One Manager's Career: How He Got There

*L*earning about the societal impacts of sport has long been a major quest for Wilson, ever since he was a young man. As with many of us, the quest began when Wilson was pursuing Asian studies as an undergraduate at Michigan State University. It was the late 60s, a time when many people were thinking about social issues, and as Wilson found himself thinking about some of these things, it was a natural progression to connect this emerging interest in society and societal issues with his already well-established interest in athletics. Having always been a competitive athlete (Wilson had grown up in Vermont, and had been a competitive skier since childhood), he had signed up for an elective course about the role of sport in society. Taking the course, he now says, had a tremendous influence on his life, for it was while studying the role of sport in society that he began to observe how the behavior that people exhibit in sports-related situations connects with other social patterns. And there were plenty of opportunities to observe the connection.

For example, Wilson was studying karate pretty seriously at the time, and he was noticing that there were a number of women joining in the classes. He was curious to know why. ("And I was even more curious about why the men in the club reacted so negatively to them," he adds) Then, as the Watergate case began to unfold, he found himself asking questions about the role of sport and its influence on societal issues, for President Nixon, as was well known, was quite adept at using sports imagery in his speeches, and Wilson was beginning to put some thoughts together as to why that was so successful.

Quite by chance, Wilson discovered that the University of Massachusetts offered graduate degrees in the history and sociology of sport, and it was at UMass, as a graduate student doing research, that Wilson began to think about information. He began to move toward librarianship, a field that—it seemed to him—could help him learn about information and information-gathering behavior, and about automation and the uses of automation in information delivery, other subjects that he had discovered he was interested in.

It was then that serendipity kicked in, for at Syracuse University, where Wilson had enrolled in the School of Information Studies to work on his library degree, Robert Taylor, a former sportswriter, was Dean. Of course Wilson got to know him. As they learned more about one another's interests, Taylor liked the idea of combining sports and librarianship, and he encouraged Wilson to slant his studies in that direction. It seemed like something of a reach ("After all," Wilson says, "how many jobs are there that require that particular combination?"), but Wilson pursued that route in his studies and eventually ended up in his present post, directing one of the finest research facilities in the sports community.

the LA Olympic Organizing Committee, the US Olympic Committee and the International Olympic Committee, 40% of any surplus—approximately US$90 million in this case—was earmarked for creating a foundation to promote youth sports in the region. The mandate, according to former Chairman David L. Wolper, was "to establish, as well as revitalize, sports programs for youngsters so they would have the opportunity to participate, learn, and compete."

That program has been a three-part one: grantmaking, programs, and the operation of the Ziffren Sports Resource Center, and no matter who you speak with at the Foundation, it becomes clear that the library is not simply a place for the well-meaning amateur (in the classic sense of the word) to find out a few facts about a favorite sport. Of course that's possible too, but the theme that comes through is that the Resource Center exists to be a focus for those interested in sports and its impact on society.

"The library staff serves thousands of people each year," according to Wolper, people whose "jobs and interests lead them to the reference desk, whether it be by phone, mail, or in person."

Certainly the numbers are impressive. For this very specialized library deals with some 7,000 user-visits each year, people who come to conduct serious research in the study of sport. Another 7,000 questions are received from remote locations throughout the United States and, since opening in 1988, some 47 other countries as well, so the research community for this particular subject is very well served.

But Wilson's role—and that of his staff—is not only to serve researchers. Among its highest-impact services are those that the Sports Research Center provides for students, especially children and young adults in the Los Angeles metropolitan area.

"This shouldn't come as a surprise," Wilson says, "for the Foundation's mission is to award grants to organizations 'serving youth through sport,' as the cover of one of our annual reports puts it. It's our work here that provides that link between the information function and 'serving youth through sport.'"

In this connection, the Resource Center plays host to many school groups, with large numbers coming on field trips from all over the Los Angeles Unified District, giving them access to the highly unusual materials that make up the collection. But just as important as having the young people come into the Foundation, the programs for youth go to the community. This year, for example, in cooperation with school administrators the Resource Center has storytellers going into the schools, telling the story of the Olympic Games. By the time the Games begin on July 19, some 15,000 kids will have had an in-person experience in hearing this amazing saga. In any organization, that level of output would be impressive. In the specialized and rarefied atmosphere of an organization as subject specific as the AAF, it's positively phenomenal.

Another of the roles that the Resource Center plays is that of a national sports library, since the United States (unlike many other countries) does not have a national sports library as part of the country's information infrastructure. As a result, many of the queries (both at the academic research level and from the general public) are the kinds of queries that would usually go to a large, national research library. It wasn't a conscious decision, to take on the role of a "national" sports library, but it seems to have happened.

"We assumed from the beginning," Wilson says, "that we would have a national impact. What we did not anticipate was the number of international users we would have. The interaction with people in other countries pushed us toward a reliance on E-mail and the Internet earlier than otherwise would have been the case. It also got us involved in the International Association for Sport Information, which in turn has given us contacts with librarians in several countries who often help us with reference questions and collection development."

As a result of these many different perspectives in their work, Wilson and his staff must work hard to keep up to date with the latest in information media, with service levels, and the like. And the wide range of focus for the services of the Resource Center, from bringing the Olympic story to schoolchildren to serving as a de facto national sports library, naturally affects the organization and management of the library. For example, to control the numbers, visitors and researchers are asked to come to the library "by appointment," meaning that, theoretically at least, people shouldn't be able to just walk in off the street. In practice, however, the friendliness of the staff and the earnest desire of each of them to provide high-quality information about what is obviously their favorite subject means that whenever it is reasonably possible that rule (like any other that might prevent the customer from having access to the information) is "bent" in order to accommodate the customer's needs.

"A few weeks ago I got a letter that I loved," Wilson recalls. "It was a thank-you note from a German student who had done research here. He thanked us for our 'efficient, friendly, nonbureaucratic assistance.' I especially liked the 'nonbureaucratic' part."

And there are other impacts from having to serve as the nominal sports library for the United States, Wilson points out.

"We've taken on a wide range of responsibilities," he says, "and that has forced us to carefully evaluate which rules and procedures are essential and which are not. For example, when the library first opened, we registered every new user and issued him or her a library card. In a lot of libraries that procedure makes sense. In our particular case, however, we learned that it didn't, so we got rid of it."

Judging from what people say about the Ziffren Sports Resource Center, Wilson and his people are being remarkably successful in doing what they've offered to do for their customers. In fact, historian Robert Edelman, writing about how he researched his book on the history of spectator sport in the Soviet Union, described in glowing terms how the library came to his rescue when he needed materials that he could not locate elsewhere.

"I can say without doubt that I have never worked in as well managed and organized a facility," Edelman wrote in a recent report about AAF, "nor have I ever been served by professionals so close to the cutting edge of modern information retrieval."

When confronted with such praise, Wilson—who is by nature a rather reserved man—seems a little embarrassed, but you can tell that he is pleased that the Resource Center is recognized as a well-managed facility.

"My job as an information manager is made much easier by the fact that our president and board genuinely believe that information plays a central role in the success of the Foundation," says Wilson. "Our job in the library is to provide a research facility that is taken seriously by athletes and scholars alike. We are expected to not only collect and organize information, but also to produce it."

The Foundation's home page is a good example, for it is nothing less than an Olympic primer, and for the 'Net surfer who wants to learn about how the Olympics came about, or what the Games are going to be like, the information posted is not only useful and interesting, it's reliable as well. And that reliability moves into the other work that Wilson does, for as Vice-President for Research for the Foundation, he is not only responsible for management with respect to the library, but he supervises the Foundation's own research efforts. A typical and very important example was in the 1989 study, "Gender Stereotyping in Televised Sports," which received national attention in both the popular media and in scholarly publications. The subject was revisited in 1994 with a follow-up report, and this and similar studies continue at the Foundation, under Wilson's leadership. More recently the library has moved into the production of interactive multimedia products, with its latest title being *An Olympic Journey: The Story of Women in the Olympic Games*, a CD-ROM distributed at no charge to schools and libraries.

So no matter how you look at it, Wayne Wilson's work is stimulating and rewarding. He not only manages a fine research facility, he incorporates its work into an organizational mission that reaches far beyond the walls of the place where it is located. On another level, he not only provides information delivery for a specifically defined customer base, he and the AAF create information, create products that bring their subject-specific information to a market that is—literally—worldwide. And in their immediate work, Wilson and his staff not only provide area school-children with high-quality information about their favorite sports (lucky kids!), they offer scholars and researchers a quality of information services that would be provided by a national sports library if there were one. And all along the continuum between these extremes, Wilson and the staff at the Paul Ziffren Sports Resource Center offer state-of-the-art popular-level services to anybody who is interested in sport and the role of sport in society. All things considered, it's a pretty heady experience, visiting the Amateur Athletic Foundation and watching Wayne Wilson and his excellent staff at work.

And it's worth a visit, for when you meet with Wayne Wilson and have him show you through the facility, you'll be very impressed with how much is being accomplished.

But don't go during the Olympic Games. Wilson won't be there.

Meet Wayne Wilson

Wayne Wilson is Vice President, Research, for the Amateur Athletic Foundation of Los Angeles, where he has been employed since 1987. He was responsible for the development of the Foundation's state-of-the-art research facility, the Paul Ziffen Sports Resource Center. Since its opening in 1988, Dr. Wilson has been responsible for all management operations for the library, including the supervision of research projects, conference planning, and related functions. Educated at Michigan State University, where he received his B.A., with a major in history, in 1972, Dr. Wilson went on to acquire the M.S. degree in Physical Education at the University of Massachusetts in 1977, followed by (at the same institution) an M.S. in History in 1979, and his Ph.D. in Sport Studies in 1981. In 1982, he was awarded his M.L.S. from the School of Information Studies at Syracuse University. Prior to coming to the Amateur Athletic Foundation, Dr. Wilson was Social Services Librarian at Northeast Louisiana University, Reference Librarian at Chapman College in Orange, CA, Reference Librarian at California State University, Long Beach, and later Director of the Library at Chapman College. He is the author of numerous articles on the history of sport, on women in sport, on library management, and on computer-assisted instruction. He was Executive Producer for the interactive videodisc *The High Jump Clinic* and, most recently, Executive Producer and Co-Writer for the AAF's *An Olympic Journey: The Story of Women in the Olympic Games*. Dr. Wilson lives in Los Angeles with his wife Jan Palchikoff, an Olympic rower, and their children Kate and Jake.

BARBARA SPIEGELMAN
At Westinghouse Energy System: TQM and competency-based
management—it's a synergistic relationship

For managers, these are interesting times. And considering the almost daily changes being propelled at us on the technology front (to say nothing of our attempts to keep up with our subject specialties), managers in the information services community are being particularly challenged.

Thankfully, there are people in the information industry who are doing good work, identifying the industry trends we all need to know about, experimenting with them, doing the "groundwork" for us, and then, when they're satisfied these things work, incorporating them into their work and letting the rest of us know what succeeds and what doesn't.

Barbara Spiegelman is one of those pioneers. At the Westinghouse Energy Systems Business Unit in Pittsburgh, PA, Spiegelman is Manager, Technical Information and Communication, and it's a position she's been able to leverage not only for the good of her own company, but for her many colleagues in the information industry who have come to rely on her solid advice and her generosity in sharing her experiences with them. Spiegelman has learned a lot as a manager, and she's been more than willing to let the rest of us benefit from her experience. What she's done with TQM and competency-based management is a case in point.

At Westinghouse Electric Corporation, in Pittsburgh and at all Westinghouse installations throughout the world, quality management and customer focus have long been hallmarks. And they continue to be so. But now there's a new emphasis, for at Westinghouse total quality management—as a management philosophy and as a management methodology—is now implemented side by side with, as Spiegelman labels it, "a more fluid, competency-based performance system."

Originally published in *InfoManage : The International Management Newsletter for the Information Services Professional* 5 (1), December, 1997.

Spiegelman, who has been affiliated with the information operation at Westinghouse since 1974, knows whereof she speaks. During those twenty-three years, she has seen the company delve deeply—and success-fully—into quality management. And like many other organizations which have studied TQM, experimented with it, and persevered until it was successful, Westinghouse has been able to point with pride to the company's accomplishments with TQM. In fact, it was Westinghouse that developed the criteria on which the now-famous Malcolm Baldridge Award is based (and, notably, which the Westinghouse Nuclear Fuel Divi-sion won in 1984). Now Westinghouse has linked that quality focus to the methodology that is fast becoming one of the hottest techniques in the management field today: competency-based performance evaluation and compensation.

For many information services managers, this collaboration of man-agement techniques—adhering to classic TQM concepts while incorpo-rate competency-based performance and compensation—makes a lot of sense. But it also represents an entirely new way of looking at managing, a new way of perceiving employees, as Spiegelman notes in the opening paragraphs of a chapter she wrote on the subject, for the seminal man-agement work, *Competencies for Special Librarians of the 21st Century*, published just this past June by the Special Libraries Association.

Spiegelman, ever modest, begins by acknowledging her influences: in their 1994 book, *Competing for the Future*, management experts Gary Hamel and C.K. Prahalad make a case for recognizing the importance of core competencies: for companies and other enterprises and organiza-tional entities, core competencies are "valued by the customers," they "enable the company to differentiate itself in the marketplace," and they often "give rise to new products and services by taking advantage of the company's unique strengths."

Spiegelman picks up on this, describing what her company is doing, and what other information managers can do with this idea. Noting that attention to core competencies encourages management to think about the company's core competencies, Spiegelman asserts that core compe-tencies can be used just as effectively to differentiate the employees' con-tribution to corporate success, a differentiation that transfers neatly into the information-delivery arena: "Core competencies grow out of the aggre-gated skills of people," Spiegelman writes. "Just as a corporation must identify, develop, and leverage its competencies, each individual within the corporation must identify and develop their own key competencies to help make the business successful."

For many information managers, particularly those already working with quality-focused programs, tackling a different approach can be a little off-putting.

But competency-based management is not necessarily a different approach to management, as Spiegelman is quick to point out. When asked about how the decision was made to go to competency-based management, she makes it clear that it isn't a separate technique.

"At Westinghouse," she says, "the focus has always been on the customer, and quality management recognizes that, which is why we incorporate TQM into our management philosophy. With competency-based management, we work with a system that is slightly different, but not separate. Competency-based performance, as a management technique, doesn't replace TQM. It works with TQM. It is a collateral activity, and exists side by side with our long-standing quality emphasis."

So one way of looking at the role of competency-based management is to think about it as a more inclusive management methodology, one that goes from (as Spiegelman describes it) focusing on what the results of employee actions are to focusing on how they go about accomplishing each of their tasks.

"It's more balanced," Spiegelman says. "When we attempt to measure performance according to the usual MBO process, we're applying absolutes, or numbers, to define variables, or human beings, and there isn't necessarily a match. Competency-based management allows us to take into consideration an employee's strengths or weaknesses, allows us to recognize that everybody has peaks and valleys. It's a more balanced appraisal system."

The balance comes, it would seem, in the very comprehensiveness of the effort. Looking at the "Full Range of Competencies" listed in Spiegelman's chapter in the SLA competencies book, a manager can't help but be impressed with the sheer breadth of competencies listed there, and the accompanying "behaviors" that have been identified that go along with them. They are obviously required for success in an information services operation in the corporate/technical environment, and it is interesting to note, as Spiegelman does, that the results are positive.

"When a staff member develops, for example, a competency in job knowledge, or communication skills, that employee understands but does not foment the political atmosphere. That's an important distinction. And that's when the results are impressive."

It's all part of a new methodology that encourage people to take responsibility for their careers—and their lives, as Spiegelman likes to acknowledge.

"We no longer live in a society where a company employs a person for life," she says, "and for employees, competency-based performance becomes a development tool, not just an MBO rating." For people who are self-directed, she notes, and clearly interested in seeking to develop the skills and competencies they need for success in the workplace, this new tool can be a boon.

And that connects—from the manager's point of view —with another advantage in working with competency-based management: "We're more able to conduct a targeted performance appraisal," Spiegelman says. "It's good for us, and it's good for the staff. In fact, now that we're more comfortable with competency-based appraisals, we feel that this was the year we got much closer to reality."

At Westinghouse, of course, this new competency-based system is in place in the company's technical library, and it is working very well indeed. In other information-related departments, the story is much the same, for competency-based management has now been incorporated into the management of the entire business unit, and all functions (including all information-delivery functions, of course) are now using competencies as a performance appraisal and compensation tool. It's a natural fit.

So there are positive gains to be made when implementing competency-based compensation, as Spiegelman has pointed out, both in the competencies book and in a chapter she wrote for *Position Descriptions in Special Libraries*, another SLA book. Spiegelman contributed a very useful essay—almost a "how-to" document—on "Writing Position Descriptions for Fair Compensation." One of her cleverest comments comes at the opening, as she acknowledges that most managers find it something of a burden, considering an already full management workload, to be asked to write position descriptions.

Not so, Spiegelman says. "When you are asked to supply a position description," she writes, "you are being given an opportunity to show the value of the position—take advantage of the invitation!" Then, putting her money where her mouth is, Spiegelman not only offers immediately applicable advice about what the position description should say, she even supplies the language, demonstrating how the new language of what she calls "Compensation-Speak" can be insinuated into the document, with important results (see sidebar on next page). It's good advice, for Spiegelman recognizes that it's through the use of language that our roles—and our work—are defined. And when librarians, records managers, and other information workers complain about senior management's lack of interest in their work, about how "they" don't understand what information workers do, she knows what to say:

"We have to educate them," she says. "There's no 'they' there! It's up to us to go to them to let them know what we do for the company."

Of course. And that's just what you would expect from someone as managerially sophisticated as Barbara Spiegelman. TQM and competency-based management are important tools for today's (and tomorrow's) information managers, and they definitely come in handy. They work for Barbara Spiegelman at Westinghouse, and they can work for the rest of us.

Revised Position Description

LIBRARY-SPEAK	COMPENSATION-SPEAK
Purpose: Provide library services to all employees, including reference, cataloging, acquisitions, literature searching, and SDIss.	**Purpose:** Proactively identify and deliver timely accurate, and cost-effective technical and business information as a basis for management decision making.
Task: Perform cost-effective SDI's.	**Task:** Implement timely, cost-effective desktop delivery system for competitor/ technical information.
Perform literature searches using Dialog STN, Dow Jones, Nexis, NewsNet, and other online databases within deadline.	Conduct research projects requiring indepth information retrieval, analysis, evaluation, and synthesis. Provide "first-cut" analysis of results.
Implement new information technologies as needed.	Anticipate and optimize the use of new/emerging information technologies, including electronic access and desktop delivery to meet company strategic objectives.
Ensure timely and accurate input to the catalog.	Design, develop, maintain, and administer information retrieval and automated systems and access channels for library operations. Coordinate the work of IS providers and library personnel to facilitate results.
Maintain accurate union list and coordinate all journal subscriptions.	Establish and maintain accurate record of current enterprise-wide investment in technical and business journals; analyze usage and recommend resource expenditures based on data.

Reprinted with permission from: Spiegelman, Barbara. 1996. "Writing Position Descriptions for Fair Compensation." In *Position Descriptions in Special Libraries*, third edition, edited by Del Sweeney with assistance from Karin Zilla. Washington, DC: Special Libraries Association.

Meet Barbara Spiegelman

Barbara M. Spiegelman received her B.A. from Chatham College and her M.L.S. from the University of Pittsburgh. She joined Westinghouse Electric Corporation in 1974. Since that time, her projects have ranged from technical indexing to database management, from videotape production to managing internal communications for a division of 350 employees, and from acting as deputy proposal manager on a $200M project to lead consultant in change management for a Business Unit of 6000 people worldwide.   Her articles, which have a strong practical and results-oriented slant, have been published in *Library Journal, American Bookseller, School Library Journal, Marketing Library Services, The SpeciaList, Library Management Quarterly*, and *OPENDialog*. Spiegelman wrote the chapter on Total Quality Management in James M. Matarazzo and Miriam A. Drake's *Information for Management: A Handbook* (Washington, DC: Special Libraries Association, 1994), and her work with TQM at Westinghouse Electric is profiled as one of two case studies in Guy St. Clair's *Total Quality Management in Information Services* (London and New Brunswick, NJ: Bowker-Saur, 1997). Her chapter, "Writing Position Descriptions for Fair Compensation" is featured in the 1996 edition of *Position Descriptions for Special Libraries*. Spiegelman is the editor of *Competencies for Special Librarians in the 21st Century*

(Washington, DC: Special Libraries Association, 1997) and author of the chapter, "Using Competencies as a Performance Appraisal and Compensation Management Tool".

Spiegelman is a member of ITIMG, the Industrial Technical Information Managers Group and of the Information Advisory Council of The Conference Board. She is an instructor in "Management of Special Libraries and Information Centers" at the University of Pittsburgh's School of Information Sciences, and a member of the school's Board of Visitors. She also serves on the Board of Directors of EIN, the Electronic Information Network, an initiative to link 62 public libraries within Allegheny County. In 1997, she received the Distinguished Alumna award from the University of Pittsburgh's School of Information Sciences. Spiegelman is also an active member of the Special Libraries Association, and has served in numerous offices for the association.

As manager of Technical Information and Communication for Westinghouse Energy Systems, Spiegelman is responsible for forty-seven employees, including the technical library, technical writing, editing, and publication management, document management, and information processing.

Spiegelman is married and has two sons and two golden retrievers.

9

PREPARING FOR THE FUTURE

*M*uch of what change management is all about—particularly in the information services arena—is preparing for the future. Anticipating what information needs will be, and establishing business plans, customer service plans, marketing plans, and similar operational guidelines (and implementing them) to meet those needs is one of the great challenges for the industry.

In this chapter, two industry leaders (now, happily, members of the same family) offer valuable insight about these matters. Both Joseph J. Fitzsimmons and Beth Duston Fitzsimmons are committed to preparing for the information future and in doing their part in structuring a society in which information is provided for future users. In an early two-part interview (published in the third and fourth issues of *InfoManage*), Joe Fitzsimmons positively describes how he expects information to be delivered ("We'll all be connected . . . and the connections will be made . . . there will be access points for all users."). In the last interview in this collection, Beth Fitzsimmons is placing her bets on content management as the information professional's primary responsibility. She contends—and makes a good case for her contention—that content management, when combined with the successful development and implementation of organizational information policy, will define the information management profession of the future.

It is not an impossible scenario, and it is already being looked at in the global information marketplace. At Berlin's Bibliothek des Kammergerichts (Library of the Higher Regional Court of Berlin), Gabriele Greve combines resourcefulness, enthusiasm, and leadership to meet the administrative and managerial challenges that have proliferated throughout German society. The future of information delivery under these conditions cannot be anything but stimulating.

Part of the stimulation comes, of course, from looking at what is going on in other industries and other disciplines, and doing what we can to apply those concepts in the information services marketplace. Robert E. Frye is intrigued by the possibilities that link the information services profession and the communications field, and he finds the commonalities fascinating as a "bridge" for solving problems and achieving goals that the two disciplines share. It's a vision of the future that has tremendous service implications, both on the local and international levels, as David R. Bender describes. His leadership in the industry comes through in the many issues he discusses in the interview in this chapter, and Bender's astute comments about a wide variety of subjects provide further stimulation. Of particular note, however, is his assertion about how information delivery has changed, and how it will be different in the future: "We're moving even further ahead now," Bender says, "beyond 'just-in-case' and 'just-in-time' information delivery, and that's where I think we're going to be in the 21st century. We're always listening to the information customers, of course, and hearing what they need, but now in addition to mediating and consulting, we're analyzing and interpreting, and *customizing*, and providing information that I like to describe as 'just-for-you'."

And we now have the enabling technology to do it, according to Sylvia Piggott. She calls the age we're moving into the "second era" of information services, because now with enabling technology we can reengineer our processes. The future of information services, Piggott says, is going to be seriously affected by what we're doing now. "We're in the age of revolution, and we have the opportunity to reinvent what the library is, and what quality, value-added library service is." It is, for Piggott and those who think like her, a challenge that is being delightfully embraced.

When Monica Ertel managed Apple's Advanced Technology Group—which included responsibility for the Apple library—she was given the task of planning the information infrastructure for the company for the future. There were two reasons why she was not concerned about planning for that future. One was the company's innovative corporate culture, and the second was the willingness of librarians to share ideas, concepts, and, when appropriate, information resources. They are two qualities that can be predictably expected to be present in any successful information operation in the future. In another 'future-planning' scenario—in a quite different environment—Susan Berg in the Rockefeller Library at the Colonial Williamsburg Foundation also looks to the community culture: "However we define it, improving access to the collections has to be the next step, and providing a virtual library will be one of the keys. . . . If we can provide [the users] with what they need electronically, at a terminal located at a remote site and at hours when the library facility itself is not available, we simply have to do it. And it's our responsibility to figure out *how* to do it."

Certainly that's the intention of Robert Nawrocki, then President of ARMA International, when he determined to use his office to sound what he characterized as a "wake-up call" for the records management field. Asserting that integrated information management will be the information delivery function of the future, Nawrocki expects practitioners to understand, among other things, the principles of organization, the use of computers as an information management tool, and how information is valued. It's a tall order, but in fact, there are those—especially young people just now moving into managerial responsibility in information services—who are enthusiastically embracing those challenges, as Martina Reich describes. The new generation of European information managers is already hard at work anticipating and addressing the challenges, and these information workers, with their confidence, their expertise, and their pride in their professionalism, are leading the way into an information future that—before long—will be heartily embraced by the information industry throughout the world.

///

Looking to the 21st century:
JOE FITZSIMMONS
and UMI take on the big issues

There isn't a better cure for the winter blahs than to spend a cold January morning talking with Joe Fitzsimmons. And while the weather outside might be freezing, the topics for this conversation were pretty hot—at least as far as information issues are concerned. In fact, that's how the interview began, with a look at some of the "hot topics" information people are thinking about today and how Fitzsimmons and University Microfilms International (UMI) are approaching those issues.

On January 1, Fitzsimmons became Chairman of UMI, after having been President and CEO since 1976, and having been with the company since 1966. Among his many duties in the new position is to look at the major information issues and address them not only, as his new job description puts it, "to leverage UMI and its parent company, Bell & Howell, to the outside world," but to participate in and develop important industry relationships with relevant professional and trade groups.

Fitzsimmons clearly delights in his new work, and the idea of concentrating his efforts outside the company is certainly one that appeals to him, but it's no small effort. If you think that being UMI's "ambassador" to the information services community is some sort of easy ride, take a look at the organizations on the list: ALA, SLA, WHCLIST, IFLA, FOLUSA (for which Fitzsimmons currently serves as President), the Coalition for Networked Information, and the Information Futures Institute. The trade groups are equally impressive, with IIA leading the list, followed by AAP, ASIDIC, ASIS, and NFAIS. It's a big task, and one which will require considerable energy and ability (and skillful scheduling agility!), but Fitzsimmons is excited about his new work.

Originally published in *InfoManage : The International Management Newsletter for the Information Services Professional* 1 (3), February, 1994.

"I am absolutely and solidly behind this change," Fitzsimmons says. "When we brought quality management into the company in 1988, one of our major initiatives was to delegate internal operations to senior people so that I could be available for more involvement on the outside. This new position brings that approach around to a practical working level."

One of his first assignments in his new role comes up almost immediately. This month, Fitzsimmons is providing an audience of Japanese information services executives some of the UMI "philosophy" that's impacting information management as the new millennium approaches. Fitzsimmons expects to include in his presentation a colorful story about an engineer who wakes early, goes into his study to bring up some preliminary information on his personal computer, and sets in motion a chain of search and retrieval events that results in full-image electronic document delivery of the materials he needs, sent to his office and routed to key personnel with whom he is connected, all before he has showered and dressed for the day. The anecdote is light-heartedly entitled "Sometime in the Future," but of course, as readers of this publication will have recognized, it's not such a futuristic scenario after all. The technology is available now, and much of it is available through UMI and its various strategic partners working in the information services marketplace.

The presentation in Japan is an example of the approach to information services that drives UMI. "For some companies," Fitzsimmons says, "international sales are just considered an export business or a by-product of the main US activity, but not at UMI. Our international marketing efforts have always been an important part of our work, a reflection of a conscious strategy for marketing in a global network."

That strategy is also seen in the "hot" information services issues Fitzsimmons talks about, for "global networking" tops the list. The term incorporates such issues as national information policies, the development of an information infrastructure, and of course the use of the Internet. And a big part of this attention is devoted to, as Fitzsimmons puts it, the "last-mile hookups," his phrase for those efforts that are currently being developed, the technical connections that will enable everybody to have access to the information they need.

"We'll all be networked," he says, and it's not an empty phrase with him. Joe Fitzsimmons truly believes that at some point every citizen will have access to the information network. "The connections will be made," he says. "They may or may not be into our individual homes, but there will be access points that are convenient to all users."

To achieve this end, UMI is doing its part in setting up an infrastructure that can provide the access. The company is currently spending a great deal of time and effort working with customers at the institutional, county and state levels to see that all communities are brought into the information picture, and recently Fitzsimmons has been giving much attention to such efforts as those of the Library of Michigan Foundation, which is in the process of raising some $6-7 million to provide access capabilities for small public libraries in outlying sections of the state. Fitzsimmons obviously believes that getting "networked" is the wave of the future for all citizens, and UMI, under his leadership, takes its role in the process very seriously.

"Part of these efforts have to go into educating the information providers," Fitzsimmons points out, a statement which leads into a discussion of another information "hot topic" in this last decade of the twentieth century. Here again, UMI is making an effort, and in his new role, part of Fitzsimmons' work will be to participate even more fully in that effort.

"Technology is being provided at a tremendous rate," he says, "and there is significant public/private development, but what we need is training for the people who are going to be showing their users how to access this networked information."

Fitzsimmons goes on to explain that within the information services field, there is plenty of support for these training efforts, especially at the senior management levels, with university presidents, provosts, and other major institutional representatives solidly lined up to support more—and better—education for information services professionals.

The resistance comes, unfortunately, from many of the information providers themselves. Why this is so could be anybody's guess, and probably many of the reasons we could come up with might not seem relevant, but there is one very relevant phenomenon that Fitzsimmons has identified.

He calls it "disintermediation," a structural change that is now taking place in the information "food chain," as it were, that frequently does away with the person who serves as a mediator between the information and the user of the information. In the creation and delivery of information in the past, Fitzsimmons notes, a mediator was required, and whether gatekeeper or interpreter, that person played an important and very crucial role in the information transfer process. Now that picture has changed, and the many component information services workers, the authors, the aggregators, the resellers, the distributors, the desk-top publishers and even the end-users are now interacting all over the place, without mediation.

In the old days, each of these "components" in the creation and delivery of information had a specific role, and the work they did—and their productivity—was specifically related to that role.

"It's not that way anymore," Fitzsimmons explains. "It used to be that everybody stayed in their niche," he says, "but not any more. Now everybody goes up and down the stream, and it's difficult to play just one role." As a case in point, he cites the recent International Online Conference in London.

"It was unbelievably exciting," Fitzsimmons says, referring to the conference and its thousands of attendees. "This conference was a boiling pot of end-users, vendors, and competitors, all focused on facets of electronic information storage, retrieval and delivery. Everybody was moving around, interacting with one another. So it's hard to play just one role anymore, say that of a 'vendor,' or any other kind of single role. And what is left out in this entire interaction is the information intermediary."

Needless to say, this new process, this disintermediation in information services, has serious implications as the information services profession seeks to determine how to educate and train information providers. The issues are frequently discussed within the profession, so another facet of Fitzsimmons' new role is to provide assistance to the system that is educating information services professionals and to bring his—and UMI's—influence to bear, so that the needed changes can be made.

At the present time, this isn't a major problem, since the door is already open. For some time Fitzsimmons has been a regular guest lecturer and adjunct faculty member in graduate information programs and in continuing education and professional development programs in the various associations, and he expects to continue these activities. Increasing the awareness of UMI's activities with the top library and information science schools is a specific priority in UMI's educational agenda, complemented by other efforts specifically directed to the University of Michigan and the University of Pittsburgh and the development of new relationships with others in the top tier of graduate library and information science programs. And of course, since he was actively involved (serving as Vice-Chair) in the 1991 White House Conference on Library and Information Services, which looked at many of these same issues, Fitzsimmons is able to bring to the task a certain level of expertise and knowledge about the subject, to say nothing of the respect he has within the community of decision makers who move in these circles.

Taking on those "big" information issues
JOE FITZSIMMONS
at UMI—Part II

When he talks about his work at UMI, Joe Fitzsimmons often begins with reference to UMI's market, which he describes as "anyone who has a need for reference information," with most of the focus, as would be expected, on serials. Electronic document delivery has been and continues to be a fundamental business strategy, with articles by the thousands being handled daily. Nowadays, the input comes in electronically with facsimile response, but that's about to change, too, as soon as the electronic transfer of full-image files becomes a practical reality.

"At UMI," Fitzsimmons notes, "we have placed a good deal of emphasis on image, as compared to ASCII text, simply because that's what most customers want. Although the full-image text is not searchable, by supplying high-quality abstracts, we can provide the user with the same level of access, we think, that he or she would get from searching an ASCII text."

That user, as Fitzsimmons points out, is more often than not an end-user, and with so much of the company's business going into major corporations and larger institutions, much effort is now being put into organizing methods for merging the internal information that the client

Originally published in *InfoManage : The International Management Newsletter for the Information Services Professional* 1 (4), March, 1994.

has onsite with the external information he or she needs from a company such as UMI. The effort recognizes, of course, the role of the end-user, and accordingly end-user support is a major component of UMI's marketing direction.

"We organize end-user focus groups to determine essential needs," Fitzsimmons says, "but much of our effort must naturally go to end-user support, which led to the creation of a new section, the Technical Customer Support Group. This is a group of fourteen people who provide support between 8:00 AM and 8:00 PM, and after hours they're available through a beeper system."

Such support pays off, for calls come in from the world-wide marketplace at the rate of some 3,000 a month and growing. To supplement this effort, the company has been involved in establishing several electronic bulletin boards, so that customers can talk to one another about their UMI products and services, and this, too, has produced impressive results in the few months that the bulletin boards have been in place.

Is this typical of UMI's approach to customer service?

"Absolutely," Fitzsimmons reponds without missing a beat. "The TQM program at UMI, started in 1988, was created specifically to help us reach our customers. And customer service at UMI is big-time. If a system goes down, the customer could go out of business. We're there to help when we're needed, and customer support is a vital part of it. If we need to, we'll fly in a support team. It's that important."

But it's not just support after the system is acquired.

"We ship a tremendous amount of sophisticated information products," Fitzsimmons remarks, "and it's important that our sales staff understand the role of the salesperson with the client. Because the decision to buy is such a major one, we consistently engage in what we call 'consultative selling,' which simply means that we want to help our customers make intelligent decisions before they buy. In many cases, the lead time before a sale can be as much as one or two years, and during that time we want to help the customer as much as we can. We lend assistance, for example, in helping customers in the grant-writing process. These and similar activities make up our 'consultative selling' concept, which we're very proud of."

Thinking about "consultative selling" and then the servicing of all those clients, including responding to those 3,000 calls coming in each month from around the world, brings the conversation around to UMI's international efforts. Always an important part of the business and growing rapidly, the company's international activities have now taken on a major new focus.

And it isn't surprising that international issues are a key component in UMI's success, for Fitzsimmons has always had a special attitude about information services issues in the global arena. In fact, when he was Chairman of the Information Industry Association in 1988, the growth of that organization's international initiative began with the founding of the Global Alliance of International Industry Associations. Now including some 27 different groups and organizations, GAIIA works to bring world-wide attention to such issues as copyright and proprietary rights, privacy rights, network development, and public and private cooperation. Although he is not as active with the group now, he is very proud of IIA's current work in this area, and makes reference to the good work being done by GAIIA and IIA's own Global Issues Council, currently chaired by Andy Prozes, the President of Southam Electronic Publishing in Don Mills, Ontario, Canada.

Back at Ann Arbor, much of the UMI international emphasis nowadays is directed toward Asia, where the market is growing at a tremendous rate and where, Fitzsimmons notes, "substantial orders are coming in from Taiwan, Hong Kong, and Singapore. Korea is right behind Taiwan, and there is major development underway in the Peoples Republic of China, so the market is there. All throughout Asia, people devour information, and this attention to information, and its value to the users, is a major component in our strategy."

Another part of that strategy is looking at the new role of the librarian or other information mediator who, in that past, has assisted the user in obtaining or interpreting the information he or she needs. In the Asian market, Fitzsimmons has observed some interesting and useful differences in the way information services professionals work, and he thinks some of those differences can be studied, with useful results, in comparison with how information workers are educated and trained in other parts of the world.

In observing business and businesspeople in Asia, Fitzsimmons notes that he admires how there is a point of view toward using information, not collecting it, and of passing it on to whoever needs it. As a result,

Fitzsimmons feels that librarians and information services professionals do a better job of, "navigating the user through the information search. They see their role as one of navigator or counselor in the information transfer process. They don't collect information or information products and materials for the sake of collecting. These people—these librarians and information professionals—see their customers as using information to make better decisions, and to help them do that, the information professionals themselves have to be able to use very sophisticated methods in delivering information to their patrons."

Is an emphasis on collections a bad thing? Some observers and commentators in the field don't worry about the growth or 'warehousing' of collections. It's the technology to access those collections that many see as the barrier. For some who are looking at these issues, it is technology which is preventing information services management from being as good as it can be. Fitzsimmons doesn't agree.

"The real issue," Fitzsimmons says, "is not with the rapid expansion of technology. It's the lack of trained people in the marketplace, the need for training people to manage the process." As Fitzsimmons sees it, we're looking at a double-barrelled situation here, for not only does society require information providers who have a basic understanding of the information transfer process, but these same people must also have, at least, a base-line understanding of the technology involved. At the present time, information workers are not sufficiently prepared in these two areas, and that lack of preparation has a lot to do with the ineffective or difficult delivery of information in the formats and technology now available.

So the next questions follow naturally: Are there solutions? Should educators in the library and information services fields be training these people to do what they need to do?

Fitzsimmons doesn't wince. And he doesn't apologize.

"Minimum standards are needed," he says, "so that information providers can use the new technology to bring the information to the user. The librarian now has a new role and different responsibilities."

It all comes together, according to many of the folks who are observing the international information services scene these days, in an attitude that combines new paradigms in information services management and new approaches to the work that librarians and other information workers do.

That attitude also includes a new awareness of the value of advocacy and support, from outside the field, to credentialize the services that information workers provide.

This new approach, this new attitude is nowhere better expressed than in Joe Fitzsimmons' work with Friends of Libraries USA, the amazingly successful organization of library friends groups that currently seeks not only to provide support for librarians and their libraries, but to educate the "friends" themselves, so that they can play a more proactive role in obtaining funding for libraries. Fitzsimmons is now the President of FOLUSA, and he and his colleagues have launched a major new initiative to bring the more than 2,500 friends groups, as he characterizes it, "from bake sales and book sales" to a new realization that if mobilized, these groups can have tremendous clout. Friends groups are located everywhere, all over the United States and abroad, and FOLUSA is working to organize and train these people, all volunteers.

"Over 80% of library funding comes from local sources," Fitzsimmons says, "and friends groups can be very effective in working with local leaders in determining the levels at which libraries and other information services organizations can be funded. In fact, it's already being done, so we know it can work. In San Francisco, for example, 'friends' raise close to a million dollars a year for the San Francisco Public Library. All together several hundred million dollars a year are raised by all the groups combined, but we need to bring that kind of talent to every friends group, and we need to train the volunteers to be able to do the work ."

The effort isn't limited to financial issues, however, for in raising support, and in offering training for library staff, Fitzsimmons and FOLUSA see themselves as changing the perceptions—and the effectiveness—of the librarians themselves. Which puts FOLUSA in the forefront in developing these new paradigms of information services and information delivery.

"Part of our objective," Fitzsimmons says, "is to see that libraries are re-defined, that libraries are not just what are usually thought of as 'traditional' libraries. To do that, to bring about this change, we must help librarians and other information workers become more skilled at marketing their services. That's our goal, to see that librarians learn to think politically and to increase support levels for libraries and other information services programs. It's what FOLUSA can do."

It's a tall order, and one that Joe Fitzsimmons is undertaking with his eyes wide open. With his usual keen interest and enthusiasm, and his experience in working with many of these issues in so many different settings, he's going to pull it off. Fitzsimmons has no doubts about succeeding, with FOLUSA or with any of these other goals that he has set for himself. For information services management, that is a very good thing indeed.

SYLVIA PIGGOTT
at Bank of Montréal: Reengineering information services for the 2nd era of the Information Age

"You Gotta Have a Gimmick."

We don't generally think of information services management in terms of that old Broadway tune, and certainly when we have a conversation with someone as gracious and well-spoken as Sylvia Piggott at the Bank of Montréal, the associations connected with the Gypsy Rose Lee story are far from our mind. But Piggott has come up with an idea that is getting some attention these days, and after all, that's what happens (in the old fashioned, classical sense of the word) with a gimmick.

But it doesn't matter what you call it. Piggott's idea—that information services as a management discipline has gone beyond its beginning stages into a "second era"—is a powerful concept that can be particularly helpful for senior management staff. As they attempt to cope with ever-changing, ever-slippery information delivery formats and media, it seems singularly appropriate for information executives to recognize that information services field isn't in its infancy or childhood any more. As a function of management and a tool for effective performance, information services (including libraries and librarianship) is all grown up now. It's time to treat it like an adult.

Originally published in *InfoManage : The International Management Newsletter for the Information Services Professional* 2 (3), February, 1995.

"Businesses and professions are reengineering as a consequence of enabling technology, and that has led us into this second era of the information age," Piggott says. "Now, libraries and other information operations can benefit from applying some of the same concepts."

Piggott is obviously very comfortable talking about the reengineering process, and she likes the idea of taking some of the same "often radical redesigns," she calls them, and putting them to work in information services.

"Reengineering involves three processes," she says, and she counts them off as if she walks around thinking about them all the time: "First, you develop a strategic vision. Then you analyze and design the reengineering process. And you follow up by implementing the process. As the processes are reengineered, jobs are reengineered as well, thereby optimizing the business and making it more competitive."

To Piggott's way of thinking, these three processes can all be applied to the information delivery process, just as they fit basic business processes, organizational structure, information technology, and job content and flow.

"What we're talking about here," she says, "is a process that is believed by some to lead to vast improvements in customer-valued productivity, and that's where we must concentrate our efforts in the library and information services community."

The emphasis fairly jumps out as Piggott warms to her subject. "Information professionals must constantly be looking for ways to optimize their services," she comments. "Especially in the corporate environment, but in fact anywhere that information and research methods contribute to some sort of satisfactory organizational success, the reengineering processes can enable library managers to structure their library or information center to deliver information using the most cost effective electronic tools and products available in the industry."

The process, it seems, can lead to the realization of Piggott's own information vision for organizations.

"It's not a complicated way of looking at things. The library or information center must seek to exist as a seamless, borderless service, a place where information can be sought wherever it exists and is used immediately by local or remote customers. Information professionals, whether they want to or not, must make the adjustment to real-time information delivery. That's what customers want. Even the delivery of information products by overnight mail is often too slow for many information customers. For them, for information to be a competitive tool, it must be real-time information."

Bringing librarians and other information providers into the reengineering effort is, of course, the much talked about information superhighway, which Piggott predicts will have a "profound effect" on the way libraries reengineer. In fact, with the technology already in place in many organizations, and with the "pioneers," as she calls them, already delivering major services remotely via fibre optics or other communications methods, real-time information delivery and the virtual library already exist as a reality. Hence Piggott's notion about the second era of information services.

"Online virtual reality and interactive learning systems using multimedia are already delivering training to remote sites of multi-national and national corporations. Obviously it's reasonable to expect library and information services to be delivered in a similar way."

Are they?

"Not yet," she says, "but in Montréal, a company called Virtual Prototypes Inc., in partnership with the ADGA Group and Hydro Quebec, has launched a $26 million project called INTERFACE. It has been designed to develop leading-edge training technology that will provide online simulation training at the exact time and place the training is needed to support the individual and the company. The library manager must be prepared to deliver information services in the same way. If librarians and other information services professionals fail to move in sync with these developments or fail to input to and impact these systems, they will find themselves at a serious disadvantage in the marketplace. These developments are going to have a real influence on the future of the business or profession for which they supply the information. Shouldn't they influence the information delivery process as well?"

Well, of course. There are few information managers who would disagree with Piggott's analysis of the big picture. But how on earth, they ask, do you bring it back to the "real" world, to the day-to-day activities, those ordinary, run-of-the-mill management demands that account for so much stress and so much frustration in the executive workplace.

Sylvia Piggott flashes the charming smile that lets you know she doesn't lose many arguments.

"Librarians who are willing and capable of reacting to the paradigm shift will thrive as they become involved in preparing for the new age of the information superhighway. Those who won't will be left behind.

"Unfortunately," Piggott says, "librarians—and many other information workers as well—tend to want to be all things to all people. While this makes us well beloved (or so we like to think) by the people we provide information for, it in fact dilutes the effect of mission-critical work.

"The librarian needs to get rid of much of what he or she does and get good at what is valued and essential for the organization the library supports. And once those mission-critical information services have been identified, they need to be expanded. That's what our organizations need from us nowadays, not some idealized fantasy that we can provide any information service or product that anybody might want."

And while there isn't exactly a villain in this piece, it soon becomes clear that this attitude, this tendency to do too much has evolved over the decades from a professional education that, in Piggott's opinion, is much too broad based. She becomes notably forceful as she expresses her opinion.

"It is imperative," she says, "that educators in the library and information services field make the shift by adjusting the curriculum to meet this challenge. If they—and the people they educate—do not make the shift, we are likely then to hear people asking, 'Who really needs libraries these days? Hardly anyone.'"

So it's a scary world out there, but it is also an amazingly exciting one, and the potential for improvement, for changing our role, is one that Sylvia Piggott embraces with much enthusiasm.

"As for information services," she says, "we are in the age of revolution, not incremental improvement, and we have the opportunity to reinvent what the library is, and what quality value-added library service is. Librarians cannot just react to the realities of today's information requirements, they have to influence them. And while this is obviously no simple task, it is a challenging one, and it puts new and thrilling opportunities before the information professional."

And for those information professionals who like things the way they are, who see no reason to change? How should these people deal with this revolution?

Again the smile, but this time a little sad and, perhaps, a little indulgent, just as a parent might indulge a well-meaning but not particularly motivated teenager.

"There's no going back,'"she says. "The world is heading in the direction of advanced technologies. More and more intelligence will be added to networks and transmission facilities.

"Site-specific work is becoming less relevant, and will become increasingly governed by the nature of the task at hand. Technologies—even the ones available now—are poised to shatter any remaining limitations on flexibility. And it will happen in the very near future.

"Besides that, complex functions are being placed within the reach of ordinary people, and they are becoming more and more self-sufficient. So we have no choice but to re-think how we do our work. And why not? There'll be work for us, plenty of work, if we have the right qualification and the right attitude."

If she's right (and it's hard to imagine Piggott not being right), information services folks don't need to worry. The second information era will need them, and they'll have a very important place in the workings of the new age of information. After all, if she's saying nothing else, Sylvia Piggott is telling those of us who work in information services to take the future into our own hands, to be in charge of our own professional destiny. For information services professionals, the future is what we make it.

Meet Sylvia Piggott

Since 1983, Manager of Business Information, Bank of Montréal in Montréal, Canada. Prior to that, Assistant to the Director of the Graduate School of Library and Information Science, McGill University. Held several positions in Special Libraries Association, including Chair of the Strategic Planning Committee, Chair of the Nominating Committee, and Director.

Since 1991, a member of the part-time faculty at Concordia University, teaching Library Automation. Sylvia Piggott writes and lectures extensively on library automation, and she is a frequent speaker at information and computer science conferences. As a leader in the field of library science, she mentors new graduates and advises on managing personal growth.

GABRIELE GREVE
at Berlin's Bibliothek des Kammergerichts: Taking the initiative
and confidently confronting the challenges

In the information services community it is a given that as society changes, information needs change. While there are those disciplines in which organizational change motivates new approaches to information delivery (the last decade's phenomenal changes in the business and finance communities come to mind), there are other disciplines in which the need for change is clearly recognized but real change is restrained or, in some cases, simply blocked. For information services executives working in organizations where change is coming slowly, a meeting with Gabriele Greve at the Library of the Higher Regional Court of Berlin can be an enlightening experience.

The responsibility for managing change comes to those who have the initiative to seek that responsibility, and Gabriele Greve has never been one to wait for things to happen to her. When she sees an opportunity, she puts her brain to work and figures out how she can take advantage of that opportunity, for her own or her organization's benefit. For example, in the library and information services community in Germany it is extremely rare for an information practitioner (the Diplome Bibliothekarin) to achieve a position of senior managerial responsibility. Such positions as the directorships of major libraries or the heads of the various library and information services institutes and organizations go to academic specialists, often chosen or appointed for their academic qualifications and/or their perceived "position" in the discipline rather than for their experience as information practitioners.

Not so with the top position at the Library of the Kammergericht, the Higher Regional Court of Berlin. Having observed that the authorities couldn't make up their minds as to whom to employ in the position,

Originally published in *InfoManage : The International Management Newsletter for the Information Services Professional* 3 (3), February, 1996.

Gabriele Greve decided to apply. She recognized that there was a need for a director who would have a combination of good management skills and practical experience, and she went after the job.

When she decided to apply, Greve had been working in legislative and parliamentary libraries for several years, first at the Kammergericht itself, where she had been employed in the reference and lending department. This of course is where she acquired her practical experience in dealing with the information customers themselves—the judges, the advocates, the law clerks, the students, and the administrative personnel, all of whom required guidance and direction in their use of the materials. Greve then worked for ten years at the Library of the Parliament of Berlin, again in the reference / lending area, followed by a stint in the cataloging section, where she was able to combine her understanding of the customers' information needs with the application of the *Prussian Instructions . . . ,* the famous and highly structured cataloging schedule used in German libraries and based on the grammar of the German language. By the time she decided to leave the Parliament Library to come to the Bibliothek des Kammergerichts, Greve had risen to the position of Assistant Director, and she felt instinctively that being manager of the library at the Higher Regional Court was a job she could do. Without waiting for an invitation (for quite frankly such an invitation would not have been offered to a practitioner), Greve took the initiative and applied for the position.

When you meet Gabriele Greve and hear about her career, you realize that her ability to move from a position of strength "outside" the established routine is not—for her—so remarkable. It's just the way she is. It was good experience for her, for the first thing she learned is that there is often opposition to someone coming in from "the outside."

"Since you're coming in to deal with what is, by definition, a problem situation," she says, "you don't have much choice but to stand back and look at the problem as objectively as you can. You try to be emotionally uninvolved, and move in to fix things."

It's not always easy, but it's a way of looking at one's work that has enabled Gabriele Greve to keep matters in perspective at the Kammergericht in Berlin. The court is one of the oldest in Germany, so old in fact that its founding date is not clearly established, but it was sometime about 1600. With approximately 200,000 volumes, the library is one of the largest court libraries in Germany, comparable in size to the library of the Federal Constitutional Court (with about 240,000 volumes) and certainly comparable—in services provided—to the country's 475,000 volume Supreme Court Library. Some 100 readers are served every day, and it is a management situation that encourages, even cries out for a manager who is not inhibited about taking the initiative.

Initiative is, after all, a combination of resourcefulness, enthusiasm, and leadership, and it's a combination that characterizes Gabriele Greve. That much becomes clear when you think about what she's doing with the other court libraries that are also part of her management responsibility. Since the opening of the Berlin Wall in 1989, administrative and managerial challenges have proliferated throughout German society, and there are few situations where the challenges are more demanding than in the courts. Not surprisingly, the demands on the libraries that serve the information needs of the courts are equally challenging, and Greve is daily confronted with new demands, new claims on her and her staff's time, new hurdles to conquer. There are 12 civil courts with libraries that are part of the information "system" that the Higher Regional Court of Berlin supports, and an independent federal appeals court is also served through the information facilities of the Bibliothek des Kammergerichts. In the past, these libraries had been at best limited in the level of services they could offer for their information customers, but now they are expected to provide library services of the very highest standard. For example, five of these libraries are located in what was formerly East Berlin, and before reunification users in those libraries sought few materials. They limited their research to only the latest books, the latest law literature, or a few of the latest commentaries. In fact, in responding to most queries, one text and one commentary was all that could be provided. Now the entire "philosophy" of information services for the courts has changed, for these inquirers now expect a greater variety of materials for their research, and they want to choose from more books, more commentaries, and a wider range of periodical literature. Information services for the courts is simply on a larger scale now, a fact which in and of itself stimulates considerable discussion among the information providers in the various libraries that serve the courts.

How does Gabriele Greve meet these challenges? And how do she and her staff deal with the massive changes that are affecting every level of German society, including information services? The answer to these questions, of course, provides another reason why visiting with Greve and the sixteen people who work with her is such a stimulating experience. A visitor soon recognizes that in addition to taking the initiative and not waiting to be invited to participate in the decision-making process, Greve is also an information services manager who comfortably brings a leadership role to the managerial function. When, for example, she received an order to create a new library for one of the courts, to establish an information agency where one had not existed before, and to provide the information services in a frighteningly short period of time (including designing the facility, organizing the staff, moving materials in, and the like), it wasn't a matter to be agonized over or to be complained about. It was a challenge, and an exciting one at that. If it meant that she and some of her staff had to show up in jeans, transport some of the materials in their own vehicles, and battle recalcitrant building employees who weren't accustomed to the "physical labor" of moving boxes of books into a library, that's what they did. Greve took it all in stride, and when asked where such activity fits into the "managerial" role, she laughs at the naïveté of the question. It's all part of the "flexibility" that is required in Germany today, in information services management as in everything else.

There are other challenges. For one thing, there is now the matter of choice, both for librarians and for the information customers. With reunification, there is more to choose from in the way of materials, cases, and, especially, new legislation. So the librarians on Gabriele Greve's staff must be willing to take responsibility for providing the information customers with more choices, and to vouch for the validity of those choices.

Staff training becomes a key component in information delivery in this new information services environment, and Greve—again demonstrating her leadership skills—takes on much of this training herself. She wants to be working with her people, showing them how to stretch themselves beyond whatever limitations or inhibitions might be holding them back. Again, it's not easy, for many of the people working in libraries in Germany today have not in the past been encouraged to go beyond the basics or to exercise themselves to deliver anything but the most rudimentary levels of service. But all that has changed now and expectations are higher. Gabriele Greve represents a new generation of library and information services managers who recognize that today's information customers—especially in an environment as information intensive as the courts—demand and expect to receive a very high level of information delivery. So Greve takes it upon herself to see that her staff is well trained. And, to ensure that she too stays current, she takes advantage of the many training programs offered by such organizations as the Deutsches Bibliotheksinstitut and other similar organizations in and around Berlin. It's this continuing training and professional development, both for herself and her staff, that is characterizing much of the success that the Bibliothek des Kammergerichts is experiencing these days.

And the list of challenges continues. Despite the beauty of the grand old edifice in which the Higher Regional Court of Berlin's Library is located, just on the edge of the lovely Charlottenburg section of the city, a move is projected. The current space is grossly inadequate for the amount of material that is housed there, and with those 100-plus readers every day, simply finding a place to sit is often a problem. Greve and her staff are already heavily involved in preparing for the move, and as soon as funds are finally appropriated (the appropriated funds for the move have been "reappropriated" to other projects for each of the past three fiscal budgets), the move will take place. The new site will be equally impressive, for the Bibliothek des Kammergerichts is going to be located in the Kontrollratsgebäude, where the highest military representatives of France, England, the U.S.S.R., and the U.S.A met in 1948 to determine the partitioning of Berlin. Not only is it an interesting building from a historical point of view, it is as attractive as the current site, and its situation on the edge of the Tiergarten is equally grand.

What it all adds up to, for Gabriele Greve and other information services managers like her, is that those "interesting times" of the Confucian adage have swept into the German library community (and especially the Berlin contingent) in great profusion. There are no "quiet times" anymore, and every day presents its own challenges and excitements. Greve doesn't mind. In fact, she finds herself intellectually and professionally stimulated by the environment in which she is working these days. But that doesn't mean she is content. Far from it, for she is quick to tell you that she is "restless" for the information services field to reach a higher plane in Germany, particularly with respect to the service demands and levels of service being expected by the courts and their research staffs. She wants better salaries for her staff, better training, better facilities, and she expects—in time—to get them. In the meantime, she provides the leadership that her employees need, and she does her best to encourage them to make the most of this exciting journey that they're making together.

Looking at information services from
a communications perspective:
It's the possibilities that intrigue
BOB FRYE

Ever since they met, *InfoManage* Editor/Publisher Guy St. Clair and
Emmy-award winning documentary film producer Robert Frye have been
exploring the connections that link their two fields. They have even gone
so far as to suggest that information services and communications might
be linked into one discipline. Now that's not necessarily a new concept,
and certainly it's been batted around among academics in these two fields
for at least a couple of decades. At Rutgers, The State University of New
Jersey, for example, graduate training in these fields was amalgamated
into The School of Communications, Information, and Library Studies in
1982, so the similarities between information services management and
communications theory have been recognized for some time.

Nevertheless, on the larger, societal scale, not much action has been
taken, and for most lay people information services and communications
are still thought of as separate and distinct fields of work. Particularly
among decision makers in organizations that benefit from the employment of information services and communications professionals, there
doesn't seem to be much motivation for linking the two fields, and yet it
would seem to be an obvious move.

In information management today we hear a lot today about the
"umbrella" theory of information services, a concept that combines librarianship, records management, archives management, MIS, and many
other disciplines, reaching all the way across the spectrum to include
information brokerage and publishing. Information services professionals
manage these operations and, in doing so, contribute essential information that enables the organization to succeed in achieving its mission and,

Originally published in *InfoManage : The International Management Newsletter for the Information Services Professional* 4 (2), January, 1997.

on an even grander scale, influence the success of the organization in functioning in society at large.

Much the same can be said about what happens in the communications field. These practitioners are the people who handle public relations, media coordination, broadcast news, advertising, and similar functions that convey to the world at large a particular point of view or perspective. But within the operational management framework, communications also includes those professionals who devise internal communications policy (and manage its implementation—a key responsibility), who structure the communications operations required for organizational success. And like information services workers, both of these groups of communications practitioners function on a larger scale. Without their efforts, the larger organization or community, however defined, would be hopelessly enmeshed in conflicting and counterproductive communications failures. The all-too-common "communications breakdown," still a serious problem in many organizations (despite the efforts of some managers), would be ubiquitous and the much-sung refrain, "They never tell us anything," would define the anarchy.

Bob Frye doesn't think it has to be that way. He has a vision about how information services and communications management can be combined and used together to enhance the corporate or organizational management process (and hence contribute to organizational success). His vision is one in which the practitioners in this new discipline are empowered by their organizations to lead to that success.

Now "vision" is one of those words we have to be careful about, and in the past, it's often been a scarce commodity in information services. The same might also be said for the communications field. On the other hand, though, there have always been those practitioners (in both disciplines) who were thinking ahead of their time, whose thinking was—in the popular cliché—"out of the box," and whose professional identities were bound up not so much in what is, but in what can be.

Bob Frye is one of those people. He's far too modest and unassuming to let you get away with calling him a "visionary," but he also has a strong track record in television production and documentary film making, two fields in which too much modesty and too much restraint can be counterproductive, so he knows how to hold his own in a conversation. And if he doesn't see himself as a visionary, there are other ways to describe what he thinks about.

"It's the possibilities," Frye says. "I've been involved with computers since 1964, and I've been in production for television and documentary films for a long time as well, and when we talk about information services and communications, it's developing and understanding the possibilities that makes things happen. We can't ignore the possibilities that are available to us, and we can't move forward unless the people who come into these fields are empowered to explore those possibilities."

In a world in which change and change management have become the *lingua franca* for both information services and communications practitioners, Frye's ideas about how the two disciplines interact and relate to one another make a lot of sense. In fact, looking beyond academia, there are probably some circumstances in which a good case could be made for merging the two disciplines, for information services and communications have much in common. For example, just as there are tensions between "traditional" information delivery practices and more "cutting-edge" techniques, so there are differences between traditional communications methodologies and the enthusiastic practitioners who are out there establishing the framework for communications management in the 21st century.

"In both disciplines," Frye says, "it's breaking down the walls between the traditional and the non-traditional that makes things happen. What we have to find is a coalescing agent, in terms of the thought process, to help us figure out how to change the way we think. We have a tendency—as human beings at this point in our development—to engage in vertical training, to use linear thinking. But for the future we need something else. We need something that gives us the ability to take ideas that come from information and move them from conceptual development to whatever the work is."

How we find that "coalescing agent," that thing that will move ideas into a finished work, is not yet clear, but for Bob Frye, there's some question if the methodologies now being so highly touted are the real thing.

"My concern for the future," he says, "is that information as we understand it is being sanitized. It's being cleaned up and stripped of the fringe matter that enables what I label the 'possibilities.' Take E-mail, for example. It's too clean. What happened to the emotional and creative pieces? How do we convey the emotion, the creativity, in an E-mail message?"

Is it knowledge management, then, this coalescing agent that is going to make information/communication practitioners successful?

"That's part of it," Frye says. "But it's more than knowledge management, for it includes an understanding that information and communication are linked, are part of the same process. Information is the raw material, the content that is transmitted or transferred. Communication, on the other hand, is part of the process. Not the mechanics, not the bells and whistles we hear so much about, but that part of the information transfer process in which the information gets moved from Point A to Point B and in the moving leads you to places you wouldn't get to otherwise. Those who understand that will win. And those who function in this environment in which information and communication are linked will grasp not only the facts but the nuances."

But that isn't happening now, and according to Frye, there are a couple of reasons why.

"For one thing," he says, "the organizational bureaucratic mindset, found in all organizations—whether they're in business, the government, or whatever—automatically slots people into little boxes. It's very confining, very restricting for their thinking and their activity. Worse than that, it encourages people to get comfortable in this restricted environment, and then it becomes hard, if not impossible, for them to dispense with the preconceived ideas that they've picked up while working in that environment. So what you get, in both information services and in the communications field, is a situation where the customer is given the essentials of the story, but is given no links to other thoughts, to the nuances. The customer would have those links if the people providing the story's essentials were given the latitude to provide the links as well. Unfortunately, most of the time the customers just ask for the essentials. And even when the customer wants more, wants to be given the fringes, to delve into the nuances, the provider is not empowered—for various reasons—to provide them."

It's this kind of thinking that sets Bob Frye apart, for despite three decades of success in broadcast news, in documentary film development and production, and, now, in the management of a company involved in World Wide Web-based communications, Frye has not yet himself succumbed to the comfortable, "easy-fit" thinking that characterizes so many executives. If anything, his enthusiasm and his sheer delight in the pursuit of possibilities in the communications and information services fields have moved him beyond the role of practitioner to that of stimulator and motivator. That much becomes obvious as he continues describing how communications and information delivery are alike:

"Think about where these two fields of study sit on the organization chart. Certainly no organization, no bureaucracy can function without some attention to information services and communications. Yet in most organizations, both disciplines sit on the side, off center, and are not really identified as key or critical in the organizations' operations, even when there's a kind of lip service about how important they are. That shouldn't be the case, but it is. Fortunately, in some organizations steps are being taken to position these functions differently, and that's a good sign.

"The problem is," Frye continues, "most of the people who have been trained to do this work—the information services practitioners, the communications people—have been trained to be observers, gatherers, and so forth. Yet they're the very people who are positioned to be major players in the corporate or organizational environment, because they see from the get-go what the story is, what the nuances are, and what the possibilities can be. They can do it, and I think they would like to do it, but they must be empowered to do it, to take this leadership role. Training is part of it, of course, because these workers must be trained to go beyond the essentials, to be the 'scouts.' And they themselves must be curious. If they're not, it's a dead deal even before it begins."

And are these the people, these curious workers, the practitioners who will be combining their efforts as communications and information services are linked?

"Of course," Frye says, and you realize that he thinks it's an absolutely obvious point and is wondering why you don't. "If you're curious, you're more than likely to be somewhat adventurous, intellectually stimulated, willing to step out of the box. In the information/communications field, these are the practitioners—the adventurous people—who will figure out how to link their two disciplines and how to use that link to provide better service for their customers."

How does it happen?

"Well, there has to be major rethinking at the corporate or organizational level, and while it's happening in some companies, it's not happening, in my opinion, in enough of them yet. It happens when people, when the practitioners, are given ownership in what the organization is doing, when CEOs permit people to have full participation in the direct function of winning. We read much these days about 'flattened' hierarchical structures, and that's one step in the right direction, it seems to me. Another is having the ability to refocus as the organization's leaders recognize that the marketplace is changing. Certainly that's what Microsoft has done in the last year as the company has moved its emphasis from the PC to the Internet. That kind of thinking is required from both managers and staff."

Frye stops and considers his next comment carefully.

"But the basic requirement, from my point of view, is that people must be permitted, encouraged, empowered to work a little more slowly, to think about what they are contributing to the process. In today's workplace, both in communications and in information services, things are moving so quickly that we don't have time—we're told—to think about what we're doing. Well, I disagree with that approach. I think we have to slow down, to have some time for reflection. Everything can't be reactive. Someone has to have the capability of grasping the whole. And why don't we do it on our own, those of us who are the practitioners? Because it's the nature of human mind: it's just too easy to be left-brain reactors instead of whole-brain participants."

So how do we get it going, this new look at what the future of a combined communications/information services discipline can bring us? Frye thinks it goes back to hiring practices.

"We must seek to hire trailblazers," he says, "people who are interested in using their intuition and their creativity to make a contribution to the organization, whatever that organization is. And we must look for practitioners who are willing to be enterprising, to be entrepreneurial within the organization. Most people want to be led. It's a matter of trailblazing, and if we hire information services/communications workers who are willing to be trailblazers, to be leaders in their organizations, we'll have that success the organizations are looking for."

In fact, for communications/information services practitioners, this is a good time to be thinking about these things, in Frye's opinion.

"We live in a time in which not only is the information/communications infrastructure being built, rebuilt, transmuted, and so forth, it's also a time in which different attitudes and different ways of thinking about things is encouraged. And it is also a matter of attitude, of keeping an open mind in order to create an environment in which one not only does one's work, one makes a contribution to the organization as well."

It's pretty heady stuff, all this thinking about the future, about change management, about moving away from distinct and discrete—and comfortable—positioning into an unknown professional scenario. Of course it's hard to change, for by keeping information services and communications management apart, by dealing with just the "essentials" of the story, as Bob Frye refers to them, we and our staffs don't have to stretch ourselves. We don't have to be concerned with the fringes and the nuances.

But guess what? It's the fringes and the nuances—and our ability to handle them, to deal with them, and to incorporate them into the information and communications packages we and our staffs are delivering—that separate out the really good information delivery and the really good communications management. And it's people like Bob Frye—bringing these ideas to us from their careers in fields like television production, documentary films, and website design—who are, in fact, leading the way. They're showing us how to incorporate the subtleties of the transaction into the transaction's final product and that, for both information services practitioners and communications practitioners, is a good sign. It will mean, ultimately, that our role is recognized for being as valuable as we've known all along it is.

Meet Bob Frye

Robert E. Frye is President and CEO of Bolthead Communications Group, Inc., an independent television and film production company concentrating on documentary programming and consulting in the communications field, and of ThinkMedia, Inc., a production company developing programming for the children's market in television, video, and non-linear computer-based formats. He has also recently become Vice-President and Managing Director of WebTop.Systems. Inc., a company organized to assist others in designing and implementing World Wide Web-based communications. His career has included work assignments in Washington and London as well as in New York, including a stint as Director of Communications Programs for the Appalachian Regional Commission, for which he oversaw the creative development of an interactive satellite project, working with NASA and other federal government agencies, utilizing the ATS-6 Experimental satellite. Frye was the Washington Producer of "ABC Evening News," and later Executive Producer of "World News This Morning" and "Good Morning, America News," and Executive Producer of "ABC World News Tonight." After he left ABC, Frye served as President & CEO of Phillips Fine Art Auctioneers, and with the creation of Bolthead Communications, began the move into independent television and film production. His latest productions, "The Journey of Butterfly," a one-hour film which tells the story of the Ghetto Terezin, and "Berlin: Journey of a City," have been highly praised as they have been shown throughout America and Europe. Bob Frye's awards include the Emmy, for a ten-part series entitled "US-USSR: A Balance of Powers," produced for "World News Tonight," and the CINE Golden Eagle for "The Journey of Butterfly" and for "KRISTALLNACHT: The Journey from 1938 to 1988," a one-hour documentary for which he was Executive Producer and Interviewer and which aired on PBS on November 9, 1988, the fiftieth anniversary of Kristallnacht. Frye is a resident of New York City, where he lives with his wife, designer and artist Diane Love.

DAVID BENDER
at the Special Libraries Association:
Visionary leadership for the information industry

Contrasts, contradictions, doing the unexpected. The Special Libraries Association has long been known as an organization of diverse and complex components. And why not? Any organization made up of 15,000-plus people who see themselves as information management specialists, knowledge managers, and information consultants, and yet still call themselves "librarians," can certainly be described as inclusive. Any organization that has 94 constituent subunits ranging in size of membership from 40 to 3,374, with subject interests as wide-ranging as business and finance, physics-astronomy-mathematics, and gay and lesbian issues has to be committed to diversity. And any such organization still operating under a single set of bylaws, after 88 years, and using a single vision statement and a single strategic plan is doing something right.

When you take all the contradictions about SLA (and there are plenty of others that could be listed) and you throw in a few other facts as well, such as the one that points out that although the association is head-quartered in the United States, it is clearly recognized throughout the world as the preeminent international organization for information services workers, or that—while the average job tenure for senior association executives is something like six years—SLA Executive Director David Bender has been running the association since 1979, you can only come to one conclusion: something right is happening at SLA.

Don't misunderstand. David Bender won't take the credit, because for him, as he's quick to point out, it's the membership that makes SLA what it is. But of course he's only human, and he is doing a good job, so he deserves some credit. And he'll smile modestly when you tell him what a good job he is doing. By and large, though, when it comes time to talk

Originally published in *InfoManage : The International Management Newsletter for the Information Services Professional* 4 (7), June, 1997.

about the association and where it's been and where it's going, Bender will rattle off a list of many people, staff members, directors, officers, external advisors, all of whom he wants to be sure get credited for SLA's success.

In fact, one of the difficulties that David Bender is having right now has to do with the membership, and the important role that member volunteers play in the various activities of the association. It's a problem, for it is through the efforts of the volunteers that SLA gets its work done, and the role of volunteers in society is changing drastically. You have to wonder how SLA would exist if it weren't for the volunteers.

"Every volunteer is a miracle," Bender says, and this man's gentle look tells you he means it. He is absolutely sincere. "Our association runs on its volunteers, and we simply couldn't be the organization we are without the volunteers who do so much work and support the efforts of the staff. But we haven't yet, even after all this time, come up with a way to make sure this value is recognized, and that continues to be a problem for me. And it is difficult for me—personally—to deal with, because it is hard to adequately recognize all our volunteers. Yet the association can't function without any of them."

So if all those contradictions and contrasts, and all that diversity, come together for a purpose, and if all those volunteers work together, what is the purpose? Can it be stated? Can it be identified?

Probably not, although long ago the association's leadership chose as its motto a phrase that still packs a punch, and in these days in the information industry, when we're all talking so much about knowledge management, the phrase probably packs a bigger punch than Dr. John A. Lapp, who coined the term in 1916, could ever have imagined.

"The basic purpose of the special library," Dr. Lapp wrote, "is to put knowledge to work." That was it. That's why SLA exists, and that phrase—putting knowledge to work—has been the slogan that has carried SLA through its many transitions, to its present position as industry leader in information organizational services.

And the transitions continue. David Bender is delighted to talk about where the association is going and what some of the coming emphasis is going to be. But when asked about what gets him excited about SLA these days, what's happening that he particularly proud of, there's a robust laugh.

"I never thought I would be giving this answer," he says, "because it's not me. I entered the information field back in its pre-computerized days.

Yet here I am, and what is in fact so exciting right now is that we're moving SLA into the future in one fell swoop. We're becoming a virtual association, and it's just about one of the most exciting projects I've ever been involved in, in my entire career."

A virtual association? A library association a virtual association? But aren't library associations supposed to be about warehousing books, about services to the disadvantaged and other social issues, about education and training and things like that?

"Sometimes," Bender says, "and sometimes not. At SLA, we have a staff that is strongly supportive of the membership, and our membership is an international, diverse membership. The staff, the association leadership, the Board of Directors and I have concluded that the best way to serve this diverse, international membership is through the creation of a virtual association.

"Now don't get too carried away," Bender cautions. "It's not a new idea, and it's been done in some other associations of course, but not in any information-related or library organization, so we're going to be leading the way. We'll be doing some serious work in this area at the senior staff retreat in July, and we'll be looking at some of the organizations that have been successful with becoming virtual. The National Association of Landscape Architects, for example, is a model we're examining. But SLA's move into the virtual association arena will be unique, for we will enter with a different model which will be pretty exciting, I think, for our members."

For one thing, there's going to be a direct chat room to the Executive Director. That the membership can't interact directly with senior association staff has long been a problem in large associations, and while Bender has been—and continues to be—notably successful with the famous "Fireside Chats" and focus groups he puts together throughout the year (he started them back in 1985 at the association's Annual Conference in Winnipeg, and they were a great success), these efforts are obviously not available to all members.

"I don't know what I've gotten myself into," Bender says with another one of those famous smiles (you can tell he's enjoying this), "and when it came time to name it, I must not have been in my right mind. We're calling it 'My Web-Footed Friend,' with a Canadian Goose as its logo. It will be up and running, at specifically arranged times, and I'll be available for realtime conversations with the association's membership."

SLA's International Future—
David Bender Describes Some of the Specific Steps

*W*ithin information services, there is widespread agreement that real success will come only to those organizations and practitioners who are willing to play in the international arena. For several years, the Special Libraries Association has been moving toward a more international focus, and Bender enjoys describing some of SLA's work in this area.

Certainly a major effort is the 2nd International Conference on Special Librarianship, scheduled for Brighton, England, October 16-22, in the year 2000. In the planning now for many years—again under Bender's personal influence—this second international conference (the first was in Hawaii in 1979) promises to provide attendees with a remarkable opportunity for investigating the flow of information in a global environment. With the theme, "The Information Age: Challenges and Opportunities," the "Conference for the Year 2000," as some of SLA's membership have dubbed it, promises to be a highlight in the industry's move toward understanding how information works at an international level. It should be an exceptional, and very worthwhile, experience.

"Of course it will be," Bender says, surprised that the idea is even verbalized. "The Brighton Conference is being managed for SLA by GIC, a multi-association Brussels company, and it will help to position SLA in the European information community. But as important as anything else, the connection with GIC will also include links to associations that are not necessarily information-oriented, a connection that

can't help but be beneficial as SLA moves toward information delivery in the next century."

The next century. Ah hah! Here it is: the futurist at work.

And what will information delivery in the 21st century be like, Dr. Bender?

Bender doesn't hesitate. He reaches across the table and pulls out a document that Lynn Woodbury, SLA's Senior Assistant Executive Director for Finance and Administration, put together for a recent meeting of the SLA's Association Office Operations Committee, which oversees the staff operation that Bender has management responsibility for. It's a document he's used before, because its phrases turn up in his speeches when he talks about the competencies of special librarians, and there's a certain kind of justice to the fact that he can use it with both staff and with fellow information professionals.

"What's going to happen," Bender says, "is that the future of information is going to call for five qualities that have been in short supply in the past. For lots of reasons, things like boundaryless behavior, speed, stretch, simplification, and competitiveness just weren't part of our ordinary operations. They weren't used among staff and workers, or among information professionals, or even within society at large.

"These qualities are going to be critical in the future, and for our profession to survive, for us to be able to continue to provide the level of information leadership we're expected to provide, those five

continued

SLA's International Future *(continued)*

attributes will become part of our work. It's easier now, of course, for we have the enabling technology that President [Sylvia] Piggott talks so much about, and we have a society that is more open to these attributes when used in the performance of one's duties, but the point is, in the future, as we special librarians attempt to do what we're expected to do, we're going to have to do it, we're going to have to manage information in terms of boundaryless behavior, speed, stretch, simplification, and competitiveness. We're going to have to put ourselves forward."

And putting ourselves forward we are. At least, SLA is. And as the association takes on more of an international focus, Bender, obviously happy about these things, describes how the 1985 move to Washington has been so good for SLA and its membership, as they seek to establish their place in the global information arena.

"For example," he says, "in the next few days, eight staff members are involved in a number of meetings with other organizations about the information picture in Latin America. What we're doing is trying to figure out how SLA can participate, as that enormous information market comes alive. In a similar vein, I'm off next week to an invitational meeting at the State Depart-

ment, to talk with the diplomatic community about information matters relating to Latin America."

Obviously the international emphasis is enhancing SLA's position in the information community at large.

"Absolutely," Bender says, without missing a beat. "And it goes on and on. President Piggott and I go in mid-May to Moscow, for we've been invited to participate in a project working with the parliamentary librarians. Jonathan Halperin, who operates a company with offices in both Moscow and Washington, is bringing us in to work with the Parliament of the Russian Republic as it attempts to organize its library/information work. What this means, of course, is that SLA will be positioned to develop some sort of Moscow entity, a "group" we're calling it, that can connect the local Moscow information community and SLA. I won't go so far to predict that there will soon be a Moscow chapter of SLA, because such an organizational focus may not be appropriate at this time in Russia. But I also won't stay that it won't ultimately lead to a Russian Chapter, because it just might. Certainly this project, with both of us participating, is a foot in the door for SLA."

It sounds like a major step forward, and certainly it's an unusual step for an information services association.

"Well, it's a step forward, all right," Bender laughs. "Wish me luck."

So Bender and his staff are working hard to look at what services can be accessed virtually, figuring out what information is to go on the website, loading it, making it secure, figuring out how to implement payment activities via the 'Net, etc. It's all the kind of thing that makes running SLA so invigorating for Bender, and it's the kind of innovative leadership that has endeared him to his many friends and supporters in the association.

Obviously, as any Chief Executive Officer can attest, such innovative activities are not always so popular, or so approved of. For example, Bender will sometimes have to remind the enthusiastic member who doesn't understand the complexities of running a $6 million, 40-member staff operation that other people and other programs could be impacted by a well-intentioned but perhaps not well-thought-out idea. It's the sort of thing that happens in any organization or any enterprise, and for the most part, Bender weathers such little blips on the management screen well. Nevertheless, it's things like moving the organization into positioning itself as a virtual association, that kind of innovative leadership, that makes Bender popular, and helps to keep him in his job.

There are, of course, problems with any grand design, and creating the virtual association for SLA is no exception: at the present time, only 83% of SLA's members can access a virtual information site, and some hard decision making is going to have to take place. The obvious answer, of course, is to provide the information in two formats, both virtually and in hard copy, but upon examination, as Bender has to reluctantly point out to some of his well-meaning advisors, some items are too expensive in both formats. The association's directory, for example, can be printed and provided as a free benefit of membership because, at present, it can be printed in such large quantities. Reduce that print run to 2,000 copies, and it's far too expensive to be a free benefit of membership.

"What it means," Bender says, "is that by developing a virtual association, you are putting SLA in a power position. And that's all well and good, and it will make a lot of people feel very proud and, yes, new members will be drawn to SLA because it will be powerful. But that also means you have to give some thought to another important consideration: not just having the power, but determining how you use the power. SLA has always been seen as a leadership organization. Going with the virtual organization emphasizes that, enhances and strengthens that, especially in terms of the international membership. Now, as an organization, you can deliver services to the same degree as if you're next door, and if SLA is a virtual association, you can be sure that the international, especially the non-North American membership, will go well beyond it's present 8–10% of the membership. So as a virtual organization, we'll be able to do much, much more than we can do now, but we must be careful, we must go gently, to ensure that the things we are doing are the right things to do for the future of information services and special librarianship."

So information delivery in the future is going to be international, and it's going to take advantage of the enabling technology. Anything else?

Bender is having a good time with this, and the grin on his face tells you this is a subject he's been thinking a lot about, and he's just been waiting to be asked.

"It's going to be focused on the customer," he says. "Of course, we try to focus on the customer now. In fact, we always have, but we haven't always succeeded. Now we'll succeed. Do you know why?

"Think about who we are," Bender says. "Think about the classic definition of the special librarian, the one we all learned years ago, that the special librarian is the person who manages a special collection for special clientele with a special need. And do you remember how, in special libraries, we led the way in moving from offering information services that were 'just-in-case' information services, when we tried to acquire and shelve everything we could get our hands on, so we would have it 'just in case' someone asked for it?"

Of course we remember. It's what librarianship was all about for many generations. Bender knows that, too, and he continues. He's on a roll now, and the story is getting good.

"Then we went forward with something we're all very proud of, the now-famous 'just-in-time' information delivery, in which we special librarians became information consultants and information explorers, listening to the clients describe what they needed, and then providing it 'just in time.'

He stops speaking for a moment, just a moment, just enough time for the emphasis to be made.

"Well, we're moving even further ahead now, and that's where I think we're going to be as we begin the 21st century. We're always listening to the information customers, of course, and hearing what they need, but now in addition to mediating and consulting, we're analyzing, and interpreting, and customizing, and providing information that I like to describe as 'just-for-you.' It's a powerful, very powerful paradigm that we're dealing with here, and that, in a nutshell, is the history (so far!) of special librarianship. We've gone from 'just-in-case' to 'just-in-time' to 'just-for-you'."

"It's all part of knowledge management, that important new discipline we're moving to, and it's something we have to do. So if there are any problems with what we do at SLA—and there are problems, as I've indicated—one of the most difficult ones, one of our most serious challenges is how we can serve the true knowledge managers, how we can make them feel part of the inside of our profession, and make them need us and want us. I think when we move to the customized information delivery we're talking about here, information delivery that is borderless and totally format independent, we'll be able to work with the knowledge management people as well. And we want to do that.

"We're doing it, quite frankly, because that's the way society is going. We don't have any choice. The information professions—librarianship, special librarianship, all of the information delivery fields—are changing so fast and moving so rapidly that if we don't develop the 'just-for-you' approach to information delivery, I'm afraid we will lose our place in the information environment. And at SLA we're not going to let that happen."

Indeed not.

With David Bender at the helm, SLA's 15,000-plus members and the international information community are well on their way to achieving, in the 21st century, that stated-but-often-elusive goal that Dr. Lapp came up with 81 years ago. The world's special librarians, working with the Special Libraries Association, are truly, finally, putting knowledge to work.

Meet David Bender

David R. Bender, Ph.D., is Executive Director, Special Libraries Association. Appointed to the position in 1979, Bender was instrumental in SLA's move from New York to Washington in 1985, and he has continued his leadership/management role for the 15,000-member professional organization, particularly in moving the association toward an international focus. Related to this, Bender serves as SLA's Alternate Delegate to the International Federation of Library Association (IFLA), and he currently is Chair of IFLA's Round Table for the Management of Library Associations.

Bender is a prolific writer, having written scores of articles for leading library publications and authored and co-authored several books. Among the most important of his writings is the seminal work, "Transborder Data Flow: An Historical Review and Consideration for the Future," which identified and emphasized trends relating to the management of international information. Published in *Special Libraries* in 1988, the article won for Bender the prestigious H.W. Wilson Company Award in 1989.

David Bender's personal interests include reading and travel (which is a good thing, for his work takes him away from his home approximately half the time). At his home, Bender can be found in his kitchen, as he is a gourmet chef, having during his sabbatical from SLA in 1988 studied successfully at the famous La Grange Cooking School near Bath, England. Bender makes his home in Washington, DC.

MONICA ERTEL
at Apple's Advanced Technology Group: Building the infrastructure
for an information-intense world . . . . and enjoying it

In a conversation with Monica Ertel, it doesn't take long for the message to come through: she likes working for Apple, she's excited about the future of information services, and she's very comfortable with the role that libraries and librarianship are playing now, and will continue to play in the delivery of information in the future.

"I started the Apple library from scratch," she says, and there's a touch of pride in her voice, for this was an idea that was a good one from the start. "There was no library, and for me it was a dream job: Apple wanted to build

Originally published in *InfoManage : The International Management Newsletter for the Information Services Professional* 4 (11), September, 1997.

a modern, state-of-the-art computerized library, and it sounded good to me. There was only one problem: I had never touched a computer!"

Working at Memorex at the time (this was 1981), Ertel was managing both the company's business library and its technical library, supervising a combined staff of four.

And if you think about that date, the fact that she was managing a library operation without computers is not so surprising after all. These were the "early days," and Steven Jobs had only introduced the Apple II just four years before, in 1977. And although all sorts of other products and technologies were being developed (IBM would bring its PC to market in 1981), the adoption of the personal computer as a ubiquitous business tool was still some time off.

Nevertheless, Monica Ertel knew a good thing when she saw it. As she began to negotiate for her new position at Apple, she identified several characteristics of this company that she liked.

For one thing, management was willing to fund the library properly. There was no embarrassment, no awkwardness about what she would be doing, and no difficult turf wars over such things as positioning, the value of information, or why the company would have a library. It was a package deal: management had decided that Apple needed a library, and she was hired to create the library the company needed. It was—for Apple and for Ertel—a classic "win-win" situation.

"On the other had, it was also a little nerve-wracking," she says with a smile. "I'm able to laugh about it now, but at the time, I had very little experience in putting together such an operation, and I have to admit I was a nervous. But I also had two very positive things going for me as I started this job, and I've always felt that our success was based on these two circumstances.

"The first was the company itself. Apple was—and continues to be (despite what you read!)—a very innovative, entrepreneurial company. People come to work for Apple because they're full of ideas, and in 1981, managers at Apple were given a pretty wide charge. It was a new company, full of bright, young employees, and they were encouraged and expected to use their brains to think of new things, to try new things. That appealed to me.

"I was given the task of setting up the company's library, and it was up to me to decide how to do it. But that's what I like about the company.

That's the way things are done: you're given a broad goal, and it is up to you to make it as large or as small as you want. We had 1,800 employees in 1981 who needed library services—we serve 10,000 now!—and I was given that as my charge, to build the library for the company, and to build it my way."

Describing the growth of her operation is a story Ertel obviously enjoys telling, and she's certainly told it before, because she knows just what her listener is thinking.

"And, yes, we did have staff meetings, and, yes, I did meet Steve Jobs, the second day I was here. He was just as you know him to be, just a little 'far out,' and that was just what I needed to see. I knew I had come to the right place."

And that right decision was reinforced later on, when John Sculley was running the company. He loved the library, Ertel says, and he even had a room in the library they all called the "John Sculley office."

"He wrote his book there," Ertel says, the book being *Odyssey: Pepsi to Apple: A Journey of Adventure, Ideas, and the Future*, Sculley's best-seller that described his ideas about business and where business is going. And as Ertel talks about Sculley's work in the library, the pride of place again comes through. "He saw the library as part of the special culture," she says. "It was. And it is."

And that second circumstance, that second reason why she knew she could create Apple's library?

"This profession we're in," she says. Without missing a beat, Monica Ertel makes it clear that being a librarian and working with librarians is one of the reasons she has been successful at Apple.

"Librarianship is a sharing profession," she says. "At first, I didn't know what I was going to be doing at Apple. I knew of course what a library was, and I had been running the two libraries at Memorex, but the idea of creating a new, modern scientific information resource was not something I had done before. But I shouldn't have been worried, for everyone I approached wanted to help. For example, I sent out a flyer to CLASS, the Cooperative Library Agency for Systems and Services, and I got an amazing response, with all kinds of good ideas and suggestions. The same thing happened when I put a notice in *InfoWorld*, and when I sent a letter to *American Libraries*."

Based on her own good experiences, Ertel realized that other librarians might be willing to share their expertise. So in 1983 she started the Apple Library Users Group (ALUG), one of the activities Ertel is most proud of.

And what is ALUG?

"It's a forum," she says, "a forum for librarians, media specialists, and other information professionals to share information with one another about how they use Apple technology. The group now has about 10,000 members, and it's very international, with members from all around the world. The common bond of all of these members is that they all work in libraries and they all use Apple computers. And they all like to share. I've never had to solicit articles for the ALUG newsletters."

Another program which Ertel established is the Apple Library of Tomorrow Program (ALOT), begun in 1988 to make hardware and software grants for innovative research and demonstration projects in all types of libraries (and some museums). And although she was originally involved in the organization of ALOT, she credits Steve Cisler with being "the guiding light" behind the enterprise, for he had joined Apple that year and began working with Ertel to focus on using existing and new technologies to integrate and expand library activities within communities.

By 1985, Monica Ertel had built the staff of the Apple library and the department was now clearly functioning as a successful management operation. It was also a time when Ertel felt she could use her talents and skills in a broader arena within Apple, so when the opportunity came along, Monica made a move, to her present position as Director of Technology Operations in Apple's Advanced Technology Group. The Library is still her responsibility, but she herself does not manage the library (that's the responsibility of Rosanne Maak, Manager, Library Operations). Ertel's current role is a broader one, just as the Advanced Technology Group's role is a broad one within the company at large (see sidebar on page 428).

When asked recently to describe her own research interests and activities (for her webpage at the Apple site), Ertel was able to successfully pull together her own ideas about information management and how they fit into her work at ATG.

"I recently read an article in which the author said that the information nirvana had become the information purgatory. He described the Internet as Gutenberg on steroids, spawning millions of pages of new content a year, much of it of uncertain lineage and some of it of dubious quality.

"I also read a recent study conducted by Reuters Business Information which had the headline 'Business People Suffering Information Indigestion,' in which business managers and senior executives said that information overload had actually affected their health and job satisfaction. This study, called 'Dying for Information,' stated that having too much information was as bad as not having enough.

"My current work interests are in the area of information technology and management. I, too, believe that we are currently in the age of over-information. My goal is to get to an information age where information will serve us and we won't be abused by an excessive amount of it.

"The goal of Apple Technology Operations is to help people live in and make sense of an information intense world. Simply put, our mission is to offer the services and infrastructure needed to turn information into knowledge.

"We do this by providing access to the world's body of published information via the Apple library using networked resources such as the Internet as well as traditional materials such as books; through actively encouraging Apple's work with universities and other research institutions; through the critical evaluation of external research opportunities and services; through providing external access to some of Apple's technological innovations; through participation in the major standards organizations and consortia; through offering advanced network design and computing services; and through offering services to help people turn all of this information into something meaningful for their lives."

Yet such noble aspirations, as Monica Ertel is the first to admit, must be coupled with the practical, day-to-day requirements for managing an information-related operation within a company that has for several years now been forced to evaluate (and re-evaluate) its operations. Apple is too important a company—and its products are too important to the information society—to be allowed to founder, as the recent attention to the Microsoft/Apple alliance demonstrates. With that agreement, as *The New York Times* stated so vividly when the story first broke, virtually every major computer hardware and software company (even companies that are competitors themselves) has now been placed firmly in the Apple camp. In fact, the entire information industry—including libraries and other information operations that make up what we call "information services"—want to see (and have a vested interest in seeing) information delivery move to that good state where the 'services and infrastructure needed to turn information into knowledge' that Monica Ertel talks about become a reality.

To get there, though, to reach that stage in information delivery that for some people is almost an idealistic goal, requires hard decision making at different levels. And with all its fine expectations, Apple, just like all the other players in the ever-expanding, ever-competitive information industry, must from time to time take a hard look at what it's doing and, if necessary, make serious cuts in spending at the corporate level.

Apple's Advanced Technology Group

*T*he mission of Apple Computer's Advanced Technology Group is to oversee the development of concept products and core technologies to be incorporated into future Apple products.

The Apple Technology Group's vision is to "enhance people's lives by developing systems that provide a rich environment for work and play, learning, and business. The emphases are on social interaction and access to knowledge through systems of hardware, software, networks, services, and content. The work is customer-centered, aimed at developing simple, smart, system-oriented, cohesive designs. ATG develops the technologies for the next generation of products that are sensitive to the special needs and capabilities of our customers who live in a rich variety of cultures around the world."

ATG's goal is to create a working environment that is:

- Creative

- Exciting

- Intellectually deep, challenging, and stimulating

- Relevant to Apple (as in "pushing the product boundaries")

We live in the future, the better to invent it. At ATG, this is done through rapid prototyping, deployment, and evaluation of systems to Apple staff and to target customers. Above all, ATG intends to create systems that:

- Are multicultural

- Are information-rich

- Span the range of devices from minimum to maximum
  —from the least expensive to the most imaginative

- Establish a new economic model for business

- Are engaging, seductive, addictive, fun

One of those times came for Ertel last spring, when Apple's management determined that several thousand positions would have to be eliminated, in order to keep Apple in the picture.

"It was a tough time," Ertel recalls, "for we were required to drastically reduce expenses. And, as in so many other companies, questions were being asked about the need for library services. 'Why should there be a library?' we were asked. 'Especially when we have the Internet?' It's happened to all of us, and it'll happen over and over again, but that doesn't mean it makes it any easier when the questions are asked.

"So the first thing I had to do was to get very proactive. I had to send information to senior management about why the Internet isn't enough, why it can't replace having content specialists, information advisors, information counselors on staff to work with the Apple staff as they seek information products. They just can't do it alone, and the library staff has to be there to help them.

"At first management simply wanted to cut out all Apple libraries, simply stating that 'There will be no more libraries.' As it turned out, we were able to get that thinking changed, and in the end, we were able to save the library, but it is a much reduced one. We had to cut six positions, reducing the library staff from 13 to 7 people, and we had to be strategic about it, so we took a look at the services we offered and came up with three options, in which we would cut services by 10%, 25%, or 50% respectively."

As it turned out, the Library Manager and Ertel are good friends, as well as being good professional colleagues, so they tackled the problem together, ultimately deciding that the best approach to dealing with the situation was simply to redesign the service.

"This was the core of the matter," Ertel says. "It was an opportunity to redesign what we had been doing and we decided to see it as such. So instead of thinking about how we were going to get along with fewer people, we took the approach that we were starting a new library, that the library would be given seven people and a certain amount of money, and that there wouldn't be an opportunity to get bigger. In that situation, what services would we offer? What would we do and what wouldn't we do?

"In our case, we decided that seven is a good number, and we decided to concentrate on the 'public service' jobs and, particularly, those jobs that brought us visibility and attention. We eliminated behind-the-scenes work: technical services, acquisition, checking in serials, and so forth. Unfortunately, these kinds of activities were not as valued by our users or by the organization as our more external activities. And if they were necessary, they could be outsourced. We outsource everything that can be outsourced, and that leaves us with a staff of information specialists, reference librarians, who are there to work with the information customers and to serve as information advisors as well as information providers. It's a system that's working, and we think we're going to succeed with it."

One of the reasons it works, Ertel quickly notes, is that once again the willingness of librarians to share information and ideas has been confirmed.

"We rely on the community of librarians, listservs, organizations. It all comes into play. I'm active both in the Information Futures Institute and in ITIMG, the Industrial Technical Information Managers Group. Not too long ago, I needed something in a hurry, a ratio about salary vs. operations. I had to have this information within four hours, and I went to my colleagues. I got tons of stuff! I think in this day and age that's just the way we do business, if we're in the information business. It just makes good sense. And it makes good sense from a management point of view as well."

So Monica Ertel is doing pretty well at Apple, and Apple is doing pretty well by her. If she has any unfulfilled ambitions at this point, she would like to see the library doing more analytical work.

"At the present time," she says, "we're in the midst of redesigning library services at Apple. It's challenging, not as easy as we thought, and often frustrating. But it's also very exciting and even fun!"

And that, when we think about it and about what Apple has brought to the international information services arena, is what Apple has come to stand for. It's comforting—and of course highly appropriate—that Apple's library management is on this track, for it's a management scenario that many information services managers would strive for, and try to put in place in their own shops: an information services operation that is challenging, that makes us stretch, and one which is, yes, sometimes frustrating. And it is also an information delivery facility that is, in the final analysis, one that is always exciting and fun. What an adventure!

Meet Monica Ertel

At the time of this interview, Monica Ertel was Director, Technology Operations, at Apple Computer's Advanced Technology Group, and is currently also the acting vice-president of ATG. Her undergraduate degree, a B.A. in Social Science, is from San Jose State University, as is her M.A., from San Jose's School of Library and Information Science. Her M.B.A. is from the University of Santa Clara.

Ertel is a member of the Information Futures Institute and, with her interest in international librarianship, of the International Federation of Library Associations (IFLA) as well. She is also an active member of the Special Libraries Association, currently serving a second term on SLA's Board of Directors. She was named a Fellow of SLA in 1996.

A prolific author, Ertel has written for most of the important professional journals in her field, and she edited, with Edward Valauskas, a popular book on information delivery for educators (*The Internet for Teachers and School Library Media Specialists: Today's Applications, Tomorrow's Prospects*), published by Neal Schuman in 1996.

As for her personal life, "My non-work time," as she puts it, "is taken up by my role as car owner and crew chief for a SpecRacer race car. I determine pit stop timing, car preparation, timing and scoring, and driver coaching. My husband John is the driver. If you're interested in coming to a local SCCA race, just let me know." And her interest in writing flows over into her personal life, for two of Ertel's poems, inspired by her participation in the 1995 United Nations Women's Conference in Beijing, China, have been published. "City of Women" and "Tiananmen Square" were included in the anthology, *Seeing the World Through Women's Eyes*, edited by Naima Richmond and Marilyn M. Cuneo and published by the Women's International League for Peace and Freedom in 1996.

ROBERT NAWROCKI
is ARMA International's president and
he's sounding a wake-up call for records managers

Chicago is one of America's most beautiful cities, and on those gorgeous cloudless late-autumn days, there are few places one would rather be. But despite the temptation to drift outdoors and savor the joys of October, few of the 2,000 delegates at the ARMA International Conference were willing to miss the Opening General Session. They had heard that the program planned by President Robert F. Nawrocki would not be the usual rousing, motivational, "let's-feel-good-about-ourselves" Opening Session. For this program, Nawrocki and the speakers he brought in were going to, as he puts it, "wake 'em up."

And wake 'em up he did. From the moment the delegates entered the hall with lively and rousing musical selections playing in the background, until the end of the session two hours later, these records managers were challenged, stimulated, threatened, and, yes, even provided with some positive "motivational" attention as well. And after two hours, they were ready to go back to work with a new and (for them) drastically realistic understanding of what they are going to be expected to accomplish in the next couple of generations.

From Nawrocki himself, conference attendees were asked to think about how the many factors impacting the records and information management profession (generally acronymned, these days, as RIM) would affect their work as they move into the 21st-century. And from the "power panel" that he had put together to talk about "The Future of Information Management," Nawrocki elicited just enough solid common sense and careful predictions to encourage the audience to participate in "the new information management profession."

Originally published in *InfoManage : The International Management Newsletter for the Information Services Professional* 5 (2), January, 1998,

It was all done, Nawrocki says, because he really did want to provide a "wake-up call" to the RIM profession.

"The members of ARMA need a wake-up call," he says. "There are changes going on in our profession—important changes—and they are changes that will affect each and every one of us. We need to begin realizing that if we don't change our profession, the way we work as RIM practitioners, others will change it for us."

And as Nawrocki sees it, connected to that idea is a more important matter, one that is being spoken about in the other information professions as well:

"The various information professions are moving towards convergence," he observes, "to an integrated information structure. The old rules about managing information by format or origin are fast disappearing, and we're going to be working by different, new rules. We're going to be asked to do things differently, to change. Take, for example, the book on core competencies that was published recently by the Special Libraries Association—it never mentions the words book, or serial. It talks about 'managing information.' This is a new way of looking at specialist librarianship, and at records management as well."

Nawrocki began to formulate his ideas about how the records management field would participate in the convergence of information disciplines while he was doing his graduate studies in library management, recently completed at The Catholic University of America in Washington, DC.

"As a student," he says, "I had the opportunity to read about other professions, and of course having worked for almost twenty years as a records manager, I had a strong sense of what was going on in the RIM field. And it occurred to me that I was in fact very lucky, for most records managers don't have the opportunity to read widely outside their profession. But I did. As a result, once I was elected President of ARMA, I felt it was imperative for me that I provide the membership with that 'wake-up call' we're all giving so much attention to. And that's why I wanted this program as our Opening General Session at the conference. I wanted the members of ARMA to hear what is going on in the information services field. And I wanted them to hear it from others."

That Nawrocki touch was in keeping with the general theme of the ARMA International Conference, "Getting Connected." For Nawrocki, though, getting connected—in this sense—is not an issue that's limited to RIM practitioners. There has to be connection all the way across the spectrum, connections among librarians, archivists, MIS staff, telecommunications people, presentation staff, and anybody else who is involved in the delivery of information.

"Of course," Nawrocki says, smiling at his visitor's naïveté. "Let's get real here. Most information professionals don't have time to stay current in their own field, much less read about other professions. We tend to be concerned about our own profession or field to the exclusion of others. The reality, though, is that as the information professions converge, each of the information services fields will have a profound effect upon the others. Just as massive clouds of space dust collide and coalesce to form new stars, so will the information services fields bump up against each other. Where those individual fields happen to intersect, they will in effect be creating our new information management profession."

Convergence doesn't come without its price, of course, and Nawrocki is keenly aware of the pressures that this kind of change puts on all information services workers, including RIM professionals.

"Indeed," he says, "unless RIM professionals have an understanding about the core competencies of the other professions, and draw upon those that apply to records and information management, the records management field will be at a competitive disadvantage. And the same can be said about the other information fields: librarianship, archives management, and so forth."

For information services managers working in the integrated information environment, Nawrocki has, in fact, been able to identify the specific areas that they need to be aware of, and in a recent presentation for a private client, he demonstrated considerable success in listing them [see sidebar on next page].

"These are the basics," he says. "When we information professionals have mastered these, we're ready to take on the integration of information. In my opinion, that's where we need to go, in the information services professions, where we need to be, and that's what I mean when I say we must be connected."

During his twenty years in records management, Bob Nawrocki has made it something of a habit to watch what's going on (which isn't surprising, when you realize that he is president of a professional organization as forceful and as influential as ARMA International). And

Integrated Information Management (IIM): Bob Nawrocki's Guidelines

*T*he professional with responsibility for integrated information management must know and be able to apply:

1. the principles of organization

2. the principles of indexing and abstracting

3. the use of computers as an information management tool (not just as a word processor or number cruncher)

4. a sound understanding of the organization one works for (and its purpose)

5. a knowledge of telecommunications (for example, the difference between a T1 line and a T3 line, or how much bandwidth is required to transfer images across a network)

6. how information is valued—from an historical standpoint and from an informational standpoint

for Nawrocki, two of the trends he's identified are of critical importance to the future of information delivery, the more important being (again to no one's surprise) electronic records management.

"There are two issues to this move toward the electronic management of records," Nawrocki says. "The first deals with a lack of corporate understanding of what records are, with understanding that records are not media specific. Organizational managers tend to view electronic records as non-records, and the fact that electronic storage is becoming cheaper does not help. In fact, it is something of a common response, when people are asked if they have any records, for them to say no. They don't have any records, at least to their knowledge, even though their 3-gigabyte hard drive is full and they have several hundred diskettes. What they don't have are any paper records, and that's what they think they're being asked about. It's remarkable how many executives who should know don't know what a record is. And of course a good number of lawyers make their living conducting electronic discovery of information.

"The second issue related to electronic records management deals with the fact that there are a number of information organizations working independently in developing methodologies for managing electronic records. There's still a great lack of coordination, and that has to change. These groups have to work together to insure that electronic records are effectively managed both in government and private industry. Until that happens, the whole subject of electronic records management is going to continue to be in flux."

Outsourcing is the other important trend Nawrocki sees influencing how information delivery is changing, and for RIM practitioners, the issues connected with outsourcing are remarkably similar to those being dealt with in specialist libraries, archives departments, and other organizational units with information delivery responsibility.

For Nawrocki, and indeed for most practitioners in the RIM field, the issues connected to the outsourcing controversy are broader and, perhaps, more personal than they are professional. For RIM practitioners (and for other frontline information staff), to have basic tasks outsourced leaves the employee wondering about what his or her work is going to entail. Nawrocki has advice for those workers:

"If you look at the traditional aspects of records management, records storage, media conversion, and even schedule development, they are highly vulnerable to outsourcing, but that does not necessarily have to be a bad thing. In fact, it's something RIM professionals can exploit. Too often records and information managers use soft money and fear to justify their positions. By extrapolating from the number of boxes in storage how many file cabinets, how much space, and how many people are needed to manage them in an office, a sizable saving can be demonstrated. But it is soft money, because you can never prove that those funds would have been expended, and the saving never shows up in the organization's bottom line. And the fear comes into play when we scare our bosses with the threat of litigation. It's often used to justify an RIM position, with the well-known stories of large companies being penalized due to poor record-keeping practices being trotted out as justification for maintaining and continuing the record-keeping programs. The reality is that many organizations will never be sued, and that a large fine will never be assessed against them.

"But RIM can survive and advance as a profession, if we look at such issues as outsourcing from another perspective, and if we are willing to show how our functions add hard value to the organizational bottom line. We do it by learning how to manage the information contained in the box, rather than the box itself. And as RIM professionals, if we're smart, we'll look at outsourcing before it becomes an issue. We'll evaluate our skills and our knowledge and we'll think about what we could do with them if we were no longer burdened by the routine tasks. This may mean, in fact, that we are the ones who put forward the suggestion of outsourcing our records center, preparing the cost comparisons, doing the analysis, and determining if outsourcing is a viable management option for the organization. Of course such an approach involves significant risk, and each of us has to determine whether or not we want to take this kind of risk. But the end result is pretty significant, for in today's organizational environment—whatever the organization—outsourcing is always a possibility. It will be raised in almost every situation in the organization, in every department, and with respect to our information units, whether it be as RIM professionals, managers of specialist libraries, archives unit heads, MIS staff, or whatever, we have to recognize that the issue of outsourcing will be brought up at some point. The question then becomes: do I want to be in control of my fate, or do I want to have someone else in control?"

This is important, and Nawrocki pauses in his comments just long enough to let his listener know that he's thought long and hard about these things, and it doesn't matter whether he's talking about outsourcing, or electronic records management, or any of the many other issues that affect RIM these days. Whatever the situation, the implications for information professionals are much larger than the specific issues being debated.

"If we are passive," he says, "and continue on without thinking about these things, someone else will write our story for us. We can't let that happen. We must be proactive in our careers, in every aspect of our work as RIM practitioners, or whatever other form in information delivery we have management responsibility for. We must been seen as the information leaders in our organizations, and not as passive followers. And in the final analysis, it isn't really very complicated. The question I ask when a subject such as outsourcing comes up is this: do you want to be known as the person called when people don't know what to do with their old records, or do you want to be known as the person who added a significant positive financial position to the organization's bottom line, because you were able to unlock the information that you are responsible for?"

It's this kind of thinking, of course, that makes Bob Nawrocki such a strong proponent of integrated information management. He came to the concept quite naturally, for having worked for so many years as an RIM practitioner, there seemed to be a certain logic in concluding that the basic principles for successful information delivery in records and information management would apply in other information-related fields as well. And Nawrocki is not shy about talking about how his thinking was influenced in this direction.

"First of all," he says, "I've had a pretty broad-based career. I've worked as a records manager, as a librarian, and as an archivist. I've worked in law firms, with state and federal government agencies, and in private industry. I feel that this broad 'spread' has given me a unique perspective on the information services field and how it is changing. And in my studies, Ken Megill—formerly at The Catholic University of America and now in private business—had a strong influence on my thinking. Ken has a way of thinking outside the box, and it's a style, an influence, that stimulates other ideas. Likewise, the writings of Tom Davenport, Watts Wacker, and Thomas E. Steward have also had a major influence on my thinking.

"But regardless of the influences, the point I am trying to make when I discuss IIM (and which I hope I'll be making in a book in the not-too-distant future) is that the future is wide open right now. RIM professionals have to begin thinking about the future and how it will affect them. RIM professionals have to be part of the dialogue, and earn (and take) their place at the table, and integrated information management gives them the opportunity to do that."

There are, of course, those who would suggest, despite the advantages being promulgated about IIM and its value to organizational success, that what is being proposed is a move backward, to a more "generalist" information delivery position, to a situation where the person with information management responsibility has to be something of a "jack-of-all-trades" as far as information is concerned.

"In some respects that might be true," Nawrocki says. "And I suppose to some extent I am proposing something of a generalist position. But that's not the total picture, for as I see it the leaders of information management in the future will be the ones who put the systems together (and when I speak about 'systems,' I'm not talking about hardware). But these leaders will rely on specialists to do what has to be done, so there will always be a place for the librarian, or the records manager, or the archives manager, at least during the long transition period. A good analogy, in fact, comes from the library world itself. At one point, as all librarians know, all librarians did original cataloging. Now those librarians have one tool, OCLC, to handle the routine material and a cataloger to deal with original cataloging when it's required, but today's cataloger has other tasks and other responsibilities and only catalogs when necessary, and cataloging is not a primary competency for that job.

"That is how I see librarians, records managers, and other information-delivery professionals in the future. They will all be available to handle certain specialized tasks that aren't handled through expert systems or by the integrated information manager, but it will be the IIM professionals who will be developing, creating, testing, and implementing the new information future. They'll be multi-disciplinary, these IIM professionals, but they will require specialists to carry out the day-to-day activities. And as the processes becomes more and more automated, the specialists may eventually disappear, but I won't go so far as to predict a speedy disappearance. And they won't disappear entirely—not any time soon.

For Robert Nawrocki, that is what integrated information management is all about: integrating the various information-related disciplines into a single information stream.

"It's going to happen," he says, "and when it does, those of us who understand the management of information will take our rightful place at the table. And we'll be happy to do so."

Meet Bob Nawrocki

Robert F. Nawrocki, CRM, is the President of ARMA International, the professional association of individuals interested in the field of records and information management. A native of Buffalo, NY, Nawrocki was awarded his B.A. (History) from SUNY College at Buffalo, his M.S.L.S. from Shippensburg State College, and his M.S.L.I.S. from The Catholic University of America. His archives credentials were awarded by the Ohio Historical Archives Commission, and he has been designated a Certified Records Manager by the Institute of Certified Records Managers. Nawrocki was employed as Librarian for The Historical Society of York County (Pennsylvania), and moved from that position to become State Records Manager for the New Jersey Department of Education. Following positions as Records Manager for the law firms of Simpson Thacher and Bartlett, and Morgan Lewis & Bockius, and as Supervisor, Records Management, GTE Federal Systems, Nawrocki later worked with Labat Anderson Inc. under contract for the Environmental Protection Agency. He currently works for Armstrong Data Services of Tysons Corner, VA, also on an EPA contract. Nawrocki serves as an Adjunct Professor, Metropolitan College of The Catholic University of America, teaching courses in Records Management Technology for the Central Intelligence Agency and on the CUA Washington, DC, campus. His personal interests include travelling with his wife Ginger (who is Cataloging Supervisor for the Prince William Public Library System), reading mystery novels, and working around their house in Manassas, VA.

MARTINA REICH
at Roland Berger & Partner: Here comes the new generation
of European Information Managers—they're confident,
they're experts, and they like what they are doing

What do we call them, these eager and lively information workers who are changing the face of information delivery in Europe? These people—information managers with such a high level of commitment to their work that their companies simply cannot succeed without them—can be spotted throughout Europe, and with the ascendancy of the European Union, their star has risen, too. These are information workers who have—with remarkable authority—taken their rightful role in the information marketplace.

But what name do we give them? How do we designate them? Of course we could call them "librarians." Or "specialist librarians" or "special librarians." And that wouldn't be too far off the mark, for many of them have been educated in library work. Martina Reich, for example, who heads up the library at Roland Berger & Partner in Munich and Madrid, has a classic education in librarianship, even though, like the others of this "new breed" of information workers, she long ago left behind the traditions of "traditional" librarianship.

On the other hand, many of these information enthusiasts (as we and their managements know) do much, much more than library work, or do something totally different, something completely removed from librarianship. So they can't be associated with "librarianship." Equally important, of course, is the fact that others of this group have never darkened the door of a library school, so "librarian" doesn't work.

"Information consultant" might do it. Or "information analyst" or "information coordinator." But we're still not there, because not all information professionals work as consultants, or analyze information, or

Originally published in *InfoManage : The International Management Newsletter for the Information Services Professional* 5 (5), April, 1998.

coordinate it. Coming from another perspective, though, "information specialist"—Reich's other title at RB&P—is a title that works, because specializing in information management is what these people are doing. They are, indeed, part of the new information management profession, and when they refer to themselves as "information specialists," people know what they mean.

"There are certain 'key success factors' which can be associated with a successful information specialist," Reich says, and she easily launches into a list that is not only comprehensive but which does, in fact, characterize these people who are making a major difference in the way information is being managed in the business community in Europe. As she speaks, it's easy to see how Reich herself is part of this group of information workers that is leading Europe's business information community into the new millennium.

"First of all," Reich says, "today's information specialist has extensive experience in information business and management, and understands the requirements of the industry he or she is working in. Obviously an extensive knowledge of internal company structures and contexts is a must, and know-how in designing in-house databases, experience in setting up user-oriented information systems, and practical experience working in the company's various offices—if there is more than one—are all qualities that will enable the serious information manager to be successful."

For Reich, and for those like her, these characteristics are all summed up in the phrase that has become almost a mantra for these information workers (and it's a phrase that Reich uses over and over again in conversations about her work): "A new challenge."

That's what these people want, and it's the phrase that's heard all the time in conversations, in formal presentations, in exchanges at professional meetings and conferences, and, as far as we know, in conversations with families and relatives. These people want to be challenged. They know that the challenges are there, in society, in business, and in all their other endeavors in the European community today, and they don't want to work in information management unless they are going to be challenged there as well.

When asked why there is so much enthusiasm among these workers about what they are doing, Reich is quick to respond.

"It's not hard to understand," she comments. "Probably more than anything else, it has to do with the quality of information these information professionals deliver. In fact, at RB&P, we advertise our commitment to quality, when we say to our customers that 'RB&P Information Center staff guarantee the quality of the information they deliver.' We know we can guarantee the quality because our information staff has the education and professional experience to know how to do it, and to do it well. For example, we conduct electronically-supported research. We also have knowledge about the various information channels. We have access to in-house know-how, we're in constant touch with important contacts, and we have access to national data, statistics, and contact partners. And equally important, we have our informal networking, which we couldn't get along without. As far as I'm concerned, these are the elements of high-quality information, and we have an obligation to bring these to our managements and to our organizations."

And those organizations make it very clear that this is the level of information delivery they want, a point of view that Reich and her colleagues in the information industry share.

"I'm convinced," she says, "about the advantages of having the right information, about how it's the right information—not something that comes 'close'—that enables the successful companies to achieve their success."

Roland Berger & Partner, by any measure, is one of those companies. With more than thirty offices worldwide, and 1,000+ employees, this management consultancy firm specializes in (and characterizes its efforts as) "relationship marketing," i.e., as having a long-standing cooperation with its clients. In fact, some 77% of the company's clients in 1996 have been with the company for many years. With its strong emphasis on strategy, and with its work generally limited to the top end of the consultancy market (that is, DM500,000.00+), it's not difficult to understand why information management and information delivery play such a significant role in the company's success, and why the very characteristics that make for success in the company are also required for success in its information staff.

Take this excerpt from a recent RB&P Annual Report, for example: "As a global top-management consultancy of German origin," the report says, "we still have our roots in Europe. And indeed, Europe stands for variety and complexity: every few hundred kilometers one encounters a different language, culture, legal system, currency and market structure as well as limited resources. All these aspects call for cooperation beyond the borders of countries and corporations. In the full sense of the term, European management culture thus entails an ability to master this multiplicity: not thinking in preconceived patterns and methods, but exercising sensitivity to different (corporate) cultures, flexible adjustment to the changing rules and the ability to operate globally without losing sight of regional particularities. Especially in the global competitive environment, this proves to be an advantage."

Certainly those ideas characterize the kind of work that Martina Reich does for the company. When she came to RB&P in 1992, to the company's central office in Munich, the company's library had existed for one year, and Reich's first assignment—managing the library's "InfoDesk"—was certainly an important job, and one that kept her very busy. But it was also, alas, "very routine," and for people who have the vision of information delivery that Martina Reich has ("I wanted to move beyond a 'traditional' paper-based library," she says), routine is not particularly conducive to job satisfaction.

"I wanted to change the focus of my work," she says, describing how she dealt with the need for more professional stimulation. "So I moved to being a half-time information specialist for one of the company's 'competency centers,' (the name we give to operational functions analogous to 'practice groups' in other consultancy firms). The one where I went, for the construction industry, turned out to be a real opportunity for me. Of course I continued to carry a 50% workload with the InfoDesk, but I found that working in this area, with my specialization in information management, was just what was needed. I became, for the construction industry competency center, one of those 'insourced information specialists' we're hearing about in the information industry. I found myself in a role that I liked very much, for I was now working in a consulting role, consulting both with the RB&P Information Center as a departmental specialist, and outside the department—during those hours that I worked at the InfoDesk—with the consultants and others throughout the firm."

The insourcing did not go unnoticed, and Reich found herself eventually offered a role as a consultant in the construction industry competency center, but she declined.

"It would have been a fascinating job, and probably would have been much fun, but what I like to do is marketing for the Information Center, for new colleagues, managers, emphasizing certain focuses, so I felt my best efforts were in this direction."

Needless to say, such experience is not gained without considerable support from others in the company, and Reich is quick to give credit where credit is due.

"First of all," she says, "recognize that this is a company that rewards enthusiasm and innovation. Think about it. The company had its thirtieth anniversary in November, 1997, and that's a pretty astounding fact, astounding because it happened in Germany. We Germans are not particularly known for risk-taking, for an entrepreneurial approach to management, but that's what this company does, and it's a corporate philosophy that reaches throughout the company, in all its offices. And since marketing and creating new products and services is so attractive to me, as an information professional, and since this is a company in which that kind of activity is encouraged, of course I wanted to continue working with the Information Center, bringing new ideas and new products to the entire corporate operation."

Reich also credits her manager, Felicitas Schneider, who came to RB&P from McKinsey.

"Felicitas is also one of those people who is always thinking ahead," Reich says, and the pleasure she takes in working with Schneider is obvious in her voice. "She has a vision about how good information delivery can be, and we work hard to see that the company gets its best work from us and the others who are connected with information management for the company."

All of this planning and visioning comes together at the company's Information Center at the corporate headquarters in Munich.

"We know that there is an over-supply of information in today's workplace," Reich says, and in saying so, gives vent to another of those attitudes that characterize the new information managers in the European business community. They view the information services facility (in this case, RB&P's "InfoCenter", as it's called) as a "filtering interface," and Reich sees her role, and that of the other information specialists, as one of moving all the information that is available through the InfoCenter in order to provide for their defined customer base the "precise information" they require for whatever evaluation process they're involved in. It's a pretty provocative (and exhilarating) prospect, but people like Martina Reich are undaunted and, in fact, find themselves thoroughly "charged up" by the possibility of what they can achieve as information specialists.

For Reich, the prospects and possibilities continue to play themselves out in ever-more-challenging (there's that word again—and it's exactly the one she wants to use!) situations. Marketing, of course, plays a big role in the process, and these new information workers understand the value of marketing the information services operation and what it can do for the company. But they also recognize that in addition to marketing the information products, services, and consultations they provide, it's necessary for them to market themselves. As Reich puts it, "information managers must have self-assurance, and self-assurance requires self-marketing. It's important," she says with a confident smile. "Outsiders will take notice."

This concentration on marketing, and being comfortable with these concepts, has its own rewards. In Reich's case, the marketing skills, and her expertise in training colleagues led to her being given the responsibility of building an information center for the Stuttgart office. It was successful, and in the summer of 1996, the next step (and, in her career path, an obvious one by now) came along and Reich was sent to Madrid to work with the RB&P office there. She had two months to train the then-current part-time librarian, but when she got there, Reich discovered plentiful opportunities for improved services (why are we not surprised, knowing what we know about her enthusiasm for her work?). Of course she threw herself into her work, and that particular job has now been extended through 1998.

"Of course there are challenges," she says. "And they came from both sides: For the Madrid office, management wanted to see how the organization could operate with a professional information center. For me, I wanted to see how I could operate in a totally different environment, a different culture, and so forth."

And it was a different scenario. For example, there were all sorts of questions having to do with how information technology is managed in a country so different from Germany, RB&P's "home" country. Then there were those very challenging situations having to do with offering a very open approach to information management in an environment in which, for many people, asking questions—and especially asking questions of a woman from a different country—posed an awkwardness or uncomfortable "feeling" for the people who required information.

How did she do it?

Reich laughs, for she knows the answer is so obvious.

"Marketing," she says. "Getting out into the company and taking a proactive, positive role in the company's basic functions. We prepared information packets without being asked, for example, and we identified special Spanish-language databases that no one else in the company knew about. In other words, we did what we would have done anywhere, but we just put a particularly local 'slant' on the effort."

It worked, and when asked about her successes in Madrid, Reich can list them quickly: "There have been changed attitudes," she says, "for we concentrated on the needs of the different project teams, organizing our work so that they received only the relevant material they needed. And then when they had it, we went back to them to make sure it was exactly what they required, and if it wasn't we kept at it until we found what they needed."

And that idea, in summary, is what the new European information specialists are all about: professional expertise, marketing proficiency, customer satisfaction, relevance, and excellence in information delivery. They're all qualities that information specialists like Martina Reich at Roland Berger & Partner are blessed with, and by incorporating these qualities into their work, these information workers are changing the very foundations of the information industry in Europe. Their managers couldn't be happier.

Meet Martina Reich

Martina Johanna Reich is Head of the Library and Information Specialist at Roland Berger & Partner GmbH, International Management Consultants, Munich and Madrid. Reich received her diploma in librarianship from the Fachhoch-schule für Bibliotheks und Dokumentationswesen in Köln, and her first professional position was as Head of the Library at the Wehrwissenschaftliche Dienststelle der Bundeswehr für ABC-Schutz, Munster. Other experience included managing the Library/Information Center at the GSF-Forschungs-zentrum für Umwelt und Gesundheit GmbH, München, and working as an Information Manager at Agiplan AG, Mülheim/Ruhr. She came to Roland Berger & Partner GmbH in 1992.

An active leader in the library/information services profession in Germany, Reich served from 1987 until 1992 as Chairman, Board of Management, Münchener Arbeits-kreis für Information und Dokumentation (MAID), and since 1989 has been a member of the Executive Board of Arbeitsger-meinschaft der Spezialbibliotheken e. V (ASpB). She taught at the Bayerische Beamtenfach-hochschule from 1990 to 1996, and she has produced a large number of publications and presentations in the field of librarianship and information science. At Online Information 1997, Reich's paper on competitor intelligence on the Internet was received with enthusiasm from attendees at the program's satellite event, "Environment and Chemistry on the Internet," held in London in December, 1997. For the next ASpB Conference in Dresden in February, 1999, Reich is organizing a seminar on "Knowledge Management for Special Librarians."

Reich's personal interests include walking in the mountains (she's an Alpine hiker), and since she's been in Spain, exploring the mountains around Madrid. Reich also likes her quiet time at home, and gardening on her typical Spanish balcony—this year specializing in roses—gives her much pleasure. She likes living in Madrid, right in the center of the city's famous "old" section, where she and her friends enjoy the lively lifestyle that makes Madrid so attractive to so many foreigners.

▐▌▌

Seamless information delivery is coming to
Colonial Williamsburg—and Library Director
SUSAN BERG
is doing her part

Even the world of historical research isn't immune to the massive changes taking place in information management. When you visit a place like Colonial Williamsburg, in beautiful Tidewater Virginia midway between Richmond and Norfolk, of course you're impressed with the charm and the stunning loveliness of the place (how could you not be?). And if information management or information delivery is your interest, you're going to be doubly impressed, with what's going on in historical research in general, and with how it's done at Colonial Williamsburg (they don't use http://www.history.org as their URL for nothing!).

But beyond those impressions, there's even more to think about, for Colonial Williamsburg is, in fact, a research-centric operation par excellence. While those visitors strolling the 18th-century streets and wandering in and out of the restored and reconstructed buildings might not realize it, those restorations and those reconstructions didn't just happen. They were scrupulously researched, and ever since the Colonial Williamsburg Foundation came into being in 1926—"to undertake the preservation and restoration of 18th-century Williamsburg"—research and the faithful attention to accurate detail has played a central role in the organization's success. In fact, that faithfulness to detail has now become something of an assumed value at Colonial Williamsburg, and it is now simply an accepted fact that the foundation cannot achieve its stated mission without research.

That's just fine with Susan Berg, the Director of the Colonial Williamsburg Foundation's new John D. Rockefeller Jr. Library. Opened in April, 1997 (along with two other buildings forming the "campus" of

Originally published in *InfoManage : The International Management Newsletter for the Information Services Professional* 5 (8), July, 1998.

Colonial Williamsburg's "University Without Walls"), the new library is a welcome addition to the organization's overall research operation.

"And 'welcome' is indeed the right word," Berg says, describing the move from the windowless second floor of an old telephone relay building. "The staff wanted—indeed, needed!—the move. We loved the idea of moving out of the crowded, tight spaces we were in, and of course we all loved the idea of having windows all around us."

There are windows, to be sure. With some 33,000 square feet (see pp. 450–451), the new research library is something of a marvel to the staff and many of the researchers, all of whom had become accustomed to stumbling all over one another as they attempted to accomplish their research objectives.

The new John D. Rockefeller Jr. Library is part of a three-part, 30-acre research campus, put together during the first half of the 1990s at a cost of some $37.5 million and conceived to serve as an appropriate resource for Colonial Williamsburg's research activities. Called the Bruton Heights School Education Center (so named for the historic school that had been on the original site), the three buildings offer some 170,000 square feet of space to serve a research staff of 185. In addition to the library, the campus also includes the Wallace Collections and Conservation Building, and the Bruton Heights School, now completely renovated and used as a conference center, for offices for the foundation's Research Division, and for facilities for Colonial Williamsburg Productions.

The jewel in the foundation's research crown, though, has to be the splendid Rockefeller Library. It is truly a beautiful place to visit, and even the casual visitor—with no particular research interest—will be delighted by the pleasing architectural design of the building, the comfortable flow of the sight-lines, the ease with which the various traffic patterns function, and, yes, the distinctive flavor that the library staff brings to its public offerings. As noted in a description of the library at that cleverly named website:

> The new library's distinct character becomes evident as soon as the visitor steps past the main reference desk. Where other libraries might make available recent copies of *The New York Times* and *The Wall Street Journal*, the John D. Rockefeller Jr. Library puts out facsimiles of the 18th-century monument of learning, Diderot's *Encyclopedie*.

Design for the Future

[The Spring, 1997, issue (Volume XIX, Number 3) of *Colonial Williamsburg: The Journal of the Colonial Williamsburg Foundation* is devoted to a compilation of articles about the new Bruton Heights School Education Center, which includes the John D. Rockefeller Jr. Library. In that issue, Susan Berg writes about how it all came about.]

Planning for the John D. Rockefeller Jr. Library began in 1991, when library staff conducted focus groups with [Colonial Williamsburg Foundation] employees to solicit suggestions and recommendations for a new building. Their ideas were incorporated into the preparation of the building program. Jay Lucker, former director of libraries at the Massachusetts Institute of Technology, served as a consultant. In February, 1994, the firm of Perry Dean Rogers & Partners was selected as architects.

The new building incorporates the collections of the old main library and two branches. A centerpiece of the Bruton Heights Education Center, north of Lafayette Street, the new library is a short walking distance from the Historic Area.

Its brick exterior complements the other buildings in the complex; however, its concave façade, vertical fenestration, and gently curved roof make it distinctive. Storage capacity will accommodate 15 years of collections growth, and the interior design supports plans for future expansion. An increased weight-load capacity will allow conversion from standard to compact shelving if it becomes necessary. The new library has enhanced security devices, which will include closed-circuit cameras as well as improved temperature and humidity controls.

The library, which contains 33,000 gross square feet, has four major sections on three levels: public services, containing circulation and reference collections (levels 2 and 3); audiovisual services (level 3); special collections (level 2); and technical services (level 1). A two-story central lobby provides visual access to the circulation and reference desk, the reference area, special collections, a book display, the exhibit area, a large conference room, and the book collections on level 3. Two group study rooms, one with audiovisual capabilities, allow employees to discuss their research with colleagues without disturbing others. A closed carrel room enables visiting scholars and employees working on extended projects to reserve carrels and to keep materials close at hand. A specially designed exhibit area provides space for small exhibitions showcasing library collections.

For reading there are individual carrels, a few well-placed tables and chairs, and a reading room for special collections materials. A 29-inch high counter with chairs runs along the west wall adjacent to the general book collection. The current periodicals room directly above the entrance is a particularly attractive area. With its expansive view of the plaza outside and window openings into the lobby below, it is a well-designed space containing fully upholstered chairs, where users can read in a relaxed setting.

One of the most important features of the Rockefeller Library will be its extensive connectivity. The building is fully wired

continued

Design of the Future *(continued)*

with electrical, voice, and data outlets. Users connected to the Internet will be able to send their research by file transfer protocol, or FTP, from the library to their own electronic mailboxes. Local area networks, or LANs, will permit staff and users multiple access to shared databases and multimedia CD-ROM products. In addition, the library will have optical-fiber outlets connected to a satellite dish for the receipt and transmittal of broadcast images.

These physical features and electronic connectivity provide the structure and support for what is most important about the building, the materials it houses. The library contains several collections concentrating on the history, architecture, archaeology, and decorative arts of the Chesapeake and of British North America.

Among the thousands of books, manuscripts, drawings, prints, and reels of microfilm, some unusual items stand out:

George Washington's journal, one of eight copies known to exist; Patrick Henry's original manuscript of his resolves against the Stamp Act of 1765, the colony's first protest against the power of Great Britain; and 18th-century Williamsburg imprints, public acts, political pamphlets, histories, religious tracts, newspapers, playbills, broadsides—even a cookbook.

The books and documents are supplemented by personal libraries from 18th-century Williamsburg families. In the architectural research collection, 50,000 drawings and several thousand photographs document the single largest historic preservation movement in the United States, the restoration of Williamsburg. These collections are available to anyone who uses the library: Foundation employees, scholars and museum professionals, students and faculty from the College of William and Mary, community residents, and visitors to Colonial Williamsburg."

And why not? It's what the library's users want to see, and such a gesture to the library's public doesn't seem to be so odd, after you've spent some time with Berg.

"We're an unusual hybrid," she says. "We're a research library that welcomes the public. Our primary mission is, of course, to serve Colonial Williamsburg's staff and visiting scholars. But we also provide an important resource for the faculty and students of the College of William and Mary, and we have been receiving more than 8,000 visits a year from the general public—even though we've been virtually invisible! With the opening of the Bruton Heights School Education Center, we are finally on the map, serving all of these constituencies more efficiently and actively than ever before."

And those constituencies include colleagues around the world who need to avail themselves of the resources available only at Colonial Williamsburg.

"Now," Berg says (and you can hear the pride in her voice as she speaks), "the library's materials are more accessible, through publications, through online catalogs, and through an expanded program of inter-library loans. In fact, since 1985, the library's exchanges with other institutions have jumped by more than 600 percent, and with the opening of the Education Center, the demand is certain to increase. We look forward to it."

How much of that demand will be met electronically is impossible to predict, but certainly, at the end of the twentieth century, the availability of those enabling technologies we hear so much about is going to influence how the Rockefeller Library meets those challenges.

And there's no question but that the technology link was a critical consideration as the Rockefeller Library was planned.

"The role of the virtual library was always kept in focus while we were putting this together," Berg says. "But whether the new library will become a 'true' virtual library remains to be seen, simply because the term 'virtual library' means different things to different people, and we have to recognize that. For one thing, in a setting like ours, a virtual library isn't created just for the external audience, the community's audience. For us, we want to bring the benefits of virtual research to the library's core users as well. The internal staff, the researchers, scientists, and curatorial staff at the Colonial Williamsburg Foundation can't always work at (library) staff hours, so having a virtual library permits these people to be able to use the library even when it is not physically accessible. And moving toward a virtual library makes a certain kind of sense in this environment, as there are some 300 OPACs located throughout the Colonial Williamsburg Foundation."

That role of providing the information the researchers need, as seamlessly as possible, is a driving force with Susan Berg as she organizes the services that the Rockefeller Library provides, and will provide in the future:

"Of course," she says. "In many ways, however we define it, improving access to the collections has to be the next step, and providing a virtual library will be one of the keys. I feel very strongly about the researcher who wants to improve performance, the craftsperson. These people—like executives in the business world— don't have a great deal of time for research, and if we can help them move the process along, I think we should do so. If that means we can provide them with what they need electronically, at a terminal located at a remote site and at hours when the library facility itself is not available, we simply have to do it. And it's our responsibility to try to figure out how to do it."

Figuring it out isn't always as easy or as direct as it seems, as Susan Berg will tell you. As early as the mid-1980s, it was clear that the particular configuration of research activities at Colonial Williamsburg—spread out over the 125-acre historic site—needed some sort of consolidation, and even the traditional library materials, housed as they were in so many different offices and studios and various work environments, needed to be brought together, to be centralized. That effort was begun in 1985, when the library had been moved into the space it was in before the new facility was built. Of course there was some resistance, as various departments wanted "their" research materials kept in a conveniently near-by (or onsite) location, but eventually most ("but not all," Berg says with a grin) of the departments began to see the wisdom of shared resources and a centralized management operation for the library.

By 1991, a white paper recommending a new library building had been written and distributed, and goals and standards—envisioning a consolidated library—were identified. Focus groups were held ("What would you like to see in the new building?" they were asked), and after much study, a master plan was prepared. Called "The Once and Future Library," the plan codified the library's goals for service, staff, collections, and so forth, and by 1994, it was time to hire the architects. The work started, and after a three-month shutdown for the move, the library was opened in the spring of 1997.

"Yes, it was important for us to be closed for three months," Berg says. "because in addition to organizing the move, I felt we had to get to know the building. So some us went to work there before the collections were moved in, to test the heating, the ventilation, air conditioning, that sort of thing. And, equally important, to my way of thinking, as a staff we had to work together. It was very important to me to work with the staff, to bring them along and to encourage them to support all these changes that were going to be taking place. All of this activity, the whole project—the planning, the construction, the move—was enormously complicated and involved all of us. In fact the project —as happens with any project of this size—eventually had taken on a life of its own, and we found ourselves referring to this experience as 'the five-year leech,' since it was draining off so much of our energies. Fortunately, though, it was finite. It would definitely come to an end, and we were able to 'end-run' some of the problems that come up in a large library move. For example, we didn't have to put things in storage, and we were able to move into the building and work with our collections onsite, rather than moving twice (which would have been awful!).

"And we did get some help," Berg continues, "for we realized early on that we were going to need some training, particularly in getting us all ready for the move. So we had a workshop on change management, but in putting together the workshop, we found to our great delight that there really wasn't that much resistance to change, in the general understanding of that term. But by having the workshop, we were able to lower the anxiety level about the move, and that was good for all of us.

Were there glitches? Did anything go wrong?

Berg smiles, and you know she's been waiting for you to ask the question.

"Well," she says, "there was one, and it turned out to be a rather consequential problem we hadn't foreseen, and it caused additional stress. It was primarily economic, for we discovered, once we were heavily into the project, that there was going to be some economic difficulty. Suddenly, within the organization at large, there was a need for cutbacks and downsizing in the foundation's overall operations, and this meant that the library would be affected as well. The number of visitors to Colonial Williamsburg had not kept up with budget predictions, and that meant that management had to do a great deal of re-thinking and re-structuring within the organization at large. But management did take a look at this—in fact worked very hard to offset the results of the economic downturn—and last year a new strategic plan was put in place. Fortunately, the efforts growing from the new strategic plan are paying off, and for the future, the prospects for the future for Colonial Williamsburg look good."

But there have been staff cuts, and that hasn't been good for service. Some work that is described in some employees' job descriptions just doesn't get done, some gets delayed, and in any case, you get a picture of service delivery that is incomplete. And the problem often comes with the work itself: the staff employed at the Rockefeller Library want to work with the collections (in many cases that's why they've come to work there) but when there are staff cuts of the magnitude that had to be put in place, you get a situation where the core functions of some jobs can't be done.

Nevertheless, within the library, there is tremendous staff support, and much pride in working at the library. In fact, because of the spacious new facility ("the windows are important," Berg points out, again!) and the all-around improvement with respect to "creature comforts" (for both library staff and users), there's been a vast improvement in the way people who work at the library think about their jobs. For example, one special amenity that Berg insisted on, and which has paid off in spades (and one that all information services managers might take note of) is the staff's own space: Located just across the hall from the staff kitchen, with its nice modern appliances and its very clean and well-kept space, is another room, glass-walled along the hallway. It's fitted out with a door that closes snugly, and when you go in, it's the perfect place to sit quietly with your professional journals and do a little catching up. And that's exactly what it's for. It's the staff's "Quiet Room," designed just for the library staff, located conveniently so you can take a cup of coffee in with you if you wish, and it's there so that staff, when they have the opportunity, can get away from the busy research areas and have a little "down time." It makes a lot of sense, in a facility that is as busy as the John D. Rockefeller Jr. Library is.

And it's that kind of thinking that went into the planning of the new facility, a way of looking at service delivery that incorporates not just a style of management, but a point of view that recognizes that such elements of service delivery as the openness of the physical space, the arrangement of the physical layout, the provision of creature comforts, and attention to staff concerns are as important (or, perhaps—dare we suggest?—*more* important) as the quality of the collections and the management of the services, products, and consultations offered by the library. It all adds up to a perfectly viable formula for quality library service, and it's something that Susan Berg and her staff at the John D. Rockefeller Jr. Library have managed to put in place with great success.

Meet Susan Berg

Susan Berg is Director, The John D. Rockefeller Jr. Library of the Colonial Williamsburg Foundation. A recognized leader in the library community, Berg has been active in the Special Libraries Association for many years. For SLA, she has chaired the Museums, Arts, and Humanities Division and she currently serves as Chair of the association's Social Sciences Division.

In her personal life, Susan Berg and her husband Sven enjoy lawn bowling (he is a serious aficionado and the couple travels extensively for lawn bowling tournaments). The two of them are also avid sailors (Berg's license plate reads: "PRA4WND"). The Bergs make their home in Williamsburg, just a few blocks from the historic area, where they take particular delight in their garden as viewed from their glass-walled living room.

BETH DUSTON FITZIMMONS:
policy development for the information future

Has Beth Fitzsimmons ever met a person she didn't like? Has she ever met a job she couldn't do? Those are the questions you find yourself asking when you're listening to Fitzsimmons talk about her career. There are few people who are as confident or as enthusiastic about their work as Beth Fitzsimmons is, and certainly there are few people in the information delivery business who are as optimistic about what the future is going to bring. Change management and the effects of change on information delivery—for people like Beth Fitzsimmons—is not a subject of concern or doubt. For her, these subjects—so frightening and so off-putting to so many other information professionals—are simply one more "piece" (one of her favorite words) of the new information environment

Originally published in *InfoManage : The International Management Newsletter for the Information Services Professional* 5 (12), November, 1998.

"Of course it's a new environment," she says, and you know the idea hasn't even bubbled to the surface before. It's just there, part of that whole move to better and better information delivery that Beth Fitzsimmons has been involved with most of her adult life. From her perspective, you don't even think about how things are changing or whether you "should" accept the new, because in information delivery—in the Fitzsimmons scheme of things —continuous improvement and doing things better are just the way the universe works.

"Of course it's new," she repeats, and you can see the enthusiasm building as she speaks. "And the really exciting challenge for us is that we get to influence the process. I often think about how we information professionals, we librarians are coming to grips with our new role in society, and I think the secret of our success is going to be in recognizing that we're the content specialists, that we're the people who enable others—our customers, our managers, the research community at large—to understand the value of the information content."

Certainly the best person for delivering that message is Beth Fitzsimmons (known as Beth Duston to many in the library and information services community, the people who knew her and worked with her before her recent marriage to Joseph J. Fitzsimmons). Of course it's a message that—for some—is fraught with dangerous pitfalls, with so many opportunities for complaining and whining and "this-is-not-they-way-we've-always-done-it" excuses that sometimes it's hard for information workers to visualize just how much better their professional lives will be, once they are recognized as content specialists.

Not for Beth Fitzsimmons, who has always been something of a ball of fire in the information services field and who is even today tackling new challenges in that exhilarating arena. As a Ph.D. candidate at George Mason University's Institute of Public Policy in Fairfax, VA, she is well along in her exploration of the "links" (another favorite word) between policy development and high-quality information delivery.

But don't be misled. This connection is not a new pursuit for Fitzsimmons, and for her, it's just one more step in that long journey toward excellence in information delivery. Throughout her career she has been seeking to match the organizational and operational policies of the places she's worked (either as an employee or as a consultant) with the identified needs of the information customers.

And she's been remarkably successful. As a scientist, Fitzsimmons became interested early in her career in the value of accurate and timely information to the scientific community, and it wasn't long before she had obtained a graduate degree in librarianship in order to focus that interest. Then, as an employee working for others in the scientific and technical research field, she discovered that she, as the company's librarian, could play an influential role in corporate decision making if her operation were recognized as a revenue-producing operation instead of being perceived (as, sadly, most organizational libraries are perceived) as an overhead operation. So, in typical Beth Fitzsimmons fashion, she did just that: she began to create products that the company could take to its clients, for a price, and thus was born the intrapreneurial librarian. It was a career path she pursued for her company for several years (and wrote about in a variety of publications for such organizations as the American Management Association) until, in 1987, it just made sense to go into business for herself. She opened Information Strategists, her consulting/information brokerage company, in Manchester, New Hampshire, moving to the Washington, DC, area in 1994.

For those who knew her, the move to Washington was not surprising. With much of her client base in the U.S. Federal Government's sci/tech community, it seemed a natural next step to be working in the area. She had, after all, chaired the group that had put together the IT system for the White House Conference on Libraries and Information Services in 1992. Her other consultancies, for such organizations as the Executive Office of the President Libraries at The White House, DTIC (the Defense Technical Information Center of the Department of Defense), OFHEO (the Office of Housing Enterprise Oversight), PTO (the Patent and Trademark Office), and, in the non-government sector, for such organizations as National Public Radio and the Association for the Advancement of Medical Instrumentation, had brought her into contact with many of the movers and shakers in the information services community in Washington. So after thinking about it for a while, Fitzsimmons realized that she had a large enough customer base in the area to make it worth her while to move her company. She had also, through her work with several federal agencies, found herself doing a great deal of work with CENDI, an organization of information managers within the Executive Branch, and that work, together with her appointment as the Chair of the U.S. Government Printing Office Committee on Depository Libraries in 1993, positioned her as one of the key players in the Washington information-services scene. Of course she should move to Washington.

And after four years "in residence," so to speak, having made the move and continuing her success in the Washington-area information services community, Fitzsimmons is more than willing to put her work in context, when she's asked about how it all ties together:

"'What is the connection?'" she repeats. "What links all this stuff that I'm doing?"

Fitzsimmons smiles as she thinks about her response, and the answer is not long in coming. It's not simply a rhetorical rumination.

"For me, the connection has to be the fact that I value information, and it goes all the way back to the days when I was the librarian at Aerodyne Research in Billerica, MA. It was while I was working there that I began to understand that the value of the information professional to the organization is that this person—the information professional—understands the value of information. From the organizational perspective, that's just about the most important thing that can happen, for organizational management and—in this case—the librarian to recognize that content is what counts, is what the company needs collected and organized and made ready for dissemination, and it's the information professional who can 'open up' that content for the organization. As I've gone through my career as a librarian and as a consultant, that's how I've had my fun, helping others manage the content."

That reference to "fun" is not out of place here, not when the comment comes from Beth Fitzsimmons. For her, optimist and genial person that she is, finding fun in her work as an information manager is only to be expected. Fitzsimmons has long delighted her friends with her enthusiasm about her work, about the solidly positive pay-offs from the various assignments she's been handed. Whether it's a White House conference or a quietly handled information search for a venture capitalist looking to find sci/tech start-ups to fund, you get the impression that as the job is completed, the client is going to be so happy Beth Fitzsimmons was hired that she's likely to be offered a follow-on project fairly quickly. She puts forward that kind of confidence and enthusiasm, and her clients pick up on it.

That enthusiasm—and certainly the confidence—come into play when Fitzsimmons describes her newest undertaking, the doctoral studies program she's currently pursuing.

"When I'm working with information policy," she says, "it's one layer above the corporate structure I learned my craft in. I've always recognized the value of information, and that is what is driving the work I'm doing now, but now I'm looking at policy at a different level, at the national, regional, state levels, that sort of thing. It's a different perspective, and it's a whole new arena for information management."

And it's a topic and a field of study (at least the piece Fitzsimmons is looking at) in which there has not been a great deal of work, and one of the questions Fitzsimmons is asked frequently has to do with information policy, with its purpose: Why is there a need for information policy?

"Yes, it is a brand-new field," Fitzsimmons says. "and it's come about because we're now recognizing the value of the content, and the whole area of information policy has evolved in order to create a sort of protection mechanism. Intellectual property is information created in an organization, created by the organization, and since we now recognize that information is valuable for economic and strategic purposes, we have to be thinking about how those protections can be organized and put in place. So of course the whole concept of information policy is brand new, and when you're asked about the 'purpose' of an information policy, the answer has to have something to do with protection: it's to protect the rights of the individual—or, in many cases, the organization—that created the information. In addition, by protecting and encouraging the intellectual endeavors of innovators, the U.S. protects its technological and competitive advantage.

"Basically that's the role of government in the whole policy arena anyway, and when we move it into the information arena, we can see how the role of policy is to protect the creators, the owners of the intellectual property, and we start looking at things like copyright, patents, trademarks, that sort of thing. And of course if anything is protected, including intellectual property, it becomes even more valuable. And that, ultimately, has to be recognized as well. If we don't protect intellectual property, it loses its value, to those who create it and those who will use it."

But there's another side to this coin, too, and Fitzsimmons doesn't ignore it.

"Absolutely," she says. "and the flip side is even worse: if there is no protection, no restraint, the creators of that property become uninterested in creating anything else, and the whole creative process slows down and—if things get bad enough—just stop altogether. And we all, as a society, end up losing our creativity, our innovation, and our enthusiasm for creating. That's not a scenario I want to see come about. I don't even want to think about it."

She is thinking about it, though, and in very specific ways, for connected to her work in information policy is the other major challenge in Fitzsimmons's professional life these days, an serendipitous opportunity that Fitzsimmons says she couldn't resist. Long a consultant at the U.S. Patent and Trademark Office, she is currently involved in a project team conducting a study of how patents, trademarks, and other intellectual property can be measured, and other similar matters as PTO tries to come to grips with GPRA. It was a chance to participate in something she wanted to be part of, and she was pleased when the project came along and she could be appointed to the team.

And she laughs as she mentions the project, for the expression on her visitor's face reveals that "GPRA" is obviously uncharted territory.

"It all comes from the mandate of the Government Performance and Results Act of 1993. That's the 'GPRA,' and it is part of Vice-President Gore's initiative for reinventing the federal government. Do you remember how, early in the Clinton administration, there was so much talk about 'reinventing government'? Well, the responsibility for this task fell to Al Gore's office, and he and his people threw themselves into it with a bang. It was talked about a great deal, and it was taken very seriously in Washington. You might not see much about it in the press these days, but the fact is, the Vice-President's project has been slowly—and in some cases not so slowly—percolating along, and GPRA was passed by the U.S. Congress to see that this initiative took hold. The act mandates that every federal agency had to have a strategic plan in place by September, 1997, and each agency is required to submit evaluation reports to Congress on a regular schedule. To send up those evaluation reports, specific measures must be adopted, and that's what our team is working with at the Patent and Trademark Office. We're attempting to identify and put in place specific measures, so PTO can tell Congress how well the agency is performing."

This is not an easy task in the scientific/technology community, Fitzsimmons says. In fact, in any sci/ tech environment it's difficult, but in the government sector the task seems to be a little more difficult.

"I can't tell you why," she says, "but it probably has to do with the inherent difficulties of quantifying measures in a research environment in which specific results are required. And it might have something to do with the general 'government' ambience, in which—as in any large organization—things move a little more slowly than in other environments. In any case, it's tough, and our group has begun by looking at things like the distinctions between outputs and outcomes. We're required, and we require our agencies, to understand the differences, and our team is using standard definitions in this work."

Such as?

Fitzsimmons doesn't miss a beat:

"Outputs," she says, "are the direct production of agency activities and effort. It's a productivity measure, and not in the final analysis so difficult to measure. You just count things. Outcomes, on the other hand, are the effects or consequences that the program is expected to have, the 'softer' (you might say) results that are usually articulated in the mission statement and planning documents and that sort of thing. Outcomes are the 'bigger-picture' goals that the agency is attempting to accomplish.

"So you can see how at the Patent and Trademark Office it's a very tricky situation. There isn't a culture of measuring outcomes, and yet that's part of what Congress wants. So we've had to step back and look at, as we put it in our study, 'What would you have if you didn't have PTO?' Developing quantitative measures for PTO outcomes becomes very difficult."

For Fitzsimmons, the exciting thing about all of this is that once performance indicators have been established for one agency or operation, the model can be adjusted, or pared down, or otherwise manipulated so that it can be used by other agencies and organizations, and that's where the project team's work fits into the overall "reinventing" scheme of things. If they come up with a model that works for PTO, it can be adopted elsewhere.

Of course there are specifics that have to be calculated in, Fitzsimmons notes.

"When you're inspecting patents," she says, "you can of course measure by number, but what is the quality of the information piece? It's that quality of the information that affects the outcomes, the effect of the work, and it's difficult to come up with a formula. So you have to find other applications and lay them over this system. There might be financial institutions, for example, or other organizations in the profit sector, in industry, in which this type of measuring is being done, and it's that type of effectiveness measure that needs to be pursued. When we find something that works in one environment, that can be beneficial for one organization, we want to take a look at it and, if it's viable, move it to another environment."

It's a path that Fitzsimmons definitely sees as opening up new challenges, yes, but also new opportunities for information managers.

"It seems very obvious to me," she says. "You become one of the team, and management and the other leaders in the organization begin to recognize the value that the information manager can bring to the organization. This is definitely something that information professionals have to get involved in, simply because there are so many things we can do once we open that mental door."

What we're talking about here is changing the culture, and the way Fitzsimmons sees it, it's not just a one-sided change. Not only is the organization opening a "mental door" by incorporating information policy into organizational measures, the information professionals, too, are opening themselves to new experiences and a new level of participation in the organizational effort. These are new contributions that librarians and other information workers can make, Fitzsimmons says. They can do things they've never done before, and the organization (and, presumably, the information workers themselves) will benefit.

"Look at it this way," she says. "As the organization moves into the realm of thinking about information—the content of information—as valuable, and you, as the information worker, understand the value of that corporate asset, you are positioned to move directly into influencing top organizational management and the way top management acquires and uses information. This was neglected in the past, both in the executive offices and in the corporate information centers. Now librarians and other information workers have the opportunity to use their knowledge and their expertise to demonstrate to management how the organization can leverage the information the organization has created. And you do it by switching off thinking about yourself as just the corporate librarian whose job is to provide external information that the company needs. The time has come for you to insist on managing the internal stuff. Most librarians and information center staff forfeit that, and that's such a wasted opportunity. If you get in there and work with management to develop an information policy, that gives you that kind of oversight responsibility and, well, you don't have to worry about job security any more. You end up being just about the most important person in the place, at least from the management perspective."

Fitzsimmons is really warming to this scenario now, and the famous Fitzsimmons enthusiasm is on the march.

"Think about it," she says. "There have been some studies showing that you can use some of these measures to identify information as a financial asset for the organization. How many of us, trained as librarians, ever expected to be managing a piece of our organization's financial assets? There's a whole new wave of interest—in the management community—in intellectual capital, and information professionals understand the importance of research to economic growth. And these information professionals are the very people who can show the organization how to handle this information. It's what we're good at. No, we're not just good at it. We excel at it, and the sooner we're working with our managers in developing this kind of information policy, the better off we'll all be!"

It all goes further, as Fitzsimmons happily points out.

"Once the policy is in place," she says, "that same policy is then used to measure the intellectual capital of a company, and there's no reason why the same policy measure can't be used in other operational units. Government, for example, can do the same thing, using established information policy to measure the intellectual capital of a town, community, and similar government agencies, just by using different inputs. It seems to me that this, for many organizations, is a plan that can have positive benefits all around."

It's a scenario that has a very appealing ring to it, there's no doubt. For part of what Fitzsimmons is suggesting is nothing more than a rallying cry for librarians and others who have provided information in the past to think about—to borrow a phrase from Al Gore—reinventing themselves.

The idea hits home, and Fitzsimmons picks it up.

"Absolutely," she says. "For so many years, I thought of myself as someone who was always begging for what I needed, begging to be given the resources that I had established were required to provide the services that the organization had to have. And once I discovered that in working with management in identifying value in the content of the information we had to find anyway, I was bringing value to the company, and not just taking resources out . . . . Well, it turned out to be the most important discovery of my career.

"Why? Because it is empowering when you have something of value to manage, and when I discovered the value of information content, and learned how to convey that value to my organization, I was no longer 'just' the librarian. Once you learn to use information you're responsible for to add value, to empower your associates, to strengthen the company, you know your professional work has meaning. And that, I suppose, is the bottom line. Knowing that what you're in control of has value. And once you know that it's all valued, you, your work, the information processes and the information content . . . . Well, that's when the work is fun."

Meet Beth Duston Fitzsimmons

Beth Duston Fitzsimmons is the President of Information Strategists, an information brokerage firm in Arlington, Virginia. Educated at Simmons College (B.S., Chemistry) and the State University of New York at Albany (M.L.S.), she is currently a doctoral student at The Institute of Public Policy at George Mason University in Fairfax, VA. Since 1975, her firm has provided a full range of information services for high tech companies. From 1993-1996, Fitzsimmons was associated with CENDI, an Executive Branch interagency working group composed of the scientific and technical information (STI) managers from the Departments of Commerce, Energy, Defense, Health and Human Services, and NASA. She has been involved in activities related to indexing, modernization, gateways, bibliographic record exchange, and machine translation, as well as other current information-related issues of importance to the scientific and technical community.

Fitzsimmons served as the information specialist for 10 years at Aerodyne Research, Inc., a contract research firm specializing in the physical sciences. The Aerodyne Information Center was selected by King Research and Infometrics, Inc. as one of the top 50 corporate libraries in the country.

She has also served as the Chairman of the Depository Library Council to the U.S. Public Printer (1993-94) and received the Public Printer's Distinguished Service Award. She was a Presidential appointee to the Advisory Board of the 2nd White House Conference on Libraries and Information Services (1991) and based on her understanding of information technology, Fitzsimmons chaired the conference's Technology Committee. She is also a member of the American Chemical Society, the Special Libraries Association, the Information Industry Association, the American Society for Information Science, and the Information Futures Institute. Her papers have appeared in management, science, library, and information publications, and she is an Editorial Consultant to InfoManage.

Fitzsimmons makes her home in Arlington, Virginia, and in Ann Arbor, Michigan, where she and her husband, Joseph J. Fitzsimmons, are active in Michigan politics. Joe Fitzsimmons, former President and later Chairman, UMI, is a past president of FOLUSA, Friends of Libraries of the United States of America. The two met when they were serving on the Advisory Board of the White House Conference on Library and Information Services in 1991.

SOURCES AND
SELECTED BIBLIOGRAPHY

Abram, Stephen A. "Adding value . . ." *InfoManage: The International Management Newsletter for the Information Services Executive.* 3 (3), February, 1996.

Albrecht, Karl. *At America's Service: How Corporations Can Revolutionize the Way They Treat Their Customers.* Homewood, IL: Dow Jones-Irwin, 1988.

Albrecht, Karl. *The Northbound Train: Finding the Purpose, Setting the Direction, and Shaping the Destiny of Your Organization.* New York: American Management Association, 1994.

Ashworth, Wilfred. 1979. *Special librarianship.* London: Clive Bingley.

Barker, Joel. *Paradigms: The Business of Discovering the Future.* New York: HarperBusiness, 1993.

Barrier, Michael. "Small Firms Put Quality First." *Nation's Business*, 80 (5), May, 1992.

Bartlett, Christopher A. and Sumantra Ghoshal. "Changing the Role of Top Management: Beyond Strategy to Purpose." *Harvard Business Review*, November-December, 1994.

Bennis, Warren. *The 21st Century Organization: Reinventing through Reengineering.* San Diego, CA: Pfeiffer & Co., 1995.

Boynton, Robert S. "The Two Tonys,"*The New Yorker* October 6, 1997.

Branin, Joseph J., ed. *Managing Change in Academic Libraries*. New York: Haworth, 1996.

Curzon, Susan C. *Managing Change*. New York: Neal-Schuman, 1989.

Dalziel, Murray M. and Stephen C. Schoonover. *Changing Ways: A Practical Tool for Implementing Change Within Organizations*. New York: American Management Association, 1988.

Davenport, Thomas H. *Process innovation: reengineering work through information technology*. Boston, MA: The Harvard Business School Press.

Drucker, Peter F. "The Age of Social Transformation." *Atlantic Monthly*, November, 1994.

Drucker, Peter F. "Discipline of Innovation." *Leader to Leader*, No. 9, Summer, 1998.

Drucker, Peter F. *Innovation and Entrepreneurship: Practice and Principles*. New York: Harper & Row, 1985.

Drucker, Peter F. *Landmarks of Tomorrow* New York: Harper, 1959.

Drucker, Peter F. *Managing for the Future: The 1990s and Beyond*. New York: Truman Talley Books, 1992.

Ferriero, David S. and Thomas L. Wilding. "Scanning the environment in strategic planning." *Masterminding Tomorrow's Information—Creative Strategies for the '90s*. Washington, DC: Special Libraries Association, 1991.

Hesselbein, Frances. *The Community of the Future*. San Francisco: Jossey-Bass, 1998.

Hesselbein, Frances. *The Leader of the Future*. San Francisco: Jossey-Bass, 1996.

Hesselbein, Frances. *The Organization of the Future*. San Francisco: Jossey-Bass, 1997.

Himmel, Ethel, and William James Wilson. *Planning for Results: A Public Library Transformation Process*. Chicago. American Library Association, 1998.

Horton, Forrest Woody. *Extending The Librarian's Domain: A Survey of Emerging Occupation Opportunities for Librarians and Information Professionals*. Washington, DC: Special Libraries Association, 1994.

Jacobs, Robert W. *Real Time Strategic Change*. San Francisco: Berrett-Koehler, 1993.

Kanter, Rosabeth Moss. *The Change Masters: Innovation and Entrepreneurship in the American Corporation.* New York: Simon and Schuster: 1983.

Kanter, Rosabeth Moss, quoted in "A Conversation with Rosabeth Moss Kanter About Leadership," by Donna J. Abernathy.*Training & Development* 52 (7), July, 1998.

Koch, Tom. *The Message is the Medium: Online All the Time for Everyone.* Westport, CT: Praeger, 1996.

Kott, Katherine. "Anxious Response to Change." Unpublished paper delivered at the conference, "Living the Future II: Organizational Changes for Success," University of Arizona Library, Tucson, AZ, April 22-24, 1998.

Kotter, John P. *Leading Change.* Cambridge, MA: Harvard Business School Press, 1996.

Kotter, John P. "Why Transformation Efforts Fail." *Harvard Business Review,* March-April, 1995.

Likins, Peter, quoted in "Living the Future II: Organizational Changes for Success," by BethAnn Zambella. *C&RL News,* 59 (7), July/August, 1998.

Mackenzie, Maureen L. "A Cognitive Look at Change Management." Unpublished paper, August, 1998.

Maurer, Rick, "Building the Capacity for Change" *Leader to Leader,* No. 8, Spring, 1998.

Orna, Elizabeth. *Practical Information Policies: How to Manage Information Flow in Organizations.* (London and Brookfield, VT: Gower, 1990).

O'Toole, James. *Leading Change: Overcoming the Idealogy of Comfort and the Tyranny of Custom.* San Francisco: Jossey-Bass, 1995.

Park, Mary Woodfill. *InfoThink: Practical Strategies for Using Information in Business.* Lanham, MD: Scarecrow Press, 1998.

Piggott, Sylvia E.A. 1995. Why Corporate Librarians Must Reengineer the Library for the New Information Age. *Special Libraries* 86 (1), Spring, 1995.

Ponzi, Len. "The Role of Information Policies in Corporate Knowledge Management." Unpublished paper, August, 1998.

Postrel, Virginia. "The Work Ethic, Redefined."*The Wall Street Journal,* September 4, 1998.

St. Clair, Guy. "Exceptional Information Delivery: The TQM/QIM/SLA Competencies Connection," *Information Outlook*, 1 (9), August, 1997.

St. Clair, Guy. *Entrepreneurial Librarianship: The Key to Effective Inormation Services*. (London and New Providence, NJ: BowkerÐSaur, 1996).

St. Clair, Guy. *Power and Influence: Enhancing Information Services Within the Organization*, (London and New Providence, NJ: Bowker-Saur, 1994).

St. Clair, Guy. "Special Libraries." *Librarianship and Information Work Worldwide 1998*. London: Bowker Saur, 1998.

Schwartz, Peter. *The Art of the Long View: Planning for the Future in an Uncertain World*. New York: Doubleday,1991.

Senge, Peter. *The Fifth Discipline: the Art and Practice of the Learning Organization*. New York: Currency Doubleday, 1990.

Senge, Peter, et al. *The Fifth Discipline Fieldbook: Strategies and Tools for Building a Learning Organization*. New York: Doubleday Currency, 1990.

Senge, Peter. "The Practice of Innovation." by *Leader to Leader*, No. 9, Summer, 1998.

Spiegelman, Barbara, ed. *Competencies for Special Librarians in the 21st Century*. Washington, DC: Special Libraries Association, 1997.

Thompson, LeRoy, Jr. *Mastering the Challenges of Change: Strategies for Each Stage in Your Organization's Life Cycle*. New York: American Management Association, 1994.

Varlejs, Jana, ed. *Agents of Change: Progress and Innovation in the Library/Information Profession*. Jefferson, NC: McFarland, 1992.

Von Dran, Gisela M., and Jennifer Cargill, eds. *Catalysts for Change: Managing Libraries in the 1990s*. New York: The Haworth Press, 1993.

Wheatley, Margaret. *Leadership and the New Science: Learning About Organizations from an Orderly Universe*. San Francisco, CA: Berrett-Koehler, 1992.

Wheatley, Margaret and Myron Kellner-Rogers. *A Simpler Way*. San Francisco, CA: Berrett-Koehler, 1996.

Wheatley, Meg, quoted in "Living the Future II: Organizational Changes for Success," by BethAnn Zambella. *C&RL News*, 59 (7), July/August, 1998.